Leonard
Koppett

A FIRESIDE BOOK
Published by Simon & Schuster
New York *London* *Toronto* *Sydney* *Tokyo* *Singapore*

The New
Thinking Fan's
Guide to
BASEBALL

SIMON & SCHUSTER/FIRESIDE

Simon & Schuster Building
Rockefeller Center
1230 Avenue of the Americas
New York, New York 10020

SIMON & SCHUSTER, FIRESIDE and
colophon are registered trademarks
of Simon & Schuster Inc.

Designed by Black Angus Design Group
Manufactured in the United States of America

1   3   5   7   9   10   8   6   4   2
1   3   5   7   9   10   8   6   4   2   PBK

Library of Congress Cataloging in Publication Data

Koppett, Leonard.
The new thinking fan's guide to baseball / Leonard Koppett.
p. cm.
"A Fireside book."
Rev. ed. of: A thinking man's guide to baseball. 1967.
1. Baseball.   I. Koppett, Leonard. Thinking man's guide to
baseball.   II. Title.
GV867.K6   1991
796.357—dc20   90-22512
                                                          CIP

ISBN 0-671-68330-6
0-671-73205-6 (pbk)

Portions of this book were published previously in *A Thinking Man's Guide
to Baseball* and in *All About Baseball*.

TO SUZANNE—AGAIN, AND STILL.

Contents

THE WHOLE BALL GAME

Introduction

Baseball's glory, many of its devotees declare, is that it is "changeless" in an otherwise bewildering, ever-changing cosmos. That's nonsense, of course. Nothing is changeless. What's true is that baseball, in the form the twentieth century has known it, has changed much less than most other facets of life, and that what has remained constant has been the central source of its appeal.

Nevertheless, it does change, and in the twenty-five years since I wrote *A Thinking Man's Guide to Baseball*, the changes have been numerous and profound. In 1966, the ten-team leagues were not split into divisions, and there were no playoff preliminaries to the World Series. Expansion itself was only five years old then, after sixty years of apparently immutable eight-team formats, and the 162-game schedule was still a novelty. We had never heard of a "designated hitter," or imagined that "artificial turf"—just installed in the unique indoor Astrodome because the grass had died without sunlight—would become widespread outdoors. There was no effective player union, no centralized promotion of the game, no cable television with all its consequences, no videotape recorders (for study of replays), and no serious thought of playing World Series and All-Star Games at night.

Other changes have been more subtle, less visible to the naked eye, but no less noticeable to those who live with baseball day by day. Relationships—player to manager, player to club, player to media,

club to media, club to fan, media to fan, player to fan, player to player—
are drastically different.

And, it goes without saying, the whole context of life outside of
baseball is entirely different than it was a quarter of a century ago, so
baseball couldn't be the same even if it tried, no matter how much it
wanted to.

Yet the basics have remained in place, and that is the stability its
practitioners and followers cherish. The principles of hitting, pitching,
and fielding, of baserunning and inning-by-inning tactics, of game and
season strategy, of making out lineups and putting together a roster
were pretty well standardized by the end of the 1920s. Techniques are
subject to fashion, refinements are made, old practices are abandoned
and rediscovered, and new ideas of value are quickly absorbed and
applied by everyone. But the fundamental shape of the game a seventy-
year-old grandparent sees with a ten-year-old grandchild is familiar
to both, and that particular shared experience is not available to a
similar range of generations in games like football, basketball, and
hockey.

Except for the designated hitter, baseball's playing rules have
stayed essentially the same since 1903. And playing rules dictate techniques and attitudes. The organizational structure, which determines
how the games are staged and how the public perceives the activity,
has not been altered significantly since 1921. That may not be "per-
manence," but it's a lot closer to it than almost anything else in our
hectic lives.

So in returning to the subject in 1990, I have to discard some and
change more of the things I wrote in 1966, but I must also keep intact
whatever I happened to get right then. I have also learned more, I
hope, in the intervening years.

Unchanged are the assumptions I made then about you, the reader:

That you would enjoy knowing more about Baseball (the capital B
indicating its organizational form from the major leagues down) than
daily newspapers and broadcasts can convey.

That you would prefer the realities, even if they seem complicated
and sometimes incomplete, to myths and clichés, however neat.

That you take baseball seriously—but never too seriously—and feel
some curiosity about its techniques as well as its personalities.

And that no matter how familiar you are with some aspects of it,
others have not come to your attention.

But another, entirely new, assumption must be added. If you are
interested enough in baseball to be reading about it now, you have
been exposed through television to more of the game's intricacies, in
greater detail, every year, than a fan of an earlier era could be in a

lifetime of going to ballparks. You have seen, through camera angles and slow motion, more of the game's mechanics than even the players themselves used to see. You have heard more explicit commentary, in real time, about what pitchers, hitters, and base runners are trying to do, from former players with firsthand knowledge and considerable ability to communicate, than even the most astute radio broadcasters were able to convey. So your level of awareness of such things must be higher than my original audience's was—and, I hope, you are therefore even more receptive to realistic discussion.

I must also repeat that this is not a "how-to," or "who-did," or "who-will-win," or "who-said-what," or "what-happened-when" book. It reveals no secrets. It does, in fact, reproduce one of the underlying modes of thought among baseball people: Repeat the obvious, repeat the well known, remind yourself and your teammates (or players, if you are a manager or coach) what they are supposed to know anyhow and probably do. The repetition is to make sure that the appropriate thought is firmly in mind at the appropriate moment—and if it isn't, failure to call attention to it should not be the reason. We see catchers and infielders holding up fingers to indicate how many out, coaches reminding runners to tag up, managers telling a hitter to make sure he gets a good pitch to hit—all commonplace reiterations that make up the day-to-day, moment-by-moment actualities of baseball's mental processes. These don't involve some sort of mystical flashes of brilliance, but only the ability, willingness, and need to concentrate on perspective, context, relevance, and focused attention.

The themes that permeate our discussion are the same as they were: interaction, human fallibility, unpredictability, effort that rarely quite matches intent. Above all, there is the dynamic aspect of reality (in baseball as in everything else) in which many related forces operate simultaneously, not as isolated events neatly following one another (as statisticians love to imagine). I think we are all more aware of this than we used to be, thanks to our constant exposure to television pictures. In 1966, I felt impelled to point out that "words, which are unavoidably static, need the help of imagination if some approximation of the true picture is to arise." That's still true of the nature of words, but our imaginations are now less dependent on language and more attuned to moving pictures than they were then.

Another paragraph, however, remains valid without changing a word. In real life, the mood and ailments of a man affect his performance. The intent of a maneuver is always an intrinsic part of its execution. Confidence and concentration, the two perpetual intangibles, often determine results to a far greater degree than do physical abilities and the hallowed "percentages." There is a great tendency, in dealing with baseball, to get bogged down in statistics and history—to treat numbers as if they were things, instead of mere records of something already finished; to fantasize about mathematical laws and averages, instead of recognizing them to be rather simple probabilities derived pragmatically from decades of accumulated experience.

That's the viewpoint I'm trying to convey, and the one I advocate for understanding baseball as a spectator and a follower. (Those who make their living from it, by playing or in business roles, have other demands and attitudes.) But my own vantage point has also shifted over the years. Aside from the obvious fact that I am much older, my status is different. I wrote then, subjectively, from the particular (and peculiar) perspective of a daily baseball writer traveling the circuit. I stopped doing that more than ten years ago, but have remained actively involved in baseball coverage more at arm's length, as it were. Even those who travel regularly now do so in a different universe than the one I knew, but I have seen and grasped aspects of the game from a distance that didn't register then: I see fewer trees blocking the vista of the forest.

The result is no less subjective, and probably just as didactic, but the canvas is broader and my awareness of how much is being left out is much greater.

Stronger than ever is my belief in a metaphorical distinction I made then. I don't think of baseball as a "science," but as an "art." Science suggests natural laws and impersonal forces, working automatically, always producing the same result when applied the proper way in the right circumstances. The laws of nature can't be broken, and defying them guarantees failure. But art suggests intuitive and purposeful manipulation of material to create a certain result. Its rules must be learned and they do apply, but they can be broken productively by the sufficiently creative artist. And that's what the outstanding players and managers seem to me to be: practicing artists.

As a working newspaperman, my relation to their craft was akin to that of a critic, chronicling their successes and failures with a certain amount of interpretation. But in a book of this sort, the key word is "guide"—an attempt to lead through, illuminate, explain, and describe the intricacies of the art, not to evaluate it. The goal is to increase the reader's capacity to enjoy what he or she has already chosen to experience.

And, as should be the case with any worthwhile guide, I find the journey and the panorama more and more rewarding each time I make the trip. Let's go.

The Game
on the
FIELD

CHAPTER
1

Hitting—The Artistic Science
(Mind over Physics)

Fear.

Fear is the fundamental factor in hitting, and hitting the ball with the bat is the fundamental act of baseball.

The fear is simple and instinctive. If a baseball, thrown hard, hits any part of your body, it hurts. If it hits certain vulnerable areas, like elbows, wrists, or face, it can cause broken bones and other serious injuries. If it hits a particular area of an unprotected head, it can kill.

A thrown baseball, in short, is a missile, and an approaching missile generates a reflexive action: Get out of the way.

This fact—and it is an unyielding fact that the reflex always exists in all humans—is the starting point for the game of baseball, and yet it is the fact least often mentioned by those who write about baseball.

All the tactics employed by pitchers, and all the problems faced by batters, are rooted in this reflex. Even historically, baseball evolved into recognizable form only when this fact was taken into account. In most primitive forms of the game, a runner between bases could be put out by being hit with a thrown ball. This meant that only a fairly soft ball could be used, or the players would soon be maimed; and a soft ball cannot be hit very far or very fast. Only when the tag play, with the ball held in a fielder's hand, was substituted did it become possible to use a ball that was hard enough to behave in a way familiar to us. There has been no basic change in the size, weight, or consistency of the ball since 1872.

The act of hitting, therefore, encompasses what seems like an emotional contradiction (which is not so unusual, psychologists tell us). It is simultaneously pleasurable and dangerous. The batter's primary desire is to hit the ball as hard as he can, and this requires "stepping into" the approaching ball with the rear foot very firmly planted. But self-preservation demands that the body move away from a ball that is going to hit it, or that *seems* to be going to hit it.

This interplay between executing a productive swing and resisting the built-in desire to dodge is the reality of every time at bat.

And the tactical consequence is, at bottom, rudimentary: Throw close, and drive the batter back; then throw over the outside part of the plate. Then, if you can alternate pitches that seem to be headed for the batter but aren't (curves) with pitches that have a straighter trajectory, you can keep the batter off balance most of the time.

Why, then, is there so little talk of fear? Why is this subject a sort of myth of omission?

One reason is that it is taken for granted. The process of becoming a capable batter begins with learning to overcome this specific fear—but it is never eliminated; it is mastered. By the time a man has become proficient enough to play professionally, he has mastered his fear to such a degree that he has nothing to discuss in such direct terms.

Another reason is that "fear" implies cowardice or lack of manliness, and as such is a loaded word. Therefore, the subject really is much discussed among professionals, but in circuitous language. They talk of "hanging in there," "standing up to the plate," "bearing down," "challenging," "fighting back."

All these are euphemisms for conquering the fear of being hit—but many of the professional eavesdroppers who communicate to the public don't bother to translate. If knowledgeable, they, like the players, take it so much for granted that they don't think of being explicit; if not knowledgeable, they don't realize to what the references really refer.

There are also deeper reasons for glossing over the naked truth. In all athletics, conquest of fear of pain is an essential element. One must learn to carry out the proper action *despite* the possibility of getting hurt. A professional football player, or boxer, or hockey player, isn't less susceptible to pain than other people; he doesn't hurt less; prick him and he bleeds. His special quality is that he is *willing* to endure the pain to gain his objective. It's true that he has conditioned himself physically to withstand some type of beating and strain—but the conditioning in itself involved self-inflicted pain.

It is no help, however, to remain conscious of the feeling of fear that one is trying to conquer. Very quickly, then, and very firmly over a long period of time, *awareness* of fear is pushed aside. A man doesn't go to bat saying to himself, This time I will not be afraid; he stopped thinking in such terms long ago. But the fact remains that he is, on the instinctive level, afraid, and how he performs in spite of this is the measure of his success.

So the participant has pushed the subject out of his conscious mind, while the spectator has either forgotten his own feelings, or never experienced them.

It is revealing, however, that once a participant passes out of the line of fire, once he has retired, the awareness surges up and becomes prominent in conversation.

Listen to Dizzy Dean, reminiscing about his great days with the Gas House Gang of the St. Louis Cardinals in the early 1930s: "I'm pitchin' against Hubbell," said Diz, "and I knock down eight men in a row. I skip Hub. Then I knock down the lead-off man again, to make an even nine."

"They'd never dare dig in the way they do now," declared Frankie Frisch, who was Dean's manager then. "If our pitchers saw a guy diggin' a ditch with his spikes the way some of these fellows do, you know where that next pitch would be."

"I remember Fitz pitching one time to Johnny Mize," said Leo Durocher, in his best flamboyant storytelling mood. "I'm managing the Dodgers, and Fitzsimmons is pitching for me, and Mize is with the Cardinals. He looks down and he yells to Mize, 'The first one is coming right here'—and he throws it *right here!*" (Leo points to his head.) "Then the next pitch is that big slow curve, right on the outside corner. Now it's 1-and-1. 'Again,' yells Fitz, and throws it right here for ball two. Then the curve, and it's 2–2. 'One more time!' Fitz hollers at him, and sure enough, he goes flying. And then strike three."

Every gathering of old baseball people is guaranteed to produce reminiscences of this sort as the evening, and the booze, wear on.

Now, these were people in the 1960s talking about the 1930s, making it plain that they thought the "youngsters" of the 1960s weren't as tough. And those youngsters, rolling their eyes upward and shaking their heads, didn't bother to hide their boredom and irritation at hearing the older generation spout such bravado.

But listen to them now, in the 1990s, talking about the 1960s.

"Don Drysdale would consider an intentional walk a waste of three pitches," says Mike Shannon. "If he wants to put you on base, he can hit you with one."

Shannon, a right-handed hitter, had to bat against Drysdale, of the

Los Angeles Dodgers, but not against Bob Gibson, Shannon's St. Louis Cardinal teammate. Ron Fairly, a left-handed hitter, had to face Gibson but not Drysdale because Ron played for the Dodgers.

"But let me tell you about Gibson," says Fairly. "Remember Derrell Thomas? He played with a lot of clubs. Well, when he was with us, he comes up to bat against Gibson this time in Dodger Stadium, and before the first pitch, starts digging around with his spikes, to get a good foothold in the batter's box. Gibson is standing on the mound, glaring down, watching him. Finally, Thomas figures he's ready, plants his back foot, and starts to step in—and Gibson yells down, 'You'd better dig it deeper!'

"Thomas, startled, knows exactly what he means—and immediately calls time, and starts pushing dirt back into the hole with his spikes. He knows he made a bad mistake."

Fairly can't stop chuckling.

"It didn't help him, of course. He went down on the next pitch anyhow."

But Shannon, Drysdale, Fairly, and Gibson—all broadcasters now—agree with the prevailing view that times have finally changed. Since the 1980s, they feel, pitchers don't throw at hitters; hitters don't know how to get out of the way; a close pitch is considered a reason to start a fight; and "intimidation" is disappearing from the game.

They are right, to a degree, for several reasons. Baseball's off-field authorities, always disturbed by the public relations aspect of overt danger, began imposing and enforcing anti–head-hunting rules (by giving umpires the right to warn and eject managers as well as offending pitchers). Pitchers now grow up without much experience in pitching inside, partly because aluminum bats make it less of an advantage. Hitters have less experience in dodging close pitches, and do get some subconscious comfort from wearing helmets. And attitudes about life in general are less cutthroat than they used to be—especially when all concerned are making lots of money the way things are.

Nevertheless, the threat always exists, and the hostile overreaction to being hit or almost hit by a pitch only proves how close to the surface the fear reaction remains.

But if it all begins with fear, it doesn't end there. That is merely the beginning.

The second fundamental fact about hitting is so self-evident that it is mentioned only as a cliché, when clichés are being derided. It's a round ball and a round bat.

Yet this unique problem in physics is what gives baseball its particular character. It doesn't come up in any other widely played game. In all the tennis-family games (including squash and even handball), a moving ball is struck by some flat surface that is large in relation to the ball. In hockey, a sliding or rolling disk is hit or guided by a flat blade. A cricket bat has three plane surfaces (and the ball may be hit in any direction). In golf, the striking surface is flat and, what's more, the ball is stationary. Even in billiards (where the balls are stationary), the striking tip of the cue is relatively flat.

In all these other games, therefore, the margin for error is much greater than in baseball. A hockey or tennis shot can be reasonably effective even if the point of contact is not quite centered on the blade. But to hit a baseball into fair territory, hard enough to have any reasonable chance of the ball falling safe, one must connect almost perfectly. A line drive can result only if the line from the center of the ball through the point of contact to the center of the bat cylinder is practically straight. The height of the area in which the bat and ball can meet squarely is something less than half an inch.

Consider the dimensions: A baseball's diameter is 2.868 inches; the bat's diameter, at its fattest part, cannot exceed 2.75 inches. A major-league fastball can approach 100 miles an hour, which means that the distance from the pitcher's hand to home plate (less than 60 feet, since the ball is released in front of the rubber) is covered in something less than half a second.

To hit the ball, of course, the batter must begin swinging his bat before the ball arrives. In other words, he must decide on the basis of the first portion of the pitch's trajectory what its final path will be, and he has approximately one-quarter of one second in which to make this decision. Then he must start the bat, judge height, lateral placement, and velocity, adjust the swing, and make contact no more than a quarter of an inch above or below the center of the ball. And while doing all this, he must keep his body from flinching if the ball seems to be coming too close.

Put that way, hitting seems impossible. It would be impossible if it were a conscious process. By and large, it is a trained reflex, the product of hundreds of thousands of swings taken from childhood on. But it is easy to see why the pitcher has so big an advantage, and why outstanding batters are so few, and why even the greatest of all never succeeded in hitting safely as much as 40 percent of the time. And that's why, at major-league levels, batting ability is considered an inborn gift.

"No batting coach," said Harry Walker, one of the first and most studious of all batting-coach specialists, "can do anything to make a man a better hitter than he is. He may, once in a while, teach a man to overcome some basic flaw in his technique, a flaw which had been robbing him of the benefits of his natural ability. Mostly, though, all the coach can do is observe a man when he's hitting well, spot what he's doing differently when he's not hitting well, and get him back to his own correct groove as quickly as possible."

And why does a hitter lose his "groove"? There may be any variety of reasons, but the basic one brings us right back to the underlying fear. If he never had to worry about avoiding a close pitch, he would simply find his best spot (close enough to the plate to have the fattest part of the bat cover the width of the strike zone, with his feet firmly planted) and depend on a grooved swing to do the work. This is what a basketball player does on the free-throw line, or a golfer in addressing the ball. But the pitcher makes sure he does have to worry, so the batter can't dig his spikes in too firmly: He must remain ready to dodge.

Each time up, and often after each pitch, the batter must find his "right" spot all over again—not only the right spot for his feet, but for his whole body position. It is easy to lose the rhythm of one's own best swing in such circumstances, especially since being ready to dodge can be a mental distraction as well. And it doesn't matter much whether the pitch comes close unintentionally (if the pitcher is wild) or intentionally. The result is the same, and the batter must be "ready."

As a specialist in coaching hitters, Harry was something of a pioneer. Until about 1950, teams usually had only three coaches assisting the manager, and they were generalists except, perhaps, for the catcher or pitcher in charge of the bullpen. Then people like Walker and Wally Moses were in the forefront of a group that taught more systematically, throughout minor-league systems as well as with a parent club.

In the 1970s, Charlie Lau emerged as a guru of hitting style, with specific theories that defied the conventional wisdom but also won converts. I'll have more to say about that when I talk about the coaching function in Chapter 7. But there's no need to argue the pros and cons of various hitting mechanics here. It's enough to recognize that they exist, that they are very complex, that they are not universally agreed upon, and that they can help you—like prayer—only if you can hit.

But the theoretical approach can produce its own oddities. Dusty Baker, who was a fine player for the Braves, Dodgers, Giants, and A's, had his disciples while still playing and emerged as a respected teacher as hitting coach with the Giants in 1989. Here he is talking to Glenn Dickey, the San Francisco columnist: "You have to be in good condition. Your legs and triceps muscles have to be strong. You have to have a small waist, so you can get your bat around and rotate your hips into the swing."

Small waist? You mean, like Babe Ruth? Hack Wilson? Jimmy Foxx? Pedro Guerrero? Harmon Killebrew?

Dusty couldn't help laughing when I teased him about it. "You know what I mean—in general," he said. And, of course, I did know, and he was right. But the point of the whole incident is that in hitting, as in so many other elements of the game we're just starting to look at, there are no flat-out generalized rules. Especially in hitting. Every person is put together differently, and every talented hitter has his own peculiar form for his own needs, as diverse as the stances of Joe DiMaggio, Ted Williams, Stan Musial, Yogi Berra, and Wade Boggs. They are artists, not technicians.

"When you see older hitters who are having trouble getting the bat around," Dusty also said, "it's usually because they've thickened around the middle."

Be that as it may, the most common saying in sports is "the legs go first." Yet, obviously, it does not apply to hitters. What goes first, as a man ages, is the hair-trigger reflex needed to control the bat properly—and, at just about the same time, the *confidence* in one's dodging reflex. Most players would never admit it, and some perhaps don't even realize it, but when a man reaches a certain age (or a certain state of satisfaction), the fear he originally conquered comes back. He becomes afraid, not (as the fans and writers assume) that he won't be able to move the bat quickly enough to hit the good pitch, but that he won't be able to move himself quickly enough to get out of the way of the bad pitch.

And this is what happens when teams get "complacent," or "tired," or in any other way lose the fine edge of highest motivation. It shows up in poor hitting. Any decrease in concentration not only makes a batter susceptible to being fooled, tactically; it loosens a little bit of the perpetual control on the fear. The defensive reflex breaks through. The head turns; the rear end moves backward; the arms hesitate; the step forward is unsure. These things may happen to an infinitesimal degree—but that's all it takes to turn a line drive into a pop-up or a foul.

Traditionally, fans think of a team as "fighting back" when it scores in the late innings to come from behind—and this vague terminology is precisely correct. That's exactly what it takes to score: added determination to stand up to the plate, with maximum concentration and minimum defensiveness.

So hitting is a tricky mechanical problem. Psychologically, it requires nerve and concentration. Is there a third basic factor? Yes indeed—luck.

It is unfashionable to talk about luck in baseball. To losers, it implies alibi; to winners, it detracts from self-esteem; to spectators and strategists, luck is an unwelcome intrusion into the illusion of an ordered universe and spoils the second-guesser's sensation of omnipotence. And to all those involved in baseball as a business—players, managers, executives—it is a wise policy to ignore luck, good and bad, in their own thinking. Their concern is always with next time—the next inning, the next game, the next season, the next pitch. To dwell on the chance factor in what has already happened undermines the will and disciplined thinking; in planning ahead, one must, by definition, exclude luck from the calculation.

Nevertheless, the reality is that luck plays an important role in almost every game. It could not be otherwise with round bats, round balls, and fields full of pebbles, ruts, clumps of grass or seams in the carpet, and odd-shaped boundary walls. Baseballs *do* take funny bounces; a ball hit weakly may drop between fielders who were properly placed; a ball may land fair or foul by a fraction of an inch; a roller may be beaten out for a hit; and the hardest possible line drive may go right into a fielder's glove instead of a foot to either side.

With these general observations out of the way, let's come to grips with the more specific aspects of hitting, as it occupies the minds of thousands of hard-thinking professionals and their eager followers.

The main concern of every hitter (and, of course, pitcher) is the strike zone. According to the rules, this is the portion of space directly above home plate (which is 17 inches wide) and bounded by the levels of the batter's knees and armpits "when he is in his natural stance."

That, at least, was the "traditional" zone. The rule book has tinkered with definitions from time to time, and it is generally agreed that during the last fifteen years or so the zone has become lower: In practical terms, a "high strike" no longer exists, and a pitch above the waist will almost always be called a ball. A couple of decades ago, this upper limit was at the level of the letters on the front of a uniform shirt. At the same time, more low pitches, not much above the ankles, are called strikes.

The current definition, rewritten in 1988, is accompanied by a diagram (for the first time). It sets the top of the strike zone at "a horizontal line at the midpoint between the top of the shoulders and the top of the uniform pants," and the lower level at "a line at the top of the knees."

Actually, that's a pretty flexible area. It differs with the height, and the degree of crouch, of every batter. It also varies, although it's not supposed to, with many umpires. But it is definite enough to work with, and it is the strike zone—his own strike zone—that each hitter must come to know. Its evolution is the key to its importance. Trial and error, in the early years, delineated which pitches could be hit solidly. If the batter has to reach out too far, or step away from a close pitch, or reach too high or too low with the bat, he doesn't have "a fair chance" to hit the ball with any degree of power. If it is in this "fair-chance" zone and the batter lets it go, he is penalized by a called strike; if it is outside it, he doesn't have to swing and the pitcher is penalized by a "ball," or one-fourth of a base on balls.

Any time a batter swings at a ball outside the strike zone, he is hurting himself in three ways: He accepts a physical disadvantage, he saves the pitcher from an unfavorable count, and he weakens the accuracy of his own future responses to balls and strikes.

Hang around managers, and you'll hear the following observations over and over, in a variety of phrasings:

"If only he'd stop trying to kill the ball!"

"When he gets to know the strike zone—"

"If he'd go with the pitch once in a while, instead of trying to pull everything—"

These are three of the cardinal sins from a coaching or observing point of view: swinging too hard, swinging at bad pitches, and refusing to hit an outside pitch to the opposite field. As a general principle, major-league hitters are expected to avoid them (although there are plenty of specific exceptions, certain occasions when it is all right or even desirable to violate each of the three precepts).

Listen to individual hitters, and you'll hear a different set of preoccupations:

"I've been in a slump—I'm pressing."

"I don't feel comfortable up there."

"Since I opened up my stance, I pick up the ball better."

"I'm getting good wood on the ball."

The hitters seem more concerned with the mechanics of hitting the ball squarely than with intent and judgment stressed by managers. But this impression is only partly correct. It is true that the individual ball player thinks, and talks, more about the mechanics than the manager does, because each individual's mechanical problems are personal and peculiar. If he is a good ball player, however, he devotes a lot of thought to the intent-and-judgment business, too. Of course, thinking is a long way from doing, and many times the batter who knows perfectly well that he shouldn't swing at a bad pitch still finds himself unable to avoid doing it. In general, though, as long as a hitter smacks the ball with satisfying solidity a good proportion of the time, he feels content; a manager, on the other hand, may be dissatisfied with a player who is hitting the ball squarely but doing so on borrowed time because of the faults he is committing.

When coaching, the teacher—it may be the manager, or a special coach, or one player helping another—deals with a much finer collection of technicalities:

"You're jerking your head."

"You're overstriding."

"Your hands are being held too low."

"You're dropping your elbow."

"You're locking your hips."

These are specific prescriptions for specific problems of specific batters. No two men swing the bat exactly the same way. Each athlete has slightly different body proportions, slightly different relative strengths in various muscles, different eyesight, different rhythm, different lifelong experiences, and different habits.

In the final analysis, again, batting is a conditioned reflex, built up over tens of thousands of repetitions against a certain level of pitching. To begin with, a natural gift must exist, in the form of that special eye-to-arms-and-hands coordination that is rare. Practice—repetition—develops this ability to a degree high enough, in a few hundred men, to get the opportunity to play in the majors at all.

Only then comes the real test: hitting in competition against the pitchers who have made a profession of foiling those reflexes.

And the only thing the batter can really do is make solid contact. He can't "get a hit" or "drive in a run": Those are consequences, things that happen only after the ball leaves the bat, dependent on the actions of others. He can intend all sorts of things, but all he can do physically is hit it squarely, not so squarely, or not at all.

So the mechanical side of hitting is largely habit: "good" habits acquired by practice, and "bad" habits slipped into unconsciously through fatigue, injury, carelessness, laziness, eagerness, complacency, worry, or experimentation. And it follows that the key psychological factor in success at bat boils down to confidence. The batter must have complete faith in his reflexes, in his ability to swing the bat exactly where and when he wants to, in his ability to hit *this* pitcher *this* time up. Only when he is convinced of these things emotionally can his conscious mind be free enough to concentrate on the mental problem of when and where to swing; and only then can he get the proper balance of tension and relaxation that allows the trained reflexes to move muscles by themselves.

One of Yogi Berra's most quoted remarks contains, simultaneously, the purest truth and the most misleading idea. Bill Dickey, one of Yogi's early coaches, tried to impress the young Yankee with the importance of thinking about what he was going to do at bat.

Yogi, always a malleable character, tried it, and popped up.

"Aarghh," he declared in disgust, "how kin ya t'ink an' hit atta same time?"

In one sense, Yogi was absolutely right. You can't. No rapid, reflexive action can be performed consciously. If you play the piano, just try thinking consciously about the next note, and the one after: It can't be done. The hands, once trained in a particular piece, go by themselves, and they stumble if thought intrudes. Or try reading a book one letter at a time and see how far you get. It's the same with hitting: You can't think *about hitting*—that is, about how you swing the bat, where it is to meet the ball, just how you will stride—while you're doing it in competition. You can, and should, remind yourself of little corrective details *just before*, and in practice, but not while doing it.

In another sense, though, a major-league hitter *must* think if he is to hit safely with any regularity. He must think about what the pitcher is likely to do, what the situation is in the inning and in the game, and what he wants to accomplish in this time at bat. In other words, he must have an *idea*, a positive approach to the immediate problem. When a hitter is simply hoping to avoid making an out—and that happens a lot—he is being "defensive." Good hitters are seldom on the defensive in this way.

Yogi, of course, could and did do this kind of thinking with the best of them; he simply didn't consider it "thinking." In his case, mental reflexes were as thoroughly attuned to baseball as his remarkable physical reflexes. He couldn't tell you how he knew what was right—but he knew, and his record reflected it.

But, if hitters have to think, *what* do they think? Do they say to themselves, Gee whiz, the score is tied and there are three men on—I gotta get a hit and win the game? Do they say, I'm gonna hit a homer into the third deck? Do they say, I see the shortstop is one step too near second, so I'll poke a single just out of his reach?

Not really—or, at least, not very often.

They think the following things, or they should, starting when they reach the on-deck circle:

1. What is this pitcher's best stuff, and what is his best *today?*
2. What sequence of pitches has he gotten me out with in the past?
3. Knowing my weaknesses—which he does—how does he usually try to exploit them with his particular equipment?
4. Which of his deliveries have been behaving properly the last couple of innings, and which haven't?
5. What is the situation in the game and what do I want to accomplish?
6. What is there about this ballpark and this day—dimensions,

wind strength and direction, visibility—that should affect my
intentions?

7. What pitch do I *want* to hit?

That's not an all-inclusive list, but it will do. Let's elaborate.

Unless a pitcher is a newcomer, there is no excuse for an experienced
batter to be unfamiliar with the pitcher's equipment. The batter knows,
from past experience, whether this opponent's basic strength is speed,
or breaking pitches, or a combination; how well this pitcher usually
changes speed on various deliveries; how reliable his control is; and
whether he uses any of the trick pitches, like knucklers or screwballs.
The batter should also be able to judge how well any single portion
of that pitcher's repertoire is functioning in this particular game.

Joe Pepitone, as a young Yankee, had a quick mind not noted for
concentration, consistency, or good judgment. Before a game at Yankee
Stadium one day, he came into the dugout from fielding practice while
a few writers were still chatting with Ralph Houk, the manager.

"What's this guy throw?" Pepi asked Houk, indicating the opposing
starting pitcher, who was starting to warm up. "Good fastball?"

Houk grunted something, and Pepi went on into the passageway
to the clubhouse.

"At least he's starting to show some interest," one of the writers
said to Houk. "That must be progress in a way."

"You don't understand," said Houk, letting go an eloquent stream
of tobacco juice. "He's asked exactly the same thing the last four times
this guy pitched against us."

This was pure Pepitone: smart enough to try to score Brownie points
with his manager in front of an audience, not smart enough to see why
he wasn't getting them, or helping himself.

The second point is equally universal. A batter must be able to
remember exactly what this pitcher did to him the last time they met,
whether it was in an earlier inning of the same game or a month before.
The pitcher (with the help of his catcher, his manager, and his coach)
most certainly remembers it. He knows exactly how he got this batter
out whenever he did get him out. The batter must be alert to the same
information, so that if a recognizable pattern develops he can catch
it—or so that he can draw intelligent conclusions from any variation
of it.

Knowing his own weaknesses, the batter knows what he has to
protect against. That every batter has a weakness is one of baseball's
dogmas. The most general categories are "high-ball hitters" and "low-
ball hitters"; almost every player will hit one better than the other,
and experienced baseball men can spot which is which by watching

even a few swings. But it gets broken down much finer than that: Some men have more trouble with inside pitches, some with outside pitches; some can hit fastballs better than slow pitches, others the other way around; various kinds of curveballs bother some more than they bother other players; and all these factors can be combined. For instance, a batter may have trouble with an inside fastball but not with an inside curve, but be able to murder a fastball over the plate or away while acting relatively helpless when confronted with a curve that catches the outside corner.

Whitey Herzog points out that a hitter who can't handle a "straight change"—off-speed fastball—may do well with an off-speed breaking ball. Distinctions can be that fine—and you'd better know them. As for the high-low differences, the statisticians over at the Elias Sports Bureau, after becoming thoroughly computerized in the 1980s, have come up with a fascinating set of numbers. They classify pitchers as ground-out or fly-out pitchers, meaning that that pitcher gets most of his outs on grounders or flies, and then break down individual hitters for their records against ground-out or fly-out pitchers. This is, of course, a reflection of the high-ball/low-ball preferences of those hitters—interacting with the conscious countermeasures of those pitchers. Just as pitchers know who is a high-ball hitter, batters know—or should—who is a high-ball pitcher.

Combining his knowledge of what the pitcher has available, how it has been behaving most recently (particularly late in a game, when a pitcher may tire), how he likes to work on the batter's weakness, and how the pitcher has given him trouble in the past, the batter is in a position to make some reasonable estimate of what pitches will be thrown to him on this time at bat. Having arrived at his reasonable estimate, the batter must apply it to his own needs. Most important is the tactical situation at the time.

In general, a batter's duties are:

1. Avoid striking out—because this is a dead loss to the offense, especially if there is anyone on base. Once the ball is hit, however weakly, it has at least a slight chance of falling safely, taking a bad bounce, or being misplayed. For this reason, batters will usually cut down on their swing—not swing as hard—after the count has reached two strikes. The harder one swings, the more chance of missing the ball. With two strikes, the batter concentrates on "getting a piece of the ball" on any pitch that looks like a possible strike. Even a foul will preserve the batter's life. The common phrase is: "Put the ball in play."

2. If there is anyone on base, advance the runner. This is a primary rule of team play, often unappreciated even by knowledgeable baseball fans and ignored by selfish players. Of course, a base hit would advance

the runner, but it's not an all-or-nothing proposition. No manager can expect even his best hitter to hit safely 40 percent of the time—but he does expect everyone to try to move the runner along 90 percent of the time.

This can be accomplished in various ways, some of which are the manager's prerogative. If he wants a sacrifice bunt, he'll signal the batter. If he wants a hit-and-run play (with the runner breaking for the next base and the batter committed to trying to get his bat on the pitch wherever it is, and to try to poke it through the infield if possible), he'll call the play from the bench.

Certain situations, however, are standard, and every batter is supposed to know them without special instructions. If there is a runner on third with less than two out, the batter's job is to get him home by hitting a deep enough fly. If there is a runner on second with nobody out, the batter is supposed to produce at least a grounder to the right side of the infield, so that the runner can get to third with only one out. (This particular situation is really an uncredited sacrifice, and the best team players often give up their chance for a hit by making sure they make this sort of out. It doesn't show in the statistics, but managers remember and appreciate it.) If there's a runner on first, it is also better to hit the ball to the right side, because it's harder to start a double play from there, but it is better still not to hit a grounder at all.

3. If there's nobody on, get on. This is the situation, usually, in which "a walk is as good as a hit." Especially with nobody or one out, in a close game, the main idea is to get an attack started. Once there's a base runner, the pitcher and defense are confronted by new problems. With nobody on, the batter can be more choosy about taking pitches right on the borderline of the strike zone, or of his own weakness, than he can when there is an obligation to move a runner along. With a man on second and nobody out, for instance, a walk most definitely is not as good as a hit (although it may be if you're four runs behind); it creates a double-play possibility with the next batter, without moving the potential run any closer to home. In that case a ground-out, which moved the runner to third, from where he could score on an out or a wild pitch or an error, may be more valuable to the team than a walk—although less valuable to the batter's personal record. And, with nobody on base, the batter can be more selective about "getting his pitch to hit." His attention, however, is on hitting the ball sharply rather than setting tape-measure distance records. He wants a single or a double or a walk, to start something.

4. If the game situation demands or allows, go for distance. With two out, usually a hitter who has even a moderate amount of power

is more justified in swinging for the fences than at other times. With two out, it would take three consecutive singles to score a run, and the chances are as much against that as they are against a 30-homer-a-year man hitting one out of the park.

More specifically, the score, inning, and identity of the batter have a lot to do with justifying the big swing, even after two strikes. For a while in 1989, the Giants had Will Clark batting third and Kevin Mitchell fourth with notable weakness in the fifth slot, no matter who occupied it (until Matt Williams came back from the minors in mid-season and helped the team to a pennant). Suppose Mitchell is up in the home half of the ninth with the Giants one run behind. Even with two strikes, it's worth trying to tie the game with one swing on a borderline pitch (but not one out of reach, of course). In fact, accepting a walk in such a situation is an evasion of responsibility by the big hitter, because the chances of the next two men getting him around are also very small.

This kind of thing comes up all the time for the better hitters. Only a limited number of men, on every team, are consistent power hitters. Late in a game, with the score close, they must try to cash in on their special ability while they have the chance, rather than leave the decision to less talented hitters who follow them.

A prime example—actual, not hypothetical—was Ted Williams. One of the greatest of all batters, this left-handed slugger was often confronted by a lopsided defensive alignment (called the "Boudreau Shift" when Lou Boudreau, managing Cleveland, made it popular, but now a standard procedure against certain power hitters). This is an extreme shift toward the right-field foul line, with the second baseman playing back in short right, the right fielder close to the foul line, the center fielder in deep right-center, the shortstop on the second-base side of second, and the third baseman halfway between second and third.

It was an invitation to Williams to poke the ball to the left side for an almost certain single. Most of the time, Williams refused to accept it, and kept swinging for the right-field fence. He was often criticized for this by all segments of baseball society from bleacher fan through Ty Cobb, and undoubtedly he did act a bit stubbornly at times. But his argument made sense, too: After all, one reason for the shift was that the defense was more afraid of a homer than a single, and by taking the single, Williams would be playing the defense's game. He might be robbed of some hits to right if he hit his normal way, but he would also hit at least some homers; if he went to the left, he wouldn't hit any homers. A homer could win a game better than a single—and if the hitter were as good as Williams was, it was worth the try.

On the other hand, Williams was also criticized for taking walks on borderline pitches when one of his extra-base hits could have done more good. In isolated strategic situations, this criticism was justified—but Williams's attitude sheds a lot of light on the nature of hitting, and is worth pondering. He insisted that "good habits" were the primary consideration for a hitter, and that the best habit was knowing exactly what the strike zone was and absolutely refusing to swing at anything outside it.

If you gave in once, Williams believed, and compromised swinging at a pitch just a little outside the strike zone, you would do it again, and then again at a pitch a little farther outside. You might hit some of those pitches safely, but you would be undermining your self-discipline and your reflexes, which were more important in the long run. You would eventually be seduced into swinging at bad pitches, and would be giving the pitchers a bigger target to throw at.

Williams, of course, was exceptional in all sorts of ways, and, anyhow, usually played in lineups that had power behind him. Since he was *so* good (.344 lifetime) his way was the right way for him. The point is that the good hitter must make deliberate and intelligent decisions about what's needed, and try to carry them out. The situations that arise are not met by automatic, textbook-listed rules, but by trying to cope with all factors involved at that particular time.

All these decisions about the batter's intentions have to be tempered by the physical surroundings and weather conditions. In a big ballpark, for instance, where it is harder to hit a home run, looking for the pitch that can be hit out of the park is self-defeating—pitchers love long, high flies if they have capable outfielders with plenty of room behind them. In a smaller park, or with a strong wind blowing straight out, free-swinging may be more profitable, and a pitcher aware of such handicaps may be worked for more walks. Far and away the most important thought of all, however, is: What pitch do I *want* to hit? This is where the artists are separated from the purposeless stick-wavers.

Just as every batter has a weakness, every batter—if he's in the majors—has a strength. And just as every batter is human, so is every pitcher. If a pitcher were able, every single time, to throw each pitch exactly where he wanted to, with the appropriate amount of force and spin, the batter would be out of business. Fortunately for baseball, no pitcher can be that consistent; sooner or later, the pitcher makes a mistake, physically if not mentally, but usually both.

Now, our hypothetical artistic hitter knows what he wants (let's say, "a ball I can pull," because it's late in the game and he has to try for an extra-base hit or even a homer). He knows that, in his case, this means any inside pitch above the waist, since he's pretty good at hitting curves as well as fastballs. He has a pretty good idea, by now, of how fast today's pitcher's fastball is, and is geared to hit it; if the pitch turns out to be a curve, he'll have time to adjust. (If he set himself up for a curve, on the other hand, a fastball would catch him unprepared.) And he knows that this pitcher, in this game, has had trouble controlling his curve and has been relying on fastballs in the last few innings.

Our hypothetical hitter also knows that, ordinarily, this pitcher likes to throw him low breaking balls, inside, a spot our hitter has trouble with. And the hitter, since he respects this pitcher, knows that the pitcher is just as aware as he is that the situation calls for a long hit.

The battle begins. The pitcher, despite past success, may not want to risk that unreliable curve; if he misses, and gets behind in the count, he will be in more danger when he has to make sure he throws strikes to avoid a walk. On the other hand, his fastball may not have quite as much steam as it had earlier in the game.

From the hitter's point of view, then, the principles are:

Make sure you recognize the desired pitch (inside and above the belt) whenever it happens.

Avoid swinging at any other kind of pitch, even if it means taking two strikes.

If the count gets to two strikes, try to foul off possible strikes that are out of the desired area. (Only the real bat artist can try this; the rest must give in.)

All this time the pitcher is trying to keep the ball down and away. In doing so, he may miss the strike zone often enough to issue a walk—which isn't what the hitter wanted, but still useful. But he may also miss the other way: He may miss by throwing the ball into the zone the hitter has chosen. In that case, the hitter "got his pitch."

He still has to hit it—and a very large number of times, a hitter will pop up or ground out or even strike out on exactly the pitch he was looking for. That's the human element. And many a game-winning hit has been made off "a good pitch," one that was thrown just where the pitcher wanted, and one that the hitter ordinarily has trouble with. In fact, it's exactly this element of uncertainty that keeps baseball interesting. Nevertheless, the odds are in favor of the batter who "gets his pitch" to hit.

What if he doesn't get it? That's when he has to "give in" to the pitcher's skill, and to try to go with the pitch. If the pitcher, in our example, succeeds in making several good pitches low and away, the best the hitter can do is accept the fact and try to meet the ball, hoping to poke a single through the opposite side.

This question of "giving in" really lies at the heart of "getting one's pitch." No single time at bat exists in isolation. The same hitters face the same pitchers many times. The hitter who can hit the ball in several directions is more likely to find the pitches he wants than one who is always trying to do one thing. If a pitcher gets stung a few times by a single to left by the left-handed home-run slugger, he will try to do something about it—and, in the process, increase the slugger's chances of getting an inside pitch by accident or design. But if the slugger keeps trying to pull the outside pitch and, as a result, is hitting harmless flies to center or easy grounders, the pitcher can keep making a sucker out of him forever. So the batter's actions each time at bat affect his chances on subsequent turns.

But common sense, also known as street smarts, has to enter into it too. Ron Fairly, in his later-life role as critic, likes to repeat what he learned through listening to masters and by his own experience.

"Why look for a pitch you know you can't hit?" he asks. "I see players do that all the time. Look only for the one you know you can handle. If you can't get around on Nolan Ryan's fastball inside, what good does it do to be mentally ready for it? Simply pass it up as long as you can. What you're looking for is something the pitcher probably doesn't want to give you in the first place; you're waiting for his mistake. But if his mistake is of a type, or to an area, that you're not good at anyhow, you still won't handle it. So don't work against yourself by looking for what won't help, even if you guess right. Look for what you *can* hit, in case you get it."

Casey Stengel had his own way of expressing almost anything. On this subject—the unwillingness of many hitters to give up trying to hit homers off pitches that were not suitable for that—he used to say: "They think they're bein' unlucky, but they'll be unlucky all their lives if they don't change."

And Hank Bauer, the right-handed bruiser who played for Stengel on the Yankees from 1949 through 1959 (on nine pennant winners in eleven years), learned the hard way. Old Yankee Stadium, of course, had an impossibly deep left center field. The left-field foul line was only 301 feet long, but the angle it made with the stands was so wide that a point some 20 feet fair was 402 feet deep, and true left center ranged from 420 to 460 feet. Bauer could hit a ball hard and far, but if he got around on an inside pitch a little too much, it would go foul, and if he didn't pull the ball right down the foul line, he couldn't reach the stands. So pitchers would feed him nice, fat, appetizing-looking deliveries just out enough over the plate so that Hank couldn't pull too sharply. He'd hit the ball 410 feet or so, and the left fielder would catch it at an easy trot.

One day, after Hank had been a Yankee for seven years or so, he hit seven drives of 400 feet or more in one doubleheader. All were caught. After the games, he was sitting in front of his locker, shaking his head. A sympathetic newspaperman came by.

"Tough luck," said the reporter.

"How about that?" said Bauer, his hoarse voice a trifle hoarser than usual. "Seven of my best shots—seven. And not even a single."

"Well," the reporter (who had been indoctrinated by Stengel long ago) suggested politely, "can you draw a conclusion?"

Hank looked up, and started to smile slowly.

"Yeah," he said. "I know what you mean. Yeah. Maybe that's right."

Bauer was past his peak as a player when this happened, but the realization stayed with him. As a manager at Kansas City and Baltimore, he became an outspoken member of the Stop-Trying-to-Pull-Every-Pitch philosophy.

If it is so plain that hitting to all fields—going with a pitch—is advantageous, why do so many players fail to acquire the skill? After all, most players aren't idiots and their livelihood is at stake. There are three main reasons why players remain resistant: greed, insecurity, and difficulty. The last two reasons are, in all fairness, pretty good ones.

Greed used to be simple to explain: "Home-run hitters drive Cadillacs" was an irrefutable slogan. All of baseball's biggest moneymakers (except pitchers)—Babe Ruth, Joe DiMaggio, Ted Williams, Willie Mays, Mickey Mantle, Stan Musial, Hank Aaron, Mike Schmidt, and Reggie Jackson—were prolific home-run hitters. Home runs are hit, fundamentally, by pulling the ball, because a hitter's power is to the side he swings from, and fences are closer at the foul line. The trouble is, the ability to hit a lot of homers is a rare one. While it is true that those who can hit a lot of homers "strike it rich," it is also true that those who try and can't, wind up with less lucrative careers than those who realize they must utilize their talents in more modest fashion. Since baseball players are not chosen for proficiency in freshman logic, the falsity of the mock syllogism "Home-run hitters drive Cadillacs, I want a Cadillac, therefore I should try for homers" escapes many of them.

This economic motivation is much weaker since the salary explosion put even utility players in the million-dollar class and the old symbolic flavor of "Cadillac" became incomprehensible. (Today's player is likely to travel in a chauffeur-driven stretch limo, or collect six-figure sports cars by the dozen.) But it does still exist. Oakland's José Canseco added half a million dollars to his 1989 asking price by achieving his 40-40 statistic in 1988—and the first 40 stood for homers. Without that, the 40 stolen bases wouldn't have had much impact. And it was still being cited as his distinguishing characteristic when he broke new ground to a $5 million-a-year level by signing a five-year contract midway through the 1990 season.

There is less blind fascination with home runs today than there used to be a generation ago, for several reasons: They aren't the glamorous novelty they seemed to fans of the 1920s and 1930s, who were the trendsetters for attitudes of the 1950s and 1960s; the surpassing of Ruth's records by Roger Maris and Hank Aaron took some of the "uniqueness" out of their emotional impact; the increasing sophistication of spectators since television, along with the revival of a running game, enhances a better perspective about "mere" home-run hitting.

Nevertheless, home-run power still distinguishes the best from the very good. It's all the other assets *plus* a lot of homers—by Canseco, or Ryne Sandberg, or Will Clark, or Don Mattingly, or Mike Schmidt, or Reggie Jackson—that defines first-magnitude stardom.

And, in a perverse way, in an age in which strikeouts are more acceptable, .220 averages are common, and low salaries are restricted to players in their first couple of seasons, a few homers on your record may seem even more appealing since the price you pay for trying and failing is so discounted.

Even so great a slugger as Mantle, at the advanced age of thirty-five, could be subject to this misplaced desire. About halfway through the 1966 season, Mickey went on a home-run spree. He hit eight home runs in a six-game swing through Boston and Washington and was suddenly the hottest story in baseball.

The Yankees returned to their stadium, with its cozy right field, and played the Red Sox, the same team Mantle had slaughtered a week before in Boston. The same right-handed pitchers worked. But Mickey, now conscious of home-run heroism (and responding to its glory after a long period of injury-caused eclipse), started swinging for the fences deliberately. He tried to pull. He tried to hit it into the third deck. And he did nothing at all. He struck out six times in three games, popped up, and got one opposite-field single. The Yankees lost three straight.

They went into the ninth inning of the fourth game of the series trailing, 2–0, about to lose their fourth in a row. But the Yankees rallied, tied the score, and had men on first and third with two out as Mantle came up.

Now it was a desperate situation for the team: The winning run was on third, and it didn't matter how it scored to end the losing streak. Any kind of hit would do it, but a long fly would be useless. All Mantle cared about was meeting the ball, poking it through the infield somehow, avoiding a strikeout at all costs.

Not concerned with distance or pulling the ball, Mickey belted it twelve rows deep into the right-field stands for a dramatic three-run homer. Having put aside home-run greed, he was able to swing naturally again—and got his homer.

Greed, after all, can be psychic as well as material. Home runs, especially long ones, are macho, and professional athletes are more likely to be inclined to that self-image than, let's say, hairdressers.

Insecurity is a much more valid obstacle. Hitting is habit—reflex, groove, automatic reaction. Every player is wary of losing his timing, and therefore his confidence. Every player has a tremendous stake in doing things exactly the way he has always done them, because these have meant success. He got to the majors by hitting a certain way, and he is immensely reluctant to change any pattern as long as he continues to have a reasonable amount of success with it.

At this point, a question arises about degree of success. The manager constantly seeks improvement; the player tends to protect what he has. Hitting .280, he can be a regular. The manager thinks that, by making a few changes, that man might hit .300, but the hitter is more likely to feel that, in trying to make changes that feel unnatural or uncomfortable, he may drop to .250. In most professional athletes these days, the fear of a drop-off in record and earning power outweighs the hope of doing better—especially since the rewards for sustaining mediocre performance are so high.

And the thing that justifies the hitter's fear of change, in his own eyes and to a significant degree objectively, is the fact that it is not easy to change. With good intentions, and honest effort, a man may still fail to master the knack of hitting to all fields. Like power, this is a skill some men have naturally more than others. A man may have sufficient bat control to hit fairly well in his natural pattern, but not so much that he can also coordinate his actions for a more deliberate, less automatic way of hitting. So most major-league hitters, acknowledging the advantages of "going with the pitch," nevertheless fail to do it much of the time.

There's a slight relationship here to the subject of bunting. Everyone should be able to bunt, right? It's so simple: Square around, face the pitcher, plant your feet, and just tap the ball out in front of the plate. (We're talking only about sacrifice bunts to advance runners, not surprise bunts to get on base.) Poor hitters above all, and especially pitchers, should be able to bunt. No single deficiency in baseball arouses as much indignation among intolerant old-timers as the inability to bunt.

Yet a startling proportion of attempted sacrifice bunts fail. Why? Because today it is *not* easy to execute a bunt under game conditions. It's easy enough in practice, but not easy when the pitcher is throwing hard in an attempt to prevent exactly that, while the first baseman and third baseman tear in at top speed to field the ball. In the context of major-league baseball life, there is little opportunity to practice bunting under competitive conditions, and therefore, what is so simple in practice is difficult to carry out in a game. Furthermore, many fields consist of artificial turf, on which the ball moves quickly and far, and making the bunt soft enough is definitely a problem.

By now, another of baseball's unacceptable dirty words—like "luck"—is entering the picture. All we have said about hitting revolves around analyzing what the pitcher might do, and adjusting the batter's desires to the pitcher's actions. The word taking form is "guessing."

A "guess hitter," in baseball society, is one to be sneered at. But, obviously, all hitters are "guessing" all the time. The distinction is one of definition. To "guess" in one sense is fatal to good hitting—in the sense that a hitter says, I've got my mind made up that this next pitch is going to be a fastball. And it is that sort of guessing that players have in mind when they criticize someone else for being a "guess hitter," or deny being one themselves.

In another sense, however, the "educated guess" is the basis of good hitting. Here the batter says to himself, For such-and-such a set of reasons, he might throw me a fastball now, and if he does, I'm ready to hit it. In the first case, the hitter mentally committed himself to something that may not happen; in the second, he alerted himself for one thing but remained ready to cope with anything else that may happen.

So far, we have ignored one of the most obvious features of hitting—the fact that some players bat right-handed and some bat left-handed.

Batting left-handed is a major advantage. For one thing, the left-handed batter, at the end of his swing, is two steps closer to first base and moving in the right direction. The right-handed batter ends his swing with his body weight toward third. He must check his momentum and set off across home plate toward first. These two steps make a great deal of difference in beating out infield hits and in avoiding the second half of what could be a double play.

For another thing, most pitchers—about 75 percent of them in the majors—are right-handed, and it is a fundamental law of baseball that left-handed batters have a better shot at right-handed pitchers, and that right-handed batters have a better crack at left-handed pitchers. This is one popular theory that is absolutely true (as a generality, that is, with plenty of significant exceptions). There are two reasons why these lefty-righty opposites work in favor of the hitter: sight and spin.

Consider the right-handed batter facing a lefty. The arm delivering the ball is coming from the first-base side of the mound, and is in a field of vision that requires less turning of the head. As the ball approaches (imagine a straight fastball), it appears to move toward the hitter laterally (as well as toward him from mound to plate). It is easier for a right-hander to judge the trajectory of such a pitch than one thrown from the third-base side of the mound. In that case, the ball's motion in the horizontal plane seems to be *away* from the batter, and the head must turn slightly to keep the ball in focus. In addition, the natural spin imparted to a baseball makes it tend to curve away from the side it was thrown from. A "normal" curve thrown by a right-hander breaks away from a right-handed batter, and toward a left-hander—and for a curve thrown by a left-hander it is the reverse. Exceptions are numerous, because of individual styles and pitches given reverse spin, but that's a subject for the next chapter. The point is, left-handed hitters do have an advantage.

But, in that case, why doesn't everyone hit left-handed? Many players who throw right-handed bat left-handed, so it doesn't seem to be that closely tied to natural left-handedness. And why aren't all left-handed hitters better than right-handed hitters?

Here, again, human factors come into play. Most right-handed people automatically start to bat right-handed, and once the habits become set, they are too hard to change, especially since these habits begin in childhood. And the left-handers have some disadvantages, too, because of the prevalence of right-handers.

A right-handed hitter, to reach the majors at all, *must* learn to do reasonably well against right-handed pitchers. If he didn't, his record would be too poor. Then, when he faces a left-hander about one-fourth of the time, the unfamiliarity of the confrontation is compensated for by the natural advantages of righty-lefty oppositeness.

The left-handed batter faces the reverse problem. He has had the advantage, most of the time, of facing "opposite" pitchers. When he has to bat against a lefty, it is both difficult *and* relatively unfamiliar. And that's why, traditionally, left-handed batters have more trouble with left-handed pitchers than righties do with righties.

But then, it should be obvious that the greatest thing in the world must be to be a switch-hitter, like Mickey Mantle. If a man can hit from both sides of the plate, the confrontation with the pitcher is *always* in his favor. Or so it would seem. It turns out, though, that things aren't exactly what they seem. This point was made by Tom Tresh, one of the young switch-hitters who came along in the wake of Mantle's example.

"It's an edge," Tresh explains, "but not as big an edge as you'd think. Hitting is rhythm, finding a groove, all that stuff. When you are a switch-hitter, you have two totally distinct batting styles. Something can go wrong with either one, independently of the other. And the constant changing may keep you from getting best set in either one. Now, every switch-hitter is better one way than the other. It's hard to say exactly how much better or worse a man might have done if he had concentrated all his life on his stronger side."

There's little incentive, of course, for a natural left-hander to learn to bat righty, since the left-handed hitter has the advantages already noted. Switch-hitters, then, are almost always natural right-handers who have learned to hit lefty also, and it is common practice to try to turn a weak-hitting but fast-running right-handed man into a switch-hitter. (It seldom works, but when it does, it saves a career—as it did for Maury Wills.)

And, of course, Pete Rose, who got more hits than anyone else, did it switch-hitting.

Another long-accepted tenet of baseball lore is that the curve ball is the hardest pitch to hit. Traditionally, the minors are full of players who never made it in the majors because "they couldn't hit a curve." A surprising number of contemporary experts—that is, expert hitters—disagree with this idea. Red Schoendienst, who was one of the most skillful hitters of his day and subsequently manager of the St. Louis Cardinals, put it this way: "The hardest pitch to hit is a fastball, and anyone who doesn't realize that is kidding himself. I mean, of course, a real good fastball. And it's hardest to hit for the simplest of reasons: You have the least time to react. A curveball travels slower. You can learn to time and plot its course, and to adjust. But if the good fastball is fast enough to keep you from getting all the way around on it, there's nothing you can do.

"What this means is that a hitter has to *set* himself for the pitcher's best fastball. It may be true that if the pitcher threw nothing but fastballs in succession, the hitter might eventually time up to it—or the pitcher would get tired—but in practice that doesn't happen. The hitter, then, has to be ready to hit the fastest pitch that pitcher can throw.

"It is only then, working *off* the fastball, that the curve becomes so hard to hit. It's not the curve itself, it's the contrast, in speed and direction, between the curve and the fastball you have to be set for. It's when a pitcher mixes things up properly that a hitter finds it so hard to hit a curveball. But if the fastball isn't very fast, or if you know the curve is coming, the curve isn't that hard to hit."

The truth, then, is once again hidden by a common expression that contains a grain of it. It's true that many big-league hitters never learn to hit a curve—*while being set for a fastball.* It's because they can't give up some degree of being set for the fastball that the curve puts them out of business.

But now we are inching over into the pitcher's area of operation: the different deliveries, what they do, how they are used, and so forth. Before going on to that, we have to consider one final aspect of the hitter's viewpoint, one to which we will return in our discussion of pitching. This is the matter of the pitcher's "motion."

A hitter does not—cannot—see the ball approach in isolation, like some object on a radarscope. He sees it in a context: A pitcher winds up, goes through a complicated motion, and out of this motion the ball suddenly appears. The hitter must react to the *totality* of windup, delivery, background, and trajectory, and this varies from pitcher to pitcher and from place to place. That is why a pitching machine has only limited usefulness in batting practice. It can reproduce, to any desired degree, the *actual* path of the ball as thrown by a pitcher, but it can't give the hitter any practice at all in identifying this actual path out of the welter of arm and leg motions produced by a live pitcher in a competitive game.

One thing a batter can look for is "rotation": As the ball spins while flying toward the plate, the red seams form a kaleidoscopic design, like a dot or a blur, which can tip off the kind of spin that implies fastball or curve. Also, an overhand fastball motion displays the white ball at the moment it leaves the hand; an overhand curve, on which the pitcher "turns the ball over," shows the hitter flesh first and then the ball.

But Stan Musial, a supreme artist in his field, told an interviewer in 1990, a generation after he had stopped playing, "They used to say that I could pick up the spin of a curveball, but I didn't do that at all. What I knew was the speed of every pitcher's fastball, and I could judge that. If it was something less, it had to be a breaking ball or a change."

Think about that for a moment: In his mental file, Musial could identify the velocity of hundreds of different men's fastballs—in less than a tenth of a second. That's why he hit .331 lifetime—which means that even *he* made outs two-thirds of the time.

So the major-league hitter confronts, endlessly, two shifting dynamics: physical and mental—the physical act of swinging the bat, and the eye-brain reflex that fires off muscular response, deals with sorting out the elements of each delivery. The decision-making process, meanwhile, controls expectation, preparation, concentration, and in-tention—the art-and-craft aspect. But both are a reactive mode, re-sponding not only to the movements made but to the thoughts generated by the one who holds the ball in his hand.

And that's the fellow who starts and controls the game—the pitcher.

CHAPTER

2

Pitching—The Scientific Art

Pitching is 75 percent of baseball—or 70 percent, or 90, or any other high number that pops into the mind of the speaker. The more popular current phrase, "pitching is the name of the game," reflects the fact that it is again more fashionable to speak in metaphors since high-powered computers have usurped the illusion of accuracy baseball statistics used to supply.

In any case, there is no disagreement about the point itself: Pitching is the most important element in the game. As a rule, the team with better pitching wins the game, and the team with the better pitching staff wins the pennant, while many a heavy-hitting lineup winds up nowhere because its pitching is poor.

This may be obscured by the glamour of day-in, day-out slugging. Many outstanding teams, like the Yankees of 1927, 1936, and a dozen other winning years, had awesome power but they also had consistently fine pitching, and it was the combination that made them so great. On the other hand, teams like the 1930 Phillies (who had eight .300 hitters and finished eighth) and the 1947 Giants (who broke all home-run records and finished fourth) show how fruitless run-making can be if the pitching isn't there for the defensive half of the inning. Yet the Dodgers of 1963, 1965, and 1966 were able to win pennants with little else than superb pitching.

Such examples could be multiplied indefinitely. Recent ones include the 1988 Dodgers, who won with pitching; the various Red Sox and Cincinnati teams that lost despite good hitting; and the 1988–1990 Oakland A's, who showed so much balance.

Walter Alston, who managed the Dodgers to their victories in the sixties, summed it up as well as anyone. "When you get consistently good pitching," he said, "you keep the score low, and you have a chance in every game. You can try to use all the ways there are to score a run, and benefit from any error or lucky break. You're never out of the game. But if your own pitching gives up a lot of runs, there will be lots of times when you're out of business early, where the only way to get back is with a lot of slugging of your own. So it's pretty hard to be lucky when your pitching is bad."

An axiom goes hand in hand with this truism: Good pitchers usually stop good hitters, rather than the other way around. The good hitters fatten up on the mediocre pitchers, but the best pitchers often complete spectacular records against the best hitters. It isn't hard to see why all this should be so. It's an inherent condition of baseball, tactically and mathematically.

Tactically, the pitcher is the most important man on the ball field because he is, essentially, the aggressor. In the truest sense, he is the "offense," because he puts the ball in play and does so according to his intentions and ability. He has the initiative—he knows where he's going to throw the ball (provided his skill doesn't fail him), exactly when, and how. His is the deliberate, calculated act, and the batter must react to it. In this sense, it is the batter who is on the defensive side of the action until and unless he hits the ball; only then does the team at bat become the attacker.

Mathematically, it's cut and dried. According to the rules, you can't win a game unless you get 27 men out; you *can* win by scoring only one run. The defensive side of baseball, therefore, requires great consistency: Nine times a game, you must get three outs in an inning. The offensive side can, and almost always does, work in fits and starts. A lucky hit, one defensive lapse, one ball tagged just right, can produce one or more runs, and any one run can win a game; but a lucky bounce, a spectacular catch, or other exceptional defensive occurrence is only 1/27th of the work needed—by definition—to complete a winning game.

That's what a pitcher thinks about—getting men out.

Let's examine some of his premises:

First, under major-league conditions, he accepts the fact that he cannot strike out every hitter. Therefore, the outs will have to be recorded by his fielders. Therefore, if he can prevent each hitter from hitting the ball too solidly, his fielders will have a chance to make the play in the vast majority of cases. The pitcher's job, then, is to do whatever he can to keep the batter from hitting the ball solidly.

How can he do this? The whole immense technique of pitching deals with this question, and we'll come back to it in detail a little further on. Suffice it to say that a pitcher can employ time (by varying the speed of his deliveries), space (by pitching high, low, inside, outside), trajectory (by making the ball curve or otherwise change direction on the way to the plate), deception (by making the hitter expect one thing while doing another), knowledge (of hitters' weaknesses and his own assets), and strategy (by limiting the batter's choice in particular situations, apart from deception).

A second premise is that pitching, physically, is an unnatural act. Hundreds of millions of years of human evolution did nothing to prepare the structure of the arm for the strain of 150 maximum-effort throwing motions in the space of a couple of hours. There are those who claim that any overhand throwing motion is contrary to nature; but whether it is or not, to use it as often and as hard as pitching requires is an abuse of normal body function. After all, the arm hangs down from the shoulder, the elbow joint turns in, and so many pitching motions require exertion in the opposite directions. All in all, pitching sets up tremendous strains in muscles, ligaments, tendons, joints, and even certain pieces of bone.

The consequence of this physical fact is that a pitcher must take care of his arm in some special fashion. He can work only so often (usually no more than once in four days, if he is a starter). He needs a trainer's assistance, in some form of rubdown or muscle-stretching massage, before he pitches and often afterward. He must be able to withstand a certain amount of inevitable pain without having his concentration suffer. He must stay in good shape in general because his whole body is involved in the rhythmic pitching motion, and because he must not succumb to fatigue late in a game. He must, in short, keep his arm physically sound in order to put into effect his knowledge of how to keep hitters from connecting.

It must seem confusing, in the light of this, to read about the pitching heroes of the nineteenth century, who posted won–lost records like 60–12 (Hoss Radbourne, in 1884) and regularly won more than 30 games. The mystery disappears, however, when one realizes how different the conditions were. Until 1884, overhand pitching wasn't even permitted; after that, until about the time of World War I, it was customary to use one baseball until it was lost, no matter how scarred or soft it became. In this dead-ball era, a complete game required perhaps half the number of pitches required today. And with little danger of a home run by any but the very best batters, pitchers didn't have to bear down as hard on every pitch, the way they do today. In short, they pitched more often because they didn't work as hard when they worked.

These physical limitations have tactical consequences. The full range of weapons available in theory is never at the disposal of any one pitcher. In individual cases, attempts to use the wrong type of delivery may hurt the arm, and very often minor injury or fatigue will prevent even a healthy pitcher from using a particular delivery as often as he would like that particular day. And, of course, the necessity for sufficient warm-up and proper rest determines every manager's thinking about who is to pitch and when.

Sandy Koufax is an example of a pitcher who ran into the first type of problem, while at the height of his powers. In 1963 and 1964, he developed a sidearm curve to use to left-handed hitters, and it gave his already overstocked arsenal an extra, especially unkind, torture weapon. But he found that using it made his elbow sore. It was only later that his arthritic condition was diagnosed, and it was clear that the sidearm pitch would have to be dropped permanently. This limited him so much that he could win only 53 games in the next two seasons— which is merely the largest number of victories posted in consecutive years by any National League left-hander in the modern era.

Sandy's teammate Maury Wills used to tell a story in his nightclub act that illustrates the kind of problem rest and warm-up cause for managers.

The Dodgers, Wills said, were playing a vital four-game series in San Francisco in August of 1965. The Dodger bullpen was slightly overworked and had to be stretched through the four-game set. Manager Walt Alston, therefore, was reluctant to order a reliever up any sooner than necessary.

In the fifth, Claude Osteen, the Dodger starter, lost his stuff abruptly, and Alston had to wave in Bob Miller.

"Look, Maury," Alston told Wills at the conference at the mound. "We need some extra time for Miller to warm up. When he gets here and takes his regular warm-up pitches, you go back to short, and then pretend you've got something in your eye. Make it good, really put on an act. Then, while we're trying to fix your eye, Miller can keep throwing."

It was a flawless plan, and Wills gave a great performance.

"I'm blinking, and staggering, and moaning," is the way Wills described it. "The umpire is convinced, and doing his best to help. The trainer is working on me. Other players are gathering around. My act is so good that Miller has time not only to get warmed up but to get tired. And what does Miller actually do? Instead of warming up, he comes over with a towel to help them get something out of my eye!"

A third premise is that a pitcher must have control—and "control" is a tricky word. There are two kinds of control: One is the ability to throw strikes, to make every variety of pitch in that pitcher's repertoire go through the strike zone with great dependability (let's say, four out of five, or nine out of ten times). This kind of control—the broad-scale control—is an absolute must for a major-league pitcher. On the days he doesn't have it, there's nothing he can do.

The other kind of control is pinpoint control, the ability to throw each pitch not merely over the plate but to a very specific spot, just so high, just so much inside or outside, and at just exactly the desired speed. This is a much rarer accomplishment, and the pitchers who have it are the true maestros of their trade.

It is obvious enough why strike-zone control is essential and pinpoint control a blessing. Unless the pitcher can deliver the ball exactly where and how he wants to, his mental success in fooling the hitter is wasted.

The fourth basic premise of pitching is "stuff." The pitcher must be able to throw the ball hard enough to make reaction time a problem for the batter. A pitch perfectly placed, but thrown so softly that the hitter can readjust his sights, will be socked just as hard as if the hitter had guessed right in the first place. At the major-league level, there is a threshold of speed that must be maintained, and all talk of "slow" or "soft" or "junk" pitches refers to *relative* speed.

That's why, incidentally, slow-stuff pitchers are often effective. Hitters are geared to the average level of speed, a level that would catch most of us motionless, and a "slow" pitch (which would seem plenty fast if you or I were trying to hit it) is hard to adjust to. It requires a check on all those built-in reflexes it took years to set. But even these "slow" pitches can't be so slow that the batter gets a chance to check himself, and then start swinging again, or to wait until it breaks and misses the strike zone.

But with regular-speed pitches, the amount of stuff on them has to be sufficient. It's not enough to throw a curve or a fastball to the right spot; it has to be a curveball that really breaks, not gently bends, and a fastball that has something on it. Otherwise, the correct intentions are nullified by physical failure.

Perhaps the most common of all pitching problems is the tendency, more often subconscious than conscious, to "ease up" or "aim the ball" in an effort to improve control. To "take something off it" as a deliberate change of speeds is one thing; to do it in an attempt to get a strike, or pitch to a particular spot, can lead to disaster. And it happens all the time, even to the best pitchers occasionally.

Our fifth and final pitching premise is the subject of "motion," touched on at the end of the chapter on hitting. The ball does not come toward the plate as an isolated object. The pitcher's windup, his kick, his arm motion, and the background all form part of the picture. Now, to the pitcher the motion has a positive and negative importance. On the positive side, it can be used to increase the deceptiveness of his delivery, by hiding the ball as long as possible, by distraction, and by intensifying some unusual angle of the trajectory (like a sidearm pitch thrown by a right-hander to a right-handed batter). On the negative side, a motion that is noticeably different for different types of pitches will tip off the alert opponent as to which pitch is coming.

Pitchers strive, therefore, to develop identical motions from which to throw all their basic deliveries, and to find a motion that strikes the best balance between their own comfort (which is the main consideration) and bewilderment of the batter.

Most pitchers whose repertoire is based on off-speed pitching—Stu Miller, Eddie Lopat, Jim Konstanty, Kent Tekulve, Fernando Valenzuela after his arm injury, Mike Boddicker—rely on motion as much as on the actual pitch to fool the hitter. But it must be stressed, again that even such pitchers have fairly respectable fastballs, fast enough to catch a hitter flat-footed when mixed in properly with the softer stuff.

Back in the 1950s, when New York still had three teams, Stu Miller worked for the Giants. They occupied the Polo Grounds, which had the shortest walls in the majors along the foul lines. This was early in Stu's career, and much was being made of his three speeds: "Slow, slower, slowest." Bill Roeder, a baseball writer for the then *World-Telegram and Sun*, decided he'd like to do a first-person story about how it felt to bat against Miller.

Roeder went to the manager, Bill Rigney, for permission.

"Nothing doing," said Rigney. "I can't afford to risk it."

Roeder, a good baseball man, could understand Rigney's reluctance.

"Look, I'm a young guy and I'm pretty agile," said Roeder. "I can get out of the way if he comes close, and you know he won't anyhow. Besides, we can fix it up so that my paper and I take full responsibility."

"It's not that," said Rigney. "But what if you got lucky and hit one over that 257-foot fence? What happens to my pitcher then? How would he ever get his confidence back?"

Thus saved from possible psychological destruction by a solicitous manager, Miller went on to considerable success in both leagues over the next decade.

But there was a grain of truth to Rigney's apprehension. Miller's slow stuff, to an amateur, would not be a disturbing contrast but a handleable problem, and the fakes and twists of Miller's motion could not deceive someone who was not accustomed to reacting to ordinary motions. Of course, with his own fastball, Miller could easily have overpowered a newspaperman, but if the experiment were performed in good faith, with Miller throwing easy, the kind of accident Rigney feared was not impossible.

Lopat, like Miller, promoted the idea that he was incredibly slow, but his real asset was a great variety of speeds with perfectly placed curves. He could buzz one fairly hard, when he wanted to, and when he did—at a moment of his choosing—he looked like Walter Johnson just by contrast.

Almost all Lopat's pitching success came as a Yankee. When he was at the end of the line, however, he found himself pitching briefly for the Baltimore Orioles, whose manager was Paul Richards. Before managing Baltimore, Richards had managed Chicago White Sox teams that were repeatedly knocked out of contention by the Yankees, with Lopat's help. Richards, a proud Texan, had one point of pride above all others: his ability to teach pitching.

When Lopat arrived, Richards offered a suggestion.

"If you do this," said Richards, showing a certain grip and motion, "I'm sure it can help you."

"This?" asked Lopat. "I have that one here, here, here, and here," he said, rapidly displaying four different degrees of spin and arm location at the release of the ball. "What do you think I've been getting you out with all these years?"

Many years later, after Lopat had served as a manager and general manager and pitching coach and superscout himself, he once spoke of another dimension of truly artistic pitching.

"I could usually tell, by watching the hitter's reactions, how he would have hit a ball even if he didn't go through with the swing," he said. "You watch his legs, arms, body, eyes—everything. Sometimes, then, you may throw a pitch, outside the strike zone, just to watch his responses; it may tell you something.

"Specifically, though, look at it this way: If you throw a fastball and he fouls it off down the first-base line (a right-handed hitter, I mean), you know he was a little late swinging at it. If he fouls it past third, you know he swung a little early. Now, if the thing you're doing is trying to prevent him from pulling the ball, you might try another one if you know he's been timing it late—if you've got that good a fastball, of course—but you'd be absolutely crazy to try another one if he had just shown he was swinging at it too soon. So what he does with one pitch, or a series of pitches, can help you decide what to do with the next one."

The scientific element in pitching is considerably greater than the scientific element in hitting, according to our original definitions. The mechanics of pitching—grip, release of the ball, arm motion, body position—are dealt with much more consciously than the mechanics of hitting, and there are more of them to master. We are not concerned here with the mechanical details of how to grip and release various types of pitches, but this is a subject of vital interest to pitchers and their coaches.

The basic pitches used, however, do need description, and before they can be described, one of baseball's hoariest arguments must be dealt with.

Does a baseball, thrown over the distance of 60 feet 6 inches from the rubber to the plate, actually curve? Or is it just an optical illusion?

The real answer is: both. It most certainly does curve, but there is also an optical illusion involved that plays an important role.

Many, many treatises have been written proving mathematically that a baseball can't possibly curve under the forces applied. Many others have explained why it can and does. The explanation most widely accepted these days, at least among physics-minded baseball people, is this: The rotation of the ball, as determined by the way the pitcher releases it, sets up differences in air resistance and pressure on opposite sides of the ball, and this makes it veer to one side or the other. This deflection becomes greater as more of the forward force is spent. At the same time, gravity is working on the ball from the moment it leaves the pitcher's hand. The result is a fairly complicated path, but decidedly bent.

But what a batter, standing alongside home plate, sees is not an *actual* path but an *apparent* path. The actual path, plotted on a graph or photographed from directly above the field, is quite different from the illusion the batter must react to. The batter's illusion is a distorted one, because the ball is moving toward him while he is stationary. When it first leaves the pitcher's hand, any change in its direction appears relatively slight; by the time it is near the plate, exactly the same amount of horizontal or vertical deflection seems much larger.

But what does the batter actually swing at? After all, it takes a finite time—brief but finite—for muscles to respond to brain-and-eye directions. Whenever the swing actually begins, it must begin sometime *before* the ball reaches the plate if bat and ball are to collide flush in the area of home plate.

What happens, then, is this: The batter follows the flight of the ball for perhaps the first 40 of the 60 feet. On the basis of its apparent trajectory over that distance, he projects what the rest of the trajectory will be, and starts to swing accordingly. None of the process is conscious, of course. The human brain is still far the most efficient computer in existence, and experience has fed the batter's computer-brain, which does its work without bothering one's awareness. He may be able, as Ted Williams is supposed to have been, actually to see the ball hit the bat, but by then it's irrelevant. The bat action had to be started sometime before. The conscious decisions (to swing or not) and the unconscious decisions (where to swing) are made when the ball is approximately two-thirds of the way home.

For all these reasons, the *apparent* break of a curveball is bigger (and more effective) from the hitter's point of view (and the catcher's and umpire's) than its actual break. This can be seen, sometimes, when television switches from a home-plate camera to a center-field camera on successive pitches. The shot from center field shows a curve breaking not as much as the shot from behind home plate. Since both cameras are relatively far from the action, however, the apparent difference is slight; to the batter on the scene, the scale of difference is much greater. The actual non-straight path veers relatively constantly and gradually—but the hitter sees the *noticeable* change disproportionately late and close-up: He sees the ball "move" only when it's near home plate.

Jay Hook, one of the most personable and least successful of the original Met pitchers, was an engineer. He once provided *The New York Times* with a learned essay, complete with diagrams and formulas, showing why a baseball curves. This prompted the baseball writers to create the following parody, on the Rodgers and Hart song "I Could Write a Book," from *Pal Joey*. The actor depicting Hook sang:

> *If they asked me I could write a book,*
> *About the way a baseball's spin makes it hook.*
> *I know all the theories, the complex math,*
> *That explains a curving ball's path.*
> *I compute compression of the air,*
> *Count gravity as one-half times Gee Tee square,*
> *But with all I know of trajectory,*
> *They keep hitting homers off me.*

Jay's problem, you see, was not the way the ball curved on the way in but the way it soared on the way out, usually 400 feet or more.

So we accept the idea that a pitcher does make a ball curve, really and truly. But how many ways, and what for? What are the basic pitches?

1. The primary pitch is a fastball. It is, to all intents and purposes, a pitch with a straight trajectory, although in reality it veers off a little bit. Because it is straight, it is the easiest pitch to throw to any par-

ticular spot—and it is the easiest path for a hitter to judge correctly. Its usefulness, then, lies in its speed. In baseball talk, however, any straight pitch is referred to as a "fastball," even if it isn't especially fast. Almost all other deliveries are lumped under the category of "breaking balls."

If a fastball is fast enough, it has a "hop" to it. This is almost entirely illusion, but it's a dilly. The pitcher is throwing from a hill, 10 inches above the level of home plate. He releases the ball at some point usually even with his head, so let's estimate this to be about 7 feet above plate level. The top of the strike zone, on the average batter, may be 4½ feet (or less, these days) above ground level. Therefore the fastball, in the course of traveling 60 feet, must drop at least 2½ feet to be a strike.

The faster a ball is thrown—the more force it has behind it—the shorter will be its time in flight and the less it will be affected by gravity during its trip from pitcher to catcher. Gravity, as televised space shots must have taught us all by now, is a constant acceleration: It exerts the same amount of downward pull in the same amount of time regardless of horizontal forces involved.

Now, the batter is accustomed, by experience, to gauging the paths of thousands of ordinary fastballs. But the extra-fast fastball, being in flight a shorter time, doesn't get pulled down *as much*. It still comes down, or it wouldn't be a strike, but it comes down *less* than the ordinary fastball. But the hitter makes his decision—remember?— when the ball is still about 20 feet away. At that point, he has no specific landmark to measure its speed against; he *expects* the rest of the path to be that of an ordinary straight fastball, and swings—but by the time the ball gets to home plate, it is *higher* than the ordinary pitch would have been. This is translated, by the hitter's mind and eye, into a "hop"—a jump.

Whether it jumps or not, a good fastball "moves" a little bit. It is called "live." A pitch with the same velocity that's absolutely straight is called "flat," and is the reason some men can throw hard and still get clobbered.

Overwhelming speed, when available, is the most effective pitch. That's what made Walter Johnson, Bob Feller, Lefty Grove, and Nolan Ryan superstars. In this respect, myth and intuition are in accordance with fact. But this truth applies only if exceptional speed is truly overwhelming.

Roger Clemens of the Boston Red Sox became one of the premier power pitchers in the middle of the 1980s, about the same time Dwight Gooden was earning the name "Dr. K" as a strikeout king with the Mets. Clemens set the major-league record by striking out 20 in one nine-inning game in April of 1986; Gooden owns the rookie record for strikeouts in a season, 276, set in 1984.

In the 1986 All-Star Game at the Astrodome, Clemens went to bat against Gooden. They were the starting pitchers. Clemens, whose 1985 season had been cut short by injury, had started 1986 with 14 straight victories and was 15–2 at this point, en route to 24–4; Gooden, who had been 24–4 in 1985, was 10–4 now.

Gooden threw Clemens a fastball. *His* fastball.

Clemens turned to Gary Carter, the catcher.

"Is he throwing as fast as I am?" Clemens asked, meaning, in effect, "Is that how fast I throw?"

"Yes he is," said Carter.

And Clemens thought to himself: There's no way a human being can hit a pitch that's thrown that hard. Having experienced it from the batter's box for himself, he decided he wouldn't have to bother with finesse and could rely on his fastball as a basic pitch from then on. It was the right conclusion—but only for someone who could throw as hard as they.

2. The second basic pitch is a curve. It would be more accurate to call the curve a family of pitches, because a curve can be thrown with many different degrees of "break"—change of path—and at many different speeds. The main characteristic of the common curve, however, is the downward component of its break. In giving it the proper spin, the pitcher gives it less forward force, and when it reaches the plate, both spin and spent force (which gives gravity that much more time to operate) work in the same direction—down and away from a hitter of the same-handedness as the pitcher.

3. The third indispensable element of a pitcher's repertoire is some sort of "change of pace"—a pitch that is enough slower than his fastball to make a strong contrast, but is not identifiable as easily and as early in its flight path as the curveball is. There are many varieties, often named after the method of grip (like the palmball), but the one indispensable element is that the motion of delivery must look like a fastball or regular curve.

Every pitcher must be able to control three pitches of the above type to be effective for any length of time. A man doesn't have to be equally proficient with all: A great fastball can be supported by a very mediocre curve and rudimentary change-up, and excellent curves can make a moderate fastball sufficient. But those are the three building blocks—throw it fast, throw it slow, make it bend. Unless a pitcher can get strikes with each of the three types when necessary, he isn't going to be a big leaguer long.

4. The slider is a cross between the fastball and the curve, and one of the most widely used pitches in baseball today. It's no longer a newcomer, the way things are measured in baseball. The fastball, curve, and change were thoroughly established weapons before the turn of the century. The slider came into general use only after World War II. The main difference between a curve and a slider is the plane in which it breaks. A slider looks like a fastball until the last moment, and then veers off to the left or right, not very much, but more than enough to avoid the batter's intended point of contact. It doesn't drop sharply as it bends, however, the way a curveball does, but stays pretty much in one plane, like a fastball.

Like the curve, the slider is also a family of pitches. It can be thrown with various degrees of break, at different speeds. Before the 1930s, when it began to be developed as a deliberate weapon (which didn't become widespread until the 1950s), it was called a "nickel curve," a derisive description of its small break, or an "outshoot." Its popularity grew because free-swinging fence-seekers, looking for fastballs, can be fooled into committing themselves to a pitch that will wind up not where they expect.

Today, it is a basic part of the repertoire, but not as large a fraction as 20 years ago because the repertoire is larger. Many situations that used to call for a slider are now met by a "splitter" or "cut fastball," which we'll come to in a moment.

5. The screwball, which is used increasingly but remains a minority pitch, is a reverse curve: Thrown left-handed, it breaks away from a right-handed hitter instead of in. For this reason, it is more popular with lefties, who have so many righties to face. Right-handers have less need to find a pitch that breaks away from left-handed hitters, and they're not looking for one that makes the right-handed hitter's task easier. The main thing, though, is that the screwball puts a tremendous strain on the arm, especially around the elbow, because the wrist is snapped in instead of out when the ball is released. Some men can't use it at all, and many who do pay a physical price if they use it too much.

6. The knuckleball is thrown with either the fingertips or the knuckles gripping the ball, and it has a minimum of spin. This brings it to the plate with almost all its force spent and extremely susceptible to random effects of air pressure and currents at that moment. Its break, therefore, is unpredictable and as much a problem for the catcher as the hitter. It is, essentially, a slow pitch, although there are some (relatively) fast knucklers, too.

7. Sinkers are varieties of fastballs and sliders, with little horizontal break and a definite downward break at the last minute. Some

pitchers have "natural" sinkers. Others have sinkers that are really spitballs.

One of the major developments of the 1980s was the spread of the split-finger fastball, or "splitter." By gripping the ball with two fingers spread far apart (the two fingers are kept side by side on an ordinary fastball), the pitcher can make his delivery dip sharply and suddenly as it nears the plate—"like falling off a table." This type of sinker gets its special effectiveness from its similarity to a fastball in arm motion, spin, and pace. Just as a slider veers off the straight line less than a curve, but enough, the split-finger drops less than a curve, but plenty. Its additional advantage is that if a hitter reacts to it as if it were a fastball (as hitters often do to the slider), he'll not only miss it altogether more often, but hit a grounder if he connects—and pitchers are always looking for grounders.

Roger Craig is widely given credit for perfecting the way to teach this pitch, although he didn't invent it. Bruce Sutter, who became a dominant relief pitcher in the late seventies, used it because his large hand enabled him to make this grip comfortably. Craig, as a pitching coach in Detroit and later as manager in San Francisco, taught it to dozens of pitchers, and to anyone who asked from other clubs. It became the most devastating pitch of the 1980s for those who could master it.

A split-finger also has less velocity than a fastball, and thus becomes a cross between a change and a sinker.

All these gradations of control are achieved by varying how tightly the ball is gripped, by the degree of wrist snap at the moment of release, by the type of grip, and by other arcane mechanical details (which vary, obviously, with the configuration of any particular pitcher's fingers). Generally speaking, the looser the ball is held, the less velocity produced by the same arm speed; the sharper the wrist snap (which also twists the elbow), the bigger the break.

And every type of wrist snap means gradual and cumulative damage to the arm. The fastball is unnatural enough, but most of the strains are put on the shoulder area (throwing overhand). Any breaking ball adds torque to the arm structure and its joints. From time to time, fashions develop in trying to protect pitchers. Some coaches will decide a slider does long-term damage, or a split-finger, or something else. (No one denies a screwball will cause more damage, more quickly.) But there is no consensus on such matters, and the plain fact is that *all* pitching is dangerous and eventually damaging to human arms. It's just that some human arms can stand it better and longer than others (which is why one young admirer of Nolan Ryan said, "I want to see his autopsy").

8. The spitball was outlawed in baseball nearly three generations ago, and, being an illegal pitch, is used by no more than one-quarter of the pitchers in the majors. Saliva or some other slippery substance, applied to fingers that hold the ball like a fastball, will allow the top of the ball to slip out of the hand first, giving it a forward rotation and a tendency to break down.

There is no question that the spitball is an effective pitch, since it seems to be a fastball until too late, and there is no question that many pitchers learn how to use it, especially in tight spots. Official Baseball, through its umpires and league presidents, prefers to ignore the whole business, which is just as well. Outlawing it in the first place, in the first flush of slugging glamour after World War I, was of questionable wisdom. Hitters moan and groan about being retired by this illegal delivery—which few pitchers admit using until they write books after they retire—but, for some strange reason, no one has ever reported hitting a home run off a spitball, and it must happen *sometimes* if pitchers throw so many. In short, it's like any other pitch: Used by a good pitcher, it's a wonderful weapon, but a poor pitcher throwing spitballs remains a poor pitcher.

Other "trick" deliveries were outlawed with the spitball, and these, no doubt, still have some unacknowledged practitioners today. In general, anything that can cut, roughen, or slicken the surface of a baseball can give a pitcher a chance to make his pitch behave in an unorthodox manner.

In the 1980s, there was a decrease in the use of spitters as the way to cheat, and an increase in dependence on "scuffed" or scarred surfaces. Such a change was part fashion, part practicality. For a while, Vaseline became more prevalent than saliva (and things to chew to promote saliva). But as time passed and older pitchers who had mastered the spitball disappeared from the coaching and scouting scene, there were fewer practitioners handing down the art. Meanwhile, a later generation of pitchers who reached the point where they needed this sort of surreptitious help found they could control a nick in the cover (where a fingernail could get a toehold, one might say) more reliably, and get more strange aerodynamic effects.

But the real weapon is psychology. The pitcher who acquires a reputation for using an illegal pitch plays it up. If he can make the hitter think he's doing something to the ball, he has distracted him from normal and proper "batter thinking." If he pretends to "load up" when he doesn't (and he might), he has performed the bottom-line function of pitching: Confuse the hitter.

Those are the standard deliveries—fastball, curve, change-up, slider, screwball, knuckler, sinker, and "trick" pitches, of which the spitball or scuffball is the most common. Each has its dangers as well as its assets.

The fastball, if fast enough, is the safest of all deliveries. If not fast enough, it's the easiest for the batter to hit, and is likely to carry farthest, because its own force adds to the force of the rebound off the bat. It is, as stated, the easiest pitch to control.

The curve can be disastrous when it "hangs," that is, doesn't break down sharply enough soon enough. Because it travels slower than a fastball, it is easier to time, and if the change of direction is too slight, look out! The precept is that curves *must* be low passing the strike zone; a "high curve" is not considered a pitch, but an abomination.

The change-up exists only by comparison with other pitches, and is therefore devastatingly effective when used correctly. The danger is obvious: If the hitter is *not* fooled, it's easy to hit.

Sliders, many people believe (and I among them), are one of the underlying factors in the increased number of homers along with the dip in batting averages. When a slider works right, it is marvelous; but when it doesn't, it's a prime candidate for gopherism. Why is a home-run ball a "gopher"? Because of the self-deprecating expression uttered by pitchers: "It'll go for extra bases or a homer." The "go-fer," especially in country accents, led to the picturesque but unrelated animal image. If a slider doesn't slide, it's just a fastball with not enough on it; and if it slides into the wrong spot, it can find the hitter's strength instead of his weakness.

The only real disadvantage of the screwball is difficulty—the difficulty of mastering the delivery, and the wear and tear on the arm. Those who can control it have great success with it, because to the automatic advantages of any good curve, it adds the tremendous one of unfamiliarity. It breaks the opposite way from almost all the other breaking pitches hitters see, and they don't see the "scroogie" often enough to become accustomed to it.

The knuckler is the most unhittable of all deliveries—and the most uncontrollable. No one, not even the pitcher, really knows which way it's going to break, and this creates two major problems. One is that it is so hard to throw strikes consistently with a knuckler (and when a man can, as Hoyt Wilhelm and Phil Niekro showed, he lasts forever). The other is that it is dangerous to use with men on base, because it gets away from the catcher so often. In fact, plenty of knuckleball pitchers have been beaten because a missed third strike put a runner on base (no, *not* Hugh Casey of the Dodgers in the 1941 World Series against Tommy Henrich and the Yankees; that famous pitch that got past Mickey Owen was probably a spitball). Even if handled by the catcher, a knuckler makes base-stealing easy.

These deliveries are the raw materials of pitching. To succeed in the majors, a man must "have" at least three. "Having" a pitch means absolutely dependable control of it, in tough situations. When a pitcher "adds" a new pitch, he usually works with it for a period of years in practice, and then in a few relatively safe game situations, before feeling that he has acquired it. There are, of course, exceptions (like Niekro, whose only worthwhile weapon was the knuckler), but they are rare.

Acquiring the raw materials is the science part of pitching, and so is the constant problem of keeping all deliveries in good working order. Injury, fatigue, carelessness, overeagerness—all the things that can put a hitter into a slump—can afflict a pitcher, causing him to lose his rhythm or pattern or groove or whatever he calls it. Usually, the pitcher or coach can eventually spot some mechanical defect to correct the situation. Pitchers will spend hours analyzing every detail of every movement when a delivery doesn't work right, and videotape has been a boon to the profession. Only then comes the art, the process of deciding what to throw when, and where. The tactics and the thinking begin here.

Fundamentally, the pitcher wants the reverse of the hitter's coin. The hitter is looking for "his" pitch to hit. The pitcher is trying to make the hitter hit "his"—the pitcher's—pitch.

What does a pitcher think about while on the mound?

First, he is always aware of the count, the number of outs, the score, and the inning. Each of these things will influence the decision on which pitch to throw.

Second, he has his "book" of each hitter's strengths and weaknesses at his mental fingertips, having reviewed each item before the game.

Third, he has firmly in mind the current state of his own equipment—which pitches are working right today and which aren't, and not only "today" but this inning.

Fourth, he is influenced by the number and location of the men on base.

Let's consider each of the above in more detail.

The first rule of effective pitching is to stay ahead of the hitter most of the time. If the first pitch is a strike, the arithmetic shifts way over in favor of the pitcher. Now he can miss the strike zone three times without issuing a base on balls, and has to hit it only once to give the hitter the problems that come with a two-strike count. In other words, if the first pitch is a strike, the pitcher has plenty of margin for error in trying to get the batter to swing at borderline strikes. Even if only one of the next four pitches finds the mark, he still has an even chance with the count 3–2.

On the other hand, if the first pitch is a ball, things are not so good. If the second pitch is also a ball, the pitcher is in a real hole with a 2–0 count; he *must* come in with three of the next four pitches, and the chances of throwing something the hitter wants are much greater. The psychological pressure of the necessity to come in with the pitch adds to the physical difficulty of throwing to the exact spot hoped for. This is especially true for inexperienced pitchers, but it is a problem for all.

A sure sign, therefore, that a pitcher is flirting with trouble is a pattern in which he is constantly behind the hitters, particularly 2–0 and 3–1. Counts of 1–0 and 2–1 aren't so bad, because the next pitch can even matters, and a pitcher with excellent control (like Warren Spahn) often reaches such a count on purpose.

Don Drysdale expresses a philosophy common to better pitchers. "You don't worry much about a hitter's weakness until you get ahead of him," says Drysdale. "First you concentrate on getting your good pitches over, to put him in a hole. You don't want to get yourself in a hole by missing a spot and falling behind in a count. So you start by making sure he has to hit your best stuff if he's going to hit you. Then, once you're ahead, you can work on his weaknesses."

And he sums it up in one of the most eloquent and profound baseball aphorisms I have ever heard: "You win going 1-and-2, you lose going 2-and-1, and the difference between 1-and-2 and 2-and-1 is a fraction of an inch."

For their part, many managers consider it an unforgivable sin if their pitcher gives up a damaging hit with the count two strikes, no balls. At that point, they feel, there is no excuse for a pitch that's well within the strike zone, or toward a hitter's strength.

Mel Ott, managing the Giants, once fined Bill Voiselle $500 when a Cardinal hit a home run off an 0–2 pitch. Voiselle, who was earning about $3,500 a year at the time, was impressed as well as appalled.

"Is that the biggest fine anyone ever got?" he asked a writer in hushed, awestruck tones.

"No, Bill," the writer had to tell him, "Babe Ruth once got fined $5,000."

"Whew!" whistled Voiselle. "I couldn't cover *that!*"

Of course, that was back in the 1940s. Today, a $3-million-a-year pitcher (like Mark Langston) is earning more than $10,000 per *inning*, and what would Voiselle have thought of that? Incidentally, this also shows the futility of trying to discipline or teach players by fining them these days. It's hard to get their attention that way.

But pitchers, of course, and many pitching coaches, object to so narrow a viewpoint on the part of managers. They point to all the times they retire a man on the 0–2 pitch by being willing to get it over.

What all this means, really, is that a pitcher won't use the same pitch—necessarily—when he's behind in the count that he would risk when he is ahead. When he is ahead, he can afford to work on the batter's weakness with maximum confidence, and can try pitches that are not his own strength. When he is behind, he may have to reject what would be the toughest pitch for that particular hitter to hit if he can't be absolutely sure of controlling it.

Hitting or missing with a pitch is another aspect of baseball that tends to become overdramatized and misunderstood. Not even the greatest pitcher can, every time, in competition, hit an exact spot in the sense of a dart hitting a target. What he is working with is a dynamic system: It isn't an abstract cross section of a strike zone that he's pitching to, but a living batter. If the direction, momentum, spin, and—for want of a better word—tendency of a pitch are correct, that's enough, even though there may be an inch or two of displacement from the idealized target.

Pitchers are taught, therefore, to make sure that they miss *in the right direction* when they do miss. For example, suppose you are facing a hitter whose weakness is low inside, but who can handle a low pitch pretty well if it is out over the plate. You aim for the inside corner at the knees, but you try to make sure that if you miss it will be *too far* inside, not the other way, which fades into the hitter's strength.

The most common instance of this sort of thing is "jamming" a hitter. If a strong pitch can be made in close, "on the fists," it can be hit only with the thin portion of the bat handle, and therefore hit weakly. A couple of inches farther out, and the fat part of the bat might send the ball out of the park. Jamming is invariably effective, but dangerous if you miss in either direction, because if the pitch hits the batter, he's on. The physical advantage lies in the fact that the batter can't extend his arms for maximum power, even if he connects. But some of the best batters don't mind being jammed, since if they do connect they are likely to foul it off and get another chance. The less skillful batter is more likely to hit a weak fair ball, or just miss.

At any rate, the count on the hitter is a major factor in the pitcher's decision on what the next pitch should be.

The outs, score, and inning have more obvious relevance. It may be easy enough to retire a particularly stubborn free-swinger by letting him hit long, catchable flies—but not with a man on third and less than two out. With a two- or three-run lead, and nobody on base, a pitch that might be hit for a home run if it isn't quite right is a good risk; with the score tied in the bottom of the ninth, it isn't. In other words, there is no such thing as the "right" pitch to a particular hitter—it all depends on the count and the situation in the game.

It also depends on the accumulated analysis of the hitter's strengths and weaknesses. It's not only a matter of which pitches a batter hits better or worse, but also where he is likely to hit any particular pitch. This varies with every pitcher; a hitter may be able to pull one pitcher's curve but not another's. Thus, every pitcher has to work out for himself a table of values, involving his own strengths and each batter's abilities. From this table, he can select the pitch that will tend to make this batter *this time* hit the ball where the pitcher wants—on the ground for a possible double play, to the left or the right, or whatever.

It's hard for the nonprofessional to remember that, in real life, it's not "a" curve that's being thrown to "a" batter, but some specific pitcher's curve to a specific batter. What counts is how *his* works to *that* hitter.

Naturally, the pitcher is aware of the state of his equipiment at that particular moment. His best pitch, in general, may be a curve—but not that day, so he uses it less and relies more on the fastball. If he's a regular pitcher, with a well-developed style, the very fact that he is deviating from his normal pattern can be put to use.

In general, pitchers think of "out" pitches—the pitch they hope the batter will swing at—and pitches they "show." For example: Rick Reuschel is pitching to Dale Murphy in Candlestick Park with one out, a man on first, score tied, sixth inning. Naturally, Reuschel would like to get a double play. His fastball, he feels, isn't the sort that's going to overpower a Murphy, so "Big Daddy," as his teammates call him, will just "show" it to him—he simply will not throw the fastball into the strike zone. It may still be very useful in at least two ways: as a contrast in speeds, to make a subsequent delivery hard to time, or as an enticement to swing at even if it is just outside the strike zone.

Here we move into the mysterious area of "setting hitters up." Some great pitchers—like Sandy Koufax—scoff at the whole idea, at least as it is often presented. The pitcher, Sandy feels, is always trying to fool the batter anyhow, and it's a two-way guessing game. If the pitcher succeeds in thinking along with the batter and fools him, fine—but the same "setting-up" sequence is meaningless if the hitter isn't thinking in the groove the pitcher assumes.

Others, though, as qualified as Koufax, wax rhapsodic about the artistry with which someone was "set up." Without splitting hairs about just which part of the process is intentional and which isn't, we can see that the sequence of pitches has a great effect on the batter.

Thus, most pitchers are told, don't throw the same thing three times in a row (because obviously the batter will get the range). By the same token, every batter knows that after two identical pitches he is not likely to get a third—and yet, a third one may prove to be the most surprising thing of all. So we're back to the guessing game.

Drysdale again: "They say don't throw soft stuff to a little hitter with men on base." (A "little" hitter means a not very good one with little power, not a small person.) "But because everybody has said that and done that, he's probably never seen a slow pitch in a tight situation, and is totally unequipped to react to it. So if you do it, exactly because you're not supposed to, it may be the best thing in the world."

The whole idea is, remember, to keep the hitter—any hitter—off balance. But if a pitcher does what Drysdale so logically advises, and that little hitter does get a hit, the pitcher will never be allowed to forget it: the Ott-Voiselle situation in another context.

There are, however, some abstract principles that work well in practice: In-and-out, on successive pitches, is a classic pattern; change of speeds is another. In all such instances, the batter's reaction to the previous pitch is still working on him as he responds to this one. Among the refinements are such esoteric practices as saving up a particular pitch, which has been withheld from this batter in previous times at bat, for a dangerous moment.

And finally, in deciding what to use at any particular time, the pitcher gives a lot of consideration to the ballpark and the weather. By now, these factors have been touched upon repeatedly. In a large park, where long flies make luscious outs, more high pitches can be risked than in a small one. The same is true if the wind is blowing in rather than out. If the wind is strong out to right field, left-handed hitters must be prevented from pulling the ball, but if the wind is strong blowing in, that may be a good way to get them out. If the day is overcast and dark, or if the lights at a night game aren't the best, speed becomes more effective. Certain times of day—like twilight anywhere, or when the grandstand shadow passes the mound at Yankee Stadium—create conditions of visibility that can help a pitcher.

One pitching decision is the center of controversy over and over again. It is the practice of throwing close to the batter's head. One common term for this is a "beanball." This implies that the pitcher is trying to hit the batter in the head, which would make the pitcher, morally speaking, an attempted murderer. A term used more often by hitters themselves (and managers, of course) is "knockdown," which has a more accurate connotation: The pitcher is making the batter drop, suddenly and desperately, to avoid being hit. Pitchers themselves invariably refer to it as a "brush-back" pitch, which paints a milder, more strategy-oriented picture of forcing the hitter to get out of the way simply to upset his timing and to prevent him from digging in too securely for subsequent pitches. Whatever you call it, it is a fundamental weapon, universally accepted as a fact of life in professional baseball.

There are all gradations of viciousness involved. When real ill-feeling develops between individual players or whole clubs, beanball wars do develop. As a means of calculated intimidation, throwing close (without intent to hit or hurt) is considered a necessity at times by every single manager I have ever spoken to, although some don't like to admit it while others (like Leo Durocher) use talk about it as psychological warfare. And even the mildest, most idealistic pitcher, who would rather lose than hurt a batter (and there have been plenty of men who feel this way), acknowledges the legitimacy of the almost prehistoric pattern of high-and-tight-then-low-and-away.

Besides, morals should cut both ways, too. Pitchers are hit by batted balls even more often than batters are hit by pitches. The ball comes off the bat faster than it went in, and almost every pitcher, at one time or another, has had to stay in and pitch with a bad bruise on the leg, body, or arm. Cracked kneecaps and other serious injuries have been suffered by pitchers on the mound.

Now, the batter, trying for a hit, really doesn't care where the ball goes. He is trying to hit as hard as he can, and often aims "back through the box," because that is a good method of keeping eye and stance ready. Whether or not the pitcher succeeds in getting out of the way is something the batter doesn't worry about.

By the same token, pitchers say, it's not their concern how a batter eludes a high inside pitch. The pitcher has as much right to throw it there as the batter does to hit the ball through the box, and it's up to the man in the line of fire to get out of the way. A pitcher throwing high and tight intends to miss—and, if he's any good at all, he wouldn't miss if he were really serious about hitting the batter. Only on the relatively rare occasions when intent to hit the batter comes up is there a real moral question.

The morality of this may be questionable, but since there is no infallible method for distinguishing between lack of control and an intentional high inside pitch, everyone concerned lives with the situation uncomplainingly most of the time. Hitters, no less than pitchers, recognize the inevitability of being thrown at from time to time, especially when they've been hitting well or hurting a particular pitcher too often. This is less accepted now than it used to be, as mentioned in the discussion of hitting. Hitters are quick to feel insulted, glower, and start for the mound; pitchers have grown up in a world, from Little League through aluminum-bat college, in which retaliation and threat are not part of the ethos. So the overt knockdown pitch is rarely seen—especially since authorities have declared it an infraction which the umpire can punish—but in a subtler way, the process goes on.

Only when there is some additional reason for rancor—personal animosity, or the feeling that a deliberate effort to injure is involved—do bitterness and recriminations arise.

There are two answers: courage and reprisal. The major-league hitter must be able to stand up to the plate just as firmly for the pitch after a knockdown pitch as before. In plain words, if he can prove that it doesn't decrease his ability to hit the next pitch, the knockdown or brush-back simply becomes another ball and therefore of no value to the pitcher. If the hitter can't prove it, he's going to get knocked down over and over in important game situations.

Reprisal is up to the opposing pitcher. You throw at our hitters, I'll throw at yours. In the final analysis, this is the code of loyalty that keeps beanballing in check most of the time. The most direct and effective reprisal—throwing at the opposing pitcher when he comes to bat—occurs infrequently; for an obvious reason all pitchers seem to be reluctant to use it, indicating that "do unto others" is a two-edged sword.

A striking example—it might be called classic—arose in September of 1969, during the hysterical pennant drive of the hitherto hapless Mets. The Chicago Cubs, managed by an aging but not forgetful Durocher, came to New York for a two-game series, leading by two and a half games. The Mets had been winning and closing the gap, but weren't yet universally accepted as a possible winner; the Cubs, who had been losing (but not too badly), were expected to polish them off once and for all.

New York's pitcher was Jerry Koosman, a left-handed fireballer (then), and he got the Cubs out in the first on a fly and two strikeouts.

Chicago's pitcher was Bill Hands, a right-hander who could also throw hard. His first pitch to the first Met batter, Tommie Agee, was a "knockdown," high and tight. Agee went sprawling and the message Durocher habitually preached—intimidation—was presumably delivered.

Agee did bounce out, and the next two Mets went out, and the first batter to face Koosman in the second was Ron Santo, the Cubs' captain and most respected clutch hitter.

Koosman's first pitch cracked Santo on the elbow.

And there was no further trouble. The retaliation was accepted for what it was: a response to the first message, saying "we can play it any way you want." The fact that Gil Hodges, the Mets' manager, had played under and against Durocher for years made it that much more certain that no misunderstanding was possible—or would be permitted. The Mets went on to win that game—as Agee hit a home run the next time up—and the next game, and the pennant, and the World Series. But that's another story.

Now we fast-forward (in 1980s language) to the first game of the 1988 World Series, in Dodger Stadium, Los Angeles. By now, Tom Seaver, who was in the Met dugout that day in 1969, is a television commentator. Here's how he saw what happened (as he recounted it a year later).

"Tim Belcher [the Dodger starter] came in on José Canseco in the first inning, and hit him on the hand, after a single with one out. He got out of the inning with the bases loaded.

"Do you remember what happened next? Dave Stewart hit Steve Sax with his very first pitch. It was clear-cut retaliation, the old code. The umpires issued their warning, and that was the end of that. But."

But?

"One out later, he committed a balk, and then got tagged by Mickey Hatcher for a two-run homer. Hatcher had hit only one home run all season. How can a hitter like him hurt a pitcher like Stewart at a time like that? And who kept killing the A's the whole Series? Hatcher." (Note: Hatcher hit .368 and another homer as the Dodgers won in five games.) "And all through the Series, the Dodgers simply outhustled and outfought them."

So?

"So the retaliation, at that time in that situation, wasn't necessary, and it came back to haunt the A's. The Dodgers were underdogs who had just survived a fabulous seven-game series with the Mets. They felt lucky to be in the Series at all. They weren't in Oakland's class in terms of talent. Waking them up that way, giving them a personal challenge to meet, was the wrong thing to do. Retaliation is part of the game, but there's a right time and wrong time, and this was the wrong time."

The trouble with intimidation, then, is that it can backfire. It can arouse hitters, who have shown they can master the fear impulse by being in the majors at all, to a sharpened concentration rather than otherwise. And it can interfere with the proper concentration of the pitcher (which was the point Seaver was making about Stewart), who had a game plan in mind when he began.

Incidentally, Canseco hit a grand-slam home run off Belcher the very next inning, so he wasn't intimidated either.

There's another aspect to the retaliation syndrome, but we'll save that until we talk about the designated hitter.

In today's pitching philosophy, the principle of pitching low rules unchallenged. With rare and special exceptions, managers want "out" pitches—the pitches intended to be hit—to be low. The reasons are many. A low pitch is most likely to be hit along the ground, and no matter how hard it's hit, a grounder (or low liner) can't be a homer. In a lively-ball era, home runs are the chief danger. Also, a grounder is more likely to be an out, since there are five infielders (counting the pitcher) defending a narrow area and only three outfielders covering a much wider span. Also, many tactical situations (like needing a double play) call for grounders. Also, almost all high pitches except high fastballs are easier to hit than low pitches; all breaking balls have a downward component as part of the break, so part of the misjudging stimulated in the hitter is to have him swing in a plane above the ball. If a breaking ball starts out too high, and comes down into the top half of the strike zone, the batter may "misjudge" it right on the nose.

Here, a whole new set of variables arises. Not all pitchers are at their best pitching low. Some hitters are low-ball hitters. What happens to the general principle in these cases? Should a pitcher do what is theoretically advantageous when his physical ability is best in another direction? Should he pitch to a hitter's strength because theory dictates that sort of pitch?

The answers, almost always, are in the realm of the pitcher's own strength. If his strong points prove incompatible with most theoretical necessities, he simply won't be around long. Aside from that, a pitcher usually resolves a questionable decision in favor of his own best weapon, and hopes it's good enough.

Once again, confidence is a key element. A pitcher must believe in his own ability to make his pitch, just as a hitter must believe in his ability to hit that pitch.

And Lefty Gomez loved to tell stories about being the starting pitcher in the very first All-Star Game in 1933. The manager was Connie Mack, and he called the usual pre-game meeting to go over the hitters. ("How come they never go *under* the hitters?" Joe Garagiola has asked.)

Gomez was skeptical. "Mr. Mack," he said, "these National League fellows are All-Stars. They haven't figured out how to pitch to them in their league for years. How are we going to do it in ten minutes?"

Mack ignored him, and started going down the list: Pepper Martin, "fastball hitter"; Frank Frisch, "fastball hitter"; Chuck Klein, "fastball hitter"; Paul Waner, "likes a fastball"; Bill Terry, "fastball hitter."

Gomez interrupted. "Mr. Mack, I think you'd better start someone else. All I've got is a fastball."

It must have been good enough, though, because Lefty pitched three shutout innings and emerged as the winning pitcher—and was the starter in the next two All-Star Games, too.

But I digress.

There is more to pitching than throwing pitches. A pitcher with fine stuff and control can still be beaten if he lets base runners run wild, or if he can't field his position to some degree.

Holding runners on, especially the runner at first base with second base unoccupied, is a major responsibility. If the runner gets too big a lead, he may steal, and thus be in scoring position for a subsequent single. Or, on a single, he may go to third, from where he can score on an out; or he might score from first on a double; or he may break up a potential double play by arriving at second in time to spill the pivotman.

The rules permit a different motion (a stretch instead of a full windup) with men on base. All the various types of balks are rules to prevent the pitcher from taking advantage of the base runner. A pitcher must, therefore, acquire complete command of his pitching repertoire from the stretch as well as from the windup, and within the framework of the balk rules. At the same time, he must not let preoccupation with the runner interfere with his concentration on the batter. Striking that balance requires a great deal of experience, and countless young pitchers have suffered defeat because they didn't have it yet.

As a fielder, the pitcher has two big responsibilities: covering first base and bunts. He must—absolutely must—get off the mound and over to first base on grounders hit to the right side. He has to run about 65 feet while the hitter runs 90, and if he doesn't make it, the trouble that follows is his own fault. And he must be agile enough in fielding bunts to prevent this from becoming a surefire weapon against him.

The lefty-righty matchups, already discussed from the hitter's point of view, have some additional meanings for pitchers.

For one thing, the layout of ballparks makes a big difference. A left-hander has a considerable natural advantage in a place like Yankee Stadium, where left and left-center fields are deeper than almost anywhere else, while right field is a tempting home-run target. The right-handed batters, who constitute the southpaw's bigger problem, will have a tough time hitting a homer; the left swingers, who have the good home-run target, have a left-handed pitcher to contend with. Boston's Fenway Park is exactly the opposite, with a short left field and a long right, so left-handed pitchers seldom have success there. (One great exception, Boston's Mel Parnell, was a screwball pitcher who could get right-handers out better than left-handers.)

For another, the left-handed pitcher has an advantage in keeping a runner close to first. In his stretch motion, he is facing first base. The right-hander, facing third, has to keep an eye on the base runner by peering over his shoulder, and has to throw across his body to throw to first. The lefty's move to first can be much more deceptive, and artists like Ford and Spahn were famous for picking men off.

For a third—and this is something I've never heard explained satisfactorily—left-handed pitchers seem to have more odd spin on their deliveries, and more trouble with control, than right-handers. This seems to be a fact; if it's a myth, it's one myth that won't be dispelled here.

How to get men out is the main subject on a pitcher's mind. The topic that ranks second is when he will pitch. If he is an established starter, he used to count on the four-day schedule that became normal in modern baseball, although now a five-day cycle is preferred. Why? It's said we know more and care more about preserving health, but Whitey Herzog, who worked in the Met farm system before becoming a manager, gives another reason too: "It started when teams cut down their number of farm clubs, and still had a lot of good pitching prospects. They could use and develop five instead of four. And a parent club, like our Mets, had lots of pitchers, so why not use them to the maximum? Once you start, it becomes the standard pattern and everyone grows into it, and the new ones come into it, and you can't go back."

A man can pitch nine innings—between 100 and 150 pitches, not counting warm-ups—every fourth day without undue strain. On one of the next two days—it varies with the pitcher—he'll do some throwing, in batting practice or on the sidelines or in the bullpen. On the third day, few pitchers throw at all. In an emergency, a starter can go with two days' rest with good results—Koufax did it in the seventh game of the 1965 World Series, as a prominent example—but he can't do it very often. It is generally considered thoroughly unwise to pitch a starter with only one day of rest, and never on successive days. Now that most major-league managers prefer to use a five-pitcher rotation for much of the season, if their personnel permits it, this rarely happens. The pitchers don't always like the five-man rotation, because fewer starts mean fewer chances to compile a winning record, but many managers are convinced it pays off in fresher arms late in the season and helps prolong careers. (On the other hand, Johnny Sain, an independent thinker and a spectacularly successful pitching coach with four different teams, believed that in certain cases some pitchers can do well with only two days off. Under him, Denny McLain won 31 games for Detroit in 1968, and Wilber Wood, a knuckleballer, pitched regularly on a three-day schedule for the Chicago White Sox in 1972 and 1973.) Late in a pennant race, most teams will revert to four.

If he is a relief pitcher, he must be ready every day—but if he works in a game, or has an extended warm-up without getting into a game, two or three days in a row, he'll probably get a day of idleness.

If he is not fully established as either, he cannot count on regularity of schedule, and this is moan material No. 1 among professional pitchers. But since a ten-man staff now has five starters and two "closers," fewer pitchers find themselves in that ambiguous situation.

What makes one man a good starter, another a good reliever?

Repertoire, physique, outlook.

Other things being equal, the better pitchers are starters. Naturally, you want your best pitcher out there most of the time, and that's the starter.

In the old days, relievers were simply those not good enough to be starters. Today, relievers are specialists, often highly paid, always much appreciated. Many men have certain abilities that can be put to good use in relief.

A reliever, for instance, may have complete command of one outstanding pitch—an overwhelming fastball, a sinker, a screwball, a knuckler. His other pitches may be mediocre to poor, but his one specialty is highly reliable and unhittable. With such an arsenal, he is not a good risk for a full game as a starter—no starter can get by relying only on one good pitch; too many mistakes crop up, and the hitters, facing him a third and fourth time, get too good a chance to lay off his specialty and hit something else. But in relief, one pitch, if it's good enough, is plenty. The relief pitcher's job is to get one or two outs in the middle of an inning with men on base, and to pitch a scoreless inning or two. Rarely will a relief pitcher face more than nine men, which means few batters will see him twice in one game.

At the same time, a reliever needs certain physical and mental attributes that even good starters often lack, at least to a degree. He must be able to get ready quickly, work often, and be at his best in the toughest spots. Because he will be brought in when sudden emergencies arise, he must be able to warm up quickly. Because he will be expected to work only an inning or two—perhaps 20 pitches—he should be able to work two, three, or four days in a row. Some arms can stand that, some can't.

Koufax, with his arthritic elbow, could never have been a relief pitcher, because he needed rest and treatment between starts. Spahn, even in his forties, could never get the right mental approach to relief pitching, because he was too immersed in his own mental processes of preparing for a game, planning how to handle each hitter, and so forth. In fact, some of the best relief pitchers have had devil-may-care personalities.

More specifically, a relief pitcher's specialty must be good enough to get a strikeout or a grounder, since, in almost all the situations he is called upon, it will be necessary to keep runners from scoring or advancing. He must, it goes without saying, be able to pitch with men on base.

Relief pitching has become systematized, and the contemporary buzzword is "role playing." A team needs two "closers," a righty and a lefty, although one of them will be of primary importance (like Dennis Eckersley with the A's). Then it needs "setup men," or middle-inning relievers, whose job is to keep the enemy at bay between the time a starter falters early and the time a closer can be brought in. Here, too, a lefty and a righty would be ideal, and these are the men who can be pressed into starting assignments when injuries or the schedule make that necessary. ("Spot starters" they've come to be called.)

To get an idea how things have evolved, consider these figures: In 1930, of all starting pitchers, 44 percent pitched a complete game. In 1950, the frequency was still 40 percent. In 1970, it was down to 22 percent. In 1988, it was 15 percent. This means a team uses three pitchers in one game more often than not.

That this is an entirely conscious managerial approach to using more pitchers is proved by an American League statistic. With the designated-hitter rule, no pitcher has to be removed for a pinch-hitter, so every pitching change is dictated strictly by pitching considerations. In 1972, the last year before the DH was adopted, American League pitchers finished 27 percent of their starts; in 1988, with the DH, they finished 16 percent.

Most pitchers are notoriously poor hitters, for two unavoidable reasons. One is lack of opportunity to develop—as pitchers, they get much less opportunity to bat, in practice and in games, from the beginning of their careers. The second is natural selection—not Darwin's, but baseball's. The special reflexes that make a good hitter are totally different from the set that makes a good pitcher. When pitchers are scouted and selected, only their pitching abilities are rated and everything else is ignored. All other players, at the beginning, are judged on their hitting potential.

But the pitcher who can hit well—Don Drysdale, Warren Spahn, Robin Roberts—has a big edge as a pitcher (in the National League). In many situations, he may stay in the game when it is his turn to hit in the late innings of a close game, and thus remain to get the victory. The ordinary pitcher, one run behind or even with the score tied sometimes, must be removed for a pinch-hitter.

While most fans recognize the necessity for rest, few realize that a pitcher can have too much rest. A starter on the four- or five-day schedule, if held out longer because of rain or blanks in the schedule or other reasons, will often have trouble with his control after four or five days' rest instead of three. Pitchers who work irregularly almost always have control trouble. Regularity seems to be an essential part of efficiency for pitchers. Even relievers can get too much rest.

Relievers, however, are involved in one of the most invisible facets of the proper care and feeding of pitchers: warming up. The box score only shows how much a man pitched in a game. In the bullpen, he may have warmed up three or four different times without being called into the game. It depends on how troublesome the game has been, and how decisive his manager is. The reliever may work the equivalent of three or four innings for several successive days in the bullpen, and never appear in a box score at all.

Finally, after all the mechanical and tactical considerations have been listed, there remain the intangible qualities that lift outstanding pitchers above the mass: applied intelligence, confidence, poise.

Pitchers are the intellectuals of the baseball community. They do much more thinking, in quantity and in depth, about the techniques of baseball than the other 60 percent of the players do. They have to. Even the worst pitcher must have a clear idea of how and where to pitch each hitter, and this automatically requires hours of mental effort. Some pretty good hitters, on the other hand, get by on instinct, paying only superficial attention to the finer points of the game.

Today, hitters help pitchers immensely by being home-run crazy. The harder they swing, the easier they are to fool, since a hard swing commits the batter sooner. Today's pitchers take full advantage of this powermania, which is one reason that the slider is so effective. If hitters concentrated more on just meeting the ball, it would be harder to get outs. As Lou Burdette put it, stating the thoughtful pitcher's case: "I make my living off the hungriness of the hitter."

Confidence, for a pitcher, means confidence in his command of his various deliveries.

"It is better," says Sandy Koufax, echoing a thought many top coaches subscribe to, "to throw a theoretically poorer pitch whole-heartedly, than to throw the so-called right pitch with a feeling of doubt—doubt that it's right, or doubt that you can make it behave well at that moment. You've got to feel sure you're doing the right thing—sure that you *want* to throw the pitch you're going to throw."

For all these reasons, pitchers are the most important and the least predictable people on a ball field. They're good one day, ineffective the next, then brilliant, then helpless. They get sore arms and other ailments that they tend to hide—because everyone is afraid of being labeled physically deficient—and sometimes they can compensate for them, and sometimes they can't.

No one can guarantee, on any one day, that the good pitcher will have his best stuff. They are, in this respect, like opera singers, who can be in good voice or not, regardless of reputation. And the poorer pitcher, every now and then, will have a day when every pitch breaks right.

This is the human factor again, the unpredictability that makes baseball possible and worthwhile day in and day out. It is also an inescapable inconsistency that drives managers crazy, as we will see in Chapter 5 when we turn our attention to the genius in the dugout.

CHAPTER

3

Fielding—The Art of Manual Labor

Fielding is the bread-and-butter activity on the ball field. For every ball he hits, a professional will catch and throw a dozen, both in practice and in games. In a sense, the fielders are the remote-control mechanisms that turn the artistic pitcher's work into put-outs. At major-league levels, fielders are expected to be as efficient as machines, making the routine play every time. They don't, in reality, because they are human, but in the calculations of the manager they are supposed to.

And to most baseball players, fielding is just about as exciting as bread and butter. Hitting is a delight. Without probing, pseudopsychoanalytically, the satisfaction most humans seem to feel when they strike a ball solidly with a stick, the fun element in hitting, is always evident. Even the most experienced players, practicing their profession and apparently blasé about everything else, can be seen enjoying themselves in practice when it's their turn in the batting cage.

But fielding is a chore. Not that there isn't a thrill of accomplishment in making a spectacular catch; any ball player responds to that. But spectacular plays are rare, and many of them are more painful than satisfying (when a tumble or collision results). Most of the time, fielders must handle precisely those routine plays that everyone takes for granted. Therefore, one mistake, after 19 perfectly executed plays, makes a man a villain, while one key hit in 20 tries will make him a hero. In the sphere of ego satisfaction, the fielder has little to gain and a lot to lose.

Furthermore, the public is relatively indifferent to fielding skill. Admiration for the leading hitters and pitchers is unbounded; admiration for a fielder, even misplaced, immediately brands the fan who expresses it an aficionado. This situation is compounded by the fact that crowds invariably react incorrectly. The plays usually cheered loudest are not nearly so difficult as many others that go unnoticed.

For instance, an infielder will leap high and spear a line drive; an outfielder, running at top speed, will reach up and make a full-extension catch a few feet from the fence; a third baseman will smother a vicious smash, and throw the batter out at first; and—absolutely guaranteed to elicit shouts of awe and a trailing murmur of appreciation—an outfielder will throw the ball 300 feet on the fly to third or home, retiring no one and very likely letting someone take an extra base.

But leaping for a line drive is the easiest play of all; there's no danger and nothing complicated to gauge. You leap, and you reach the ball or you don't. The third baseman's play on a smash is dangerous, but it's also in the "you do or you don't" category. An outfielder's long run is not necessarily less routine than a short run, because 99 times out of 100 he knows when he starts whether or not the ball will be within range of his speed, and once the ball is within reach a one-handed catch is not only no particular strain but standard procedure. And the world-record discus throws some outfielders unfurl are strictly show-off propositions.

Even more realistically, all professional players know that teams choose players for their hitting ability. The two great exceptions are shortstop and catching, but even here, if one shortstop can outhit another by 50 points, he'll get the job unless his fielding skill is downright inadequate.

And here a contradiction arises. All managers, in conversation, stress the importance of defenses, the fact that a poor fielder "can't be hidden," the principle that poor fielding will lose many more games than good hitting will win. Yet they seek hitters, and often decide to sacrifice at least some defense for power.

By the same token, the majors are full of players who recognize that their fundamental success or failure depends on their hitting—but who, for that very reason, work hard to keep their fielding skills at the highest level. They will hit as well as they can, and there's not much they can do to improve their batting records; but they can, by practice and concentration, keep their fielding near 100 percent efficiency, and thus save their positions from only slightly better hitters who don't field as well.

This is because fielding skill is teachable and learnable, to a greater degree than either hitting (which is mostly inborn) or pitching (which involves a lot of learning, but only after the special gift of "a good arm" is present).

Naturally, fielders need the basic athletic endowments, and those who can run faster, throw harder, and react quicker have the advantages. However, the differences in endowment are comparatively slight for fielding duties, and the difference made by steady application is considerable.

In fielding, the mental work is paramount. The thinking done by pitchers and batters is primarily concerned with outguessing each other, but a fielder does not have to outguess a moving baseball; he has to anticipate which way it is likely to move before it starts. His mechanical responsibilities—catching and throwing—are coarser and less difficult than the fine-scale reflexes employed in batting or pitching, so that the most important part of the fielder's task is to be properly prepared for what comes up.

Sustained concentration is the key to effective defense in all sports. Anyone (or almost anyone—one can think of exceptions) can manage to extend his attention span through one whole time at bat, or while shooting at the basket or running with the football. The fully effective fielder, though, must focus his thoughts and alert his body about 150 times a game—before every single pitch his pitcher throws, even though the ball will actually be hit to him only a few times. Consistency, not occasional brilliance, is his goal.

And what do fielders concentrate on?

Where to play.

Since individual hitters have discernible characteristics, and hit a certain type of pitch in more or less the same direction, the alignment of the defense must remain flexible. A right fielder may play close to the foul line for one hitter, way over in right-center for another, in close for a third, back deep for a fourth. Every other fielder (except the catcher and pitcher) must also shift his position according to the batter, the type of pitch being thrown, the situation in the inning, and the score of the game.

These refinements are generally lost on the fan, who does have a vague notion that fielders do shift positions. The fan can see "infield in," and outfielders moving very deep, and the extreme shifts employed against hitters like Ted Williams, Willie McCovey, and so forth. But that's about all. The details are seldom realized.

Yet these details are what make up the chief mental activity of the entire game. Each fielder, if he is paying attention, has an idea of where he should be playing on every batter in every situation, according to that day's pitcher. Managers and coaches, in the dugout, are watching constantly to see if the players are right, and will move them if they are not. Much of the season-long shoptalk concerns where to place the fielders on particular hitters.

The blend of individualism and teamwork peculiar to baseball is seen at its best in the way the defense operates. In clubhouse meetings, the broad strategy of where to play whom is decided. But each individual fielder has to make his own adjustments, according to his knowledge of his own capabilities. An outfielder who is fast, and good at going back, can play shallower than one who is slower; the slower one realizes he is going to let some singles drop in front of him, but he still has to protect against the bigger danger of a ball going over his head. A shortstop with a strong arm can play deeper, but a shortstop who has exceptional quickness in getting rid of the ball (as Phil Rizzuto used to) can make up for lack of throwing power. Clubhouse meetings are not long enough to discuss every possible variation for every fielder in detail, so each man must know his own job.

One of the fundamental changes in baseball over the last twenty years has been the universal use of charts for defensive purposes. Every pitch in every game is marked down to be collated for pitching analysis—but every ball that's hit is also plotted on a diagram of the field for fielding analysis. You now have specific information on how often each batter hits each type of pitch (and off which pitcher), in which direction, and either on the ground or in the air, so you can play his "tendencies" in any situation. This is baseball's equivalent of basketball's shot-location chart or football's play diagrams.

One consequence is generally better defense. In principle, the charts don't contain anything the best baseball brains didn't always keep in their minds anyhow—but now the result of this "best" analysis is available to everyone, and transmitted by coaches to players during play to a greater extent. In other words, what the "smartest" players used to do and ordinary players missed is now imparted to ordinary players. An "eye-in-the-sky"—a coach or scout with a walkie-talkie up in the stands—can check alignments that aren't so easily visible from the dugout, and he tells the bench when someone has to be moved.

But the charts, of course, have their limitations. They are only a mechanical device. They're no better than the information and interpretation they contain ("garbage in, garbage out" still applies), and they are inherently weighted toward past circumstances that may no longer apply. You still have to decide, as a living being, the best thing to do *now*, this time, here, against this opponent.

One of those who doesn't consider charts a panacea is Willie Mays, whose opinions on fielding are of special value. Willie was usually admired as a great "instinctive" player whose prodigies were the result of God-given abilities, and that was certainly part of the truth. But he was also an exceptionally intelligent, analytic, quick-thinking, and astute player, able to perform his fielding wonders (and baserunning achievements) because of his mind, not just his legs.

"I would always know," he said recently, "exactly how every one of my pitchers was going to pitch each hitter. And that would change with the count. Then, knowing what the pitcher was trying to make the batter do, I'd position myself and even lean or get a head start in the right direction on the basis of what the batter could do with that pitch. The percentage was always in my favor. If the pitcher made the wrong pitch, or the batter somehow hit the ball against the odds, okay, we'd get beat on that play; but the majority of the time, things would go the way they were supposed to, and we'd get all those outs.

"For instance, I knew Sal Maglie would drive hitters back from the plate, and that the hitters knew that. So they wouldn't be dug in as hard against him as against some other pitcher. Now, a guy who would ordinarily be a dead pull hitter wouldn't be as likely to pull Maglie— so I'd play him accordingly when Maglie was pitching, and more to pull the next day against somebody else. And if, during a game, my pitcher changed his style or strategy—let's say, his curve wasn't working—I'd be aware of that too, and adjust.

"So I'd tell the left and right fielders to play off me—my adjustment could tell them what adjustment they had to make."

This is the same kind of thinking, of course, that enabled Mays to be effective at bat, and on the bases. It may be hard to "think and hit at the same time," but it's essential to "think and field." A baseball field with 300-foot foul lines has about 90,000 square feet of fair territory, and only seven players (not the pitcher and catcher) are allowed to line up anywhere they please. Placement makes all the difference.

When Ron Fairly was playing right field for the Dodgers behind Drysdale, they had their own system.

"Don knew exactly where he wanted me on every pitch to every hitter," Fairly recalls, "and, of course, I had a general idea of what he wanted. But every now and then he'd want me to move. So he would stand at the back of the mound, before the pitch, rubbing up the ball or something like that, and stare out at me. When I saw that, I'd start to move—I knew whether he meant toward the line or away from it from my general idea—and I'd keep moving as long as he stared at me. When I got to the spot he wanted, he'd look away, and I'd stop.

"Now I was in exactly the right place. If the batter then hit the ball out of my reach, that was Drysdale's fault—he hadn't done what he'd intended with the pitch. But if I hadn't been where I was supposed to be, that would be my fault."

A striking example of what the fan is up against when he tries to penetrate this mysterious area for second-guessing or for just plain fun came up in 1966 in Atlanta. This was mid-June, and the Mets were leading by one run in the last of the ninth. The Braves filled the bases, and Jack Hamilton, a right-hander, had to pitch to Henry Aaron with two out. Aaron was leading the league in home runs and runs batted in.

In the press box, I thought I saw something strange. Ed Kranepool, the Met first baseman, was playing close to the right-field foul line, while the second baseman was shaded toward second. In other words, there was a big hole in the right side, and all we experts knew that Aaron frequently hit to right and right-center, much more so than most right-handed sluggers. I couldn't figure out what Kranepool was protecting against, since a single to the outfield would score two runs anyhow and win the game for Atlanta. As it happened, Aaron made the final out by hitting a fly to straightaway center.

After the game, I asked manager Wes Westrum about Kranepool.

"No, he was just where we wanted him to be," said Wes.

"But doesn't Aaron hit to right and right-center?" I asked.

"Not this year," replied Westrum—and in three words he hammered home the lesson hardest for the fan to absorb: Current form is everything; what is a man doing *now?*

"He's been going for homers this year," Wes went on, "trying to pull much more than he ever did. And it's not that easy for a man to adjust his swing back and forth. So we felt that if he hit the ball to the right side, it would more likely be only because he didn't hit it well, swung late, or something like that, and in that case it might be closer to the line. But if he met it well enough, he would be trying to pull it. By keeping the pitch outside, we could make him hit it to center while trying to pull, which is what he did. But even if he had tried deliberately to go the other way, he would be doing it against an outside pitch—so again, the place for Kranepool was way over to the right."

And that's the reality of major-league baseball, once again: Think of all the possibilities, anticipate the more likely ones, and trust to fate that the unlikely ones won't pop up to beat you too often.

Positioning the fielder is only the first half, however, of the mental process in defense. The other half is anticipating which play to make.

Assume that I am properly placed and the ball is hit to me. Assume that I handle it flawlessly. What must I do with it?

I'm supposed to know:

1. The speed of the batter, going to first.
2. The speed of all base runners.
3. The needs of the strategic situation: Must a potential tying run be cut off at home? At third? At second? Is a possible double play more important than the lead runner? Is the chance of throwing out the man going from first to third good enough to risk the batter's reaching second?
4. My own capabilities: Where will my best play be if the ball is hit slowly? Sharply? To the extremities of my range, right and left? How much can I get on the ball throwing off balance?
5. The capabilities of my teammates.

All this is supposed to be clear in my mind before the pitch is made. Also, I'm supposed to be clear about my alternatives if the ball is not hit to me. Where do I go to back up a play? What base do I cover? What sort of help can I give to some other fielder?

And slight (sometimes not so slight) changes in each of these decisions come up with every new pitch.

Those fielders, therefore, aren't just standing around waiting to be awakened by the sound of the ball hitting the bat. They are thinking all the time—at least they are supposed to be. Being human, they are subject to distraction, most often by brooding over the last time they made out, occasionally by personal worries, now and then by sheer mind-wandering. But such lapses are rare. Most of the time, most players are tending to business quite seriously.

Each position has its own characteristics. Let's go down the list, examining the qualities that go into making a good fielder, and the principal duties involved.

Catcher

Aside from the pitcher, he's the most important player in the game for obvious reasons: He handles the ball all the time, he calls pitches (thinking along the same lines as the pitcher), he quarterbacks the infield (since he is the only player on his team facing all the others), and, when called upon, he must make the most important put-out of all, the one that prevents a run.

A catcher must have a reasonably strong arm, to prevent base-stealing and excessive bunting. Major-league catchers are usually judged first by the quality of the arm.

He must also, not quite so obviously, be a good receiver. That means he must be able to catch low pitches, since good pitching is low pitching. Now, many low pitches will hit the dirt before they reach the catcher, or just as they do, and smothering these is a prime responsibility when there are men on base. He must not only smother them, but catch them, because the runner might be going.

When Chris Cannizzaro was a regular catcher for the New York Mets, manager Casey Stengel was full of praise for his arm. As time went on, a flaw in Cannizzaro became apparent: While it was true he could really fire the ball to second, it was also true that he had to catch it first—and too often, Chris couldn't hold the pitch on which someone was running.

"I got one that can throw, but can't catch," Stengel complained, "and one that can catch but can't throw. And one who can hit but can't do either."

It was a trying time with the Mets, because they had comparable problems at seven other positions.

A catcher does not have to be able to run fast, because he doesn't have far to run. (He does run down to back up first base on grounders to the right side, but because of the throwing angles involved he doesn't exactly have to keep pace with the batter.) However, he does have to be able to move very quickly for the first few strides, in order to handle bunts, and be quick with his hands. Yogi Berra was outstanding at pouncing on bunts.

And, of course, he must be sure-handed and sure-moving on all foul pop-ups behind and to the side of home plate. This is a difficult play a large proportion of the time, and the pitcher feels he has earned an out when the batter hits one, so the pressure on the catcher to record the out is considerable.

Foul tips are another story. If you hold one on the third strike, the batter is out—but it is more luck than anything else if you do. The reaction is just too fast to be conscious, in all but a few cases. Usually, a foul tip that is held is simply one that wasn't deflected very much, and the catcher's glove was in the right place to start with.

Then there is the matter of "handling the pitcher." This has nothing to do with fielding skill, but with psychology, rapport, intelligent calling of pitches, pacing, even personality. It's important, but it's largely subjective.

With all these important things for the catcher to do, his weakness in hitting can be borne if he is outstanding at everything else. Nevertheless, the "best" catchers in everyone's opinion are the ones who hit very well and do the other things adequately. Today, with a universal shortage of good catchers, defensive value is the prime consideration, but a catcher who can hit remains a most coveted commodity.

First Base

Many clumsy men have played first base because they were powerful hitters. Traditionally, it is a position that can be used to keep a power hitter who is a poor fielder (like Dick Stuart, Zeke Bonura, and Lou Gehrig at the beginning of his career) in the lineup. Essentially, he must only catch thrown balls, master some limited footwork, field a few grounders, and handle some bunts. He doesn't need a good arm, because he seldom makes important throws. Many hard-hitting outfielders are moved to first base when they slow down.

But such situations are merely bowing to necessity. While it may be true that a poor first baseman will do less harm there than in some other positions, it is a certainty that a good first baseman is of great defensive value.

His most important maneuver is the stretch. By stretching far into the infield to take a throw, he can have the ball in his glove a fraction of a second sooner than if he stood up straight and waited for it to cover the additional four feet or so. That split second can be the difference between safe and out, especially at the completion of a double play.

When there is a runner on first and no one on second, the first baseman must "keep the runner on." That is, he must be anchored at first base until the pitcher commits himself to throwing home, so that the runner doesn't get too big a lead. If he did get too big a lead, he might steal, or spoil a double play, or take an extra base on a hit. As the pitcher starts to throw home, the first baseman backpedals, or charges in if it is a bunt situation. All this makes it unlikely that he will be able to field a sharp grounder unless it is right at him, so this situation gives the batter (especially a lefty) a good target for a ground single.

At other times, and even with a man on first in many situations ordered by the manager, the first baseman plays back, some 20 feet behind the bag. Late in a close game, he will tend to protect the foul line, to prevent a double between him and the line even at the risk of giving up the more likely single through the hole to his right.

A left-handed thrower is perfectly at home at first base, since it makes no difference in catching throws, and he has one distinct advantage on the one type of throwing play that comes up—to second base, on a grounder to his normal position or on a bunt.

On most teams, the first baseman acts as cutoff man for throws home from right field. The cutoff man's job is to intercept the throw if it is apparent that the man won't be out at home, and thereby to prevent some other runner from taking an extra base.

Second Base

On a diagram, the second baseman has the same position to the right of second base as the shortstop has to the left of it. In reality, their positions are quite different.

The crucial play for a second baseman is the double-play pivot. To complete a double play, he must take the throw to second with his back or side toward first, and simultaneously turn, avoid the runner, get rid of the ball quickly, and put enough steam on an accurate throw. Second basemen of quality are judged by how well they "can make the double play." In traditional thinking, a second baseman doesn't need a strong arm, because his throws to first are short ones. But many infielders, and managers, challenge this idea. They believe that a strong arm is so helpful in the double-play situation that it is an important factor in judging a man's suitability to play second. A strong arm is also valuable because a second baseman will be the relay man on throws from the outfield when a ball is hit to deep right or center.

Durability and a certain amount of acrobatic talent are needed, too, because the second baseman is often knocked over, from the blind side, by the runner sliding into second.

Naturally, a second baseman must be able to move quickly to either side, since he has a lot of territory to cover laterally. And he has to be able to go back for looping flies in all directions. But most of all, he needs guts. The real measure of double plays, says Whitey Herzog, is not how many you make, but how many you don't make when you could have. "And we don't have a statistic for those," he notes.

Shortstop

The shortstop is the most important player after the pitcher and catcher. He is the key man on the infield, for the simple reason that 75 percent of the batters are right-handed. More grounders will be hit to the shortstop over a period of time than to any other infielder.

He must have a strong arm, because his throws to first are fairly long—150 feet or more "from the hole" toward third. Because he has to throw farther, he must get rid of the ball quicker and get more on it than the second or third baseman. He, too, is the relay man from the outfield when the ball is hit to center or left.

The greater his range the better, but more than any other infielder, the shortstop covers ground with his head as well as his legs. His knowledge of the hitters, and variation of position, is of maximum importance. He has less chance than the second baseman to recover from a lunging stop to make a throw, so it is more important that he field a ball from a stance that makes a throw possible.

Lou Boudreau, Dick Groat, Alvin Dark, and Cal Ripken were outstanding examples of shortstops who had no exceptional gift in speed afoot or throwing ability, but whose knowledge of where to play made them exceptionally effective. Of course, all were outstanding hitters, or they wouldn't have been given the opportunity to play short on the basis of their fielding equipment alone.

The shortstop's double-play problem is simpler than the second baseman's, because he comes across the bag facing first, but the shortstop must be a master of timing to start the double play correctly.

Third Base

Outstanding fielders at third are relatively rare, because this is another position where a big hitter can be carried without fatally crippling the defense. But the outstanding ones are or were something to see—Brooks Robinson, Clete Boyer, Pie Traynor, Billy Cox, Mike Schmidt.

The third baseman's most important play is the bunt, or the accidentally topped slow roller toward third. He must be able to come in quickly, field a tricky hopper surely, and fire to first.

The harder-hit grounders, right at him or to either side, are "do-or-don't" plays most of the time.

It is widely believed that a third baseman needs an exceptionally strong arm. Obviously, it's valuable, because every once in a while he must make a long throw from deep behind third—a distance comparable to the shortstop's throw from the hole.

But even on this play, he is closer to the plate than the shortstop, and therefore the ball reaches him sooner, and therefore he has more time to make the throw. On most other plays, when he is lined up even with the bag at third or up to 20 feet behind it and in wide (toward short), a batted ball reaches him in plenty of time for a careful throw, and the distance is seldom more than 130 feet. The *need* for a strong arm at third (as distinct from desirability) can be classified as a myth.

Accuracy is far more important than power, and the ability to throw straight while off balance is vital to the coming-in plays.

All the infielders must have "good hands." Sure-handedness in fielding grounders seems to be based on a degree of relaxation. The hands are loose and sort of absorb the ball. Stiff, tense hands are sure to make errors, particularly at important moments. And "good hands" must be quick, because a high proportion of grounders take minute bad hops. Everyone can see the spectacular bad bounce that suddenly goes completely past a fielder with a drastic change in trajectory. But in every game, several apparently routine grounders skip or skid or otherwise shift direction at the last moment, and hands must react reflexively.

The third baseman, because he is closer to the plate and has more time, can succeed more often than other infielders in making the play by blocking the ball and then retrieving. Many a third baseman (like Pepper Martin) made a reputation for "fielding with his chest."

We can summarize infield requirements this way:

The first baseman needs elasticity and a sure glove; the second baseman needs guts and agility; the shortstop needs brains and agility; the third baseman needs reflexes and guts.

Outfield

The one indispensable quality for a good outfielder is speed. He must be able to run. There's a lot of ground out there and he has to cover it. That's a *good* outfielder. There are lots of mediocre-to-bad outfielders playing regularly because they can hit. You have to have hitters in your lineup somewhere, and if your hitters can't field, they'll do the least harm in the outfield—specifically, in left field.

Every professional ball player, it is taken for granted, can judge and catch a routine fly. Outfielders become specialists in four other respects: in how far they can go, in how well they adapt to the special visibility and wind conditions of various parks, in how they handle line drives, and in how they throw.

The center fielder has to be the best man available. He has the most ground to cover, he needs a strong arm, he must be able to come up throwing from either side, he must be able to come in fast to cover the looping-fly territory not quite covered by the second baseman ard shortstop, and he must back up right-center and left-center. He will frequently have throws to third and home from right-center, and will have more chances (of every type) than the right or left fielder. In defensive importance, he ranks behind the catcher, pitcher, and shortstop. In fact, some managers maintain he is more important than the shortstop. An infielder's mistake costs one base, an outfielder's three.

The right fielder needs a strong arm, even stronger than the center fielder, because his vital throws will be to third and to home from fairly deep right.

The left fielder can have a moderately weak arm, since the throw to third is a short one, and the throw home (while no shorter than the one from right field) leads to an easier situation for the catcher (who sees both the ball and the runner coming from the same direction, instead of having to catch the ball and turn).

Left-handers are common in right and center, but unusual in left, although that's a convention hard to take too seriously. It has to do with the fact that a left-handed left fielder, if he fields a ball between him and the foul line, has to turn his body before he can throw to second base, so that some possible singles may become doubles.

The main thing for all outfielders is "getting a jump." This is a compound of instinct, reflex, experienced guesswork, and practice. Willie Mays was so exceptional an outfielder in his youth because he got such a fantastic jump—a start in the right direction the moment the ball is hit. Sometimes, knowing the type of pitch being made and the batter's proclivities, Willie would start even as the pitch was on the way to the plate, as he has told us above.

In the 1954 World Series, Mays made one of his most famous catches. In the first game, at the Polo Grounds, the Cleveland Indians had two on and nobody out in the eighth inning, with the score tied. Vic Wertz smacked one high and deep to center, toward the bleachers 435 feet away. Willie raced back, caught it over his shoulder a step or two from the wall, and whirled a throw back to the infield. It was hailed subsequently as the "No. 1 sports thrill of 1954" and described as incredible.

And yet, to those of us who had watched Mays all season, there was no doubt that he had the ball all the way, as soon as he moved. From the press box, when the ball was hit, one couldn't tell whether or not it was going to reach the wall; but, after the first glance at Mays, one *knew* that Willie was going to catch it if it stayed within the playing field.

Now, Willie was exceptional, and the catch was understandably startling to those who weren't familiar with his abilities—but the point is that he "made" the play in the first step, not the last. Once Willie got "the good jump," the ball was his, provided it didn't carry to a barrier.

Every day, in every game, on a more routine scale, the same thing is happening. An outfielder's range is determined more by how soon he can start (in the right direction, of course) than by how fast he can run once he's under way.

A ball that "stays up," however far from home plate it goes, is seldom a problem. It's the line drives that are hard to handle. A liner directly at a fielder is hard to judge correctly, because there is so little apparent trajectory to let the brain's three-dimensional perceptions work on. If it's curving just a little bit, you may find out too late; by the time it reaches the outfielder, 300 feet from home, that slight shift may be a couple of feet. Most liners to right or left have some degree of curve to them (being either sliced or hooked), and when a fielder switches from one field to another, he has some adjusting to do. If a liner is not directly at a fielder, it takes a lot of hustle to get in front of it to keep it from becoming an extra-base hit. The "good jump" really counts in holding such drives to singles.

Throwing to the right base is the outfielder's main mental concern. Here he must make an instantaneous decision about the speed of the runners, his own body position as he gets the ball, the length of the throw, the strategic situation, and his own throwing ability at that moment. He must be sure he has a good chance to get the lead runner out; if not, he is giving the trailing runner an extra base by making a futile throw.

The cardinal sin, then, is overthrowing the cutoff man. High throws look spectacular, but the low throws, even if they bounce, are the better ones, because a cutoff man then has a chance to change the direction of the play. The lead man may get to third, or score, but another runner or the batter may be cut down for a lifesaving out.

In my opinion, there was a deterioration of the general level of outfield play in the late 1980s. I have no idea why, but almost all the scouts, coaches, and managers I discussed this with agreed with the observation. The drop in quality centered on two aspects: throwing to the wrong base (or at least failing to throw to the right base), and hanging on to catchable balls when the fielder's legs have brought him within reach of it. Jimmy Piersall, an established expert, thinks that too-large gloves cause drops.

One possible explanation is simply experience: There are more and more players in the majors who have played fewer minor-league games, and defensive play—like everything else between the foul lines—is a matter of accumulated, repetitive, trained reflex. You can't "practice" game situations; you have to play X number of games. The X has become smaller with more college cutting into the start of a minor-league career, and with fewer minor-league games played by those promising enough to be brought up to the majors.

Another explanation is the general acceptance of less concentration and shorter attention span, not only among athletes, but throughout society. As noted, fielding requires longer periods of maintaining top concentration than batting and pitching do—and job security, enhanced by expansion and high salaries, does not promote sharpened faculties.

It has even become something of a joke. Before All-Star Games, they've revived entertainment that once was frequently used before night games (when night games were something special). They have home-run–hitting contests, a relay-from-the-outfield involving three or four players, and a catcher's throw-for-accuracy to second base.

In 1988 in Oakland, in front of a big crowd at the public workout the day before the game, they had these activities, and the relay-from-the-outfield drew a tremendous cheer from the responsive spectators. Players are very crowd-aware.

I formed a mental image of one of the young All-Star participants, in the clubhouse afterward, saying to his manager, "Hey, you know, that's a pretty good play. Why don't we try it sometime in a game?"

When I described this thought to Bill Rigney, Al Rosen, Roger Craig, Tony LaRussa, and Sparky Anderson, they just smiled.

But they didn't dispute the point.

The final aspect of fielding is equipment.

Gloves today bear no resemblance to those used before World War II. They are vastly superior, and even different in conception. The old gloves, although they increased in size as they evolved from the 1880s on, were still basically designed to protect the hand from pounding and injury. The ball was still actually caught in the "pocket," which touched the palm, and was gripped by the fingers. Today's gloves are literally traps, and the ball is caught in a snare between the thumb and forefinger. The fingers are used more to manipulate the glove than actually to grip the ball through it. As a result, today's fielders hold virtually every ball they reach. And one reason outfielders use only the gloved hand on routine catches is that the big glove leaves nowhere for the bare hand to go.

In 1990, authorities decided to enforce rule-book restrictions on glove size, but as of mid-season it seemed a non-issue getting little attention.

Sunglasses have been used for decades, by infielders as well as outfielders. They come with a strap that fits around the back of the head, and the lenses are attached to a hinge at the top of the glasses frame. The fielder doesn't look through them until he has to look up into the sky; then, with a finger, he flicks the lenses down. In most parks, the area around home plate, where the outfielder must look to see the start of the ball's flight, is in shadow, so to have the glasses down all the time would cut out too much light.

Only the catcher wears pads, for protection from foul tips, but sooner or later players will be wearing batting helmets in the field, as they already do while running the bases. It's not flattering, but many outfielders look as if they could use batting helmets. Pitchers certainly could, along with hockey-goalie masks.

It is possible, after all, to get hit with a batted ball if the sun blinds you—a fairly common occurrence that happened in its most severe form to Willie Davis in the second game of the 1966 World Series. He lost two in a row that way, and made a wild throw off the second one, to give the Baltimore Orioles three runs, breaking up a 0–0 game Sandy Koufax was involved in. It was the turning point of the series and the Orioles went on to beat the Dodgers in four straight.

In the same Baltimore Memorial Stadium in which the Orioles completed their sweep, Yogi Berra was hit by a fly ball in practice in 1962. Yogi's catching career had all but ended, and he was back in the outfield in those days. With the sun low on the rim of the stadium before a night game, Yogi got careless and was conked on the forehead.

The blow opened a gash, and although there was no serious injury, there was a lot of blood. They ran out to right field with towels, and Yogi started to walk to the clubhouse, holding a bloody towel to his head and looking like one of the victims in *The Vikings*. (When Yogi saw that movie, years later, his comment on the graphic swordplay was: "I'm glad I don't live in them days.")

As Yogi passed under the broadcasting booth, en route to the dugout, Phil Rizzuto saw him. Phil was now a Yankee broadcaster, his playing career years behind him, but he was still a "teammate" of Yogi's in several business enterprises the two had in New Jersey, where they lived.

Rizzuto looked down at the apparently mortally wounded Berra, and called: "Yogi, speak to me, it's your partner. You wanna sell?"

Not included in the equipment is sympathy.

CHAPTER

4

Baserunning—Achieving Foot-to-Brain Coordination

To the connoisseur, the most exciting baseball action happens on the bases. It is the one aspect of the game completely free of luck. The base runner who steals or takes an extra base on a hit or an out has no bad bounce to contend with, no infinitesimal physics of spin or ball-against-bat to deal with. Only his mind, his skill, and his speed afoot are involved, and these are constants.

It is also, apparently, the most instinctive part of the game. Great base runners seem to be born, or at least trained in the earliest, formative stages of their baseball experience. The basic ideas of when to run and when not to, of course, can be taught to anyone. But the two things that really count—instantaneous grasp of the situation, and the ability to go from a standstill to top speed in the first step—are rarely acquired and only slightly improved even by years of practice.

Base-stealing was a primary offensive weapon in baseball until Babe Ruth started hitting home runs by the gross in the 1920s. Up to that time, the baseball itself was "deader" than the one used today— it didn't carry as far, because of its construction, and because one battered ball was kept in action longer. Scores were lower, one run meant more, and home runs were few. Standard procedure was for the man on first to try to steal second, so that he could score on a single. Pitcher and catcher developed techniques to prevent this, as one of their main concerns, but even so the risk was worthwhile, because if the runner didn't reach second, the chance of scoring was so small.

All players, then, were expected to be reasonably adept at stealing, even slow ones, just as they were expected to be able to catch the ball and throw it.

Babe Ruth changed all that. By making the home run so glamorous—and proving that it was so possible—he led the owners into introducing a livelier ball, which gave more players the opportunity to be home-run hitters. Once home runs became frequent, base-stealing became comparatively obsolete. Now the risk of being thrown out was too great, since the man at bat might hit a two-run homer. With decreased use, the need for mastering base-stealing skills disappeared. By the middle of the 1930s, only a few specialists in each league practiced the art.

It's not entirely a coincidence that Ty Cobb, who compiled the best batting record in baseball history (a .367 average for 24 seasons starting in 1905), was also the best base stealer (until now). In his day, the two weapons went hand in hand, just as in later times we expected any really great hitter (Mays, Mantle, Williams, DiMaggio, Aaron, Musial) to have a high home-run output. Since his hits had put him on base more often than anyone else, Cobb had more opportunities to steal, and he made the most of them.

And Babe Ruth himself came out of the same era. A little-remembered aspect of a very famous World Series game is worth pondering, because it gives the modern fan a glimpse of how completely different the attitude toward base-stealing used to be.

The seventh game of the 1926 World Series is one of the most frequently retold events of baseball history. The Yankees were playing the St. Louis Cardinals, who had just won their first pennant, in the still new and incomplete Yankee Stadium (which had been opened in 1923). Grover Cleveland Alexander, one of the greatest of all pitchers but now near the end of his career and thirty-nine years old, had beaten the Yankees in the sixth game to bring about this showdown game.

Every baseball fan has heard (and a popular movie has depicted) how Alexander came out of the bullpen and struck out Tony Lazzeri in the seventh game. The Cardinals were leading, 3–2, and the Yankees had the bases loaded with two out when Alexander relieved Jess Haines. (In the movie version of this story, Alexander was portrayed by Ronald Reagan.)

What very few baseball fans know is what happened afterward. It was, after all, only the seventh inning, not the ninth, when Lazzeri fanned. Alex got through the eighth and got the first two outs in the ninth—and then walked Ruth, who had already hit four home runs in that World Series.

The score was still 3–2. A home run would win for the Yankees. The batter was Bob Meusel, a right-handed batter who had led the league in homers the year before.

But Meusel never got a chance. Ruth tried to steal second, on the first pitch, and was thrown out, ending the Series.

Such an attempt today would be inconceivable by such a man. A pinch-runner would be used if the manager wanted to play it that way; then it was the normal way to play baseball. As Ruth told Tom Meany, a young sportswriter, in the locker room after the game: "Well, I wasn't doing any blanking good where I was," meaning first base.

Other aspects of baserunning didn't decline as much as stealing did after the Ruthian Revolution, but they did to a degree. The hit-and-run play became less important, not so much because of the base runners but because fewer batters could execute their part of it as they concentrated more and more on free-swinging for the fences. (The runners were also important, though, because on a hit-and-run play, the runner has to have a good chance of stealing the base in case the batter misses the ball.)

Attempts to stretch singles into doubles by daring baserunning also decreased, because, again, the risk of being thrown out wasn't worth it when a subsequent homer could score the man from first. Least affected was the attempt to go from first to third on a single, but even here there was a shade more willingness to stop at second (in doubtful situations).

In short, the emphasis shifted from maximum *advance* to maximum *men on.* It became more important to have as many men as possible safely on base when the home run did come up than to risk losing some of them for the sake of an extra base. It would be a double loss: Not only would a runner be wiped out, but another out would be recorded, which might keep a home-run hitter from getting another swipe later in the game.

Like most changes, though, this one took effect gradually. Ten years after the lively ball had been installed, the major-league players were men who had been brought up in the old style (like Ruth himself). Only in the mid-1930s did the population of the majors shift to men who had never had to concentrate much on baserunning, and by the time World War II ended, stealing was strictly an exciting specialty for such stars as Jackie Robinson.

Then, just as the 1960s began, a skinny little twenty-eight-year-old man of exceptional determination revived the moribund art in its full glory. His name was Maurice Morning Wills, and he had spent almost a decade getting nowhere in his chosen profession.

Wills is the man who finally broke Cobb's record (set in 1915) by stealing 104 bases in 1962. If ever a record seemed unassailable, it was Cobb's mark of 96 stolen bases in one season. The game had simply changed too much. Between 1928 and 1959, only three players (one of them twice) had been able to steal even *half* as many as that. Then Luis Aparicio, a slim Venezuelan with the Chicago White Sox, started (in 1959) to steal 50 or more a year.

But Aparicio didn't make the impact on the baseball world that Wills did, because his totals were only high, not undreamed of. When Wills stole 50 bases to lead the National League in 1960, it was the highest total any National Leaguer had posted since 1923—nine years before Wills was born. When, two years later, he stole more than twice as many, it was a far more startling achievement to baseball insiders than the breaking of Ruth's home-run record by Roger Maris the year before.

The story of Maury Wills is interesting enough as a typical success-of-the-underdog biography. But it deserved—and eventually got—thoughtful attention from many ball players, and it certainly had an important effect on the attitudes of many players. For managers, Maury provided an object lesson to be used with certain types of players, and his efforts revived awareness of baserunning among fans and reporters. He didn't change baseball back to what it was before Ruth—nothing could do that—but he did bring about a shift of emphasis. It spread to his teammates and then, after the Dodger World Series victories of 1963 and 1965, to other teams.

Wills was born in Washington, D.C., and went to work in the lowest link of the Dodger chain at Hornell, New York, when he was not yet nineteen. He was a right-handed hitter who played the infield and pitched occasionally, and he didn't do badly. In 1951, however, a black man could not yet take rapid advancement for granted; Robinson had broken the color line with the Dodgers only four years before. To the outstanding talents—like Willie Mays, who reached the Giants that season, and Don Newcombe and Larry Doby—the barriers were down, but the ordinary black player still faced a practical, if unacknowledged, quota. If he was good enough to beat out a white regular, okay—but in those days there was little room for the merely equally good black.

And there was nothing outstanding about Maury. He hit well enough at the Class D level—.280 his first year, .300 his second—but he obviously had no power and little special attractiveness to a Dodger organization whose parent club had eight home-run–hitting regulars in cozy Ebbets Field.

Wills moved on to Pueblo, Miami, back to Pueblo, Fort Worth, Pueblo again, and finally Seattle, one step below the majors. His statistics were always respectable, but his power insufficient. He had settled at shortstop by now, where he was a pretty good fielder but not spectacular.

But in 1958, the whole baseball world changed.

The Dodgers moved from Brooklyn to Los Angeles, where they had to play in a football stadium, the Coliseum, which had lopsided dimensions for baseball with no left field and an impossibly deep right field. At the same time, Robinson had retired; Pee Wee Reese was through as the regular shortstop; Roy Campanella had been crippled in an automobile accident; Gil Hodges and Carl Furillo were aging. Suddenly, there were all sorts of new needs and opportunities for the Dodgers.

The chief Dodgers farm club was now Spokane, and that's where Wills was. The manager was Bobby Bragan, who had already managed two major-league clubs. The Dodgers were still not terribly interested in Wills, and another club—the Detroit Tigers—had turned him down. Maury was no kid anymore, in an era when $50,000-bonus youngsters were getting more and more attention. He had not yet earned as much as $7,000 in any one year of playing baseball. And not one baseball fan in a million, outside of the Pacific Coast League, would have recognized his name.

Then Bragan made a suggestion.

Maury's main asset was speed. Obviously, he had good bat control and the ability to meet the ball, because his averages were always respectable. What if he became a switch-hitter? Batting lefty three-quarters of the time (against the 75 percent of the pitchers who were right-handed) would put his speed to best use: Being closer to first base, he would beat out more infield hits; he could bunt for hits much more effectively; and by reaching first base more often, he would get more opportunities to steal.

Maury tried it.

We can appreciate, after our discussions about batting, what strength of purpose it must have taken for a man to attempt this kind of change in his eighth year as a professional. Just to accept the fact that he was going nowhere the way he was required a kind of firm-mindedness that many players with poor records don't have.

What Wills had to an exceptional degree was desire to succeed. Given the threshold of physical ability any professional ball player needs, Wills made his career from that point on by his mental discipline, perfectionism, alertness, and willingness to make the utmost demands on himself.

He learned to hit left-handed. Since he didn't have any power anyhow, he didn't have to worry about swinging hard. He could wait to the last moment, smack the ball sharply through the infield, and a good proportion of the time beat it out if he tapped it weakly. By swinging down and smacking the ball so that it would take a high, long first bounce off a hard infield (a chopping-motion technique to which Casey Stengel, a lifelong advocate, gave the immortal name "butcher boy"), Maury could get a hit while the fielder helplessly waited for the ball to come to him.

To do this, however, Maury had to be a leading student of pitching. With his handicaps and his style, he had to hit intelligently, not instinctively. This required, again, mental application in studying all pitchers at all times and a good eye for the strike zone, two things that imply strong mental discipline.

Then Maury applied the same outlook to baserunning.

He studied and analyzed every rival pitcher's move to first base just as thoroughly as the most analytic hitters did the pitcher's pitching motion. In his mental "book," Maury came to know exactly when each individual pitcher was going to throw to first, when he was going to bluff, and when—most important of all—he reached a point in his motion that committed him to throwing to the plate.

With this knowledge, and with tireless vigilance for the tiniest deviation from familiar patterns, Maury could take the biggest possible lead without being picked off—and, when stealing, could be on his way to second at the earliest possible moment.

It is an axiom of big-league baseball that a runner steals "on the pitcher," not "on the catcher." At lower levels of competition, this is not true. If the catcher's arm is weak or inaccurate, the base runner will be safe even if he doesn't get the best start imaginable. In the majors, though, while some catchers have better arms than others, all can make the routine play, or they don't get the chance to catch in the majors. The difference, then, lies in how good a "jump" the runner can get—how big a lead, and how soon he can get moving.

It's the pitcher's responsibility to keep the runner under control. Most of his throws to first are not an intention, or even a hope, to get an out; they are a means of making the runner come back if he has taken too big a lead. And to a large extent, a pitcher can keep a runner pinned just by looking at him. If, within the context of the balk rules, the pitcher can keep the possibility of a throw to first open until the last moment, and then make his pitch to the plate with a rapid motion, the runner has very little time in which to make his decision, shift his weight, start his legs moving, and pick up speed.

It's often said, then, that a base is stolen in the first stride, not in the last, unless the catcher makes a bad throw.

Wills perfected these techniques. He did have the gift of a great "first step" (which is also such a great asset to basketball players and football running backs). And he made the most of it. Many, many other men have the same innate ability, but don't develop it; and very few put in the mental effort, the tireless observation, that makes such baserunning possible. By the middle of 1959, he was a Dodger; by October, he was in the World Series. By 1962, he was a star.

And by 1966, after he had helped the Dodgers to three pennants in four years, he had permanently influenced baseball thinking. Other players rediscovered the possibilities of the steal, and managers began to permit and encourage it—and look for players who could do it. Eventually Lou Brock, and then Rickey Henderson, eclipsed Wills's records, and a dozen other players routinely incorporated a 50-steal level into their games.

More important, though, was the change in managerial attitudes. Three in particular both used and talked up the running game: Chuck Tanner, Whitey Herzog, and Billy Martin. But the effect was universal. Earl Weaver, whose Baltimore teams dominated the American League through the 1970s, became identified with the idea of "playing for a big inning" and preferring the three-run homer, because he had personnel who could play that way, but the very fact that he was singled out for a particular philosophy revealed the change: From the 1930s through the 1960s, it wouldn't have been worth comment.

Of course, two basic changes had crept into the game at the same time, making it easier to see the advantages of running. One was people, and the other was fields. Artificial turf, when it spread to the base path itself, improved traction and running speed. But the player population in general was running faster, especially those exceptionally talented athletes who were most likely to excel at any phase they concentrated on. The distance was the same. The speed of the thrown ball, from pitcher to catcher and catcher to second, was the same. But if the runner were now a step or more faster, on the average, the odds shifted in favor of the steal attempt.

So the profile of the game changed again (and, again, gradually). In 1919, in every 100 games, there were 186 stolen bases and 39 home runs. In 1949, there were 59 stolen bases and 138 home runs. By 1959, there were still only 69 stolen bases and 182 home runs. But by 1979, stolen bases were up to 142—and home runs still plentiful at 164. Today's baseball is more balanced than ever, with homers and stolen bases showing up with essentially equal frequency—which is great for the spectators, since this maximizes action and keeps scoring up.

And Wills is the one who started the trend. It probably would have happened anyhow, eventually, because of the changes in speed and surface already noted; but the historical fact is that he was the one who made the impact when the time was ripe.

There is a third factor, also deeply involved with spirit and will. Stealing means sliding, and sliding means pain, frequent minor injuries, and always the risk of a more serious injury. To play the type of game Wills did requires stealing whenever possible, keeping on the pressure, establishing a pattern of daring—and this means running when you are already hurt, when the scrapes and bruises and ankle twists are not healed. And the more times you slide into a base, the more times you may collide with or be spiked by the man defending it.

So the steps in stealing are:

1. Get on. "You can't steal first base."
2. Know the pitcher's moves.
3. Be able to spot any lapse in concentration, and take advantage of it.
4. Know the pitching pattern, to find the best pitch to steal on and to avoid pitchouts.
5. Get a good jump.
6. Know how to slide, to avoid a tag even if the ball is there in time.

All these are things that can be learned, or at least improved. Getting on means taking the base on balls by having a good eye, and swinging to meet the ball, not to kill it. Studying pitchers is just that—study, concentration, dedication, not a gift from heaven. Sliding is practice—hard, unpleasant practice. There are various types of slides, to be used consciously according to the position of the ball and the baseman; the idea is to give the man taking the tag the smallest target to touch—a toe or a hand.

Choosing the right pitch on which to steal is a matter that shades into team play, and in this Wills had adept teammates who, in turn, adjusted to or adopted Maury's way of doing things. The manager, too, is fundamentally involved, in giving (in the case of a Wills) the runner free rein to use his judgment. The ordinary player doesn't steal unless he's given permission—a permission similar to the "hit" sign to a batter in that it doesn't *order* the runner to go, but only *allows* him if he thinks he can. The runner is obliged, of course, to try to arrange it so he can, and 99 times out of 100 he will go when given the sign—if he gets it.

The "right" pitch involves the count on the hitter, the type of delivery the pitcher uses, and the psychological battle between runner and pitcher (which includes the catcher, who is thinking with the pitcher).

If the count is 0–2—no balls, two strikes—it is obviously a bad time to steal, since the catcher won't hesitate to call for a pitchout just in case. (A pitchout is thrown deliberately wide of the plate, so that the batter can't reach it and so that the catcher can make a quick, unobstructed throw to second.) With that count, the pitcher can waste a ball, or even two.

By the same token, with the count 2–0—two balls, no strikes—the pitcher is very concerned with making the next pitch a strike, so the runner's opportunity is that much greater. What's more, the batter can even afford to help by swinging at the pitch and missing; it's only one strike on him and he might bother the catcher making the throw.

The type of pitch makes a big difference, too. A knuckleball is an invitation to steal, because the catcher has his hands full trying to hold it, let alone throw it. *Any* kind of slow pitch is easier to steal on than a fastball, because it takes the ball longer to reach home plate, and the catcher can't throw the ball until it does. A breaking pitch, especially a low breaking pitch, also helps the runner by traveling slower and by giving the catcher an extra problem.

If a left-hander is at bat, the runner on first is at least partially blocked out from the catcher (and with a righty, the runner on third). If a pitch is low to the third-base side of the plate, the right-handed catcher (and all catchers are right-handed) will need a fraction of a second more to get into throwing position than if the pitch is to the first-base side. (And why are catchers always right-handed? Because, since most batters are right-handed, there is less chance of the batter getting in the way of the catcher's throwing motion. But this may be more traditional than necessary.)

The base runner, then, by doing the kind of thinking that the man at bat and the pitcher are doing, may find a moment of maximum advantage to steal on.

One quality has been omitted from this whole discussion, and significantly so. A good base stealer, or any good base runner, does *not* have to be exceptionally fast. That's one of the most widespread misconceptions. He can't be slower than average, of course, but every team has some men on it (often pitchers) who can beat the best base runner in a foot race. It's not a question of how fast you can run; some sprinters are terrible base runners. It's a matter of deciding exactly when, and starting quickly, and sliding well.

Wills, or any other outstanding base stealer, brings his team many indirect benefits. All are predicated on his percentage of success, however; if he were getting thrown out half the time or more, he would be killing more rallies than he was helping. Most of the good ones run to a percentage of success of .700 or more; they are safe on more than 70 percent of their attempts.

What are these team benefits?

Most of all, a threatening base runner, like Robinson, Wills, Mays, Aparicio, Brock, or Henderson, bothers pitchers. The pitcher worries about him, throws over, looks. All this can interfere with the pitcher's concentration on the hitter. It can spoil his aim. Many a walk has been issued, and many a home-run ball served up, because of a base runner's harassment.

This situation has changed over the years. In the 1930–70 period, when the home-run style bred out the base runners among hitters, pitchers did not have to master the techniques of keeping runners in check that were necessary in the 1900–30 period. So when Jackie Robinson and Maury Wills and Luis Aparicio started re-using the weapon, many pitchers were so unaccustomed to worrying about a runner that their concentration was less affected. Since the revival of base-stealing (which includes the presence of more fast runners), pitchers are extremely runner-conscious, and also face stricter (and more haphazard) application of the balk rule, and are even more susceptible to being distracted than the dead-ball pitchers were—with the hazard of home runs being hit off mistakes. One reason games are much longer, in elapsed time, is the attention paid to base runners' leads.

Second, the better base runner can keep the first baseman pinned to the bag a trifle longer, thus keeping the right-side hole open a trifle longer. He can force the shortstop or second baseman to play a trifle closer in, since to get the double play they may have to move a little faster. Playing in more, they leave more room for a grounder to go through for a hit. These are small edges, measured in inches, but inches can decide the game.

Third, the good base runner, by his success, increases the efficiency of the offense. The same number of hits can produce more runs.

Fourth, he can upset the entire defense. Fielders may hurry throws and relays, infielders and outfielders may be too hasty trying to pick up a grounder. The catcher, most of all, may be rushed on a bunt play or on an attempted steal or on a pickoff, and may throw the ball away. A small number of such incidents has a large effect on the steadiness of the opposition.

Fifth is the other side of the coin: His alertness and daring can be contagious, can lift the spirit of his own team, can make teammates bear down harder. An air of aggressive excitement can be transmitted to the whole team.

So far, most of our attention has been on stealing, which remains the province of specialists even though the specialty has enjoyed a revival and an expansion. When baseball scoring decreased, stealing a base became more important and a more worthwhile risk—for exactly the same reasons that the skill was developed in dead-ball days. Nevertheless, just as only a few men are truly suited for hitting homers consistently, only a few have the potential for stealing 40 bases a year.

But the other aspects of baserunning apply to everyone.

Coaches at first and third are supposed to help base runners. In most situations, there is little they can do. Most of the time it is up to the runner to see where the ball is hit, estimate how far he can advance, and do so without hesitation. He must take into account the effectiveness of the arm of the fielder involved, the position of the ball with respect to the fielder in terms of how long it will take to retrieve the ball and throw it, and his own established speed (modified by the amount of jump he had).

The base runner must consider the score and the number of outs to determine what sort of risk is worthwhile and what isn't. Trailing by four runs, with one out in the bottom of the ninth, there's not much sense in trying to go from first to third on a marginal hit, because the runs that matter must still get on and score after you; the big thing is to avoid even the remote possibility of an out. Trailing by one run, in the same situation, it's definitely worth a try, because then you can score the tying run, and avert a defeat, on an out.

The most common responsibility faced by every runner—slow or fast, big or little, bright or dumb—is to try to break up a double play. This is baseball's muscle play. The man from first must try to slide into second hard enough to spill the pivotman and prevent him from making an accurate throw to first. This means, first of all, getting there soon enough, and then being willing to mix it up without too meticulous a concern for the exact location of the bag itself. Too blatant a knockdown too far from the bag is punished by umpires (as an automatic double play) more than it was twenty years ago, but the amount of leeway given is still considerable. In any case, the runner doesn't umpire: He gets his man and takes his chances. Games, and pennants, are decided on the success or failure to break up a double play.

The same necessity, but a different means, applies in this situation: Men on first and third, none out, the batter bounces to the third baseman or the pitcher. The man on third *must* break for home. If he doesn't, the fielder will start a second-to-first double play and the runner at third will still be there. If he breaks for home, they will have to make a play on him to prevent a run from scoring. He will be a sure out, but only one out, and his team will still be left with men on first and second.

If the man on third is a good and creative base runner, he will manage to get into a chase, and to elude being put out until the other two runners reach second and third. This is hard to do in the specific example given, but it is a general rule: When a runner is caught between bases, he must dodge back and forth long enough to permit the other runners to advance as far as possible.

Always, there is a fine line of judgment: Aggressive baserunning brings tremendous rewards, in extra bases and runs and in forced errors by the opposition; too much daring results in giving the opposition undeserved outs, gets the opposition out of trouble, and wastes your own hits.

Unfortunately, for the dedicated but truth-seeking second-guesser, those judgments all hinge on the angle of vision of the players on the field, and it is hard to condemn mistakes correctly. It may have been plain enough to me, in the press box, that Kevin Mitchell had no chance to score on that hit to left-center, but it may have looked entirely different to both Mitchell, as he left second base, and to the third-base coach, also at ground level.

There is another responsibility every base runner has, and it is remarkable how often he fails to discharge it: He must catch all the signs flashed to him. If the batter is going to sacrifice, or hit-and-run, the runner must be notified; just as the batter is signaled by the third-base coach relaying the manager's instructions, so the runner is signaled, by a coach, or from the bench, or by the batter.

If the runner misreads the sign, it's instant trouble. The batter bunts, the runner is standing flat-footed off first, and an out has been wasted (and possibly a double play made). If the runner thinks the bunt is on and it isn't, there he goes chugging into a sure out at second, or finds himself unable to get back to first.

From the manager's point of view, stealing and hit-and-run merge into a larger concept called "starting." On certain pitches, in certain situations, the manager may want to "start" the runner from first base without the classic hit-and-run play in mind. He may feel that this way he can avoid a double play, or get an extra base. He weighs all the factors—the speed of his man, the pitcher's abilities, the game situation, the position of the fielders, the pitch he thinks is coming up, and so forth.

There is one automatic starting situation known to every baseball fan: two out and a 3–2 count on the hitter. In this case, the runner on first cannot be put out once the pitcher throws: It will be ball four, a foul, or a hit, or the batter will make the third out anyhow.

But on many other occasions in a game, not at all automatic, the manager will "start" the base runner for some purpose. And that's one more reason managers burn at hitters who swing too hard and miss, hanging up a runner.

Almost all the situations we've talked about involve a runner at first. Most of the action takes place there, because that is where options exist. A runner on second will rarely try to steal third, because the gain—to score on a subsequent out instead of on a hit, which would score the man from second anyhow—is not proportional to the risk. The catcher must throw only 90 feet to third instead of 127 feet to second. And stealing home is strictly a desperation measure or a grandiose gesture.

Wills was criticized for stealing bases "when it isn't necessary," and accused of "showboating"—an accusation discernibly tinged with race prejudice in the baseball world. (Even in 1989, in the American League Championship Series, some Toronto players made that charge concerning Oakland's Rickey Henderson. Toronto's manager, Cito Gaston, is also black—and was not one of those who complained.) Maury's reply, aside from self-justification and the emotions he arouses, gives more insight into the real nature of baseball than the views of his critics. "My game is running," he said, "and I have to do it at every opportunity, both to keep myself sharp and to keep the opposition on edge. Besides, when can you have too many runs? Is a home-run hitter criticized for hitting a home run after the score is 10–1? If our team is ahead 10–1—and how often is it?—I'd still like to help make it 11–1 by stealing my way into scoring position. I've got no guarantee the other team won't score nine more runs."

That's the baseball we're talking about: played by humans, with varying abilities, trying to make the winning plays in the situations that exist *at the time*—not in abstract situations after the fact.

On the other hand, some men should *not* try to steal even when they can. The outstanding example was Mickey Mantle. Exceptionally fast most of his career, Mickey also had all the baserunning instincts in the highest degree. He could, almost literally, steal a base whenever he put his mind to it; and the relatively few times that it could mean victory, he would. But Mickey's entire career was plagued by leg injuries, and it would have been plain foolishness to allow him to take the pounding and risk the injuries that frequent stealing would entail. He was too valuable in other ways, as a slugger and a fielder, to be lost for two weeks because he was injured when stealing a base.

In 1990, this was a pertinent and timely issue for José Canseco, whose 40 steals in 1988, along with 42 homers, had projected him into a new category of glamour. In June, he negotiated the largest contract in baseball history (up to then)—$23.5 million for the next five years—and while negotiating it, was on the disabled list with a back problem that required hospitalization in traction. He had talked to the press of having a 50–50 (homers–steals) season some year. But with the kind of five-year investment he and the club had just agreed to, it would be stupid and unforgivable to subject his back to the kind of strain and risk statistics-seeking (as distinct from game-winning) steals entail.

For his teammate Rickey Henderson, who will go to the Hall of Fame as base-stealing champion, the risk is an inherent part of his game (although he has other skills, too). For Canseco, his central claim to greatness will be power, not baserunning, so the risk is not worthwhile.

Besides, Mantle, like Canseco now, usually played on teams that had plenty of power, and daring baserunning simply never made sense with that sort of lineup. This is illustrated by Willie Mays, perhaps the most innately talented base runner of all, and as blessed with good health as Mantle was crippled. Willie led the National League in base-stealing before Wills arrived—in seasons when the Giants were relatively weak. When the Giant lineup became loaded with sluggers again, like Orlando Cepeda and Willie McCovey, to drive Willie in, the risks of stealing were no longer in the team's interest, and his totals shrank.

With Wills, it was different: He had to take the pounding, because running was his asset. If he got hurt and couldn't play, his services were lost—but if he didn't run, they were lost anyhow. The Mantles, Mayses, and Henry Aarons have too much hitting ability to run indiscriminately, even though they could.

The revival of "running" baseball—not really a counterrevolution against the home-run era, but a slight shift in values—is also the product of an improved level of pitching and an increased number of parks with large playing areas.

After all, the old-fashioned single-bunt-steal-single offense evolved in baseball because the pitcher was supreme. In the dead-ball era, runs came hard. In the lively-ball era since 1920, with limitations on trick deliveries, a brand-new white baseball put into play every moment, and lots of short fences, the pitcher was on the defensive. Running could be ignored, because swinging for the fences paid off.

In the 1960s, however, the balance began shifting back toward pitching. Why? Eddie Stanky, a superb baseball analyst who spent years scouting between stints as manager of the Cardinals and White Sox, had a simple answer: "Pitching can be taught more effectively than hitting can," he said. "Today's youngsters are well schooled, well trained, looked after, and advised. We work with hitters as much as with pitchers, but by the nature of things, pitchers get better results. So the day of bad pitching is gone forever. Outstanding pitchers are still rare, but the level of the second-flight pitchers is way up."

And the ever-increasing use of relief pitchers amplifies the effect.

When pitching is better, runs are harder to get. When runs are harder to get, the offense has to try something different. On top of that, Dodger Stadium, Candlestick Park, the Astrodome, Shea Stadium, and the many other new stadiums are less conducive to homers than Ebbets Field, the Polo Grounds, or old Busch Stadium used to be.

It's not a coincidence that Wills achieved what he did on a team that had some of the greatest pitchers ever assembled on one staff—Sandy Koufax, Don Drysdale, Johnny Podres, Ron Perranoski. They kept pitching shutouts, one-run games, two-run games. With pitchers like that, a couple of runs can be enough to win, and the Wills style of offense is designed to produce a couple of runs a game even if the opposing pitcher is overpowering, too. If, on the other hand, Wills played on a team with poor pitching, so that the other team could feel confident of scoring five or six runs a game, the opposition wouldn't worry about Wills. Let him steal if he's three runs behind; what good will it do, if enough other men are retired? He might still post a fancy statistic, but all the indirect, victory-producing values of his style would evaporate if his own pitchers didn't produce close, low scoring games all the time.

So even in the most personal of all baseball actions, baserunning—where no ball or bat must be controlled, just your own body and will—extensive interrelations and team considerations pop up at every step. That unique blend of individual responsibility and team effect is, as Branch Rickey loved to point out, the combination that makes baseball so distinctive among team games.

CHAPTER

5

Managing—The Art of Worrying

Every player, in his secret heart, wants to manage someday. Every fan, in the privacy of his mind, already does. The second-guess is the lifeblood of baseball's appeal to the fan, and the field manager of a team is the man to be second-guessed. The actions of individual players, while also susceptible to second-guessing, all hinge on the physical performance of their duties. You can be glad or sorry that someone struck out, but you can't really second-guess him because he *wanted* the home run just as much as anyone.

But the manager—ah, he does nothing but make decisions and issue orders. All his activities are mental. Therefore, he is the ideal object for second-guessing. If things work out right, obviously he must be a genius for having planned it that way; if they don't, he's a stupid idiot who should be fired. Often, he can go from genius to imbecile and back to genius again in the space of one inning.

What does a manager really *do?* We will consider the following questions about managers:

Just how important is a manager, as far as affecting the number of victories a team winds up with?

How important is his "handling of men," and just what does this entail?

What are his actual duties, day by day and inning by inning?

What are the qualities a good manager must have?

Let's take these topics in order.

How much difference to a team's record does a manager make? Ten victories over the course of a season? Twenty? Two? None? The best answer I ever heard to this question was given by Bill White, in the spring of 1964 in Florida. He was the first baseman and one of the elder statesmen of the Cardinals then, and Yogi Berra was just beginning his first one-year term as manager of the Yankees. Johnny Keane was managing the Cardinals, and no one dreamed at that time that Keane would succeed Yogi as Yankee manager after the Cardinals defeated the Yankees in the World Series that fall. There was a lot of speculation about how Yogi would do as a manager, and White's opinion was sought in due course.

The question was phrased: "How much difference does a manager make?"

White's answer was: "It depends on the manager."

This wasn't evasiveness, but profundity—an indication even then that this was a man whose mind would be appreciated enough, a quarter of a century later, to have club owners pluck him out of a broadcasting booth and make him National League president.

Some managers make no difference at all. Others help a team win several games it might not have won. Others can create situations that lead to many lost games. It all depends on how the manager in question operates.

Most managers have little effect on the team's won–lost record, because most clubs reflect their basic talent over the course of a full season. That doesn't mean that most managers make identical decisions, and that everything would turn out the same way whoever managed. It does mean that, given certain material in the form of the accumulated abilities of the players, managers with different styles will get similar results. Sparky Anderson might operate in a fashion that would lead to victory in Tuesday's game, but lose Wednesday's; Tommy Lasorda in the same circumstances might lose Tuesday but win Wednesday. On the average, their clubs will finish as high or as low as their material warrants.

This is because baseball's basic tactics and strategy are simply not that complicated. To the professional, who has spent his life playing and studying the game, the alternatives in almost every situation are clearly known from experience. If there is any significant advantage to be gained by a maneuver (like sacrificing after the first man gets on late in the game with the score tied), all baseball people know it with equal thoroughness. If, in many situations, the alternatives are 50–50, it's a guess anyhow.

But it is the *first* guess, and that's the distinguishing characteristic of the manager's craft. He gets the first guess, the only guess that will lead to the tangible result. No one can ever know, afterward, what would have happened if the manager didn't change pitchers, or didn't order the hit-and-run when he did; everybody—including the manager—knows how it turned out when the play is all over. So most qualified people—any experienced player on up through managers—know all the stock situations and would make similar decisions in similar circumstances.

Some managers, however, go beyond the ordinary bounds. They are so sharp at making split-second decisions during a game that their players (and rivals) become convinced that this quickness turns half a dozen imminent defeats into victories. Leo Durocher earned that reputation.

Other managers impress their players as being slow in this respect, or perhaps disruptive in some way. It is generally believed that a bad manager can cause more defeats than a good manager can steal victories. And, as with players, different abilities in managers lead to success in different situations. A manager may be ideal for one group of players, not so good for another. This isn't true nearly as often as most players would like to believe, but it does happen sometimes. By and large, however, many managers have relatively little to do with winning and losing in the short run. The ones who have great effect are the exceptional ones.

This is contrary to the myth, and contrary to the underlying wish of the fan who gets his kicks out of second-guessing the manager. If the manager's second-guessable decisions don't make that much difference, a lot of fun goes out of blaming him for mistakes or vicariously sharing his triumphs. And it is also contrary to the interests of the majority of players, who like the emotional comfort of blaming their troubles on the manager, even when they keep the complaint to themselves.

Taken at face value, however, the above remarks can be misleading. The context must be understood: *Provided* that the manager is a thoroughly qualified baseball man, and *provided* that he has a fairly free hand in making decisions, *then* almost any manager will get comparable results with given material. Differences in style tend to cancel out.

What is essential is that there *be* a manager.

Only one man can run a ball club. He doesn't have to be the smartest man in the organization, or the most experienced, certainly not the best liked, and almost certainly in no way unique—but he does have to be the boss.

Someone has to make the final decisions on who will play, who will pitch, what the batting order will be. Someone has to give the order for a bunt, a hit or take, a pinch-hitter. That someone is the manager. He can take advice, share his thought processes, delegate some rights, but at bottom the final yes-no decisions are his, just like the president of the United States.

Every team has a manager in fact, even if not in name. The Chicago Cubs tried for several years to operate with a system of several coaches of equal authority. Actually, during games, one of them always performed managing functions. They didn't take a vote on whether to order a hit-and-run play or not. The decisions may have been made by different men at different times, but at any given moment there was only one manager, whatever he was called.

What the Cub system did undermine was the equally important climate of authority a manager creates. Aside from the strategic and tactical decisions, the manager is responsible for *all* decisions—discipline, training habits, practice procedures, and assignments of personnel. He may do a lot or a little in each of these areas, but the players under him consider him the source of all orders and permissions. On the Cubs, this unity of command was lacking. One coach might prefer one player, and ask for one sort of performance, while another had other leanings.

"It's different, all right," said Don Zimmer one day. Zimmer had played for many managers before landing in the Cub system of ten coaches. "Instead of getting into one doghouse, you can get into ten." Eventually, as a manager himself, Zim got a chance to build his own kennels.

Getting into a manager's doghouse, or staying out of one, is a subject that goes right to the heart of the biggest cliché and yet deepest truth about managing: The main task is "handling men." In this case, we are dealing with mythological elements encrusting the carcass of an older, exploded myth. Thanks to increased emphasis on dressing-room coverage, interviews, debunking realism in reporting, and the sheer repetitiveness of radio and television, most fans realize these days that a manager is not simply a glorified chess master, or a wizard pushing buttons, or a mastermind outsmarting mere mortals. The image of a supergeneral plotting victory and avoiding defeat, which was part and parcel of John McGraw's public character as "Little Napoleon," is ancient history.

Instead, everyone talks knowingly of the much more sophisticated notion of "handling men." The manager must "get the most out of his men." Every man is different and has different problems, so each one "must be handled differently." As generalities, such ideas are true enough, but left as generalities they lead to some absurd viewpoints. Pretty soon the second-guessers are absorbed in judging morale instead of ability, psychology instead of strategy, personality instead of performance, the peripheral influences instead of the central events.

Of course a manager must handle men; every boss must. Of course every person is different, and is best treated accordingly. Of course a manager must try to get the best results out of the collection of abilities at his disposal. So must an orchestra conductor. Realizing only this much doesn't lead to much enlightenment.

The real question is, what does "handling men" mean in terms of managing a ball club? Where does it start, and where does it end? Current conceptions about the manager's role tend to cast him as some sort of psychoanalyst, priest, top sergeant, father, brother, and judge, all rolled into one.

With *very* few exceptions, the following propositions apply to every big-league manager:

He cannot change the fundamental character of any player. The lazy ones remain lazy, the conscientious ones are conscientious from the beginning. Men may change their own characters, and life can affect them, and a manager can be one of many interrelated influences—but the problem characters under one manager invariably turn out to be problem characters under another. This doesn't mean a manager won't change or help the behavior of a player who has acquired—even deservedly—a bad reputation elsewhere. The right manager can and does. What he can't change is an *authentically* bad character.

He cannot change the basic level of ability of any player. There are no "secrets" or miracle-working instructional gimmicks in baseball. Managers and coaches can, and do, recognize what a player does that keeps him from reaching his potential, and can show him how to improve. But only the player himself can make that improvement, by willing application (a reaction rooted in character), and he can only improve so much.

He cannot "inspire" anybody, the way Knute Rockne is supposed to have inspired football teams with half-time harangues. This is a profession, a livelihood, serious business engaged in by adults. All know the stakes involved each day as well as the manager does. Besides, what must be executed on the ball field isn't helped much by inspiration; in body-contact games like football and hockey, high emotions can bring forth useful extra effort, but in baseball, where all vital skills are of the fine-scale, hair-trigger, reflex type, a binge of passion can do more harm than good. Again, this doesn't mean he can't motivate, lead, help, and guide; in fact, he must. But rah-rah pep talks, or magic psychological tricks, are not the way.

He cannot devise any special, new, surprising strategy, or substantially affect the pattern of offense and defense, as football and basketball coaches can, because all the broad possibilities of baseball strategy were worked out and systematized long ago. All the strategic options in baseball involve "when," not "what." Our friend Yogi Berra, toward the end of his first year as manager of the Yankees (1964), summed it up neatly. His team had lost the first game of the World Series to the Cardinals, and the usual proportion of the 600 or so sportswriters and newscasters on hand asked Yogi the standard silly question before the second game: "Now that you're down, one game to zero, what do you plan to do?"

"Not much," said Yogi. "It ain't like football. You can't make up no trick plays."

Here, too, there are distinctions. The better manager figures out countless ways, day by day, to get an edge in the fine-tuning aspects of pitch-by-pitch play and analysis. But he can't invent new "formations" or design totally new approaches to basic baseball tactics, as is possible in other sports from time to time.

And he can't, in matters of discipline and training, exercise the sort of autocratic control over every detail of off-field behavior that a big-time college football coach takes for granted. He can try, but he can't succeed in imposing it. The nature of both the game (played daily for nearly seven months, counting training) and the players (professionals whose ages range from twenty to forty and whose salaries may run from $100,000 to $3 million) simply won't permit it.

In this respect, we have an important difference from relationships that used to exist. Before free-agency salaries created a new structure, starting in the late 1970s, every manager had virtually every player's career at his mercy, and every player knew it. Dominant stars, like Ruth, DiMaggio, and Williams, were relatively few in number and still prisoners of the reserve system. If a player didn't please the manager— got into that doghouse—he could be benched, sent to the minors, traded, or even released, with an immediate effect on his livelihood. The player also accepted, psychologically, the basic American principle that his boss made more money than he did and that this authenticated the boss's authority.

Nowadays, few managers get paid as much as any of their regulars, and a player with a three-year $9 million contract does not consider the manager his "boss," any more than a superstar movie actor considers the director of a particular picture his "boss." He accepts the manager's authority to make decisions concerning that enterprise— the game and season—but in matters of discipline and career, he deals (through a high-powered agent) with club owners or presidents, not the man in the dugout. Managers must now "sell" rather than "order" their instructions. It's as essential as ever that a manager succeed in establishing and maintaining his authority, but he must do it by more subtle—and creative—means than his predecessors had to use.

And finally, perhaps most of all, he cannot, in Charlie Dressen's immortal phrase, "guide that ball." He can tell a pitcher what to throw, but he can't make the ball go there; he can tell a hitter when to swing, but he can't make him hit the ball. He can frequently have the right thought, followed by an unproductive result (we'll come to an example soon); very rarely does a wrong thought lead to accidental benefits.

If he cannot do all those things, what *can* he do?

He can, and pretty well must, earn the respect of his players—respect for his technical baseball knowledge, and respect for his integrity in dealing with them as a boss.

He can, and must, maintain sufficient discipline to keep it clear that he is the boss (in the limited sense noted above). He may or may not use fines, curfews, little rules or maxims, strict work schedules, and minor punishments to this end, but one way or another he must meet the challenge whenever his authority is flouted.

He can recognize the varying needs of different characters, and treat them accordingly—without creating a group of special, privileged cases. He must know who has to be pushed, to be encouraged, who can take criticism, who can't, who needs help, and who can't be helped—all without turning into a babysitter, or a tyrant, or an unapproachable autocrat, or a friendly buttinski.

He can evaluate correctly each player's capacities, and try to use them in ways that bring the team maximum benefit. This is probably the most important single contribution he can make.

And he can run the game—the individual game.

If these are the manager's legitimate responsibilities, our chances to second-guess him become unsatisfyingly meager. About the sorts of things mentioned above, the fan in the stands can have practically no knowledge, even if he reads faithfully every word printed in the sports pages and listens to every word uttered on radio and television. The manager might be, in reality, totally wrong, but the fan's opportunity to see that he's wrong is nonexistent.

Am I suggesting, then, that we abandon second-guessing? In a book addressed to intellectual appreciation of baseball, of all places? Not exactly. I merely advocate keeping this undeniably delightful pastime in perspective. Second-guessing is fun, and that's all it should be; taking it seriously is self-deception. The man making the first guess has weighed, 999 times out of 1,000, all the relevant factors, on the basis of his experience. His reasoning powers, within the framework of baseball, are usually impeccable. Having weighed everything, he makes a decision. It may work out right, it may not, but his *reasons* for making it are usually sound.

This is not to say that all managers have the same answers, and that a computer would do as well. Some guess right a much higher proportion of the time than others—but rarely because they reason better. The difference lies in the capacity to notice small things, recognize subtle patterns, remember applicable situations. Thus a Leo Durocher might—just might—think of something that Walt Alston wouldn't; but the chance that a fan (or a writer) has noticed some element that the professional hasn't is nil. Seeing what he considers a stupid move, the fan may be aware of a half-dozen elements in a situation, and may be drawing the right conclusion from them. If the manager got another answer, however, it is because he is aware of another half-dozen factors that the fan didn't think of and probably couldn't possibly have known about.

A beat baseball writer has a better opportunity than the ordinary fan to think along in this way—and can check it out by direct questions. Invariably, when you go to a manager and say, "In that situation, considering A, B, C, and D, why didn't you do so-and-so?" the manager can reply, "You're absolutely right about A, B, C, and D and the conclusion you drew from that; but you didn't also consider E, F, G, and H, and that leads you to a different conclusion."

We saw how that works back in Chapter 3 on fielding, in the where-do-you-play-Aaron incident.

With this stipulation—that our information is necessarily limited and that we mustn't come to believe that we're *really* right when the manager is wrong—let's second-guess to our heart's content.

Better still, let's first-guess. When watching a game, get on record—to a friend, or in your own mind—what you think the manager should do *before* the play happens. Then keep track, over a period of time, how often the manager's way came out right when you differed. It requires a little intellectual self-discipline to do this honestly, and some humility will result, but a great deal of enlightenment will result also. Soon you'll feel in the game more than ever, and in return for abandoning dogmatic condemnation of that stupid manager, you will gain the excitement of thinking along with both managers more realistically. It's like double-crostics: Once you get the hang of doing them, plain old crossword puzzles seem one-dimensional and uninteresting.

So, in order to go beyond the old-fashioned "he shoulda had him bunt!" type of second-guessing, let's break down the manager's responsibilities and duties. Let's see what he really thinks about.

There are two totally distinct segments to his job: while the game is on, and all the rest of the time. Consider the second segment first.

A manager works all year round. As far as the front office is concerned, his responsibility lies in getting the best possible performance on the field from the players supplied. Procurement of players is the province of the general manager, training them to major-league level is the province of the farm system, finding and evaluating them is the business of the scouts.

During the winter, the manager divides his time between public relations work for the club—personal appearances at dinners, interviews, etc.—and numerous conferences concerning personnel. He is briefed repeatedly on the players in the minor-league system; he is consulted about possible trades (but *only* consulted for his opinion of the men involved); he confers with the general manager about the players already on the big-league club's roster, about his plans for them in the coming year, about changes he'd like to make.

He has a voice in choosing the majority, if not all, of his coaches. He takes a hand in off-season contact with players who have problems—special conditioning after an operation, special work for a man who may be asked to change positions, perhaps a pep talk where needed. If the club has an instructional team operating in late fall–early winter for rookies and a few convalescing veterans, he keeps an eye on its activities.

He lays out the work schedule for spring training—when players will report, which players (in addition to roster men) he wants to look at, what sort of calisthenics they'll do, how the pitchers will work, what special practice will be given to selected players.

As the season is beginning and subsequently, he orders the rules of life around the clubhouse. He is consulted by the groundskeepers on how the field should be tailored, hard or soft. He tells the road secretary which alternatives to choose in making the road trips, whether to leave right after a game, or the next morning, or any other such detail.

There is one subject, though, that the manager steers clear of: player salaries. With few exceptions nowadays, the manager does not get involved in the annual argument over money. That's strictly between the player and the front office. (In the past, managers had much of the authority general managers now have, and they did sign their own players.) Today, a manager tells the general manager who did a good job and why, and who didn't, but he stays out of the negotiations.

While all this is being done, the manager thinks. Almost all his waking hours (which get longer when things go wrong because sleep becomes elusive), he thinks about one problem or another, one way or another to squeeze out a few more runs, a little better pitching.

He must decide which players to keep when roster limits go into effect. He must plan his pitching rotation, for starters, a couple of weeks ahead and readjust it constantly as one pitcher gets knocked out, another gets arm trouble, another goes bad, and rain interferes. He has to keep his bullpen strong and ready, without killing it by ordering too many warm-ups too soon, and still avoid getting caught in an emergency with no one warmed up.

He has to choose his regulars, platoon his not-quite-regulars, and find ways to give his substitutes enough work to keep them sharp when an emergency puts them in action. He has to settle on a batting order, change it when necessary, and decide when to leave it alone.

Through all this, he clings to three recurrent themes, themes that have infinite applications: You can't please everybody, there's always tomorrow, and in the long run the breaks even up.

The conviction that luck cancels out over a period of time is necessary to keep firm the belief in baseball's entire structure of "percentage play." You must choose, over and over, the move that *figures* to be right, even though it just backfired three times in a row on flukes. Baseball men define "panic" as the abandonment of percentage moves in the face of a losing streak. A manager is able to avoid this panic only if he keeps reminding himself that things even up—even if they really don't, in his case.

The awareness that there's always tomorrow, always another game, another season, enters into all the plans of a manager. No game exists in isolation, until and unless it is the last day of the season and his team is tied for first place. Whatever is done to win today's game must be weighed against the price that might be paid. Thus the relief ace, who has already worked three days in a row, may be kept out the fourth day even though he might have made victory possible. Winning today, and then having your relief ace out for a month with arm trouble, is not an intelligent way to proceed. The risks must be measured against the gains, and vice versa.

Here the handling-of-men facet of managing is prominent. A young player, his confidence fragile, must be brought along gently. Perhaps, in a particular case, he needs to be thrown in over his head, but that's what the manager has to decide. Things must be done with him and for him that may not be, in theory, the best things to do in that particular game. For instance, a potential star may be allowed to bat sometimes for the sake of experience and confidence, instead of being removed for a pinch-hitter. An older player may be rested in the second half of a doubleheader or after a night game, or to avoid artificial turf, even though it decreases the chances of winning that particular game.

And all such cases must be handled with a certain amount of tact, foresight, and calm.

Remembering that there's always tomorrow is important psychologically, too, for both manager and players. Even the best baseball team loses 50 or more games a season. Taking defeat *too* hard will only lead to more defeats. By the same token, thinking the world is your oyster because you won the last six in a row is a sure path to complacency, excessive self-esteem, relaxation of effort, and defeat. Today's hero is tomorrow's bum so often, and the other way around, that all baseball men learn to keep plugging away in defeat and not to "get too gay" in victory.

The most frequent reminder, though, is that you can't please everyone. The manager must learn not to try. There is no way 25 men, whose livelihoods depend on records compiled on the field, can be kept happy in a game that calls for only nine players. Aside from arithmetic, a basic conflict of interest exists: The player, by the very nature of things, is concerned with his own success; the manager must always think of the success of the whole.

Almost all athletes believe that when they play their best, the team benefits most. This sounds like unassailable logic, but it's a whopping oversimplification of reality. In many situations, the conditions that enable one man to do his best interfere with the necessities of others. Every player tends to believe that what's good for him is good for the team; the manager knows that what's good for the team may not be good at all for several players.

This is seen most clearly with pitchers. Here are seven or eight men with starting potential and relatively equal overall potential. (Let's say you already have two clearly identified top starters and one top reliever.) Only three others can start regularly (in a five-man rotation). Each of the eight is convinced he can perform best working on a regular five-day starting schedule—and correctly so. Yet five of them will not get that chance—and those five are still needed, to fill out the bullpen, to start in case of injury, for special circumstances, and so forth. The manager will apportion assignments in a way he thinks will produce the best result for the team over a full season—but that guarantees that at least a couple of those pitchers will have their personal careers damaged, or at least unfulfilled. (This, incidentally, is one of the soundest moral arguments in favor of free agency, which enables a player to choose a more favorable situation at least sometimes.) But what's best for each pitcher is clearly not what's best for the team.

At other positions, players simply hate to be platooned. In the old days, the universal principle was "find your eight best men and play them every day." Many managers pay lip service to that idea today—

but one may be permitted to suspect that they do this more because they know it soothes their players to hear it than because they really intend to do it. Sure, it's great to keep things that simple when every one of your eight men is clearly the best available at his position. But most teams have two or three positions with no one man available to handle all situations reasonably well. They platoon at these positions because they must, to take advantage of the partial skills of two incomplete ball players.

It has been proved, again and again, that intelligent platooning enhances the career and the total income of players who are not solid stars, and that it helps a team win. Yet players hate it, because most believe privately they could be stars if given the chance. This is a healthy belief, enabling the player to give his best—but it may not be a fact. The manager is the man who must act on the fact when it conflicts with the player's belief.

This can be stated in another, more provocative, way: A manager's job is to take away players' alibis. No one enjoys accepting blame when something goes wrong—and in baseball, by its nature, most batters are failing most of the time and so are most pitchers (in the sense of permitting a run). It is a universal tendency to look for an external reason, an excuse or at least a justification, whether animate (other people) or inanimate (the sun got in my eyes). But improvement, or minimizing the repetition of failure, can come only from facing up to whatever controllable self-cause is involved. It's the manager who has to do this, constantly, to people who are more comfortable accepting their habitual level. And in the high-salary era, a man so lavishly praised and rewarded for a level already achieved is all the more prepared to accept his own alibis for not living up to or surpassing it. The manager is the one who must make him confront a weakness or a lapse, thus threatening his self-esteem.

Under such circumstances, few managers can be liked, or liked for long. As long as the team wins a pennant, everyone may be happy and consider the manager a helluva fella; but 24 out of 26 teams must, by definition, lose the pennant every year. Sooner or later, every team has its bad spell, and then the complaining about the manager begins. If nothing else, he's the handiest excuse for every individual player's failures.

The longer a man manages, the longer he stays with one club, the surer he is to wind up being disliked by a majority of his players. A few years after retirement, these same players may feel real affection and appreciation for him, but not while they are playing. It shouldn't be surprising. In other walks of life, how many men love their bosses? They can respect and even admire them, but liking them is difficult, especially in highly competitive endeavors in which it is the boss's function to drive you to the limits of your ability.

The manager-player relationship goes through various stages. The rookie accepts the manager's authority as a matter of course. To him, the manager represents "Do it my way or you'll get sent back to the minors."

The experienced but marginal player is in a similar position—please the boss or move on.

The experienced, established player tends to be loyal and conscientious—with secret reservations. In salary and importance, he outranks the manager these days. In his own mind, he is storing up the opinions by which he'll try to manage someday, and he has probably worked under several different managers. He obeys all the rules, but he expects to be left alone as much as possible, and he rarely places the manager on a pedestal.

The aging player is the toughest problem of all. The manager is the man who must recognize, and tell him, that he's losing it. The very same fierce competitiveness that made a player outstanding now prevents him, for a while at least, from giving in to the inevitable slowing down. From the human point of view, this is certainly understandable and perhaps gallant; and the emotions of the fans are all on the side of the familiar old-timer's reputation. Yet the manager must tell the star, by actions if not by words, that he's not the man he used to be, before the star can accept this for himself.

No, managers are rarely liked. That's why it's all the more important that they be respected.

What earns them respect?

Baseball judgment and fairness, with a touch of fear thrown in.

By fairness, players mean that a manager treats the whole squad equally—a minimum of privileges for the highly paid stars, a concern for the dignified treatment of the scrubs. Punishment and discipline should be applied impartially, and achievements should earn the same praise and reward whoever makes them. There should be no favoritism. Jobs should be assigned on the basis of ability, not personality. Criticism should be made without adding humiliation to it.

The manager who does these things is considered a fair man by his players (and by the rival players his players talk to). But this objectivity, which makes fair treatment possible, presupposes good baseball judgment. And what is that? Essentially, it's the ability to predict correctly the results that specific actions and tendencies will produce.

First of all, this requires the ability to spot every player's strong and weak points, and to predict reliably the consequences of each. A manager must anticipate how the opposition will take advantage of weakness, and how it will try to counteract strength, and then seek countermeasures accordingly.

Second is the ability to recognize, instantaneously, all or most of the relevant factors in game situations, not just a few—who's the hitter, what does the pitcher have, where are the fielders playing, the count, the score, the inning, the opposing manager's way of thinking and available options, his own available options, and the effect of all this on what may arise a couple of innings later.

As we've already seen, it's not much of a trick, to a professional, to think of the right strategic moves in a given situation; the real trick is to *define* the situation correctly by taking into account all the contingencies.

Third is the ability to maneuver those men available in a way that takes maximum advantage of their assets and minimizes their liabilities. The hitter with an insurmountable weakness can be "rested" against the type of pitching that bothers him most; the good pinch-hitter must be used at the right time, not too soon and not too late. There's a well-worn anecdote about this, dating from the 1930s when Casey Stengel was managing in Brooklyn. He had a round catcher named Babe Phelps who was a powerful left-handed hitter. The Dodgers were losing by four runs, 5–1 or some such score, in the fifth inning, and Casey sent Phelps up to pinch-hit with the bases loaded. Babe promptly hit a home run which tied the score. It remained tied until the ninth, when the other team scored and the Dodgers came to bat in the bottom half with no strong pinch-hitters left. Sure enough, someone got on, and there was no one to drive him in. "Ya bum ya," one of the few (there were never many in those days) faithful on hand yelled at Stengel, "why didn't ya save Phelps?" Casey, having retold this story a thousand times, once added: "The fella had a point. I shoulda had him hit a five-run homer the first time up."

Liking the manager, then, is a pleasant bonus when it occurs, but neither necessary nor important to the success of a club. Respect is essential, and respect results when most of a manager's decisions prove to be sound. The players are watching like hawks—second-guessing more persistently, more knowledgeably, and more mercilessly than any fan—and they either become convinced or they don't.

Durocher is an outstanding example. Many of the men who played under him and despised him the most on a personal basis remained the most vocal admirers of his managing. Stengel, too, was widely detested by players (who, in retrospect in later years, often spoke highly of him).

Other managers can be well liked—and unsuccessful. One reason is that "nice guys" often find it difficult to be sufficiently heartless and severe in their judgments, and strict enough to keep control. Give a group of ball players the slightest opening, and they'll take advantage of a manager's leniency in shameless fashion. You don't have to be a rat to be a good manager—but every good manager must do things occasionally that make him seem like a rat to some players.

This was the issue behind Leo Durocher's most famous quote, "Nice guys finish last." There are conflicting versions of how it actually came about, and the line I give now is different from the one I described twenty-five years ago, although the underlying sense is the same.

Mel Ott, the epitome of a "nice guy," had accomplished nothing as manager of the Giants. Leo, who had won a pennant with the Dodgers in 1941 and had had other contenders, was notoriously nasty and had served a year's suspension (unjustly) for consorting with gangsters, been boycotted by church people, and been involved in brawls that required police intervention. When Leo replaced Ott as manager of the Giants in the middle of the 1948 season, it was probably the greatest psychic shock in baseball history for fans of both clubs and elsewhere.

One day at Ebbets Field (in the version given me by people who were there but are now dead), some writers were needling Leo about being nice. Leo is supposed to have pointed at Ott, across the way in the visiting dugout, and said, "There's Ott—he's a nice guy, and he's in last place."

It came out in translation as "Nice guys finish last," and Leo certainly adopted the phrase whether or not he actually said it that way, and it became a byword of cynicism. But it can be interpreted more broadly. It doesn't say nice guys *must* finish last, or can't finish first; it just makes the point that being nice is irrelevant, and won't prevent you from finishing last, and can even make it more difficult to finish first. But any number of nice guys have actually finished first, and plenty of unattractive ones have finished last. The important—and valid—point is that niceness is not a determinant either way. But paying too much attention to being nice when it's time to be hard-headed can certainly interfere with winning.

All right, then. We have an idea of what a manager thinks about and how he operates the year round. What does he actually do with respect to a baseball game?

He begins by choosing his pitcher and making out a batting order. The pitching decision has probably been made several days before, as part of a rotation pattern. The batting order must be thought through every single day, even if it ends up the same as yesterday's.

There are traditions about batting orders, some valid. Pitchers bat ninth, for two reasons: They are the poorest hitters, and therefore you want them to come to bat less often; and, when and if a pinch-hitter for the pitcher does something positive late in the game, the top of the batting order—that is, the better hitters—will follow him.

There are other traditions. The leadoff man must be good at getting on base and a good base runner, but doesn't need much power. The second hitter should be adept at bunting, hit-and-run, and other runner-advancing techniques. The third, fourth, and fifth hitters are the long-distance, power hitters, capable of knocking in runs. The sixth, seventh, and eighth hitters are then arranged as well as can be.

The reasons for these traditions are sound. Only in the first inning of a game is the leadoff man guaranteed to lead off, but the first inning is something special, not merely one of nine. If you can get the lead, most subsequent strategy shifts in your favor; your pitcher has a margin for error, the opposition's offense is denied certain risks (primarily on the bases). Besides, in the average game, the batting order will be worked through four times, so the order in which the first few men bat amounts to one-fourth rather than one-ninth of the offensive opportunity.

In addition, the leadoff man leads off a subsequent inning a disproportionate amount of the time. Because the pitcher is so poor a hitter, and because the defense intends to take full advantage of that fact, a pitcher will turn out to be the final out of an inning more often than random numerical distribution would indicate.

Also, if a pitcher happens to lead off an inning, he is likely to make out, so the leadoff man will be in what amounts to a leadoff situation in a curtailed inning (with only two outs coming). Since there are only three possibilities—a leadoff man can come to bat with none out, one out, or two out—the proper batting order has a chance to operate in two-thirds of the possibilities.

So the first man has to get on, by a walk or a hit, and he has to be a good enough base runner to bother the pitcher, perhaps steal second, certainly reach third on a hit to right or right-center, and certainly score from second on an outfield single once he gets that far.

The second man must be able to hit to right field, to bunt well, to control the bat well enough to be reliable on the hit-and-run play (when he must swing at pitches he'd prefer to pass up), and also to run well. What's more, both these first two men must have pretty good batting averages, or the whole idea is shot.

The No. 3 hitter, traditionally, is the best hitter on the team, the one who combines high average with power. If the first two men have done their jobs, there is someone on base for him to drive in; in any event, he is guaranteed of getting a chance to hit in the first inning, even if the first two men make out.

Behind the top three come the power men, who may have deficiencies in speed or batting average. But, in principle, when they do connect, there will be runners on ahead of them.

The man who bats eighth, often the catcher or the shortstop (since these men are chosen more for their defensive skills than their offensive abilities), is in an unenviable position. The pitcher will bat next, so the opposing pitcher will make sure the eighth-place hitter doesn't get much good to swing at. Especially with two out, the man on the mound can risk issuing a walk, since the pitcher who bats will probably provide the third out. Our eighth-place hitter isn't the most talented batter to begin with, or he wouldn't be hitting eighth. Now he finds himself teased by ordinary pitchers and mercilessly borne down on by the best ones (who are eager to save the pitcher for an easy first out the next inning). Life is seldom a joy for the eighth-place hitter.

In the American League, starting in 1973, the eighth-place hitter became the ninth-place hitter, and he gained a bit from the shift. With the adoption of the designated-hitter rule, which removed pitchers from the batting order, the weakest "regular" hitter was dropped to ninth place and the designated hitter inserted wherever the manager thought best. Now the weakest hitter would be followed by the leadoff man, not by a sure-out pitcher, so it was not advisable to risk walking him. This meant he would get more "good" pitches to hit, while the new No. 8 hitter (now the second-worst regular, as the No. 7 used to be) couldn't be treated so cavalierly because following him was a regular, albeit a less dangerous one.

Getting more good pitches to hit when you are a poor hitter to begin with, however, is only a marginal opportunity. Gene Mauch, always the analyst, put it most directly. "I always know who the weakest hitter on the other team is," he explained, "because the opposing manager tells me by listing him ninth." So there is a difference, but it's not enough to alter the principles that apply to the rest of the batting order.

All these things are traditions, but not rules. They are idealizations, abstractions of qualities, more than anything. In real life, the manager must adapt the players he actually has to the needs of the day. He may not have a good leadoff man, and his best hitter may lack power, or his whole lineup may lack power, or he may have a bunch of free-swingers who can't run at all. More often, the best fielders are not the best hitters, and the manager has to choose which contribution will mean more to the team.

Here's what can come up: You have two slow-footed outfielders, both poor fielders, both awesome sluggers. They have to play, because their bats are too valuable to do without. Your infield is pretty good defensively and a little weak offensively. Now, you *must* have a center fielder who has exceptional range, to take up the slack for your two sluggers in left and right. Perhaps he can't hit more than .172, but you have to have him out there. You may also have another outfielder, who can hit .280 and do a better-than-average defensive job by one-man standards, who can't possibly cover as much ground as the caddy who hits .172. Very often, you decide to play the poorer all-around player, because he can cover center field and a half, over the other one. And you can guess how lovable that makes you to the pretty good player who is now languishing on the bench.

Getting back to the batting order, you have to take into consideration several other factors, besides the theoretically desirable pattern and the adjustments made to your players' limitations. The lefty-righty business is important. You need some sort of balance. If *all* your hitters are left-handed, a left-handed pitcher would have a terrific edge against you. If your lineup has four left-handed hitters in a row, it might prove to be a sitting duck for a good left-handed relief pitcher. Also, in deciding who is to play, you have to try to hold back at least two pretty good hitters, a lefty and a righty, for pinch-hitting late in the game. If *all* your good hitters are in the starting lineup, the decisive rally may develop in such a way that you have no sufficiently dangerous batter to take the one crack that can win the game.

So a manager, in devising his batting order, gives a lot of thought to sequences within the order: Who will bat after whom, what will happen if there's a change of pitcher at this point, and so on. If you have two slow-footed, heavy-hitting right-handers, you're just asking for rally-killing double plays by batting them consecutively. If you have a good left-handed pull hitter, you can almost eliminate the need for bunting with him by having a good base runner hit right in front of him. If you have a good bunter, he's wasted if the man before him can't run. And so on and so forth.

Stengel, in his glory years with the Yankees, had a wealth of talent and made platooning famous. He would, sometimes, lay out twelve lineup cards on his desk, as in solitaire. He would fill in the two names he was sure of—Mantle and Berra—on each card, and then he'd go to work. He would play out, in his mind, a dozen possible versions of the game coming up, and try to anticipate situations that might arise.

Your final batting order, then, will take account of the opposing pitcher and his equipment; the type of strength the opposition has in the bullpen; the lefty-righty balance and the power-speed balance available in your own club; the optimum offensive-defensive compromises; and the possible pinch-hitting moves you might make. (Roger

Craig, managing the Giants, developed a neat message to give his players. "I always use my nine best players," he'd say, "and you're one of them—today.")

You sign the lineup card, give it to the umpires, discuss ground rules, take up a favorite position in the dugout, and the game begins.

You have already gone over, in detail, how you expect your pitcher to pitch to every hitter, and where you expect the fielders to play. (This is usually done in a clubhouse meeting before the first game of a series, but it is also a continuing conversation.) Now you quickly check: Are they doing it? Are the fielders in the right spots, according to the hitter, the count, and the stuff being thrown? Is your pitcher getting the ball where he wants it?

Most of your attention, during the defensive half of the inning, is on your own pitcher. You watch his motion, and how his pitches behave. You'll be able to tell—amazingly well if you are a qualified manager—when he tires, or loses control, or loses his stuff. Hits may be falling safe against him, but if he's "throwing good," you'll let him weather the storm. Or he may be getting them out, but not showing the control or stuff he should have; in that case, you'll have the bullpen working at the first sign of trouble.

When you have to change pitchers, finally, you make the decision before you leave the dugout. Rarely does a manager let a pitcher talk him into letting him remain, and every manager can cite instances of being sorry when he did.

On the subject of changing pitchers, the second-guessers have a field day. Yet most fans have a completely backward view of the situation. It's not a question of taking a pitcher out, which is the way most fans look at it; it's a question of bringing someone in. The manager must always be thinking about the next play, not the last one. He stakes his judgment on how the *next* batter will be retired. It may be true that his pitcher has been getting hammered, but unless the manager is sure that the *new* pitcher represents a chance to do better, there's no sense changing.

So the moment of decision rests on *who* is in the bullpen, what kind of shape he is in, and who the other team will send to bat to face the relief pitcher. If a team has a great, reliable, healthy reliever, starters will be taken out much sooner than if it doesn't.

This is true of every move a manager makes: In his mind, it's a chance to improve the situation; otherwise, he doesn't make it. And he must always remember to save someone for tomorrow, too.

When the manager's team is at bat, he is much more active. He is calling the plays from the bench, just as so many football coaches do. He flashes the signal to the third-base coach, who flashes it to the batter, to hit or take a given pitch. This is an art in itself. It requires great experience and intuition to use this power constructively. Some hitters can be left pretty much on their own, some can't; what's more, the same hitter may need a tighter rein against one kind of pitching than against another. But it is the manager's unquestioned prerogative to give this order.

It is an order fraught with misunderstanding, even by many players. Batters want to hit; they want to swing at the first pitch they like; they want to avoid getting into a two-strike situation at all costs. Yet the manager, often, wants them to take pitches for tactical reasons. He may see the rival pitcher getting tired. He may want his own pitcher, who just ran the bases, to get a breather. He may, as an intruder into the pitcher-batter battle of wits, recognize a pattern better than his own (less experienced) hitter, and force him to lay off a pitch he knows won't be a good one to swing at.

It's the less intelligent hitter in the first place who gets the most guidance, and he's the one chafing most under a "take" sign. A take sign means, "don't swing, period." If it's a called strike, that's too bad, but don't swing. The hit sign, however, means "you have permission to swing *if you want to.*" There is a regrettable tendency for hitters to interpret, not quite consciously, a hit sign as an *order* to swing, and they proceed to swing at the next pitch even if it isn't a desirable one.

Some take situations used to be considered standard: a 3–0 count, often a 3–1 count. When it's 3–0, the pitcher must throw three consecutive strikes. His chances of missing with one of them are high. He might miss with the first or second, which would be a walk. Swinging at a 3–0 pitch, even though it may look so easy to hit, is doing the pitcher a favor, getting him out of a jam. It's still a round ball and a round bat, and the odds are against any one swing being a base hit. And when the count gets to 3–1 and 3–2, the pitcher still must offer a good pitch to hit. Nevertheless, with more and more emphasis on slugging, today's managers let men "hit" on 3–0 fairly frequently— and pitchers no longer assume the hitter will be taking. A breaking pitch on 3–0, once rare, is common now.

A fascinating instance of the subtleties involved came up in a routine game in 1965. It offered a fine illustration of how managers think.

The Yankees were playing at home. It was the last of the ninth, two out, and the score was tied. Elston Howard was the runner at first base. Ray Barker, a left-handed batter, was pinch-hitting. The count went to 3–1.

Johnny Keane, the Yankee manager, made Barker take the next pitch. It was strike two. Then Barker hit a line-drive double to left-center, scoring Howard from first base and winning the game.

"Barker never did understand why we made him take that 3–1 pitch, until we explained it to him afterward," Keane recalls. "Thinking just as a hitter, he'd much rather get a chance to swing at that pitch, since the pitcher had to come in with it.

"But with Howard, who's a slow runner, at first base, Barker would have had to hit a home run to win the game for us; there was no way he could score Howard from first with a long single or a double.

"However, once the count went to 3–2, Howard could break from first with the pitch, and be halfway to second by the time the ball was hit—and that's exactly what happened. With a running start, Ellie scored and the game was over. But if Barker had hit the ball to the exact same spot on a 3–1 pitch, Ellie wouldn't have started running until the ball was hit, and he would have had to stop at third.

"On the other hand, if the pitch had been ball four, the walk to Barker would have pushed Howard into scoring position automatically, and a single by the next man could have won the game."

This example is doubly interesting.

It appeared in my book when it first came out in 1967. Several managers subsequently told me they disagreed with that kind of thinking so strongly that they doubt I got right what Keane was actually saying. I am absolutely sure I recorded correctly what Keane told me (no tapes exist), but I can't swear there might not have been some other element in the situation that he left out, or I missed. What it does show, however, is that managerial thinking is not a monolithic application of "right" or "wrong" moves. Managers differ, and the same manager might think differently on different occasions. Once again: art, not science.

Now here's the other example I promised earlier in this chapter.

In 1984, Frank Robinson was managing the San Francisco Giants and Joe Torre the Atlanta Braves. The Giants were well into a bad year, in which Robinson would be fired. The Braves had been division champions in 1982 and runners-up in 1983. This game came up on June 6, a Wednesday afternoon, in San Francisco's Candlestick Park.

Bob Brenly hit a grand-slam homer for the Giants early, and Jeff Robinson, a rookie, pitched well for the Giants. But the Braves pecked away and by the top of the eighth inning were trailing only 4–3. With two out, the young pitcher walked the No. 7 Atlanta hitter, then got the third out. In the bottom half, manager Robinson lifted him for a pinch-hitter and started the ninth with Greg Minton, an experienced and supposedly top-drawer reliever. The Braves tied the game and won it in the eleventh, and the manager took a beating from the second-guessers about taking out the rookie. His explanation—"He'd gone far enough and you don't want to take a chance with young arms"—was stock public relations baloney, swallowed whole (although criticized) by what we used to call "the scribes."

But look at what really went on:

With a one-run lead and four outs to go, a main goal of the Giants was to make sure Dale Murphy, Atlanta's superstar, didn't get up again with a chance to decide the game with one swing. No one else was that threatening—and Murphy, the No. 4 hitter, was six slots away with four outs to get.

So that seemingly innocent two-out walk to the No. 7 hitter was a telltale of trouble. It was one of those don't-walk-anyone-at-any-price situations; if he gets a hit off you, okay, but don't give gifts. If he ends the inning, the ninth has to start with two pinch-hitters, and Murphy can't get up unless at least three men reach base. Because of the walk, even though the next hitter was retired, Murphy was one turn closer to coming up with the game on the line. The walk told manager Robinson that pitcher Robinson, out of fatigue or inexperience or whatever, was unable to put the ball where he wanted it. Why, then, take the chance of having the same thing happen at the start of the ninth, and have to bring in a reliever with the tying run already on? Why not simply start the inning with the reliever you'd have to count on anyhow?

That's why he took out the starter.

Minton promptly yielded a leadoff single in the ninth. A force-out (which could have been a double play) and another out brought Gerald Perry (left-handed) up with two out, the tying run on first—and Murphy on deck.

Robinson had two choices: Let right-handed Minton pitch to Perry, or bring in left-handed Gary Lavelle, his true stopper, knowing that right-handed Bob Watson would hit for Perry. He chose Lavelle (partly because Minton had already failed to retire the leadoff pinch-hitter, Mike Jorgensen, who was left-handed).

And Watson slammed a long double, tying the game at 4–4.

Well, it wasn't lost yet, and with first base open, Murphy wasn't going to be allowed to beat you. He was walked intentionally, and Lavelle got Chris Chambliss (left-handed) out.

In the tenth, Robinson outguessed Torre twice on pitchouts, but his hitters couldn't produce a run. In the eleventh, he called a pitchout that cut down the Atlanta leadoff man after he got on. Lavelle had two out, nobody on, and Murphy still three batters away.

By now, the third slot in the order (where Watson had it) was occupied by the pitcher, Steve Bedrosian, an overpowering reliever. If

Lavelle could get Alex Trevino (not a terrible threat) out, Torre would have to hit for Bedrosian leading off the twelfth, and the Giants would get a shot at someone less imposing.

Lavelle did get Trevino to hit an easy grounder—and Brad Wellman made a wild throw to first.

Torre was unwilling to take Bedrosian out for a hitter, so the Giants still had the upper hand. But Bedrosian did get the bat on the ball, and a dribbler toward third went for a hit when Fran Murray couldn't make a clean play.

Now it was two on, two out—and right-handed Murphy facing Lavelle, with no bullpen options left for Robinson.

Lavelle promptly threw ball one and ball two.

Rather than give Murphy a shot at *that*, Robinson ordered an unorthodox intentional pass, even though it meant filling the bases. Let Lavelle face Chambliss, whom he had retired in the ninth. Robinson didn't think Chambliss had a good chance to get a hit off Lavelle.

He may have been right, but Lavelle didn't put the question to a test. He walked Chambliss, forcing in the tie-breaking run.

And Bedrosian closed out the 5–4 victory in the bottom of the eleventh.

Here was a game in which Robinson kept guessing right—at least five times—and getting beat because pitchers couldn't throw a strike, fielders couldn't pick up the ball, and his own hitters couldn't do anything.

That's the difference between making the right decision and getting the right result. One doesn't guarantee the other. It's a game played by humans.

Pitch by pitch, through a game, a manager thinks this way. He decides, at the last possible instant, whether to order a bunt or a hit-and-run, responding to what he thinks the defense isn't set for. He tries to do the unexpected in standard situations, but the unexpected within the context of factors adding up in his favor. That is, *ideally* the manager does that. In practice, most managers are very much aware of the second-guessers—not so much the second-guessers in the stands, but those on his own bench, in the press box, and in his front office.

Most men are not heroes, and there are fewer mental heroes than physical heroes, certainly in athletics. The manager knows all the orthodox moves. If he makes an orthodox move and loses, no one can criticize him; if he goes "against the book" and wins, he's a genius— maybe—but if he goes against it and loses, the second-guessers may never let him up. Too often, too many managers play it safe: They go by the book not out of maximum conviction at that moment that the play is called for, but because it's the safest way to lose in an uncertain situation.

Aggressive, drama-oriented men—like Gene Mauch of the Phillies, Expos, and Angels—would call this a question of "guts." It is debatable, however, whether caution is the exact opposite of courage. Let's say that most managers accept the fact that discretion—at least, some discretion—is the better part of staying a manager.

What's the best single qualification for being a manager?

Being independently wealthy.

Casey Stengel worked in such circumstances, as a Yankee and a Met, and other men have. It is a great liberating force. He might have been right or wrong, but Casey never had to stop to think how it would look. He could act on any crazy, or brilliant, or far-out hunch or idea, and it would work or it wouldn't, but his job would not be at stake— and if his job could be lost on such grounds, he couldn't care less.

If you're not independently wealthy, and have a family, it takes an extraordinary amount of mental discipline to ignore the fact that your decisions are constantly subject to criticism that can cost you your job. The human mind is remarkably efficient at finding sincere justifications for going by the book in such circumstances. And, in all fairness to the cautious ones, "gutsiness" can get just as far out of line. One can get too eager in proving one's contempt for the orthodox, and do things that are not really productive but do look daring. A rebel may acquire a stake in remaining a rebel. Being a brilliant freethinker is fine—if you can guarantee brilliance along with the freedom.

And here we are sliding back into the psychological areas, which remain the most important ones for a manager.

There's a discernible difference between the outlooks of older and younger managers.

The older men, like Stengel, believed that men can frequently be driven to do their best by abuse. They came out of an era that made no bones about employer-employee relationships, and that didn't believe in pampering. There is little to indicate that they were wrong in applying the whip in so combative, aggressive, physical, and essentially primitive an activity as professional athletics.

The generation that followed—Ralph Houk, who replaced Stengel, Mauch, Al Dark, Sparky Anderson, Chuck Tanner—ran the full range of personality differences, but they accepted the modern reality that players demand and need gentler treatment. They stressed alertness, mental agility, the technical side of baseball, and professed interest in the happiness of their players. They didn't live up to all their ideas, but these were their ideas. Their basic tenet seemed to be: Never criticize a player in public, never embarrass him.

The next generation—Tony La Russa, Whitey Herzog, Dick Howser, Roger Craig, Tommy Lasorda—went even further down the positive-reinforcement path. And they are right, since they deal with a new generation of wealthy, independent, and sensitive young men.

Not all men are equally easy to classify, and not all conform to the public image that grows around them. Billy Martin, one of the very best modern (and all-time) managers, certainly deserved the word "feisty," and didn't hesitate to criticize a player (having drawn his ideas from his spiritual father, Stengel). But to a much greater degree than the outside world (meaning the media) realized, Martin "protected" his players in his own way, and was selective about the kind of thing he criticized. His troubled relationships, on one club after another, were almost entirely with the people above him—general managers and owners—and with the outside world, not with his own players.

Dick Williams, on the other hand, alienated players everywhere he went until even a management that supported him had to let him go. He moved around a lot, like Martin; he knew how to win, like Martin; but he was too intolerant of characteristics he didn't respect to get along, for any length of time, with a younger generation that had entirely different sets of values and habits.

And it is thought-provoking that managers seem to change as they grow older. An Al Lopez and a Birdie Tebbetts, who had "good-guy" labels when they started, didn't have them ten years later and yet were probably better managers. Perhaps the age of the man, rather than his era, is a big factor: At first, the manager is close to his playing days, surrounded by contemporaries, mindful of his own gripes as a player, eager to do "better"; after a decade or two of managing, he has seen how little difference "happiness" makes, how unchangeable characters are, how inventive alibis can be, how many promises never materialize. He learns that it is never possible to explain everything to everyone, and stops trying. He says, "We'll do it *this* way," and lets it go at that.

And, if he has the players, he'll win. If he doesn't, he won't. Williams, again, was a prime example.

Houk, in three years as Yankee manager, won three pennants. His regime was an era of exceptional good feeling. He was one manager players honestly liked. His credo was "confidence building" and he was a whiz at it. Strategically, he was orthodox and conservative, which worked fine, because he had the best team. But when he returned, two years later, to a weak Yankee team, he finished last. Later, in Detroit and Boston, he built some strong foundations, but never actually won again.

Another manager who generated deep affection among his men was

Fred Hutchinson, whom no one regarded as a dazzling tactician. The best way to describe Hutch is to list whatever qualities imply the best meaning of the term "a man," and let it go at that.

Yet Houk and Hutch both produced a little plain, physical fear in the men who respected and liked them so much. They had the physique, and the nature, that convinced you it would not be a good idea to get them mad. They did have a few monumental rages, and after that they were obeyed on trust. Athletes, after all, are bound to be impressed by muscle.

So even the nice guys have to have something going for them. Walter Alston was in the same category: mild, a gentleman, patient, certainly pedestrian in his thinking, strictly by-the-book—but convincingly able to pop you one if it came to a showdown.

The ultimate difference between managing and playing, then, is this: The player must *do*, and it doesn't really matter what he thinks; the manager must *think*, and he shouldn't really be judged only by what players do.

A decision is right or it isn't on the basis of the factors weighed *before* the result takes place. If a manager is thinking right, consistently, things will work out right most of the time, but they'll often go wrong, too.

The sensible question in evaluating a manager is: How good were the grounds for the decisions he made?

If he changes pitchers, he has made a good or a bad move *before* the next batter hits a home run. The question is *why* was a home run hit? Was the pitcher the wrong man for some valid reason, or did he throw the wrong pitch, or was he instructed badly—or did the batter just hit a home run despite the percentages in the pitcher's favor? And did the manager have any real alternative to this particular pitching change?

Great players will make a mediocre manager a genius. Second-rate players will make a genius a losing manager. All the manager can do is get the right ideas; it doesn't follow that his fellas will be able to beat the other fellas in nine innings.

Back in 1982, I suddenly found myself editor-in-chief of a whole newspaper, the *Peninsula Times Tribune* in Palo Alto, California, where I had settled. With no previous business managerial experience of any sort, I had to rely on the only guidelines I had—observing, talking with, and writing about the coaches and managers I'd known in the sports world. And when I'd run into some who were still around—Houk, Anderson, Martin, Tanner, Herzog, Rigney—I'd make a point of acknowledging my debt.

"I have to thank you," I'd say, "because all I had to go on was the good lessons I had learned from you—you know, think ahead, get the right guy in the right spot, evaluate your people, and all that. And you know something? It didn't work for me, either."

And they'd laugh. They knew what I meant, all right.

In 1951, the Yankees and Indians had a thrilling pennant race. Down the stretch, Al Lopez, the Cleveland manager, decided to use his three aces, Bob Lemon, Early Wynn, and Mike Garcia, for the last three weeks of the season, pitching with two days' rest. They did fine. But the Yankees won 20 of their last 24 games and beat out the Indians anyhow. That was when Stengel, a close friend of Lopez, permitted himself a public comment on Lopez's handling of pitchers.

"Well, yes, I see where he's doing that," said Stengel. "They say you can never do that, but he is, and it's a good idea, but sometimes it doesn't always work."

That's managing in a nutshell: the endless search for ideas that always work sometimes.

And that's why there's really a very simple answer to our original question.

What do managers *really* do?

Worry.

Constantly.

For a living.

CHAPTER
6

Signs and Signals—The Art of Communication

Signals—giving them, taking them, missing them, and understanding them—constitute the greatest gulf between the experience of the professional and the fan. To the ball player, they are second nature and a subject of greatest awareness while a game is on. To the fan, they remain a dimly perceived activity, despite periodic explanations.

The need for signals is inescapable. The pitcher and catcher must be in agreement on what's to be thrown, while the hitter must be kept in the dark. The bunt and hit-and-run must be agreed upon by hitter and runner, without tipping off the defense.

Signals, then, must be simple, in order to be reliably received, yet complicated enough to keep the opposition from cracking the code. That, at least, is the theory.

Pitcher-catcher signals are traditional—with variations. The ordinary vocabulary is: one finger for a fastball, two fingers for a curve, three for a change-up. All the special pitches can be covered by these general categories, according to the particular pitcher's equipment.

In order to keep one of the coaches on the coaching lines, or a runner on first, from seeing the signal, the catcher places his hand along the inside of his right thigh while crouching, thus shielding his fingers. But when there is a runner on second base, he can see the signal as plainly as the pitcher.

That's when the complications come in.

The answer is sequences. The catcher flashes one finger, then two, then two. Which is the meaningful sign? Perhaps the first sign, one finger, meant "throw the first of the next two signs"—that is, two fingers, or a curve. Perhaps it has been decided beforehand that the third signal, or the first, will be the "key" to a second set of signals to be given.

All that matters, really, is to keep the pattern complicated enough to prevent the man on second from deducing the code by watching half a dozen pitches and correlating them with their signs.

The pitcher often helps. He may have a prearranged plan with the catcher for shaking off signs—as a decoy. This is often directed more at the hitter, as psychological warfare, than at signal-stealers. When a pitcher indicates he's dissatisfied with what the catcher called for, the batter may start thinking—while he's thinking, he may be a trifle off balance mentally. In that case, there never was any real disagreement between pitcher and catcher; it's all an act.

Every couple of years, a big fuss arises about more elaborate signal-stealing, by means of an agent with binoculars in center field. There has never been a specific rule against this, but it is generally considered unethical, because the home team can arrange it while the visiting team cannot. (A favorite hiding place was the scoreboard, before these million-dollar electronic marvels replaced the human-occupied types located in center field.)

Still, there is an element of self-protection that is considered proper in baseball, and the simple defense against sign-stealers, however placed or equipped, is to use deceptive signals. The same attitude is taken by most baseball men concerning throwing at hitters: Judicious retaliation will keep the situation under control better than rules or admonishments.

And here we have one of the basic limitations on sign-stealing: It can be awfully dangerous if it backfires. If the batter is told that a fastball is coming, and it turns out to be a curve, he may wind up looking foolish; but if he is told curve and it turns out to be an inside fastball, he may wind up unconscious.

If a pitcher gets the idea that his signals are being intercepted, and the hitters seem a little too sure of what's coming, all he has to do is reverse matters for a couple of deliveries: Throw one good fastball off a curve signal, and the reliability of the other team's cryptanalysis is destroyed.

Signals can be reversed at any time—every day, every inning, between pitches. It's even possible to make the other side think you are changing your signs when you're not, so don't assume every time you see a catcher go out to talk to a pitcher that they are changing their signs. It may be a decoy, or a misunderstanding between them, or a plan to set up several pitches in sequence, or a discussion of something about the hitter.

But who really decides what pitch is to be thrown? The catcher? The pitcher? The manager?

There are no simple and unambiguous answers to this question. It is analogous to the quarterback's play-calling in football. In the final analysis, the manager or coach is always the boss, but there are also great advantages to having an experienced player, actually in combat, making the decisions. (In a Rolaids commercial, former Mets manager Davey Johnson is shown in the dugout musing, "I hope he doesn't throw him a curve." If that's what he hopes, why doesn't he simply call time and give the order for no curve?)

Some managers do call the pitches from the bench, signaling the catcher what to signal the pitcher; all managers do it at some point. The main consideration is the experience of the pitcher and catcher, and confidence in their judgment. An older, established pitcher working with a young catcher will obviously take the lead; if the opposite is true, it will be the other way around.

Most of the time, however, the catcher and pitcher are simply thinking along the same channels. The same knowledge—of hitter, of situation, of the pitcher's equipment and its behavior that day—leads them to the same conclusions. In a showdown, though, the pitcher always has the last word: He's the one who has to throw the ball, and if he is not convinced that he's throwing the right thing, he's asking for trouble.

Joe Garagiola, who was a pretty good major-league catcher before he turned to the banquet circuit and radio-television for a much better living, stresses the inanity of some pseudo-expert reactions. Talk that a catcher "called a great game" is just as silly as blaming "a bad call" for the home run that was hit. The pitcher is doing the throwing, and the responsibility is his. Great pitchers make brilliant catchers, and poor pitchers make dumb ones.

Sandy Koufax relates an incident that shows the degree of rapport achieved by pitchers and catchers who have worked together a lot. In the 1963 World Series, Sandy struck out 15 Yankees in winning the first game, and now, in Chavez Ravine, he was one out away from winning the fourth game for a Series sweep. He was leading 2–1 with two out in the ninth, and the batter was Mickey Mantle. The only Yankee run had been scored on Mantle's home run his last time up.

The count went to two strikes. The catcher was John Roseboro.

"I could see John put down two fingers, for the curve," says Sandy, "and I could see him just start, as if he were uncertain, to wiggle them. That would mean, take something off the pitch. A change curve at a time like that was some idea—but I was sort of thinking the same thing. If it didn't work, if Mantle hit it out and tied the score, we would turn out to be dead wrong in theory. And yet I had the feeling that it would be the right thing. So even as John was still sort of hesitantly suggesting it, I gave him a quick nod. Well, now everything was great. We were in it together. Understand, what was worrying John was that I might feel uncertain about *throwing* that pitch; he had no doubt it was the pitch he wanted. But once I showed him that I was thinking the same way, he had every confidence in it."

What Sandy threw wouldn't have been a "change curve" for any other pitcher, because it still had so much on it. But it was something softer than the most explosive curves Sandy had been throwing the whole Series

It was strike three.

Now, one of the oldest supposedly unforgivable acts in baseball is to let a man get a hit when the count is two strikes, no balls. The idea is that the pitcher then has three balls to work with, and shouldn't throw a pitch the batter can get hold of. Remember Bill Voiselle?

Where this shades into myth—and a myth shared by some professionals unconsciously—is that with an 0–2 count you're not supposed to throw a strike. Of course you are. In fact, if 0–2 is such an advantage (which it is), it's the ideal pitch on which to get a man out—and every now and then, the pitch intended to get him out may be hit safely.

But many managers, older ones in particular, consider it a sin if a pitcher gets hurt in that situation. Actually, it's a completely one-sided and unfair criticism: They say nothing if the man makes out, but blame the pitcher if the man gets a hit.

Criticism would be legitimate, of course, when the pitcher threw the wrong *kind* of pitch 0–2. He has maximum opportunity to work on the batter's weakness, or use his own strength. If he fails to do that and *then* gets hit, he's in the doghouse for fair.

The pitcher-catcher signals are a subject in themselves. Things go wrong, inevitably, but very rarely. When a pitcher "crosses up" a catcher, a wild pitch or passed ball is often the result, but it happens a small proportion of the time.

The other signals—to batter and runner—have a much, much higher mortality rate. For the average player, the hardest thing in the world to achieve is a high level of concentration, and it is lack of concentration that leads to missed signals.

Most signs are body-movement signs, and since most situations are yes–no two-valued—bunt or don't bunt, hit or take, run or stay—a simple enough gesture will serve. For example, skin touching skin may mean "take": If the coach rubs his chin or claps his hands, that's the sign. A sign may be more specific: hand brushing the letters across the chest.

Again, if the signs were given too simply, in a discoverable pattern, they would be worthless. So all the many motions a coach makes are intended to camouflage the real sign. Once again, there is some key— let's say, only if his feet are wide apart is the skin-on-skin signal in force.

When Alvin Dark managed Charley Finley's Oakland A's, Charley insisted one night that Alvin show him all the team's signs. Dark went through them, slowly and in detail, for about an hour, explaining each.

"Okay," said Finley, "now give them to me the way you would in a game."

Dark ran through some basic sequences.

Finley didn't get any—not one.

He wasn't dumb—just not conditioned to it.

A good player, then, *always* looks at the coach for a sign, even if he knows there isn't any; that's part of the long-range protection of the code. And a good player knows how to pick up the sign quickly, reliably, unobtrusively. After all, if he stares long enough at the coach, the opposition will see plainly that *something* is being ordered, and it's often easy enough to figure out what.

Since all the crucial strategic decisions depend on *when* rather than *what*—which pitch to bunt on, when is the defense deployed best for a hit-and-run—managers often wait until the last moment to decide. Then a sign must be given and received quickly.

Equally important are the signals that take a play *off*. Suppose something changes. Suppose the defense shifts before the pitcher has even begun his stretch. It must be possible to change the sign, to cancel the original signal. Missing the off sign causes as much trouble as missing original signs.

Here the human factors run rampant. One of Garagiola's stock stories—true or not—involves Dick Hall, who was a rookie outfielder on the last-place Pittsburgh Pirates of the early 1950s. Garagiola was on this team, Fred Haney was the manager, Branch Rickey the boss. Hall, a bright young man out of Swarthmore, eventually became an outstanding relief pitcher with Baltimore (in the 1960s), but at this point he was just a kid and fair game for a Garagiola anecdote in the making.

According to Joe, here's what took place:

Before Hall went to bat, Haney said to him: "If you get on, I'll want you to steal. Now this is the steal sign: I touch the bill of my cap, like this. Got it? Bill of my cap means steal. You see me do that, you run. Right?"

"Right," said the Phi Beta Kappa.

Sure enough, Hall singled. On the first pitch, Haney gave him the steal sign.

Hall didn't run.

On the second pitch, Haney gave the steal sign.

Hall didn't run.

The same thing happened on the next two pitches.

Finally the next batter grounded into a double play that Hall could do nothing about, since he was slow leaving first base.

After the inning, Haney called Hall aside. Calmly and patiently, Haney said, "Did you see me touch the bill of my cap?"

"Yes, sir."

"Do you know what that meant?"

"Yes, sir."

"You know that's the steal sign?"

"Yes, sir."

"You saw me give it?"

"Yes, sir."

"Well, whyinhell didn't you run?"

"I didn't think you meant it."

That's told as a joke, but a fascinating bit of crucial baseball history was clarified by a missed-sign story told almost forty years after the event in a videocassette made in 1989.

In the final game of the 1950 season, the Brooklyn Dodgers trailed Philadelphia by one game when the teams met at Ebbets Field. A Dodger victory would mean a tie for first and a three-game playoff for the pennant. A Phillie victory would end the race. The game reached the bottom of the ninth 1–1, with Robin Roberts pitching (in his third start in five days). Cal Abrams walked and Pee Wee Reese singled. Duke Snider lined a single to center, only to have Abrams thrown out at the plate by a wide margin. Jackie Robinson was walked intentionally (the runners having taken second and third on the throw home), but Carl Furillo popped up and Gil Hodges flied out. A three-run homer by Dick Sisler in the top of the tenth made the Phillies champions.

The futile dash for the plate by Abrams became one of the classic tragedies of Brooklyn baseball lore. Why didn't he stop at third? And how could Richie Ashburn, a star in other respects but known for his weak arm, have made the play he did?

"I only found out what really happened several years later," said Abrams into the camera in 1989. "The Phillies put on a play to pick me off second, or at least drive me back. The infielders missed the sign and didn't cover—but Ashburn, in center, did see it and broke in to back up second base, and the pitcher pitched. So Snider's hit was fielded by him on one short hop almost right behind the infield.

"As I'm approaching third, the coach is waving me in, but suddenly he switches to a signal I've never seen before, a sort of halfhearted wave or wiggle. What happened was that when he looked out to center field, where Ashburn should have been, he saw how close he really was, and it was too late to stop me."

Pictures show him out by about 10 feet. But if they had tried the pickoff play that was called for, the whole situation would not have arisen; and if the shortstop or second baseman had at least moved toward the bag, even with the pitcher throwing home, Abrams would have been bluffed back to second and would have stopped at third if Snider hit the ball exactly the way he did. That would have left the game up to Robinson with the bases full and nobody out.

So the missed sign won a pennant.

Just as intellect or obliviousnes can be an obstacle in some situations, physical problems can arise in others. Ryne Duren, whose blazing fastball made him an outstanding relief pitcher for several years, was almost unbelievably nearsighted, and he did all he could to exaggerate the impression of semiblindness he created. (It was a great asset to have batters wondering whether the launcher of this lethal fastball could see the man at the plate.) Ryne wore lenses so thick they looked like "sawed-off ends of Coke bottles," and his poor vision was common knowledge and a standing gag.

With all this, you can imagine how bad a hitter Duren was: Not only was he a pitcher with natural lack of hitting talent and no chance to practice, but he couldn't see the ball.

In 1964, Ryne was with the Phillies. In spring training, he was pitching in a B-squad game against some Met rookies, and everything was very informal. Gene Mauch, the Philadelphia manager, was talking to sportswriters as much as he was paying attention to the game.

Now it came up to the top of the ninth inning, with the score tied. The first Philadelphia batter got on, and Duren was due to be the third hitter in the inning. If the second man got on, Mauch would want a bunt.

"Hey, Ryne," called out Mauch, as Duren headed for the on-deck circle. "You know the bunt sign?"

"I *know* it," replied Duren, "but I can't guarantee I'll *see* it."

There is also the danger of giving unintended signs inadvertently. A manager or a coach must be careful at all times. If skin-on-skin is a signal, a thoughtless scratch of the cheek at the wrong moment can have unexpected consequences.

One of the more bizarre instances of this occurred in Pittsburgh when Leo Durocher was managing the Giants in the early 1950s. Leo had managed to get himself thrown out of the game by some thin-skinned umpire, and had gone up to the press box for the remainder of the game. There he chose a seat next to Barney Kremenko, a tall red-headed man who worked for the then *New York Journal-American* and just happened to be the most clearly identifiable New York writer sitting in full view of the Giant dugout. Every now and then Leo would ask Barney to make a certain movement, and Barney would oblige.

The game reached its exciting stages with the Giants at bat. Barney, innocently enough, started to take off his glasses to wipe them.

"Hey, stop that!" yelled Durocher. "You just gave the steal signal!"

Fortunately, the Giants won the pennant anyhow.

Almost as important is the nonsecret communication that goes on all the time, sometimes not as much as it should: plain talk. Teamwork involves a good deal of talk between players, and between a player and a coach.

Most of it is devoted to reminders. Alertness in a game calls for endless repetition of the obvious—just in case someone's mind is wandering. The catcher will usually remind the infield how many men are out, after every out. At the same time, the coach will remind the base runner of the same thing, and perhaps something about the right fielder's strong arm. Infielders may remind each other about how they intend to make a possible play, although they've made the same play with each other hundreds of times. Catchers will remind pitchers, again and again, how they intend to work on the next batter. The pitcher knows perfectly well—but one more repetition can't hurt.

Whenever you see men on the same team talk to each other, chances are it's some sort of reminder.

The other main topic is calling plays. On a high pop-up, one infielder can act as traffic cop for others as all converge. On bunt plays, the catcher must always tell the pitcher which base to throw to, because the catcher is facing the bases and the pitcher isn't.

In a crowded, noisy park, the cry "I got it" may not be heard, or it may be misunderstood as "you got it." A collision can result. A standard practice on balls hit to the outfield is: The man who is going to take it is the man who calls; if you don't intend to catch it, keep still; if you yell, keep going for the ball, no matter how far. That way, comprehending words is unnecessary; if you hear *anything*, veer off. If you don't, keep going.

My favorite in this category belongs to the original hapless Mets of 1962. Richie Ashburn, the center fielder then nearing retirement, foresaw danger because Elio Chacon, the shortstop, didn't speak English. So Ashburn got someone to teach him how to say "I got it" in Spanish— "Yo tengo," or something. On the next pop fly into left center, Richie came running in screaming "Yo tengo!" Chacon obediently veered away—and Ashburn got knocked halfway to the stands by the left fielder, Frank Thomas, who knew nothing from Spanish.

Talk can also be used, especially by catchers, to try to distract hitters. Sometimes that works remarkably well. Garagiola was good at it, and his boyhood friend Yogi Berra was one of the best. But then, Yogi was a remarkably garrulous, gregarious, gossipy sort who just couldn't keep still on a ball field no matter where he was. Late in his career, when he wound up playing left field, he kept chatting with fans in the stands and occupants of the nearest bullpen.

Yogi's talkativeness once produced an unforeseen problem, and this story illustrates how inexhaustible is the ball player's ability to pick up any trait at all and use it to advantage. During Stengel's first five years with the Yankees—all pennant-winning years—Casey had exceptional success with hit-and-run plays in unorthodox situations. Yogi, although he was a catcher, was a pretty fast runner, and Casey liked to hit-and-run with Yogi on first.

Then, inexplicably, the play started backfiring. Several times in succession, when Yogi would take off from first, there would be a pitchout and he would be thrown out. Signals were changed, security was checked, but still the opposition was spotting the play. Stengel would have decided that his methods were simply being figured out, except for one thing—it was happening mostly with Yogi on first.

After much thought, the Yankees finally realized what was happening. As a rule, Yogi would always be deep in conversation with the first baseman—how was the wife, what sort of football team would Notre Dame have this year, and so forth. Given the hit-and-run sign, Yogi would begin to concentrate on getting a good lead—and shut up. The opposition had noticed that when Yogi became still, he was preparing to run.

The solution was to tell Yogi to keep quiet all the time; and when that quickly proved impossible, to keep talking all the time.

Even silence, therefore, can be eloquent on a ball field. And this is the answer to those who say baseball is such a "slow" game. It is, in terms of physical activity, compared to football or basketball or hockey—but that doesn't mean nothing is happening. Most of the apparently purposeless action between pitches isn't purposeless at all. The fan who has the opportunity to watch every day and become familiar with the idiosyncrasies and motives of his home team's players is fortunate, because then he can get a type of pleasure from baseball that the more active, several-things-happening-at-once games can't provide.

CHAPTER

7

The Bench—Invisible Means
of Support

According to the rule book, a baseball team is composed of nine men.

According to real life in the major leagues, a team has 25 players, all thoroughly needed—although in recent years, as an economy measure, they have tried to limit the active list to 24.

According to the rule book, no one is allowed in the dugout during a game but active players in uniform, the manager (even if he chooses to wear civies), and trainers in uniform.

According to television networks, their cameras belong in dugouts, too, if that will make an attractive angle to shoot from. And if they can persuade the baseball people to accept the practices pro football accepted some time ago, they'd like to interview the manager and players between pitches, too.

Why shouldn't they? What goes on in the dugout that's so private, anyhow? And why does it take 25 men to play a nine-position game?

These are the topics we'll touch upon as we deal with the fifth and final dimension of a baseball game: the bench.

Originally, substitutes were just that. In the 1880s, when professional baseball was working out its future form by trial and error, a team had only 11 men—eight regulars, two pitchers, and a substitute. (Pitchers could pitch every other day then because overhand pitching was not allowed.) Later the squad became 15 men, as more pitchers had to be added. Before World War II, the active limit in the majors was 23. Since the war, it has been 25. (The voluntary limit of 24 is actually made meaningless by greater use of "disabled lists.") To be more exact, a club is allowed to have 40 men on its roster, some of whom must be farmed out. By opening day, the "active" list must be cut to 25 men, who are eligible to play in official games, and it stays that way until September 1. From September 1 to the end of the season, all 40 may play.

The normal distribution became ten pitchers, six or seven infielders, five or six outfielders, and three catchers. This is a very flexible arrangement, fluctuating with the talent available and affected by front-office considerations (when a player can't be farmed out but is too desirable to be abandoned). A team may carry eleven pitchers, or nine; many get by with only two catchers; many utility men can play both infield and outfield. (If the designated-hitter rule applies, your proportions may differ, since you may choose to have one pitcher less, or keep a man who can't really play anywhere defensively but can hit well, or keep a defensive specialist because pinch-hitters will be used so seldom.)

But there are sound reasons for the standard pattern. Take pitching, for instance: You need four or five regular starters, who need the full three or four days of rest; you need at least two others capable of starting, because the schedule will sometimes call for more than four games in four days, and because all four regulars are not likely to get through a whole season without injury; you need at least two capable relief pitchers, a left-hander and a right-hander, for late-game crises, and if they are to be available more or less every day, they can never start. That adds up to eight or nine, which is the minimum. Two more may be young pitchers in the process of development, or older men backstopping the other functions, and serving as setup men (or middle-inning relievers).

Or take catchers. Many catchers are not good hitters, but worth playing because they are good receivers. In the seventh inning, let's say, you might want to pinch-hit for the catcher. Now your second catcher has to go into action in the eighth. But suppose he gets hurt; you can't play the game, especially in extra innings, without an experienced receiver, one who can handle pitchers and keep base runners under control. So you need a third catcher for insurance. (Here we see one of the less noticed benefits of having a first-string catcher who is an outstanding hitter; since you won't pinch-hit for him if he's Yogi Berra or Roy Campanella or Johnny Bench or Carlton Fisk or Gary Carter or Gabby Hartnett or Bill Dickey, one extra catcher may be all you need.)

Outfielders are usually chosen for their hitting. If you have a slugger who is a very poor fielder, you probably want a good defensive outfielder on the bench, to put into the game in the late innings if you have the lead. Infielders, especially shortstops, are more often chosen for fielding skill. Occasionally, then, you may want to pinch-hit for a regular infielder when you are trailing. Then you need another good fielder to put in so that whatever lead your pinch-hitter provided won't be frittered away again.

Relief pitchers fall into different categories. The stars are "closers," a "hammer" that nails down a victory. These are the late-inning crisis specialists, able to work out of the toughest and most threatening situations, but also used at the end of a game to forestall a threat. The manager doesn't want to use his hammer earlier than the eighth inning, and not unless he has a lead to protect; to use him otherwise would be to waste his availability for the next such situation, so he won't even be asked to warm up until the late innings. Rollie Fingers, Goose Gossage, Dennis Eckersley, Bruce Sutter, and Dave Righetti are prototype closers of the modern era.

Ideally, you would have a lefty and a righty for such a chore, but increasingly the practice is to choose one who is so clearly your best that the righty-lefty part doesn't matter. But the other—righty or lefty—is then your closer when No. 1 has worked too much, or when a game has gone into extra innings anyhow, or to get a key out earlier in the seventh or eighth.

The other category is "setup" men. We used to call them "middle-inning relievers." Their job is to hold the fort when the starter is either knocked out or pitched out, to prevent further scoring and keep your team in the game until you can get to the closer. These are, obviously, your least proficient talents, not meeting your requirements for starting or closing. But when circumstances dictate (through injury or otherwise), these have to serve as spot starters or emergency closers.

A new category began to emerge in the late 1980s, in my opinion, although I heard little talk about it in clubhouses. I call this a "seventh-inning closer." This is a setup man who is used like a closer to shut off a sixth- or seventh-inning emergency, even if another setup man is required to bridge the gap to the star closer. Specialization is an ever-expanding process.

When a game starts, most of the extra pitchers and catchers go down to the bullpen. One pitcher who will not be used—yesterday's starter, or tomorrow's, or perhaps one who is nursing an injury—will remain in the dugout and keep a chart of every pitch thrown in the game. It will show, for every opposing batter, what sort of pitch was thrown, what part of the strike zone it found or missed, and where the ball was hit. This is raw material for future analysis.

Every team has some players who develop the knack of stealing signals or "reading" pitchers. Reading a pitcher means spotting some idiosyncrasy or inconsistency in his movements that tips off the type of pitch he's going to throw. The catcher's signals to the pitcher are, of course, invisible from the bench (because the catcher hides his hands between his legs when he crouches). But the coaches' signals, being relayed to the opposing batter, are there for everyone to see. If the other team's intention to bunt or hit-and-run or steal can be intercepted, it can be put to use. This is espionage, pure and simple.

Therefore, at least one player on the bench is busy studying the opposition at all times, trying to crack codes. He may pick up something useful for that game, or for the future, but he works at it. At the same time, the other team is doing likewise, and another player on our team may be studying our own tipoffs as a preventive measure— a sort of counterespionage or internal security check.

Not only the pitcher can give away information. An infielder, by shifting position too soon, or a characteristic gesture, may reveal what's coming. A famous instance happened in the 1920 World Series between the Dodgers and Cleveland. Brooklyn's best pitcher was Burleigh Grimes, a spitball specialist (when this was still legal). His second baseman, Pete Kilduff, developed the habit of grabbing a handful of dirt every time the catcher signaled for a spitball, to counteract the slipperiness of the wet ball if it happened to be hit to him. The Indians spotted this half-conscious habit, and knew when to let the spitball go by to wait for something easier to hit, or to catch it before it broke. Grimes shut them out the first time he faced them, but then they beat him twice.

Sometimes the spy-counterspy activity can get out of hand, with hilarious (from the winner's point of view) results. A delicious incident came up in Washington in 1963. It was August, and the Yankees had a firm grip on first place, but their pitching staff was rocky, and there was still plenty of time for trouble to develop. Whitey Ford pitched the first game of a twi-night doubleheader, and lost. Now Stan Williams was pitching the second game for the Yankees, and pitching his heart out, but it was still 0–0 in the top of the eighth. The idea of losing a doubleheader to the inept Senators made the Yankees distinctly uncomfortable.

Then the Yankees scored. Here's what we saw from the press box: Tony Kubek singled, broke for second, and continued to third when the catcher's throw sailed over second base into center field. Bobby Richardson poked a single through a drawn-in infield and the Yankees had a run. It turned out to be the only run, and Williams had an important 1–0 victory.

And here's what manager Ralph Houk revealed a few days later:

Before the inning began, while the teams were changing sides, Houk spoke to both Kubek and Richardson in the dugout. "If Tony gets on," Houk told them, "Bobby, you hit-and-run on the first pitch. I'm not even going to give a signal. Just go up and do it."

Sure enough, Kubek got on.

"My intention," Houk explained to us, "was to make extra sure that no one could miss a sign, or that Washington couldn't read it. Sometimes you can read another team just by the hesitation, by the way the players act, without even actually getting the signal itself. I didn't want anything to go wrong."

Houk overlooked only one thing. He neglected to tell Frank Crosetti, his third-base coach, that he had already talked to Kubek and Richardson. And that was natural enough, because Crosetti was probably on his way to the coaching line before the fielders had returned to the dugout as the teams were changing sides.

So there was Kubek, on first base, nobody out, score 0–0, top of the eighth. Coming to bat was Richardson, one of the best hit-and-run men in the business. The possibility was obvious to both sides. The question was, which pitch?

Crosetti looked into the dugout for a sign. There had to be one— either hit-and-run, or a take sign so that there could be a hit-and-run on a subsequent pitch. Or perhaps the manager wanted a sacrifice bunt. The coach doesn't make decisions, he transmits them. Crosetti looked.

No sign.

Crosetti looked again.

No sign.

Whatever was happening, it seemed obvious that Houk was not putting on any sort of play, and evidently the hitter was on his own.

So Crosetti decided he might as well distract the Senators with some decoy signs. If there was no play on, it wouldn't matter what motions Crosetti made, but the Senators wouldn't know that.

As Richardson stepped in to hit, Crosetti started giving phantom signals. He put on a magnificent act.

The Washington catcher saw these meaningless contortions, and leaped in the wrong direction to a correct conclusion. He interpreted Crosetti's gyrations as a hit-and-run sign.

So he called for a pitchout.

The pitcher threw. Kubek broke for second. It was a fine pitchout, at least two feet wide of the plate. The Senators had caught the Yankees dead to rights. Kubek would be out by 10 feet.

Richardson did the only thing he could do. He flung his bat at the ball, hoping at least to deflect it foul, to save Kubek's running life.

The bat missed the ball.

The catcher made a perfect throw to second.

But the Senator second baseman and shortstop got their own signals mixed. In such situations, they are supposed to have it made up between them, before the play, which one will cover the bag. This time both started, both hesitated, both stopped—and the ball flew right over the base with neither fielder within 15 feet of it.

Kubek, who had stumbled a bit leaving first, just kept running and made third easily.

Houk, having nearly swallowed his cud of tobacco, breathed easier.

Crosetti looked for the next sign.

The Washington catcher (it was Jim Retzer) was so mad he couldn't see straight.

And the Washington manager, Gil Hodges, had no choice. At that stage of the game, he had to bring his infield in for a possible play at the plate.

Then Richardson hit his single and the mighty Yankees had another victory.

Add up the heroes in that play: Houk, Crosetti, and two Washington infielders made mistakes; neither Richardson (unable to hit the ball) nor Kubek (who didn't get the best possible jump) carried out their play well; the only man who was dead right—for the wrong reason—was Retzer, and it was his play that lost the game.

After all, if he had minded his own business, Richardson might have popped up on that first pitch.

That's a good story to relate when someone tells you how incredibly scientific baseball is. It is—sometimes. Mostly, though, it's a game played by fallible men.

In the dugout, then, furious thinking is going on all the time. The manager is watching every pitch, plotting his moves. (He has to think two or three innings ahead about possible pinch-hitters and pitching changes on both sides.) The pitcher keeping the chart is writing down every pitch. The sign-stealers and tipoff watchers are plying their trade. In addition, the manager who wants extra security may use another player to flash the signs to the coaches. That is, he tells this player verbally, and it's the player who crosses his legs or touches his cap or rubs his chin, and it's the player the coaches look at.

Three functions are left: shouting encouragement at your own players, insults at the opposition, and complaints at the umpires. The requirements are uncomplicated—a voice that carries, a rudimentary competence at making phrases, and a low level of inhibition.

Taunting the opposition is called "jockeying" (because the bench jockey is "riding" his victim, get it?), and it is a dying art, by and large. The majority of players nowadays are too sophisticated to respond deeply to hackneyed insults. At their salaries, and especially if they started with fancy bonuses, they may still be afraid of sticks and stones but words never hurt them. Since the purpose of jockeying is to distract the man being jockeyed, this lack of response makes it futile. At the same time, much less real animosity exists between players of rival teams than was standard in the old days. Today's players, bound by pension plans and the organization-man outlook on life, feel very much like colleagues in a profession, and channel their antagonism into game actions, not personal remarks. More and more, the jockey's shouts are trying to get a laugh rather than arouse anger.

The physical setup in a dugout deserves mention.

In most of the new parks, dugouts are quite long and spacious. In old ones, they tend to be shallow and crowded. Usually, a tunnel leads to the clubhouse, and just inside the dugout end of this tunnel is a toilet. This is a favorite spot for sneaking a smoke, since it is against policy to be seen smoking on the bench. There is always a water cooler, at one end of the dugout or the other, and I have never seen one that didn't have at least several dents in it: A water cooler is the natural recipient of a violent kick from some player who has just struck out.

Bats, which used to be kept in a tray in front of the dugout, nowadays are stacked in a vertical or horizontal set of cubbyholes. Plastic batting helmets lie around near the bats, or in their own cubbyholes.

Most dugouts are equipped with a telephone connection to the bullpen. In most larger parks, the bullpens are located somewhere beyond the outfield fence, but in smaller and older parks, they may be in foul territory beyond the dugouts in left and right fields.

Because the floor of the dugout is often two or three steps below ground level, and because the infield has a hump, sloping down gradually in all directions from the pitching mound, a man sitting in the dugout cannot see the entire field. From the dugout on the first-base side, the feet of the third baseman and shortstop, and the whole lower half of the left fielder's body, will be blocked off; and the right-field corner is completely invisible, blocked by the end of the dugout. Even if one stands in the front of the dugout instead of sitting down, unless one gets up on the top step, parts of the field will not be visible. Some of the newer parks, especially those indoors, have dugout floors at ground level.

The angle of vision affects the view of pitching, too. Baseball men can tell with great accuracy the variation in speed of a pitch, since they see it from the side. They can tell exactly how high or how low a pitch is (unless the batter's body blocks it off too much). But they can't possibly see how far inside or outside a pitch comes. They automatically deduce this from the actions of the batter and catcher, but they can't judge the position of the ball itself.

Batters returning to the dugout, after making out or after scoring, make three types of comments most of the time: self-condemnation, alibis, and sharing of information.

"I'm a stupid so-and-so, I ought to give this game up," a man who popped up might say, bouncing his helmet off the steps.

"He's doctoring the ball," a man who struck out might say.

"He's got nothing," a man might say after hitting a 400-foot out to dead center—just as the pitcher wanted him to.

"He's really breaking that curve off today," a victim might report, building up the confidence of his teammates.

"Where was that pitch?" a hitter who has just been called out on strikes might ask his teammates. (That's one of the good questions—he was at the plate, they were in the dugout, and he's asking *them*.)

"What'd he throw you that time?" a manager might ask a hitter who bounced out—not because the manager doesn't know, but because he wants the hitter to think about it.

From an emotional point of view, one of the hardest things for both dugouts to take is a soft-stuff pitcher having a good day. Both managers die. They can see how easy the slow pitches look, and even though their minds tell them that the timing and various little curves give the batters problems, their instincts still tell them that stuff should be murdered. So the manager whose team is being stifled fumes; he can't see why his hitters don't beat that pitcher's brains out. And the manager whose pitcher is doing it, while gratefully accepting the results, also can't see why the hitters don't beat his pitcher's brains out. It's a nerve-wracking game for everyone but the pitcher.

As a close game progresses, the tension in a dugout mounts. The men who are likely to pinch-hit, or go in for defense, are as aware as the manager of when they are likely to be called upon. They get themselves ready mentally, and perhaps do some knee bends or stretches. (A fielder, if he knows a half inning ahead, may dash down to the bullpen to throw a bit.) Sometimes an established pinch-hitter will sneak back into the clubhouse to swing the bat awhile. Now that clubhouses have television sets, reserves go back there more often.

The moment of drama comes when the manager says: "Smirkilo-wicz—go up there and hit." The manager will also give his man reminders or instructions about what the pitcher is likely to do, and how the manager wants his man to hit.

One of the stock Casey Stengel stories stems from his Boston period. In 1939, Casey was managing the Braves (who were called the Bees then). They got involved in an extra-inning game with the Dodgers in

Boston. In the fourteenth inning, the Braves got a man to second base and Casey looked around for a pinch-runner. He found a rookie named Otto Huber. Sure enough, Al Lopez singled, and here came Huber around third with the winning run—only to fall flat on his face halfway home. He was tagged out, the game went on through the twentieth inning, and ended in a tie.

"The next day," Stengel recounted, "I looked at this man's shoes, and the spikes were worn all the way down, almost flat. They buy their own shoes, you know. But in his locker was a brand-new pair.

" 'That the best equipment you got?' I asked him, meanin' the old shoes, of course.

" 'No,' he sez to me, 'but these old ones are more comfortable for my feet, and I had them on because I didn't think you were gonna use me.'

"Can you imagine? For the next three years, whenever I wanted to use a hitter or a runner, I'd call him over first and make him show me his spikes."

A manager, you see, always has to be thinking.

Stengel was always thinking, but sometimes his thinking got mischievous. When he was with the Yankees, his third-base coach was Crosetti—the same Crosetti who had that problem arise with Houk in Washington. With Casey, Crosetti had a different problem. In one-sided games—and the good Yankee teams had quite a few of them—Stengel would hide behind a post when Crosetti would look in for a signal. Why? Just to liven things up.

Another Stengel idea, however, illustrates a shrewder approach. In his years with the Yankees, he had one of the best pinch-hitters of all time at his disposal—Johnny Mize, too old to play regularly but a devastating batter. Casey would send Mize out into the on-deck circle, to advertise to the opposing pitcher that he was going to bat next. More than once, this all-too-visible threat bothered the concentration of the pitcher, as much as a brilliant base runner would, and the man at bat got a walk or a good pitch to hit thanks to Mize's presence.

Two aspects of dugout conversation are constants: profanity and a manager's caustic criticism of a player for something that has just happened. Neither is as strong as it used to be. Colorful originality in cursing seems to have been undermined by universally rising levels of education, and growing camaraderie in a prosperous profession has diminished motivation. Plenty of bad language is used, but the vocabulary is contracting and the spirit behind it perfunctory—or simply conformist.

As for the bawling out, modern managers are dedicated to the idea of holding their feelings in and saving their remarks for a more private occasion. They are only partially successful in carrying out this re-solve—and the older managers, like Stengel, Dressen, and Durocher, never did make such a resolve.

Meanwhile, out in the bullpen—

A fine, detailed, entertaining, and authoritative description of bull-pen conversation and time-passing exists. A book by Jim Brosnan, called *Pennant Race*, grew out of notes he kept while having a successful year as a relief pitcher in 1961 for the Cincinnati Reds, who won the pennant. It is recommended reading on this subject, a treasure for future anthropological archeologists interested in baseball.

For our purposes, it is enough to note that the chief characteristics of life in the bullpen are:

1. Worry—most of the fellows out there aren't going too well. (The star reliever usually doesn't arrive until his working time ap-proaches.)
2. Moaning and groaning, second-guessing, daydreaming—since most of the fellows out there aren't going too well.
3. Telling lies.
4. Scouting the stands, better known in all walks of American life as girl watching.
5. Freedom of speech—a privilege limited in the dugout by the presence of the manager, who acts stuffy about keeping one's mind on the game. (The experienced manager no longer expects *all* his players to do that, but he does ask, at least, that his own brainwork be free of distraction.)

However, at least one man takes bullpen hours seriously, usually two: the coach and the No. 1 relief pitcher. They concentrate on being ready when the call comes, and follow early developments in batters' patterns for later reference.

And, of course, if a young man *wants* to watch everything that happens and thereby learn and improve, it's allowed.

Why is it called the bullpen? Many explanations exist in baseball lore, all somehow lacking in conviction. But there's no mystery why the name remains appropriate: More bull is thrown there than any-where else in the ballpark except the press box.

We've just mentioned in passing a key and too often neglected word—"coaches." If the manager is the combat unit's captain, the coaches are his lieutenants, and their importance can't be overesti-mated. Without good coaches, no good manager can function; one of the main factors in being a good manager is the ability to choose good coaches and work with them properly. They can't, of course, make players any better than they are; but if any group of players is performing up to its potential standard, you can be sure there are coaches on hand who are doing their job right.

Years ago, a coach was often seen as simply a buddy of the manager, or a flunky. This was never true, but to whatever extent that image had validity, it no longer does. The "buddy" part is not insignificant, though. Every manager needs at least one personally compatible confidant. He has to keep a certain distance from his players, even the biggest star (perhaps especially the biggest star). His contact with the front office is sporadic and serious. In eight months of daily baseball life, spent almost entirely in ballparks, hotel rooms, and airplanes, he must have—for the sake of sanity and therefore of efficient operation—someone with whom he can feel completely relaxed. He needs an associate he can trust absolutely, with whom he can share ideas, speak the same language, vent feelings, consider private judgments that may or may not be acted upon, have some fun, release tension, get advice, and experience even unspoken understanding.

So the buddy element should not be sneered at. But a buddy need not lack competence of his own. Just the opposite. It's the manager's confidence in his friend's competence that led him to make the choice.

And as department heads (to civilianize our metaphor), today's coaches have specific functions and responsibilities.

The usual complement is four: a third-base coach, who, because of that position, acts as second-in-command; a first-base coach; a pitching coach (who may be the most important of all); and a bench assistant. Those are their in-game assignments.

They can also be classified as a pitching coach, a hitting coach, an infield specialist, an outfield expert, and a baserunning guru, in overlapping fashion. The hitting coach may be the first-base coach. The manager may have been an infielder or outfielder. The pitching coach may have been a catcher. But one way or another, all these aspects of the game have to be covered. They will also pitch batting practice, hit fungoes to the infield and outfield, and generally supervise. But often the staff is not restricted to four. There is that eye-in-the-sky, an extra coach who communicates with the bench (talking to the one we designated as "bench assistant"). There may be an extra bullpen coach helping the pitching coach. There may be a special hitting instructor. Today's baseball organizations do not skimp on support personnel the way they used to, habitually, until about fifteen years ago.

What do coaches do? Teach, communicate, observe, report, perform designated mechanical tasks, and contribute to the decision-making process. The word "coaching" implies instruction. In other sports, the boss is called "head coach" because the position grew out of a tradition of teaching the game. In baseball, he's the "manager" because, originally, that's exactly what he was: He managed the club, finding and signing players and handling the business arrangements, as well as conducting the games and training. He has become, strictly speaking, a "head coach," but the title of "manager" (or "field manager" to avoid ambiguity with "general manager") has stuck. But coaches are just that.

The pitching coach is more important than ever since the concept of using an entire staff—several pitchers a game—has become universal. He not only monitors the mechanics, thinking, and conditioning of each individual pitcher; he blocks out their working schedule (in practice as well as for games), manipulates their readiness, and (most important of all) represents their interests in discussions with the manager. Pitchers develop a tremendous sense of loyalty to a good pitching coach; they miss that dependence when they don't have one.

Handling pitchers—that is, organizing and utilizing an entire staff—was always a manager's prime concern, but it is more fundamental than ever in the modern multi-pitcher game. The final decisions are still his, but ability to rely on his pitching coach is essential. If the pitching coach is not the manager's closest friend on the club (and he often is), he has the next-closest relationship.

The third-base coach has great tactical responsibilities. He, after all, is making the instantaneous decisions in sending a runner to the only place that can affect the outcome of the game, home plate. He's also the chief relayer of signals from the bench.

The first-base coach also relays signals, and tries to help the runner at first base, but his in-game role has less impact. It's an especially good spot for the hitting coach, since it gives him a good observation post for studying his own hitters and opposing pitchers.

In recent years, hitting coaches have emerged as recognized specialists approaching the visibility of pitching coaches. Much of this is due to the attention that was given to Charlie Lau, who developed some unconventional theories and wrote two influential books in the course of working with the Kansas City Royals in the 1970s and the New York Yankees and Chicago White Sox after that. One of his most dedicated disciples, Walt Hriniak, had well-publicized success with the Red Sox through the 1980s and the White Sox in 1989 and 1990.

Their method stresses a certain way of standing and using the hands to get better coverage of the outside portion of the strike zone, where most pitchers like to work most of the time. It involves a certain amount of sacrificing power for average. One of Lau's most vocal converts was George Brett, and an endorsement like that certainly got everyone's attention.

While their method has many admirers, it also has many doubters. Books and lectures by Ted Williams express quite different views, and there are others. There always were, but only recently have fans become aware of such details, thanks to the media explosion. To us, the technicalities don't matter here. What seems clear is that there is no such thing as "a" theory of hitting; whatever the theory, some players will find it helpful and some won't. Since so much of hitting is based on confidence, almost any formula that a particular player finds thoroughly convincing and comfortable is likely to help for that reason alone.

Every batter has his own mix of peculiarities, yet every batter is subject to certain general principles of balance, movement, etc. The real job is to find that individual's "right" mix. Whitey Herzog, who was the Kansas City manager under whom Lau worked, never fully accepted his theories (and doesn't to this day), but fully appreciated his work and his results. ("Brett," says Whitey, "would be a great hitter no matter what anyone told him.") Tony La Russa, on the other hand, has great respect for the Lau theories, and managed the White Sox when Lau was there.

In my opinion, Dusty Baker comes closest to the truth when he says: "I've studied them all, and I see some things I believe in in one method and some in another—and some things are good for one player and not for another. The basics are the basics, and we all have to teach those, but after that you have to tailor it to the individual."

And Will Clark, who earned a reputation as an "intelligent" hitter at a relatively young age, makes another point about the modern approach. "It's possible to overanalyze anything," he says. "What counts is being able to do it. The more tapes I watch—and I watch a lot— the more I find that what's helpful is noticing tendencies and patterns rather than mechanics."

In this realm, baseball has also adopted procedures that have their roots in football: technical aids and coaches with more specialized functions, more amenable to utilizing theory instead of handed-down maxims. The coaches have become less like master craftsmen training apprentices and more like professors dealing with advanced students.

But their greatest contributions to team success are on the human level. They are the buffer between player and management. They see everything that's going on. They know, better than anyone, who hustles and who doesn't, who fools around, who's hiding an injury, who needs some kind of help. A player can confide in a coach in ways he can't in a manager or a teammate; a coach can bawl out, or mollify, or encourage, or instruct, or joke with a player in ways the manager can't.

152 ◆ LEONARD KOPPETT

And coaches can keep the manager informed, discreetly, about what needs attention.

If the manager is, to some degree, a father figure (our metaphors are endless), the coaches are uncles and older brothers who may be more comfortable to deal with (or may not be). If the manager is the pilot, the coaches are the flight crew. And if the manager is the president, the coaches are the cabinet.

And to the baseball writer smart enough to appreciate them, they are the greatest source in the world. If you can gain and keep their confidence, you'll learn more about what's really happening from them than from anyone else.

So the bench—the dugout and bullpen, but really the men who occupy them—is an integral part of baseball. In a sense, it's the fifth dimension of the game. The first four are tangible and familiar: hitting, pitching, fielding, and baserunning. The bench is a less tangible aspect, but inseparably a part of the whole. Strategically, good pinch-hitters and reliable relief pitchers are indispensable to a modern pennant winner. In the play of the game, the dugout is central headquarters, source of decisions and orders. In human terms, it's where most players spend most of their time.

It is the manager's own little castle, and few men who have tasted dominion over it ever give it up without regret.

CHAPTER

8

The Designated Hitter

In A.D. 1973, which was Year 134 of the Abner Doubleday Myth, Year 128 of historically established, recognizable baseball rules, Year 104 of certified professionalism, and Year 98 of the major leagues, the most startling single change in the playing rules was adopted by half the major-league population. The American League installed a "designated hitter," a man who would not play in the field but would come to bat instead of the pitcher, who would not bat.

What made it so startling was that for the first time, the "nine" became a "ten"; and, for the first time, specialized functions of offense and defense were permitted by the rules (as they had been for a long time in football, and had always been inherent for goalies in games like hockey, soccer, and lacrosse).

But, in keeping with baseball's tradition-bound, unchanging, stable-to-the-point-of-rigidity character, this most radical of changes was one that made a remarkably small amount of difference. And even so, only one of the two leagues went along with it.

The designated-hitter concept was born of desperation. By 1968 hitting had fallen to such a deplorable level that even the authorities could see that something had to be done. An endless succession of 2–1, 1–0, and 3–0 games may satisfy managers and other professionals who can appreciate the arcane art of frustrating a hitter, but they bore the customers to death. For the spectator, the action begins when the ball is hit—people running, catching, throwing, sliding; and the competitive excitement comes from the hope or fear that the lead will change hands. In the days when 7–5 was a normal score, the rooters of a team trailing by three runs felt realistic hope right into the ninth inning, even if the rally never materialized. In the late 1960s, as soon as the score became 2–0, the issue seemed decided, even if it didn't turn out that way.

So the need for more hitting was finally accepted when the levels of batting averages and runs scored sank to the levels of 1908, in the deadest of dead-ball eras.

The first response was to lower the mound and restore the strike zone, which had been foolishly enlarged in 1963. But that didn't change the basic trend downward, although it provided temporary relief; and especially in the American League, where things were worse on every level than in the National, the feeling grew that something more was needed.

The designated hitter is a permanent pinch-hitter. The vast majority of pitchers, for all the notable exceptions, are pretty sure outs. Even if they hit safely, it's a surprise, and there's no anticipation of a rally with a pitcher at bat. But, under the traditional nine-player concept, if you put up a better hitter, you have to take the pitcher out. Since day-in, day-out baseball success rests on having an effective pitching staff, you simply can't afford to use up pitchers in this way.

So the idea of letting someone bat instead of the pitcher came up, stimulated by the obvious aging of sluggers like Mickey Mantle and Willie Mays, and the shortage of obvious new drawing cards. Perhaps a rule like this might let them linger longer, just as hitters, and sell tickets.

The idea was tried in the minors. It was a rousing success, according to most fans and executives who experienced it.

So, naturally, it was abandoned.

By the end of the 1972 season, however, the American League seemed to be hitting bottom. Once the "superior" league, it was now hitting less than the National, drawing a couple of million fewer customers than the National, and scoring just as little as it was in 1968. Its big campaign for revolution consisted of getting the National to agree to inter-league play; the more prosperous National simply laughed. So the American, determined to do something on its own, adopted the designated hitter. The National laughed at that, too, but at least its participation wasn't necessary.

But note the problem and the nature of the "solution."

The problem was that there weren't enough hitting stars (like Ruth, Williams, DiMaggio, and Mantle in the past) to excite the spectators, and there wasn't enough hitting by ordinary players to make the games attractive. Baseball fans, being as conservative as anyone about their game, still considered a .380 batting average something super and a .320 batting average (for a league leader) unimpressive.

You would think, then, that the kind of change to make, if any, would be one that would help the best hitters improve their records and make the mediocre hitters a little more effective.

Instead, they chose a solution that did nothing at all for the eight "regular" players. And though it did inject some strength into the ninth slot in the batting order, it also allowed a good pitcher—one who gets the good hitters out and prevents them from hitting .380—to stay in the game even if he's losing 2–1.

The new rule did increase offense. It couldn't do otherwise. But it also ducked the true problems. It did remove a weak spot from the batting order, but it did nothing to help the other eight slots.

Nevertheless, it was a success: Attendance in the league went up, and for the first time in ten years the American hit a little more than the National—but only a little. The American's batting average went up from .239 to .259—but the National's, without the new rule, also went up from .248 to .254; so obviously part of the increase was due to some general cause not related to the designated hitter. Even so, the batting levels in both leagues were still lower than what had been considered normal up to about 1950.

That's from the standpoint of the end result. What did the designated hitter mean in terms of "quality"?

Those who opposed it made three principal arguments. One, it destroys the "complete-player" concept so dear to baseball hearts. Two, it reduces the number and kinds of decisions a manager must make (about removing a pitcher for a pinch-hitter), and decreases material for second-guessing, a basic delight of the fans. Three, it doesn't do enough good (if you admit that more scoring is good) to make the first two losses worthwhile.

Those who liked the designated hitter started at the other end: They said that any increase in offense is better than none, and that the opportunity for the good pitcher to keep pitching in a close game, or the ability to leave a good relief pitcher in for several innings even if his team is trailing, is a plus in itself. They scoffed at the "strategy" involved, since 90 percent of the pinch-hitting decisions are as painfully obvious as the "strategy" of having the weak-hitting pitchers bunt whenever possible; and they doubted the relevance, in an age of specialization, of the "myth" of the complete ball player, since clever managers manipulate their personnel anyway to use special skills (as in the use of relief pitchers). To the loss of "pinch-hit strategy," they offered the increase in "hit-and-run" strategy possible with a nine-hitter lineup.

"One thing I've noticed," said Ralph Houk, in favor of the DH that first year, "is that every inning is a potential scoring inning. You used to have two or three innings in a game in which you felt, just by seeing where the pitcher was going to come up, that it was unlikely anything would get started or keep going. Now you have a potential sequence of hitters every time anyone gets on."

Billy Martin, who was managing the Tigers in 1973, didn't like it as well. "I think it does cut down on the strategy," he said. "What it does do is help a mediocre team. On the Tigers, we had lots of good hitters, and we couldn't get the full benefit of having better pinch-hitters than the other team. It's the team that doesn't have many pinch-hitters that benefits."

All that was when the rule was first adopted. By the end of 1988, we had a sixteen-year sample of actual results, enough to draw conclusions instead of speculating about possible effects.

My conclusion is: It makes amazingly little difference.

And I think I can document it.

First of all, it neither increases offense dramatically nor affects strategy drastically.

Second, the National League has steadfastly refused to try it, so we've had two leagues using different playing rules during a time when baseball's popularity, prosperity, and prestige have grown to unprecedented heights—thus the "impossible" divergence has proved both sustainable and harmless. For that matter, in 1973, it seemed inconceivable that the two major leagues could be different in size—but they have been since the American went to 14 teams in 1977. It seems that "inconceivable" is determined by the limits on one's imagination, not by external reality.

Third, the effect on prolonging the careers of surefire box-office sluggers has been negligible: There haven't been that many who were that appealing, that's not the way tickets are marketed in this sophisticated marketing age, and they always did hang around as long as they could hit. It is a convenience and a plus in certain situations, but a minor matter all in all. Mostly, it gives a slightly injured regular a chance to rest and still bat.

Fourth, the alarming possibility that pitchers, safe from retaliation because they never have to go to bat, would become head-hunters throwing at hitters never materialized. One reason is that retaliation never did involve throwing at the offending pitcher; one threw at the best hitters on the offending club. If you want the pitcher personally, you bunt toward first and try to spike him when he comes over to cover. Both correctives remain available, and are used.

The prediction was that the DH would raise the league batting average by 20 points, and in the first year, it did exactly that: The American League went from .239 to .259. But this was easy to calculate. Pitchers, collectively, hit perhaps .100; all others hit about .260. The pitcher's slot comes up one-ninth of the time. A team has about 5,400 at-bats in a season, 600 per slot. If eight slots hit .260 and the ninth hits .160 less, it should take 20 points off each of the other eight; if all nine hit .260, the average is .260. (This is flawed reasoning and inaccurate arithmetic, but it shows you how even sloppy thinking in the right direction can give you a realistic answer.)

At any rate, we have the actual record, and here's what it shows, in four-year segments:

		American League	National League	Difference in Favor of AL
1969–72	(no DH)	.246	.252	−6
1973–76	(DH in AL)	.258	.255	+3
1977–80	(DH in AL)	.265	.259	+6
1981–84	(DH in AL)	.263	.256	+7
1985–88	(DH in AL)	.263	.253	+10

So the American League has hit the expected level, and stayed there. The National League hasn't changed much. But all those differences are too small to make a major impact on what I call the "profile" of the game—what the spectator sees, day in and day out.

By plunging more deeply into the numbers, you find:

In every 20 games, in the league *with* the DH, you get seven more hits, nine more runs, 4.5 more homers, and one more hit batsman than in the National League. You get five fewer strikeouts, five fewer stolen bases, three fewer sacrifice bunts, and one fewer left on base.

In every 20 games. Is that your idea of a big difference?

As for strategy, the DH certainly simplifies decisions for the manager, but most of these are of the thinking-ahead variety that the fan can't participate in. Whether or not to hit for a pitcher, or bring in a new one to pitch, can be second-guessed only when it's actually time to make (or not make) the move, and 90 percent of the time the issue is cut-and-dried: If you're behind in the last three innings, you hit for your pitcher; if you're ahead, you don't; if it's a tie, you might or might not. But a truly ambiguous situation doesn't arise once a week. The manager has to worry about warming up a pitcher unnecessarily, but you can't.

So if you prefer seeing a few more sacrifice bunts, strikeouts, and steals, go to National League games. If you want a few more homers and a little more scoring, go to American League games. But don't expect anything startling either way.

What about inter-league play? Doesn't a DH mess up the World Series, and even exhibition games?

Not so's you would notice. At first, the World Series was simply played under the "old rules." Then they tried alternating years, one year with the DH, one year without. (It proved important: The Cincinnati Reds might not have won the seventh game of the 1975 World Series if the Red Sox had not been forced to remove a pitcher for a pinch-hitter and go too deeply into their bullpen—or they might have anyhow.) Now they use the DH in the American League home games and not the National League home games, and follow the same pattern in spring exhibitions.

And in the All-Star Game, where it would make perfect sense, they don't use it at all.

It has become a badge of respectability, like George Bush's Pledge of Allegiance gimmick in the 1988 presidential campaign, to deplore the DH (unless you have some business connection with the American League). This view is brandished as proof of artistic purity by commissioners and others of the older generation. (After all, a commissioner could forbid it, couldn't he, if he really felt it was against "the best interests of baseball"?) But it's all harmless rhetoric. The fact is, only the National League holds out; the minor leagues and even the colleges use the DH, and baseball remains perfectly recognizable. I say it's not worth bothering about, either way: Eliminate it, make it universal, or leave things the way they are, and it won't matter.

But two other predictions of 1973 have not been borne out. It was thought that managers would choose, at least sometimes, to put a good-hitting pitcher into the batting order (like a Don Drysdale or a Bob Gibson) and have an extra man to use at will. But they haven't.

Darrell Johnson, who managed the Red Sox and Mariners and was a catcher in his playing days, explains why: "No matter how good a hitter a pitcher is naturally, an everyday player, even your weakest hitter, has a better chance in four trips to the plate. Pitchers simply don't get enough chance to hit seriously, against live pitching, to keep their skill sharp, regardless of natural ability. And they haven't kept it sharp for years, all the time they've been pitching, not just between starts. The odds are against them."

The other prediction was that the DH might be the first step toward freer substitution in baseball, following a trend that set in long ago in other sports. Charley Finley advocated a "designated runner"; and, in principle, why couldn't you use a better hitter for the shortstop, the catcher, or anyone else and have (like football) maximum offensive and defensive efficiency? You could—but no one is suggesting it, and there seems to be neither reason nor desire to tamper with the game that much. It may not be perfectly changeless, but it's not *that* changeable.

Okay, what exactly is the designated-hitter rule? How does it work?

The DH can be placed anywhere in the batting order, not necessarily ninth. At the start of the game, the manager hands in a nine-man batting order. One of the nine is the designated hitter. None of the nine is the pitcher. The pitcher is the tenth name on the list.

The designated hitter *may not* be used in place of another player (the shortstop or catcher, for instance) with the pitcher also batting. He may be used only for the pitcher.

Once the game starts, the regular nine-man batting order (with the designated hitter and without the pitcher) is followed in the normal way. The pitcher, then, never has to be removed from the game unless the manager wants to remove him for pitching reasons.

Suppose the manager wants to use a pinch-hitter for the designated hitter. He can, in the normal way. Then the pinch-hitter becomes the designated hitter for the rest of the game, taking his proper turn in the batting order but never playing in the field. This kind of substitution can be made as often as one likes, just as it can with any other position in the batting order.

Now suppose the manager wants the designated hitter to play some position in the field. For example, Ron Hassey of the Oakland A's is today's designated hitter, and Terry Steinbach is catching. In the fifth inning, Steinbach injures his leg and manager Tony La Russa wants Hassey to catch. At that point, the designated hitter evaporates. Hassey becomes the regular catcher, keeping his same spot in the batting order. And the pitcher, whoever he is at the moment, must now come to bat in the spot vacated by Steinbach when he left the game.

From that point on, either the pitcher bats for himself or he must be removed from the game entirely if another pinch-hitter hits for him, just as under traditional rules.

Many varieties of a "permanent pinch-hitter" are possible. The version the American League chose was liberal and complicated. It was liberal in the sense that it permitted the man who started the game as a designated hitter to move into a fielding position later, thus eliminating the problem of keeping a catcher (or any other player) in reserve for emergencies. A "never-in-the-field" type of rule would have confronted a manager with more values to weigh when deciding whether or not to use a designated hitter that day. Under the rule that was adopted, it became automatic to use one every day.

But as I've said, any designated-hitter rule ducks the real problem (if you consider it a problem). To get significantly more offense, and enhance the attractiveness of hitting stars, you have to do something for the good hitters, not replace a helpless one (the pitcher) with a mediocre one. (In sixteen years, the American League's designated hitters as a group have exceeded the total league average only three times, each time by 1 point; in the other thirteen years, they have averaged 7 points lower.)

An eight-man batting order would do it: Simply have no pitcher's slot at all. That would bring the better hitters up more often. Imagine what (from a home-run fan's point of view) a José Canseco or Will Clark or Don Mattingly or Wade Boggs could do with another 70–100 times at bat. And how many more exciting half-innings might there be?

Ah, but that would invalidate all the old statistics and ruin baseball, wouldn't it?

You mean, the way 162 games, divisional play, unbalanced schedules, night games, artificial turf, expansion, and free agency ruined baseball?

The most important thing about the DH was that it was something new—and they tried it.

CHAPTER
9

The Umpires

And now—the bad guys. The umpires, No game can take place without them, so they are at once the most essential and the most neglected element of the game on the field.

"Kill the Umpire" is regarded as an expression of some underlying mystique in American culture. We seem to take pride in our irrational response to the one impartial element of the contest, as if it somehow relates to our love of freedom, independence of thought, and individuality. The contradiction that Europeans and South Americans, supposedly more willing to accept authority, actually get far more violent and often try literally to "kill a referee" in a disputed soccer match is just ignored. Hating the umpire is as American as the hot dog that drips mustard on your neighbor while you shout your opinion at the object of that hatred.

This attitude is shared, by and large, by players and club officials, even though they really know better. More today than in the past, participants accept the idea that an umpire is doing his objective best; but on the emotional level, it's hard to resist blaming the umpire for a play that turns out wrong—especially if the umpire really is wrong, which does happen.

As far as the fan is concerned—the fan rooting in a given direction, that is—the umpire cannot be right. If a play happens in favor of your team, the umpire has merely done his job by calling it correctly and he, as a person, is nonexistent. If the play goes against you, the umpire is suddenly the center of attention and obviously at fault.

Let's try to consider them realistically.

Umpires are human, just as human as the ball players. This means that they do make mistakes occasionally, that they have varying degrees of skill in different directions, and that they have feelings and ideas. In major-league baseball, the umpire has attained a position of unquestioned impartiality, much more than in any other major spectator sport. His integrity is beyond question, and no one has seriously questioned a big-league umpire's honesty in at least sixty years.

Competence is another question. Umpiring a baseball game is a much easier task, in some respects, than refereeing football, hockey, or basketball. There is not, in baseball, the simultaneous movement of many bodies in a confined space; whatever comes up for decision comes up alone, usually at a predictable location. With almost no exceptions, the baseball umpire can make his call while standing still, able to get a good look.

In one respect, however, the baseball umpire has a tougher job: Absolutely everything he calls is in the open, subject to second-guessing. In the other games, it is taken for granted that the official can call only a certain proportion of all the technical violations that actually occur; in baseball, there is no such thing. *Everything* that calls for an umpire's decision is called, right or wrong.

As a result, umpires can display distinct personalities, and it is a shame that today's charcoal-gray approach to baseball has all but eliminated the personal flair from major-league umpiring. The umpires of a generation or more ago were fewer in number but much more present in the fan's awareness. There is, it is true, the extreme called-strike gesture of Joe West, satirized mercilessly in the movie *The Naked Gun;* but it's an exception that proves the rule.

Bill Klem, of course was famous and unignorable as a tyrant in the National League between the world wars. Small, strong-willed, combative, he expressed an important principle: "I never called one wrong." An umpire *should* feel that way, at the time he makes a call. Another version, ascribed to many umpires, has the impatient player asking, "What was it, safe or out?" and the umpire answering, "It ain't nothing until I call it." This exaggerated definiteness, in Klem's case, was accompanied by personal sensitivity. The nickname "Catfish," used in his presence, would send him into a rage (and send the player who uttered it to the showers), because Bill's face did, in all fairness, resemble a catfish.

Leo Durocher tells of being at bat in St. Louis with Klem umpiring.

Leo was young and new to the league. In a box near first base, someone was giving Klem the business, and Klem couldn't catch who it was out of the corner of his eye. Naturally, he wouldn't turn to look.

"Take a pitch, kid," he ordered Leo, "and see if you can spot the guy who's yelling at me."

"Sure, Mr. Klem," said Leo, as obliging a fellow then as always (in his own stories).

Klem called a ball, and Leo started to point with his bat at the offending voice.

"Don't point, you dumb blankety-blank fresh busher," Klem yelled, seeing his air of aloofness thus given away. "And that was a strike."

Then there was Art Passarella, who used to umpire in the American League in the 1940s. Talkative and friendly, he was one of the best umpires to be stuck in a club car with. But players would accuse him of showboating, of putting on an act. They might have been right—because Passarella went to Hollywood and became an actor. The last time he was seen umpiring, by a large number of people, was in a movie with Cary Grant and Doris Day, in a scene that included (as guest extras) Mickey Mantle, Roger Maris, and Yogi Berra.

The universal theme of good officiating—consistency—applies most of all in baseball. Calling balls and strikes is strictly a matter of judgment, built on conventions. Unless the umpire has a very firm strike zone, both pitcher and hitter are at a loss. He must call the same pitches the same way all the time.

The strike zone itself is flexible. It changes with every hitter. Two men may be the same size, but one may have a smaller strike zone because of a habitual (but it must be habitual) crouch.

For many years, it was well established that National League umpires had a "lower" strike zone than American League umpires. That is, they were more likely to call a borderline low pitch (at the knees) a strike, and less likely to call the borderline high pitch (above the letters) a strike. Sometimes, the difference between conceptions in the two leagues could be as much as two inches. That's why some hitters and pitchers, perhaps, had better success in one league than the other. A low-ball hitter, for example, would suffer less in the National League than a man who couldn't hit the low pitch; a low-ball pitcher might have trouble adjusting to the American League, because he might not get as many low strikes, and then get clobbered when he came up with the ball in an attempt to compensate.

The difference was attributed to, at least partly, a difference in working style. National League umpires wore chest protectors under their jackets, and could crouch between the batter's and the catcher's heads or shoulders; American Leaguers used a large, external protector, and peered more directly over the top of the catcher. Perhaps the different angle of vision altered perceptions.

But nowadays, both leagues use similar equipment and methods, and the difference is considered less distinct. In this, as in many other respects, the homogenization of the two leagues continues gradually along a path that has been followed this whole century.

In any case, the actual strike zone is not the same as the theoretical one. Ideally, the strike zone would be three-dimensional, covering not only height and the width of the plate (17 inches) but its depth as well. The plate is a pentagon in shape, fitting into the junction of the foul lines. It is 12 inches on each side along the lines, and about 8½ inches on the sides extending into the field toward the pitcher. A curving pitch that catches the back edge of the plate, or a high pitch that is too high at the front edge of the plate but low enough before it passes the back point, *should* be a strike. In real life, such gradations are a little too fine to handle. The umpire draws an imaginary rectangle that is two-dimensional at the front of the plate, and judges pitches by that. Pitchers know that he does, and accept it.

It's the vertical component that's flexible. It used to be, traditionally, "knees to the shoulders," which was vague enough. Then it became "knees to armpits." The current definition in the rule book, as already noted, has a drawing to illustrate a rather legalistic statement: "The STRIKE ZONE is that area over home plate the upper limit of which is a horizontal line at the midpoint between the top of the shoulders and the top of the uniform pants, and the lower level is a line at the top of the knees."

Then it adds the kicker: "The Strike Zone shall be determined from the batter's stance as the batter is prepared to swing at a pitched ball."

If a man crouches, his knees get pretty close to the ground (making a "low" strike, which pitchers love). And where exactly is the "top" of the knee? And how does an umpire determine the "midpoint" between the belt and the shoulders, with a protractor or a sextant? What if the player hitches up his pants, or his belt sags beneath a small paunch, does the "midpoint" move? What if one shoulder is held higher than the other?

Not only is this not science, it's not even art. It's simply gut feeling crystallized by experience and general agreement—human beings knowing what they intend, and adjusting to each other and unavoidable imprecision. Anyhow, the more important variation deals with width: The preferred location for most pitches is the low outside corner (and sometimes low inside); if an umpire "widens" his strike zone, the hitters are in trouble. They not only have more difficult pitches to try to hit, but they get as a called strike what their conditioning has taught them to see as a ball. In the last generation, these borderline pitches have come to be referred to as "on the black," because the white-rubber home plate has a black border where it is set into the ground. If you take that seriously, of course, you're making the strike zone wider than just 17 inches, which is what the white part is supposed to be.

So the key element, in practice, is consistency. A good umpire establishes his strike zone, that day, and calls everything accurately with respect to it—and does so every time he works. Tomorrow's strike zone may be a trifle different, with another umpire, but if he in turn is consistent about it, there's little complaint.

Less capable umpires aren't entirely reliable even in those terms. They may be influenced by where a catcher catches the ball. If he gets it at his shoe tops, the pitcher's contention that it was high enough at the front of the plate may not be honored. And they are less consistent.

Aside from balls and strikes, almost all umpire decisions fall into two categories: safe or out on the bases (including home), and the position of the ball (fair or foul, in the stands or out, caught or trapped).

At first base, the umpire glues his eyes on the bag and listens for the ball hitting the first baseman's mitt. This two-sense measurement is the surest way to determine whether the runner is safe or not. (A tie, says the rule book, is resolved in favor of the runner.)

At second base, the two frequent plays are double-play pivots and steals. On the double play, the umpire must decide whether the pivotman had the ball in his possession while his foot was in contact with the base, not before or after. Here there is a tremendous leeway, by convention: The fielder is trying to avoid being hit by the base runner, and the umpire is not there to promote collisions by being a stickler for mathematical accuracy. Any reasonably well-executed pivot is allowed unless the umpire feels that wandering off the bag is the thing that made the play possible. On steals, the umpire must look at two things: when the runner actually reaches the base, and when the tag is made. The tag may be late, or it may miss, or the runner's feet may pass over the bag before contact is made.

On such plays, umpires are almost always right. They are right on top of the action, and have the best angle. When stop-action replays came into television, there was much fuss about such electronic second-guessing of umpires' decisions; if you watch a lot of replays, however, you'll come away impressed that the umpire is right in the vast majority of cases.

Among themselves, umpires talk shop about two subjects: rules and position. Naturally, they must know the rule book inside out. But the technique of their craft consists of anticipating plays and getting planted in the right spot to call them, close enough to see everything, but out of the way, and in the proper direction, so that the view won't be obstructed at the crucial moment by one of the players.

What can umpires be blamed for legitimately?

Lack of hustle—failure to stay alert at all times and to move into the proper position to call a play.

Inconsistency—in calling balls and strikes.

Arrogance—refusing to listen to a reasonable complaint about an unusual play, or refusing to get help from another umpire on a play he didn't see.

Umpires do help each other. They have signals. For instance, on a half-swing, the plate umpire may be uncertain whether or not the batter actually broke his wrists. A glance at the first-base or third-base umpire, and a gesture, can settle it.

In the 1980s, this particular play got out of hand. Traditionally, a batter was considered to be swinging at the ball if he "broke his wrists," that is, performed the snapping action that turns the bat and speeds its head through the point of possible contact. If he turned his body, and the bat did pass through the strike zone but the wrists didn't turn, it was considered no swing. However (and this is my own interpretation, unbuttressed by any documentation I can find), authorities found it embarrassing when television close-ups and replays showed the barrel of the bat passing over home plate, regardless of the batter's movement or intention. They then made this the definition of a "half-swing," multiplying the frequency of the incident, the ambiguity from the plate umpire's vantage point, and the frustrations of the batters (especially the better ones, making the latest decision to lay off a pitch). Now the first- or third-base umpire can be appealed to by the defensive team, and make the call directly, which they do with individualistic gestures that make the most of their instant on camera.

I think I know who's going to break Nolan Ryan's strikeout record one day: some first-base umpire.

In this case, the home-plate umpire is abdicating his ball-strike responsibility to a colleague (on purpose, not irresponsibly). But in most other cases, umpires hate to overrule another umpire, even when he's wrong, because they don't like to "show up" each other.

I once saw a game in the Coliseum in Los Angeles. Bob Skinner, a left-handed batter for Pittsburgh, sliced a high drive along that short left-field foul line. There were five umpires working the game, the fifth one at the base of the left-field wall. The umpire at third base, spinning around to watch the ball, stepped on the base, or on the third baseman's foot, and fell into fair territory.

The ball went into the stands foul by at least 20 feet. The umpire who would normally make the call was lying on the ground, making no gesture at all. Skinner, and the runner in front of him, circled the bases for a two-run homer. The third-base umpire couldn't possibly have followed the flight of the ball—yet none of the others would overrule him, and he was too embarrassed to admit he couldn't make the call. There was a 20-minute argument, which the Dodgers lost. The two-run homer stood, and Pittsburgh won the game 4–2.

On the other hand, umpires take so much abuse from players and managers that much of their refusal to listen is justified. If players weren't such wolf-criers, their few legitimate complaints might get attention. Although, they might not; a large school of thought exists that advocates constant harassment of umpires. "If you let them alone, they'll walk all over you," this school says. "You have to stay on them to make them give you an even break. You complain long enough and at least they'll pay attention; if you don't and the other side does, the other team will get the best of it." It's a moot point—undoubtedly true of some umpires and not others.

At bottom is personality. It takes a certain kind of personality to want to be an umpire, and a good deal of thick skin to stay one. Constantly under pressure and repeatedly insulted, umpires demand one thing above all: outward respect. A player will be thrown out of a game not on the merits of an argument, but for a word that shows up the umpire in front of other players, or a gesture that shows him up to the crowd. It's summed up by the comment attributed to many umpires—a batter is called out on strikes, he flings the bat high into the air as a public demonstration of his disgust, and the umpire says: "If that bat comes down, you're out of the game."

A pugnacious personality, needed to do the job, is going to lead a man into the types of trouble pugnacious personalities get into. An umpire must establish his authority. Then, when he does miss a call or two, these mistakes will be accepted in remarkably good grace by players who have come to respect his effort, his fairness, and his competence.

In no circumstances, however, must an umpire permit himself to carry a grudge, if he is to remain a decent umpire.

Much used to be made of the isolation and loneliness of an umpire's life. This was part of the myth promoted in the Judge Landis era. Landis had been made commissioner to counteract the damage done to public confidence by the "Black Sox" scandal. Landis exuded stern morality, and even racetracks were supposed to be off limits for baseball people. An owner who had racetrack interests was vetoed by Landis, in the guise of keeping baseball pure. In this context, umpires had to make special travel arrangements to avoid spending the night on the same train as a ball club, to live in separate hotels, frequent different restaurants, and so forth.

Today, all this is ignored. Some of baseball's most powerful and distinguished owners—John Galbreath and Joan Payson, for instance—were racetrack people. And umpires get around as best they can, often getting a ride on some club's chartered plane, because no comparable convenient public transportation is available. And baseball's integrity has survived such social contact very nicely.

Until the 1980s, baseball's treatment of the umpire could be summed up by one word: disgraceful. They were underpaid, inefficiently supervised, and often insufficiently backed by their bosses, the league presidents. They did exert absolute authority during a game, but were not made important enough the rest of the time. They were left behind in pension arrangements, paid as little as possible, and fired on whim.

"As little as possible" meant, if you can believe it, between $9,000 and $17,000, with a few rare exceptions above $20,000, as late as 1970. By that time even umpires had learned the lesson that if they wanted more money, they had better organize. They did, and they actually called a strike of sorts at the start of the 1970 playoffs. It lasted one day and did get them higher rates of pay for playoff and World Series games, and eventually a somewhat better overall contract. But after more strike action, they established an effective union that has won them better pay, more time off, and better working conditions.

One consequence of the unionization of umpires, many people believe, is an attitudinal change for the worse. That they have a better sense of job security, and fairer compensation, is their right and all to the good. But, at least in some cases, this has enabled them to act on injured sensibilities to an excessive degree. They seem less tolerant of argument, too quick to eject players (who are, after all, the attraction people paid to see), too often a bit too arrogant. (Chasing a manager is different: Not once in a thousand times is a manager thrown out of a game for arguing without being aware of exactly what he's doing. Umpires know this and recognize the technique, so more tolerance would just prolong things, since the manager would keep at it until he accomplished his goal. But players, almost always, are reacting with honest, uncontrollable emotion, and should be disciplined only for the most overt crowd-inciting actions.)

What has happened, I believe, is a combination of circumstances. There are more umpires, thanks to expansion and the practice of giving them time off, so naturally "the very best" are a smaller fraction of the total—just as with players. A "weaker" umpire means a less consistent one, and it's the inconsistency that produces complaint. But with every game on television somewhere, and with game clips available for endless reshowings, umpires—being human—are more sensitive to "being shown up," and become quicker on the trigger and less inclined to healthy debate. This, plus the added sense of group security, puts them in an "I'll show you who's boss" mode more than necessary, and more than in the past.

Still, with millions of dollars riding on the winning or losing of a pennant, crucial decisions are left daily to umpires being paid less than the player minimum.

That's an example of how baseball runs its business.

CHAPTER
10

The Playing Field

Up to now we've dealt with the people who play and stage baseball games, and the implements they use. But every game has to take place somewhere, and the field itself plays a greater role in baseball than in other sports. Each ballpark is different, and the difference must be adjusted to all the time.

There are (in 1990) 26 major-league parks. When expansion comes, as scheduled in the early 1990s, there will be at least a couple more, and new ones are being readied in Baltimore and Chicago. We can group them by type, but even within a type, each has distinct characteristics that affect the games played there.

Players have a saying, "between the lines," referring to the seriousness with which they take anything that happens within the field of play during a game that counts in the standings. It's an avowal of professionalism in the best sense. The "lines" are the two foul lines.

But only part of the field, within the lines, is uniform under the rules. The 90-foot square with a base at each corner and the pitching distance (60 feet 6 inches from the front of the pitcher's slab to the back of home plate, where the foul lines intersect) are always the same. But the distances to various parts of the outfield barrier, in fair territory, vary from park to park. So do the height, composition, and contours of the outfield fences. So do the amount and shape of foul territory, where the ball is in play. So does the construction of upper stands and light towers, which bear on sight lines and visibility in significant ways.

These variations help make baseball fascinating to watch, as well as to play, but they also go to the heart of the game's philosophy. The idea is to win *this* game, on *this* field, under *these* conditions, at *this* time. The conditions are supposed to be the same for both teams, but only here and now, not at all times everywhere. The home team can design contours and tailor the ground surface to suit itself (within stipulated limits), but once it does, it must leave the facility that way for the entire season.

We'll look at ballparks from two distinct points of view, to which we'll attach the fancy names "venue" and "ambience." By *venue* I mean the physical layout of those features that affect play. By *ambience* I mean the atmosphere the surroundings create for spectators and players (who are no less sensitive to atmosphere than fans).

First, the venue issue. The elements to be considered, in order of importance, are (1) playing surface, (2) atmospheric conditions (meaning wind, sun, temperature, and so forth, not the emotional "atmosphere" that goes with ambience), (3) outfield contours, (4) foul ground, and (5) visibility.

1. The playing surface can be natural grass or artificial turf. Traditional baseball techniques have evolved and been perfected on grass (and dirt). It is a significantly different game when played on a "carpet." A batted or thrown ball bounces higher and moves faster and at different angles on an artificial surface, so fielders must place themselves differently, pitchers must select different pitches at certain times, and batters must swing differently. Running speed is enhanced. Physical wear and tear on the legs is increased.

Artificial turf was developed to solve practical problems; no one ever considered it preferable from an artistic point of view. When the Houston Astrodome was first built, it contained grass and a transparent glass roof. It turned out that the sunlight through that roof was blinding, so it had to be made opaque, and that in turn killed the grass. The carpet developed to make it usable took the trade name Astroturf for that reason.

At about the same time, cities were building "multi-purpose" stadiums, intended to accommodate football and other tenants. The old baseball parks had always rented their facilities to football teams, but the gridiron had to be squeezed in, and of course the best sideline seats weren't properly placed. The new stadiums, since professional football had become so important by 1960, used movable sections of the stands to set up appropriate configurations for each. But moving the stands, as well as playing more football, meant tearing up fields that didn't always recover well, especially in the fall. Artificial turf was an attractive solution to this constant-use problem and, presumably, more economical.

A side benefit emerged. Rain doesn't stop football games, but it frequently interrupts or postpones baseball games. Heavy rain may leave a grass-and-dirt field too soggy to use until it dries out many hours or a day later. Artificial turf can be made to drain and dry much quicker. Not only can play be resumed when the rain lets up, but pre-game rain may not force postponement.

Also, at first, the artificial turf was used to cover only those areas normally covered by grass—the outfield and the inner infield square (except for the mound)—with the wide base-path area (which I think of as "the parachute") left as dirt. Then it was found that the whole field could be carpeted with dirt cutouts only in the immediate vicinity of the bases. That altered the behavior of batted balls not only in the outfield but in the whole infield. Today, all artificial fields have only the cutouts.

In the National League, half of the twelve parks have an artificial surface: Montreal, Philadelphia, Pittsburgh, St. Louis, Houston, and Cincinnati. Los Angeles, San Francisco, San Diego, Atlanta, New York, and Chicago have grass.

In the American League, only four of the fourteen parks use artificial turf: Kansas City, Seattle, Minnesota, and Toronto. It's grass in Oakland, Anaheim, Texas, Chicago, Milwaukee, Cleveland, Detroit, Baltimore, New York, and Boston.

But not all artificial fields are the same: They can be harder or softer, and in different states of repair. They don't produce many bad bounces, but they do produce some, not only where the carpet meets the edge of a cutout, but where there are seams or zippers in the carpet itself (which has to be put down in sections).

Grass fields, of course, have a much wider range of variation. Taller grass will slow down the ball considerably. The dirt portion of the infield can be adjusted to "faster" or "slower" by the type of dirt and firmness of packing. At times, bare spots can develop in grass portions.

No other aspect of playing conditions changes the demands and results of a baseball game as much as the surface. Baseball on the carpet is a drastically different game—better or worse, according to your taste, but never the same as it is on a natural field.

2. The second determining factor starts with: roof or no roof? Indoors or out?

Before the Astrodome, playing baseball at all indoors seemed out of the question (although Walter O'Malley's plan, in 1955, for a downtown ballpark in Brooklyn, before he moved the Dodgers to Los Angeles, envisioned a domed stadium).

Houston, Seattle, and Minnesota are permanent indoor fixtures; the first two have a hard-structure roof, the one in Minnesota an air-pressure–supported plastic bubble. Toronto and Montreal have retractable roof arrangements, but since they are intended to be in the open-air mode only when the weather is nice, they can be considered indoor parks for all practical purposes.

They have, of course, artificial surfaces.

But they also have, of necessity, air conditioning, and that means no wind, no rain, and a controlled comfortable temperature. And no sun shining into a fielder's eyes.

So this is the first great category of difference: Indoor and outdoor parks. The five indoor parks provide uniform and stable atmospheric conditions, which become no factor in tactics. That doesn't mean the ball won't "carry" better in some indoor parks than in others; it does. Atmospherics is a tricky science, even indoors. But in any one of those parks, conditions are consistent from day to day.

In the twenty-one outdoor parks, this is not true. Every day is different, depending on the weather. Which way is the wind blowing? How hard? Is it hot or freezing? Damp? Drizzly? Humid? All such circumstances must be taken into account by players and managers.

For the outdoor parks, then, specific location is important. Chicago's Wrigley Field, Cleveland's Municipal Stadium, and San Francisco's Candlestick Park are particularly susceptile to wind blowing off a large body of water (Lake Michigan, Lake Erie, and San Francisco Bay, respectively).

Others are not that much farther from a large body of water geographically—Chicago's South-Side park for the White Sox, Detroit, Milwaukee, Oakland, Boston, Baltimore—but somehow seem to be more sheltered.

New York's Yankee Stadium, Philadelphia's Veterans Stadium, Busch Stadium in St. Louis, Three Rivers in Pittsburgh, and Riverfront in Cincinnati are right next to rivers, but not visibly affected by them. Shea Stadium is right next to Long Island Sound, and produced terrible football weather in the fall, which is one reason the Jets moved out. But after April and before post-season games, it isn't exceptional.

Atlanta, Texas (in Arlington, between Dallas and Fort Worth), San Diego, Anaheim, Los Angeles, and Kansas City are more or less land-locked.

Sudden storms, or major changes in weather during a game, are common in the mid-continent areas. A particular day's weather is more likely to be fairly stable in the coastal cities.

Atlanta is the only city as high as 1,000 feet above sea level, which may or may not have aerodynamic consequences for home runs (which certainly fly out easily in that ballpark). But if or when Denver (5,000 feet) or Phoenix (1,100 feet in a desert climate) are included, local atmospheric conditions will be important.

Statisticians have consistently ignored such factors, but they obviously play a role. The necessary mathematical assumption that "it all evens out" may or may not be true. Players know that in Oakland or San Francisco, for example, the batted ball behaves differently not only in night games versus day games, but in early versus late innings of one game, depending on the time. So a hung curve in one inning may be a 360-foot out, and exactly the same pitch hit exactly the same way at point of impact may be a grand-slam home run in another inning. Until and unless we can have minute-by-minute recording of wind force and direction, barometric pressure, and humidity in every ballpark during actual play, coordinated with pitch-by-pitch records, statistical analysis will continue to be only a rough (very rough) approximation of reality.

Thank goodness.

3. That ballparks vary in shape is, in my view, one of the glories of the game. Those who feel it would be more "fair" to have them all alike overlook the atmospheric and surface differences we have just discussed. Linear distance from home to fence, or height of the fence, is not everything. Identical dimensions would not make parks in different locations identical.

But there are more important factors. An asymmetrical park, where one field is longer than another, makes possible the game's artistry. It gives the pitcher something to work with, to try to make the batter hit the ball in a preferred direction, and it gives the batter a preferred target to shoot at when the pitcher makes a mistake. And it dictates the alignment of fielders.

In the early days, the ball was dead and couldn't be hit very far, and crowds rarely exceeded 25,000, so grandstands that extended only part of the way down each foul line were big enough. It made relatively little difference how far away the outfield fence was placed because balls rarely reached it. A home run, itself rare, was usually an inside-the-park phenomenon.

Exceptions always exist. During 1883, the Chicago White Stockings (now the Cubs) occupied what was then called Lake Front Park (off Michigan Avenue at Washington and Randolph streets). Each foul line was a little less than 200 feet long. A six-foot fence in center field was only 300 feet from home. But the right-field fence of wood and tarpaulin was nearly 40 feet high. In the 1882 and 1883 seasons, the entire National League had hit 126 and 124 home runs. In 1884, the White Stockings hit 142 themselves, with four players getting between 21 and 27 each, while the other seven teams put together hit 180 (many of them as visitors to Chicago). The next year, the team moved into another park (short foul lines but very long center, like New York's defunct Polo Grounds) and produced 54 homers.

Nevertheless, when Babe Ruth first emerged as a home-run champion in 1919 with 29 homers in Boston, it was Ned Williamson's record of 27 in 1884 that he broke.

And even that isn't the whole story. The Lake Front Park dimensions didn't suddenly change when the 1884 season began: The rules did. Over the fence used to be a ground-rule double there; that year, they called it a home run.

It's an important lesson in statistics, which we'll return to in a later chapter: Don't draw conclusions about numbers without finding out what they represent.

Anyhow, homers were still not an important factor in the game when a new wave of building the first steel-and-concrete grandstands started around 1910. The dominant consideration was real estate. Ballparks were being built in outlying urban areas along developing transportation lines, trolley cars, or (in New York) subways. The parcel put together often had the shape of a city block, but most city blocks are rectangles, not squares. Whichever corner you used for home plate, one foul line would be shorter than the other. And until crowds became large enough to need bleacher seats backing the outfield, the outfield fences could border the property line. Result: large, lopsided playing areas.

As time went on, even those original buildings went through many transformations—adding seats, adding upper decks, surrounding the outfield with bleachers and then double-decking those (thus reducing the outfield playing area).

From that era, three parks remain in use: Boston's Fenway (opened in 1912), Detroit's Tiger Stadium (on the same site since 1901, but not built up to its present general appearance until the 1930s), and Chicago's Wrigley Field (built in 1914 for the Federal League team and taken over by the Cubs in 1916).

Yankee Stadium was built, to specifications, in 1923 as the biggest ballpark in the world, designed for 80,000 seats. It was made narrow at the home plate end, to put the spectators close to the action, and short in the right-field direction, to accommodate Ruth's bat. The result was a huge left-center area. It was completely rebuilt, in the same general shape but with more reasonable distances, in the early 1970s.

Cleveland's Municipal Stadium, another huge 80,000-seat oval (but symmetrical), dates from 1932. The Indians used it only for Sunday and holiday (and eventually night) games until 1947. It had no inner outfield fence until then, so its power alleys in right- and left-center were 435 feet and center was 450. Now it has ordinary and symmetric playing dimensions within an eight-foot canvas fence.

The other twenty-one parks, counting Chicago's replacement for Comiskey on the South Side, are all post–World War II creations.

One set is the "cookie-cutter" multi-purpose style so unsatisfactory to traditionally minded baseball fans. These are nearly circular ovals that create huge foul territory and place even the good seats far from home plate and the infield, and are unrelentingly symmetrical around the outfield. New York's Shea Stadium, Atlanta, St. Louis, Pittsburgh, Cincinnati, San Diego (with variations, using square corners), Philadelphia, Oakland, and the five indoor stadiums fall in this category.

Dodger Stadium in Los Angeles, Anaheim Stadium, Candlestick Park in San Francisco, and Royals Stadium in Kansas City were built exclusively for baseball, so they have the narrow home-plate end pioneered by Yankee Stadium. The ones in Los Angeles and Kansas City have been kept that way and are absolute gems, unspoiled even by the presence of symmetric outfield dimensions. Anaheim and Candlestick have been enlarged and adjusted to accommodate football, making them hybrid multi-purpose facilities.

Milwaukee's County Stadium and Arlington Stadium in Texas are enlarged minor-league parks. They have traditional playing-field configurations. The new parks in Baltimore and Chicago aren't in operation as of this writing, but the one in Baltimore is designed to be asymmetric (for the reasons I, among others, advocate).

4. Foul ground is of profound importance to the play of a game and the players' records. If there's a lot of it behind home plate and along the two baselines, foul pops that would give the batter another chance if they reached the seats may be caught. In places like Oakland and Atlanta, there might be two or three such cases a game. That's a tremendous amount.

Foul area gets narrower as it approaches the foul pole itself, but this varies. If you put home plate in the corner of a square, foul territory would stay of constant width. That means a "foul homer" type of fly can be caught for an out. (Yes, if it were deep enough to be a homer, it would have reached the stands in foul ground; but in most parks, this kind of drive does give the hitter another chance.) Exactly where the stands prevent a fielder from catching a foul ball is an important characteristic of every park.

5. Visibility is another variable. How the sun blinds a fielder is only the most obvious (and oldest) difficulty. The rule book says: "It

is desirable that the line from home base through the pitcher's plate to second base shall run East-Northeast." That's so the setting sun, in mid-afternooon and later, won't shine into the eyes of the hitter (or pitcher) in mid-latitude Northern Hemisphere locations. When I covered a morning game on a Labor Day in Pittsburgh one time, the hitters couldn't see at all for the first few innings, since the sun was still above center field.

In practice, ballparks do face in different directions, so either right field or left field may be the worst sun field. But all have complications.

The way the double-decked stands cast a shadow, especially as the shadow moves from home plate out toward the pitcher, affects how well hitters can see. So does the background behind center field. If such a bleacher were full of fans in white shirts (which was often the case), the hitter would have a hard time seeing the white ball as the pitcher released it overhand. Now, at the insistence of the player union, some sort of dark (usually green) background is provided, either structurally or by canvas, even if it means sacrificing a few ticket sales. Light clothing on people seated behind third base can still make problems for the first baseman trying to catch a throw across the infield on bright days.

People still laugh at the remark made by Billy Loes that he "lost a ground ball in the sun" in a World Series game at Ebbets Field, but he was telling the truth. The back of the lower stands was open to the street, and in the fall, the sun, low on the horizon, would shine through. One high bounce, and the pitcher suddenly looking up to catch it could be momentarily blinded.

At night, the lights can blind fielders if the angle of vision is an unfortunate one. Losing a ball in the lights is as common as losing it in the sun used to be, and sunglasses help less. The recent design of setting lights into a stadium rim, instead of on towers extending above the roof, reduces this particular hazard.

My favorite visibility story involves Gil McDougald, who played second, third, and short for the New York Yankees in various World Series during the 1950s. Yankee Stadium's left field was a notorious hazard in October, when the sun set earlier and took a lower path across the heavens than during the summertime; the sun would hit the third-base/home-plate roof of the third deck at such an angle that a blinding haze would develop as one looked in from the left-field area.

After one of the World Series games in which Gil had been the shortstop, he told us, "The sun has moved, you know."

What?

"The sun. It's moved. It doesn't set in the same place it used to."

Was he crazy? How could the sun move?

"If it's not the sun, it's the ballpark, and I don't think *it's* moved," insisted Gil, flushing red and sounding testy.

We gave him up as a hopeless nut. We knew ball players were ignorant and uneducated, but not to know that the earth and sun are fixed in their orbits? What was the use of talking to him?

But he was right.

That year, for the first time, the shift from standard time to daylight saving time had been set back to late October, instead of late September. The World Series game, starting at 1 P.M. as usual, was actually taking place an hour earlier, sun time, since our clocks were still on daylight saving time.

And the sun, of course, was one hour away—15 degrees along its path—from its former position in any given inning.

The sun had moved.

This taught me not to be in such a hurry to assume someone else is stupid, and never to doubt Gil McDougald again.

Starting games around 5 o'clock local time, for television's need, adulterates the integrity of performance in All-Star, playoff, and World Series games. In twilight, neither natural nor artificial light (and the lights are usually turned on) takes full effect. Visibility for hitters is so poor that the result is simply an unfair test of competitiveness in a sport where the pitcher has the edge anyhow.

So we can sum up the venue aspect. Half the parks have cookie-cutter characteristics: symmetrical ovals. Half are better designed for baseball in that the home-plate end is narrowed, and/or the outfields are less uniform.

The ambience is, in the final analysis, a personal preference. Generally speaking, we like what we associate with past good times. Which ballpark experiences we enjoy depend less on the physical layout than on the circumstances—who was with us, when, and what happened. In places as well built and well maintained as Dodger Stadium, Anaheim Stadium, Royals Stadium, and others I no longer know first-hand, anyone's enjoyment must be enhanced. And I am among those who find cookie-cutter parks, because of their shape, less interesting than the old parks used to be. (Ebbets Field was a square bandbox, breeding homers; Forbes Field in Pittsburgh was lopsided; Crosley Field in Cincinnati had that sloping terrace to harass outfielders; the Polo Grounds, with 250-foot foul lines and a 500-foot center, was unique; and so forth.)

But I don't relate to the ridiculous romanticizing of the "old" places—Fenway and Wrigley in particular—which became so fashionable in the 1980s that people seriously considered modeling new parks after them. The associations people have to them, and what happened within them, are entirely valid. But as working buildings, they were considered aging and unsatisfactory twenty-five years ago, and remain second-rate in terms of size, economical operation, access, and physical comfort. That they draw as well as they do merely confirms baseball's revived popularity brought about by the belated discovery of modern marketing efforts. They'll have to be replaced soon no matter what. To glorify them because they survived—when their owners were prepared to abandon them years ago and didn't only because plans for something better fell through—is to miss the point. What's needed is the preservation of the values they acquired accidentally—a certain amount of asymmetry, and seats close to the field—in contemporary architectural plans.

What creates ambience is people. Each city has its own attitudes, its own population mix, its own history. Philadelphia fans have a reputation for nastiness, to their own as well as to visiting teams. Brooklyn fans, notoriously loyal, weren't so loyal until the team started to win (in the years before Larry MacPhail took over, they were averaging 6,000 a game). Los Angeles fans leave in the seventh inning, regardless of the score, to beat traffic. Detroit fans are regarded as knowledgeable and intense, New York fans knowledgeable and nasty, Boston fans bitter, Chicago fans long-suffering, Minnesotans not so knowledgeable but polite, St. Louis fans terminally sentimental, and so on.

In the last couple of decades, however, club managements have pretty much taken control of the atmosphere in their parks. It started with the new Astrodome scoreboard clueing in spectators when to cheer and what to say. But by now, most parks have elaborate electronic boards that bombard us every second with ads, notes, cheer-leading instructions, acknowledgment of groups in attendance, birthday wishes, and actual television replays, all accompanied by recorded music. (The day of the individual organist, responding live to events and playing old-fashioned music between innings, is all but gone.) The result is that the remaining self-starters in the stands are overwhelmed by the obedient majority.

It's not accidental, it's not all negative, and it's not likely to change. First of all, clubs now have entire departments devoted to "promotion," whose duties include crowd control and crowd amusement. Special days—Bat Day, Cap Day, Old-timers Day, Half-Price Night—turn up about once a week, although Ladies' Day, once the ultimate in creative marketing, is no longer acceptable since being labelled (incorrectly) as sexist. When you sell group and season tickets to the extent clubs now do, you have direct contact with a large fraction of your customers in a way that wasn't possible or even thought worthwhile thirty years ago.

In the process, you gain a necessary command over large crowds, and that requires a different approach to policing than in the past, especially before the age of permissiveness about public behavior. If a team has a home attendance of 2.4 million, it's averaging 30,000 a night (and the major-league average club attendance in 1989 was over 2 million). In the old-old days, you were lucky to get 30,000 once a home stand, for some special occasion. Even as recently as 1970, the average club attendance for a year was less than 1.2 million, little more than half the current levels.

With a large crowd on hand at virtually every game, the opportunity for rowdiness is increased, and one way to combat it is to direct the energies of the masses—in other words, keep 'em busy. At the same time, marketing is geared to making a visit to the ballpark "a fun experience," not just a chance to root, root, root for the home team, and all this ancillary activity is part of the package. (I loved it when Pat Gallagher, in charge of such things for the San Francisco Giants, brought in a tiger from nearby Marine World Africa–U.S.A., for a pre-game romp around the outfield—and the big pussycat settled down in short-center field with a stubborn expression. It took expert persuasion to get him—I think it was a him—out, and I always ask Pat when he's going to have the tiger back. When the 1989 earthquake hit Candlestick Park just before a World Series game, I accused him of carrying promotional gimmicks too far.)

But that brings us back to ambience, in the sense of crowd participation. It is a precept of modern sports lore that "getting the crowd into the game" is a major goal and major advantage for the home team, and that its roar makes a difference to events on the field.

In basketball, I have no doubt that crowd noise affects the officiating. In football, the players keep saying it inspires them to greater suicidal effort (except when they can't hear the signals), and who am I to question their assertion? But I don't believe it means a lot in baseball—except to the extent, perhaps, that today's young players have been brainwashed into believing it helps and therefore it does. In fact, when I started covering baseball, the better players took professional pride in not being aware of crowds. No one denied that there's ego gratification in being cheered by thousands, but what really mattered was remaining focused on your play. They didn't need inspiration, just good execution. I imagine today's young people feel differently, just as they find displays of joy and formalized post-game congratulations a natural way to act. Their predecessors would have considered such actions bad taste and self-aggrandizement.

Baseball is not, as we have seen, explosive physical effort aided by excessive emotional highs (which produce inevitable emotional lows).

Tennis players and golfers, trying to concentrate on hitting a ball, demand—and get—quiet. Football players are trying to hit nothing smaller than a full-size (or outsize) human being. Basketball and hockey players are involved in nonstop frenzy while in action. But baseball players are engaged in fine-skill, high-concentration, split-second movements from a standing start, amid crowd noise that is allowed and encouraged, so they have to develop their shut-out-the-distraction mechanism more than their animal-response-to-cheers mechanism.

That doesn't mean crowd noise isn't important. To the television people, it's an essential background to their show. (In radio broadcasting, they used recorded crowd noise when recreating away games; it's needed the way a laugh track is needed for a comedy show.) Fans certainly enjoy believing that yelling helps their team win, and the crowd itself generates excitement.

One of the features of sports that attracts customers is the feeling one gets from being part of a festive gathering. And the crowd is conscious of this. As Red Smith liked to point out, every time a scoreboard flashes the news that "tonight's crowd of 38,417 is a record for this home stand," the assemblage invariably gives itself a nice round of applause.

But the players have work to do, between the lines.

For me, associations to a fairly empty ballpark are richest. Part of that is nostalgic resonance, since when I was going to New York ballparks as a child, they rarely had big crowds (and you could sit just about anywhere you wanted). But more important is my professional orientation. I arrive hours before game time, when it is echo-empty except for the people who work there, and I finish work long after the crowd has left. There's a strange kind of intimacy, a feeling of belonging, that's similar to being backstage in a theater. If the players think of their true habitat as "between the lines," I think of mine as "inside the gates."

And a lot goes on inside those gates besides ball games. As we shall see.

Behind the
SCENES

CHAPTER

11

The Media

Players perform the game. Club and league organizations make it possible for them to perform by creating the context. But the only reason for having a game at all, and the only way to make money out of it, is to let a large number of interested people know it is taking place, and how it came out.

That means that representatives of what we now call "the media" are every bit as essential to the whole enterprise as the players and the signers of checks. Without some way to convey information to the public about past, present, and prospective events, the entire activity would evaporate. Millions might still play ball games, as they do every day all over the world, but Organized Baseball as commercial mass entertainment could not exist without intermediaries to communicate with the masses wishing to be entertained.

"Media" is the plural of "medium," which means the instrumentality used to convey information. Radio waves are the medium by which radio and television are transmitted. Printed matter is the medium of newspapers and books. In this usage, "media" is short for "news media," a general term adopted a generation ago by publicity people careful not to insult newspaper and radio people getting the same release by having it labeled for one or the other.

(You can also say, as a clever ball player told me once, that "medium" means not rare and not well done, a perfect description of the baseball writer; but there are wise guys everywhere.)

Originally, newspapers were the only medium that counted, and the generic name was "the press." A natural alliance between baseball and the press was central to the development of both institutions in the nineteenth century. We'll get back to that. And a generation ago, when writing my book, I could neatly divide "the press box" (us knowledgeable, witty, humble, underpaid but independent daily-newspaper baseball writers) from "government radio" (those glib, hardworking, wildly overpaid celebrities who broadcast only the message their ball club and sponsors wanted them to) and make them separate chapters.

Of all the changes in baseball, however, the greatest has been in the nature of news media, baseball's relationship to it (somehow the word has become grammatically singular), and, indeed, the relationship of the media to the world at large. Today we need a different approach to the subject.

Consider four categories, in order of their importance to the baseball business: television, radio, newspapers, and other publications (meaning magazines and books).

Television brings you the actual event, as it unfolds, and makes you an insider with unprecedented intimacy: You get close-ups, replays, stop-action, the best possible viewing angles, and other insights never available from even the best seat in the ballpark—all accompanied by expert commentary in real time.

Radio also operates in real time, and delivers the same detailed information as television, but only as a verbal description: The mental images you form as a listener are determined entirely by your own experience and imagination.

Newspapers supply basic information about the games you didn't watch or hear when they occurred, as well as summaries, amplifications, and commentary concerning the ones you did. They also give you, in a small and convenient package, all sorts of related subject matter from outside the period of the game itself, in general "filling in the blanks."

(At this point, we're treating television and radio only in their play-by-play mode; sports segments of regular broadcasting news programs, or special features, overlap print media functions).

Magazines and books focus in greater depth on a small number of specific circumstances and personalities deemed of special interest, operating on an entirely different time scale.

Each serves its own primary purpose in baseball's scheme of things (as distinct from their own purposes), and we can make a table:

Medium	Mission	Direct Benefit
Television	Stimulate interest in future games and telecasts	Big bucks for broadcast rights
Radio	Sell tickets more directly	Smaller but significant bucks
Newspapers	Advertise (for free) upcoming broadcasts and game times	Circulation of information within the industry as well as to the public, maintaining continuity of interest
Magazines and Books	Incidental publicity	Virtually none

By far the most important difference is in the third column. Television and radio pay a fee, directly to the ball club, for the right to broadcast. They are co-producers of the event, partners of the management, with a direct stake in the event's commercial success. They have privileges they paid for, and exclusivity of a proprietary right. They are in the business they are describing.

The print media are not part of the business, have no comparable stake in its success, and assert their right to be present and cover a public event on journalistic grounds. They are not intrinsically entitled to cooperation (which they get because it is in the promoter's self-interest to give it), and have no obligation to "help" the promotion.

So it's not surprising that the practitioners of such diverse functions lead different lives, hold different attitudes, and are perceived differently.

By players, club officials, and most fans, newspaper reporters and columnists are seen as outsiders and natural enemies. They dig up "dirt," ask "stupid" (that is, embarrassing) questions, have no loyalty to the club, don't know what's "really" going on (having been kept in the dark by the assiduous efforts of those making the charge), and are interested only in creating trouble "to sell papers" (a particularly ludicrous misconception we'll deal with in a moment). Most players feel they must be always on guard in talking to the press, because they are sure to be misquoted—or, much worse, accurately quoted.

(All this applies, to a degree, to "independent" broadcasters, the ones doing news and features for local stations. The modifying factor is a player's sense of security when he talks into a microphone, feeling that at least only his own words and voice will be used. It's a naive comfort. Modern technology's vocabulary includes the word "splice.")

Broadcasters, on the other hand, are accepted as employees of the same organization as the players. (Network broadcasters, who show up sporadically and at major events, have the same relationship to the league as a whole as local play-by-play stations do to the individual club.) They can be trusted. Their loyalty is clear. If there is "dirt" they can be relied upon to suppress or at least offer justification for it. Often they give gifts or cash for brief interviews, and they are supplying "exposure," which can generate additional income and ego gratification. For a sympathetic shoulder to cry on, a broadcaster is as good as a family member (sometimes better), and a hostile broadcaster can be ignored with impunity because that position inhibits nasty comment—which the print people don't hesitate to make.

Self-images and behavioral patterns are equally far apart.

Broadcasters make much more money than writers, sometimes ten times as much. They are show-business personalities, recognizable by voice and face, asked for autographs, paid for personal appearances, and handled by agents and managers (and therefore sharing that experience with today's players). But their job security is nil: They serve at the whim of club, station, network, advertising agency, and sponsor managements. Like all peformers, they can go from star to has-been—or from nobody to star—in a moment.

They are primarily salesmen. They must have a knack, or develop a skill, for selling a product. They must be able to read commercials convincingly, plug ticket sales and "promos" (ads for other shows and allied products), and ad-lib tie-in product references. (They must toss in a "This Bud's for you" as individual wisdom dictates, and the wiser they are, the more often they do it.) Also, they must constantly sell themselves (figuratively) to the people who hire and fire them, and sell the drama of the game to keep the audience tuned in.

In addition, they are at the mercy of others while working. The announcer, while talking, wears a little earpiece through which come instructions, suggestions, corrections, second-guesses, and distractions from some program director. On television, whichever picture the director in the truck chooses to send (manager scratching his chin), the announcer must refer to it, no matter what other train of thought he may have started.

It takes a certain kind of personality and mental toughness to remain successsful in such a field—and considerable ability to adapt to the desires and demands of other people. They tend to be (or become) sensitive to atmosphere, political cross-currents, appearances, and pecking orders in ways newspaper people seldom have to. They fully earn whatever high pay they get.

But they are not, despite their eagerness to be seen that way, journalists. (Again, we're talking of game broadcasts, not news programs.) They lack the necessary presumption of disinterested objectivity. They take pride in being "impartial," but in the very use of that word (which is not the same as "objective") they reveal their consciousness of the partiality implicit in their position. And most have little journalistic background, where one's sense of objectivity and fact-checking is fostered by daily experience. The ex-players not only have none, but come from a lifetime of an "us-versus-them" environment; most non-player announcers rose through broadcasting ranks by displaying skills— selling, diction, quick and accurate eye-to-mouth reflexes—other than news judgment. Even those who come out of journalism schools seldom spend much time in news-gathering environments before moving into the play-by-play world.

Newspaper writers, especially those who remain in that field for any length of time, have a different viewpoint. They are certainly not more virtuous or intellectually honest; they are simply working in response to another set of imperatives. Newspapers, no less than the electronic media, live off advertising revenue, and the writer is "selling" his paper no less than the announcer is selling his program. But it's another sort of selling, with different consequences.

What sells a daily newspaper is habit, and the only thing that can create and keep the reader habit is long-term reliability and pertinence. Lively, objective reporting—of baseball or anything else—is needed to sell papers. So that's what employers demand, and what an effective reporter tries to supply. The myth about "sensationalizing the news to make headlines" had validity fifty years ago, when several newspapers competed for attention on the same corner newsstand and other means of news dissemination were not significant. In a radio-television age, with virtually no competitive newspaper situations in major cities—and no corner newsstands—shock headlines are useless. They still work on magazine covers and supermarket checkout-counter tabloids, but they don't affect the circulation or revenue potential of standard newspapers at all. Credibility is a newspaper's lifeblood; moment-to-moment drama—"don't touch that dial!" is now "don't zap the channel!"—is television's.

So the writer's long suit—irreverence—is essentially denied to the broadcaster, and the writer knows it. He sees himself (or she sees herself, now that we have many women working so well in sports) as something of an intellectual (compared to ball players, at least); ready to weigh, question, and doubt; willing to criticize, uninfluenced by considerations of friendship; more knowledgeable about the whole situation than those who wear one-club blinders; unswayed by emotion the way fans are; and witty, clever, literate, accurate, quick, honest, loyal (to his or her paper), and brave—ask any writer—but not necessarily courteous and kind. And never reverent.

This, too, takes a certain kind of personality, and those who find the above profile uncongenial move on to something else. Writers tend to care less about how they look and dress. (In television, those are crucial career considerations.) They revel in their independence: No director is telling them what to write while they're doing it, and second-guessing back at the office is relatively trivial. Their deadlines come up only a couple of times in every twenty-four hours, so they can organize their time and working procedures with great degrees of freedom. The ego satisfaction of a byline is not necessarily less than that of a screen credit, and the job security is terrific. Competent reporters may be shifted to more or less attractive assignments from time to time, but they don't get fired until and unless they do something really terrible.

Those are the seductive elements that keep them in the newspaper business. Many become bitter about the low pay, not only in comparison to their electronic counterparts, but, in the last twenty years, with respect to what the athletes have attained. Those who feel the broadcasters "do the same thing" are simply wrong, as we've just seen. And if you can perform the same service the $3-million ball player is providing, who's stopping you? But being a writer doesn't make one more logical than other humans, or less unreasonable in emotional response; it only means you *try* to be less unreasonable in what you write.

And the two groups follow different paths in their daily routines.

A writer comes to the ballpark two or three hours before game time, to circulate. He may spend some time in each clubhouse and dugout, talking to players and managers. He may do so out around the batting cage. And he may sit around the press hospitality room until game time, visiting with other media types, scouts, club employees, and whoever else hangs around that cozy facility.

During the game, he or she will probably be in the press box, a mezzanine-level area restricted for their use. In old ballparks, it may be cramped and uncomfortable, in newer ones anything from not quite adequate to sumptuous, but what counts is a chair, a little desk space, and a vantage point behind home plate and reasonably high. This is not necessarily the best or most enjoyable angle for watching a baseball game; the scouts watch pitching down at ground level, and being near first or third base is closer to the action and more fun. But to cover a game, you don't need the best possible look at some plays, at the cost of a poor look at others. You need a reasonably good look at *all* plays that can arise, and the traditional press-box location provides that.

The ambience of press boxes has changed tremendously in the last twenty years. It used to be more lively, more informal, more congenial, more exclusive, and much noisier. The Baseball Writers Association of America, formed in 1908 expressly to demand and protect working facilities for writers, won dominion of major-league press boxes and guarded them jealously for more than half a century: no women, no radio people, no unauthorized visitors, no free-lance authors, and very few inhibitions. When Western Union (long since gone) started replacing male telegraphers with women teletype operators in the 1950s, the gender line was broken. As local radio and free-lancers proliferated, their legitimate needs had to be met somehow. As teams moved into new cities, local politicians and power brokers could not be resisted. And, most of all, as clubs developed large and highly capable public relations departments, they inevitably took control of all facilities.

Meanwhile, the "regular" writer population was dwindling as so many big-city newspapers went out of business, while suburban papers (covering less consistently and often only at home) grew. Newspaper editors began shifting assignments more frequently, and writers were given major-league beats at an earlier age more often. Both tradition and practicality lost their force. Today, the BBWAA still has its rights in theory, but in practice press boxes are run by club P.R. personnel (with due deference to established perks and procedures).

But the P.R. department's prime concern is—correctly—to keep everybody satisfied, not just beat writers. And its chief effort has to be directed at radio and television, on the air live for all three hours of the game. So the public-address system announcements given to the press box are full of material chosen for its radio-TV suitability, which the print media get as a by-product.

When I started out, in the late 1940s, the only statistics most writers had were the ones they kept themselves. (A "pitcher's book," recording results and statistical highlights of each day's games, took about an hour of homework to keep up.) But because of radio, which needed elaborate statistics on every batter (to fill time), a club statistician would mimeograph such a sheet every day, and we would get it too. In time, a page of "notes" was added. But as late as the 1970s, two mimeographed sheets from each team constituted the "handout." Nowadays, thanks to computers and duplicating machines, when I go to a press box I get twelve sheets of paper printed on both sides—twenty-four pages!—of stats and notes. No matter how disciplined the writer tries to be, he winds up using too many of them—but the consumers, conditioned by the electronic media and their other life experiences, seem to like them. Tastes, as well as conditions, do change.

During a game, the writer keeps score, chats, makes notes, grumbles, exchanges jokes, (dozes?), and consumes coffee, soft drinks, ice cream, hot dogs, or whatever other food is made available. If it's a night game and he works for a morning paper, he probably has to write some "running"—an account of innings in progress—that will be replaced later by a complete story.

When the game ends, he rushes down to the clubhouse, collects a few necessary quotes, and comes back upstairs to produce his final story. It will usually be less than 1,000 words, but he'll also send a "notes" story or "sidebar" of less than that. An hour or two after the game, he's ready to leave. He has been in the ballpark approximately seven hours.

Since all newspapers became computerized, the writer uses a portable terminal (there are many models, most smaller than a portable typewriter used to be). There are telephones and telephone jacks to which the terminal can be connected—when the story is written and ready for transmission—for sending to the office. Is this a faster way to get stories in? Not really. The telegraphers who used to send my stuff a paragraph or a page at a time sent the last word only moments after I'd typed it. What's incomparably faster is the process inside the newspaper office. The old way, it had to be reproduced on paper and given to a typesetter who operated a linotype machine, and then the metal type had to be gathered into page forms. This way, the story goes directly from the portable terminal through the phone line into the central computer, which zips it into type ready to be photographed.

The toughest part is a day game after a night game. You get to the park at, let's say, 5 P.M. Friday, leave at midnight, and you have to be back there at about 10 A.M. Saturday. That's not so bad at home but complications arise on the road, especially if time zones are involved. But few of today's writers are asked to work eight straight months, from spring training through World Series, with only an occasional day off, the way earlier generations did. Extra days off after a road trip, and even in-season vacation weeks, have become standard; and since the worst scheduling abuses have been eliminated by the Players Association, the writers and other camp followers also escape some of the unreasonable routines that typified the 1960s.

The radio-TV folks work only a few feet away, but in a different world. If there is a favored location—directly in line with the batter and pitcher—it will be given to television more often than not. Broadcasters get a little more desk and leg room in their booths, but they do have to share space with the engineer, producer, and perhaps an ad agency representative. The floor is a snake pit of wires and cables. But a broadcasting booth's occupancy is strictly limited to people who belong there, because its principals are actually performing—live— not simply preparing to write.

The distinction between radio and television announcing has been pretty much washed out. On club broadcasting crews, most members take turns at each medium, although they do have main assignments. The general pattern is: All games, home and away, are on radio; many road games are televised back to the home city; in most places, few if any home games are televised free, but in cities that have superstations (local stations sending their programs nationwide to cable systems) most home games are—New York (WWOR), Atlanta (TBS), Chicago (WGN), for instance. In other cases, home games are carried directly on cable in their own areas, to customers who pay for the service.

So a club may have from four to eight broadcasters involved in various program packages and a large support staff of camera operators and technicians.

A broadcaster's pre-game activity on the field and in the clubhouse is much like a writer's, except when pre-game interviews (live or taped for later use) must be done. He must be in place in the booth well before the first pitch; a writer does not have to be.

During the game, there is no comparison: The broadcaster is on. He must maintain a level of concentration writers don't need and seldom attain. He must be "in the game" the way a player is, paying attention to every pitch. This is not only harder work, but it leaves the broadcaster with more specific knowledge and sharper evaluations of every player than most writers ever achieve—especially if the broadcaster is an ex-player. The price (and there is always a price) may be less sense of perspective, the habit of seeing the trees and not the forest. What's more, the broadcaster has no eraser or "delete" key: Anything and everything he says goes to the public, live, instantly. Mangled syntax, mispronunciations, outright mistakes, silly observations, malaprops—all are out there for critics to jump upon.

In the course of a game, a broadcaster may speak 20,000 to 30,000 words—perhaps 50 of these book pages—without being able to take anything back. A writer will file perhaps 2,000 a day, and the ones that reach the public have gone through his own second thoughts and a couple of editors. Picking on broadcaster errors, therefore, always seems to me to be a particularly cheap shot.

And broadcasters learn to be less upright about imperfections as time goes on. Tim McCarver, doing a Met game from Dodger Stadium one time, made me an admirer when he said, "There's a long fly to left field" while the camera clearly showed the shortstop camped under the pop fly and taking one step in. As the ball came down, McCarver said, without missing a beat, "And the wind blows it all the way back in to the shortstop." Ralph Kiner, his partner, could be heard chuckling. The camera went immediately to the center-field flag pole and showed the flag, as limp as possible, hanging down enfolding the pole. McCarver, following the lead of the monitor and the rule that the words must refer to the picture, took it completely in stride.

"Look at that," he said. "That wind is blowing straight down."

But this difference—the publication's ability to make a correction before the error is public—goes to the heart of the functional difference between the media. The broadcaster, like the camera, must bring you what happens as it happens, not knowing what will happen next: the essence of reactivity. The writer can, and must, select what to pass on after he knows how everything came out: the essence of editing. The broadcaster cannot use editorial judgment; the writer must. So writers have more practice at deciding what's important and sifting out from a mass of impressions; broadcasters have to give you all they can as it occurs whether it turns out to be important or not.

After a game (or after a post-game show), the broadcaster is finished, but a writer's actual work is just beginning. That's a time advantage for the broadcaster. But what the broadcaster faces every day that writers do not is the dread institution known as "meetings." Radio and television people have meetings every time they turn around, and at a big event like the World Series, the announcers may be called to a breakfast meeting, a pre-game meeting, a post-game meeting, and then a pre-breakfast meeting. Their producers and directors make game plans as seriously as football coaches. Even when that little earpiece isn't plugged in, a broadcaster is never far from Big Brother's voice.

Chuck Milton (that's Charles H. Milton III) was much younger and lower in the CBS hierarchy when he went down to do a spring training Yankee game in 1967, when CBS also owned the Yankees. His sports broadcasting experience as a director had been mostly with National Football League games. He sought out manager Ralph Houk in the dugout well before game time.

"Can you tell us your game plan today?" asked Chuck, wanting to be fully prepared.

Houk gave him a funny look, then said, "Well, I think we'll try to keep it close for a while, and I'll have my starter throw three scoreless innings, then have Pepitone hit a three-run homer around the fifth, and pull away after that."

Chuck seemed to be drinking it all in until we started to laugh. We still tease him about it. But he was merely being conscientious.

And over the years, I found out why the person in charge of a show is called a "producer." It's because he makes such a big production out of everything.

Disparity of function naturally produces conflict of interest. The electronic reporters want immediacy, and carry equipment—from a handheld microphone to bulky cameras, lights, and sound booms—to transmit what they get instantly. The newspaper story can't be delivered to the reader until hours later. So the two groups get in each other's way, physically. As a writer, what I want is as relaxed a conversational exchange as possible, to promote frankness and specificity. The microphone people want the actual voice of the player, no matter how vapid his remarks. In the jostling for position, the writers lost, long ago.

Why did they lose? Because the original baseball-newspaper alliance has lost importance. It still exists, but on a reduced scale.

Professional baseball started to take shape in the later 1860s, right after the Civil War, at a time when the modern newspaper was also just beginning to take on forms familiar to us. Baseball promoters needed exposure to advertise their games. Newspapers needed stories that would interest readers day after day. As more spectator interest developed, and as games became scheduled every day, the two needs meshed. To find out how yesterday's game came out, you had to buy the paper, and there was a new game every day for six months. But every account of yesterday's game was a large free ad for today's and tomorrow's. A growing audience for baseball would mean not only more ticket buyers but more newspaper buyers.

Both sets of businessmen were fully aware of these advantages. Clubs welcomed writers and gladly picked up the expenses for a road trip, provided them with a working area (the press box), helped them arrange transmission facilities, and—most important—insisted that their managers and players make themselves accessible to this publicity-generating process. Newspapers welcomed the prestige they acquired as insiders in "the national game," and while they gleefully ridiculed individuals and losing teams, they rarely if ever attacked the *existence* of a local team or its business practices.

The next step, solidifying the alliance, was the most natural of all. By serving each other's interests, they had created and were magnifying a venue for holding public attention—and politicians zeroed in on the opportunity to bask in reflected glory. Speaking well of the local club was a way to reach voters. Attending a game (like Opening Day) not only displayed the politician before a large crowd, but got his name and possibly a picture into the paper. Newspapers and politicians, no less than club owners, wanted baseball to thrive—and all benefited when it did.

And until the 1960s, club managements understood that newspapers were their lifeblood, and treated them with appropriate deference. Once television got rolling, however, the world changed—not just baseball, but everything in commercial and political life as well.

Television needed baseball for the same reason newspapers did at first: to sell sets. It had to ride piggyback on something already popular. To do that, it was willing to pay a lot of money for exclusive rights. In the nineteenth century, baseball and newspapers were growing simultaneously, from small-money beginnings. In the middle of the twentieth century, both were the Establishment that television had to buy into.

Once it did, however, and began reaching enough people, it emerged as the dominant force. The exposure that baseball had been able to get only from newspapers was now available, more vividly, by means of television—which was also paying ever greater sums of money for the privilege. It became of much less concern to ball clubs what newspapers did about them; it became essential to cement the new alliance with television, because if baseball didn't, someone else would—as baseball found out when the NFL took off in the 1960s.

Oddly enough, this didn't make newspapers (of which there were fewer, but the survivors more powerful than ever) unimportant. It simply shifted their usefulness. Yesterday's game story as an advertisement for today's game is a way of plugging today's telecast. One of the things radio and television outlets pay for when they buy broadcasting rights is the fact that their program—the ball game—will be written about in the papers every day. You can't get coverage like that for a sitcom or miniseries, or occasional events like the Olympics (which hold the stage only for a few weeks every four years). So ball clubs still prize their newspaper connection, and are not prepared to abandon it. But in any conflict between the demands of television and anything else—starting time, clubhouse access, credentials, work locations—the decision is in favor of television every time.

Finally, there is the famous "press room," now totally misnamed. It is a "hopsitality room" used by the club for club purposes, to which the press is also admitted almost incidentally. Press rooms were that, originally: some spot in the ballpark where writers could gather, store equipment, and write post-game stories when open-air press boxes made it impractical to go back up there after a night game. And it was natural enough to supply a few drinks and a little food for the working stiffs trapped so long inside a ballpark, and a congenial place for management and a couple of coaches to drop in on the way home. When Larry MacPhail took over the Brooklyn Dodgers in 1938 and began revolutionizing baseball promotion in many ways, the press room—"Larry's Saloon"—was one of his pioneering efforts.

Like Rock Hunter, the press room was spoiled by its success. After World War II, it became central headquarters for all those who had business with the ball club: their own office force, the radio and television technicians, the advertising agency reps, visiting scouts, equipment salesmen, visiting celebrities, local politicians, free-lancers. As night games became prevalent, it made sense (and was plain decency) to serve a better meal to people whose duties gave them no other choice but concession-stand hot dogs. The better the facility was made, the better it stimulated conversation and information exchange, the more it acquired an insider's glamour, the larger proportion of its population became people other than "the press." In today's press rooms, club employees outnumber newspaper people about three to one.

But that, too, is evolution at work. And one of the inescapable changes is that every individual grows older.

When I was a young writer, first breaking in, and got assigned to a big glamorous sports event, the question that would come to my mind was, "Will they give me one of the really good seats in the main press box?"

Later, as my priorities changed, the first question was, "Do they have real good food in the press room?"

Later, the first question became: "Do they have an elevator?"

Eventually, I reached Stage 4. "Will the seat they give me make it easy to get to the rest room?"

There's a fifth stage, which comes in two segments. "If I doze off, (1) will anybody notice? And (2) do I care if they do?"

CHAPTER
12

The Road

Baseball, like any sport, has incessant travel built into it—there must be a visiting team for every game. Baseball life "on the road" used to be special and unusual to a greater degree than it is now. Travel requirements have not changed; the rest of the world has. The kind of perpetual movement baseball involves is no longer so unusual, since millions of other business people do it routinely. And the special qualities that went with being part of a tight-knit group experiencing common hardships and joys have become greatly attenuated, if not destroyed, by affluence and individuality.

Federico Fellini's beautiful film *La Strada (The Road)* was reviewed by A. H. Weiler for *The New York Times* in 1956 with this comment: "Like life itself, it is seemingly aimless, disjointed on occasion and full of truth and poetry. Like the principals, it wanders along a sad and sometimes comic path while accentuating man's loneliness and need for love."

That's the road, all right.

Loneliness is the element unappreciated, or never understood, by those who know all other facets of baseball but have not lived this one. Just as conquering fear is the fundamental but rarely cited basis of hitting, handling loneliness is the fundamental unmentionable of baseball life. It takes all sorts of forms, but the underlying condition is always there: You are spending your time separated from the people and circumstances you prefer, not occasionally but endlessly. If you can't learn to deal with the feelings and situations that creates, you can't stay in the profession and be effective—as player, as coach, as writer, as broadcaster, or as anything else.

It is common enough to acknowledge the "fatigue factor" in being on the road: jet lag, disrupted routines, uncomfortable hotel beds, irregular meals, and so forth. This is true enough. But the real problem is "mental fatigue." The hours between the end of one game and the start of the next, as well as those spent in transit, can be totally purposeless, in personal terms, unless one makes a conscious effort to resist the sense of drift. The perpetual cycle of be here at such-and-such a time (and don't be late), then be there at another exact time, with little obligatory activity in between and always the awareness of the disconnection from spouse, children, friends, and personal interests—it wears you down.

We combat such pressures the way people always have. Some do more drinking. Some men chase women (and, as we have come to acknowledge, not only women). Some start nonstop card games. Some stare at television. Some eat too much and too often. Some get irritable, others withdrawn. Some strengthen their religious leanings. Some get into serious trouble with local authorities. Some use drugs other than alcohol. Some—few—use the time productively to read, study, sightsee, meet new people, and broaden their personalities.

But no one is unaffected. No one follows the same life pattern that person would in a live-at-home situation most of us consider normal.

In baseball, all this stultifying instability is magnified. For most players, the road is a double whammy. Their "home city"—of the team they work for—usually is not their actual home, so in effect they are on the road for eight months once spring training begins. They may bring their wives and children to stay with them during two summer months, when there is no school back at their real home, but this is still camping out and anyhow, half of that time, the players are traveling elsewhere. And for many younger players, who play winter ball in the Caribbean or go to various development camps, it's a twelve-month cycle.

In football, a team averages only two days "away" every two weeks in a four-month schedule after a month of training camp. In basketball and hockey, it's worse in one way—every trip is a one-night stand—but not as bad in another, since you don't play every day (the average is a little more than three a week). Tennis players and golfers, as independent contractors, may be circling the globe all year long, but it's a week at every stop and they can control their own arrangements.

It's the persistence of the baseball grind—play every day, move on every third day if on the road, rarely stay longer than ten days at home—that intensifies these effects.

A great compensating factor is togetherness: You're part of a team, either directly or more tenuously but significantly as a writer. Or it should be. But this has been greatly weakened over the years. Let me cite eight reasons: air travel, affluence, electronic communication, social friction, fewer newspapers, player-writer hostility, night games, and expansion.

When virtually all games were played in the afternoon and all travel was by train, togetherness was fostered automatically. On a train, people mingle in club cars, diners, and pullman seats, all conducive to conversation and continuing the card games. Trains arrive and leave from midtown locations, near hotels reached by cabs (shared) or a short walk. In the hotel, before day games, most tended to have breakfast in the same coffee shop at more or less the same time, and to hang around the lobby before going to the ballpark. After a game, there was an evening in which to socialize—go out to dinner, take in a movie, visit friends, prowl bars, whatever—and much lobby traffic going and coming. Groups and cliques not only formed naturally, but became easily identifiable. Almost everyone knew what everyone else was doing.

But there was more. Every player had a roommate (an economic necessity). Limited meal money restricted the places players would go. And—this is *very* important—writers and players belonged essentially to the same economic class; that is, the difference in their earning power wasn't so great that their life-styles were incompatible. They had the same attitudes about what was expensive, the same concerns about how their families were living, and respected one another as fellow wage-earners—some better off than others, and a few (like Babe Ruth) out of the reach of others, but in their own minds all were part of the same business and the same level of society.

Another factor was shameful, and can't be justified retroactively, but was a fact of life: It was an all-white, all-male environment, by and large oblivious to what that meant. It was an indefensible affront to the excluded, which had enormous social costs. But it did make easier the in-group mentality of those included.

Finally, there were only ten major-league cities, half of them with a team in each league. You kept returning to the same small number of places every few weeks: the Chase Hotel in St. Louis, the Kenmore in Boston, the Book Cadillac in Detroit. You got to know the security people, the secretaries, the ushers, and other ballpark and hotel personnel through frequent contact—and telegraphers, headwaiters, fans, even some taxi drivers. And, of course, you came across other teams' players and writers again and again after relatively brief intervals.

Such conditions fostered togetherness. Today's conditions destroy it.

Air travel, even in charters, is an isolating experience: You stay in your own seat. As I have often written, a train is a rolling hotel, a plane is a flying bus; where would you rather spend your time? And you don't share cabs to airports and ballparks, you ride a team bus—and most clubs segregate writers (and broadcasters) in their own bus. And airports, during waiting time, are less conducive to mingling than movie-palace-style railroad stations used to be.

Hotels are different, too. Many don't have lobbies, and nobody hangs out in them. The television set, the ice/soft-drink/snack machines, and redecoration have shifted the focus of hotel life to inside one's room. And each room has one occupant, since the players have won the right to have a private room if they want one, and at a $500,000-a-year average salary level can afford to pay the difference. They can also afford all the room service they want, obtaining still more privacy.

Players are now in the celebrity category, not just by being indentifiable (they were always that) but by adopting the life-style of the rich and famous. Each has a coterie—agent, business manager, accountant, barber, gofer, relatives, business partners—with a stake in that player's mood, importance, and prosperity, just as movie stars did in Hollywood's heyday. Younger players who haven't reached that stage of income yet take for granted that they want to and will, and see themselves as members of a class who simply haven't got there yet.

What can such people, in their twenties and early thirties, feel in common with a fortyish sportswriter who doesn't even earn a six-figure salary? If the writer had anything on the ball, wouldn't he be doing better? And since I'm so important, and make so much money (which proves it), and get paid for just signing my name and for indirect uses of it, isn't the writer simply a parasite using my words and my importance to enhance his stories? Because I am a fine person, I'll be polite and friendly, and cooperate when convenient, but who really needs these creeps?

Such attitudes are no antidote to road loneliness (not even for the player, although he seldom realizes that). And the reaction of the writers is predictable: Who needs *those* creeps? They ask the questions they have to (pad or tape recorder in hand), transact all necessary business, maintain surface friendliness (as a professional necessity)—and go their own way. Q.E.D.

And their new working conditions promote isolation. When transmission was by Western Union or some other intermediary, you had to stay in the ballpark to file, or, after writing in your room, take the story to a Western Union office. Now you plug your laptop computer into your phone, and never leave the room.

Furthermore, night ball leaves you with nowhere to go. Even the players don't get away from the ballpark until 11 P.M. or so after a 7:30 game; writers finish work after midnight. Good restaurants have closed. Movies or shows are out of the question. Local acquaintances have gone to bed. Even room service shuts down in most hotels. You can find a bar, a coffee shop, or trouble—or turn on the TV and go to bed. You certainly don't dare go out for a walk. The high-income ball players or broadcaster may arrange a party in his room or suite (yes, suite), but he's selective about who's invited.

Writers are also more isolated because they are fewer in number, and a journalistic in-culture that used to exist is no more. When New York had ten papers in the city proper, and half a dozen suburbans, the traveling party (with each of three clubs) was a dozen writers or so, and at most three broadcasters. Now there may be four or five beat writers on a trip, while broadcasters flit in and out (from a group of ten) according to how the over-the-air, cable, network, and other schedule determinants work. Socializing with players and coaches was always a very limited part of life on the road for writers; now their own in-group is reduced, and they don't seem to like each other as much anyhow.

Concerns change. What you worried about, each time you were assigned to a hotel room, used to be: Does it have air conditioning? Does the radio (later TV) work? Now the key questions are: Does it have a three-prong outlet for my computer terminal? Does the phone have a removable jack, or is it the right shape for my transmission attachment? Does this hotel give bonus frequent-flyer points?

This last has become a dominant theme. The custom is that a team makes all travel arrangements, simply adding the name of the assigned writer to its ticket and hotel room lists, and eventually bills the paper—a bookkeeping exchange that makes no difference whatever to the writer, who would get his expenses paid anyhow. (In the old days, clubs picked up the tab by never forwarding the bill. When newspapers became fewer but more prosperous, and ball clubs less dependent on their publicity, both sides discovered that this was unethical.)

Since bonus mileage, however, many writers insist on making their own flight arrangements (which they have every right to do) and hand in their own expense accounts, and sometimes choose different hotels than the club stays at. This, too, does not promote togetherness.

And our society, in general, is more fragmented than it used to be.

It's idle to pretend racial and ethnic frictions aren't common. They are. In the past, blacks were simply excluded and Latins were few. Now blacks and Latins make up perhaps a third of the major-league population. But blacks, whites, Latins, and others haven't been getting along with one another all that well in our central cities, suburbs, and work places for many years, and tend to socialize within their own groups and cultures when left alone. Why should it be—how could it be—any different in sports? Even within the white community, we have more group antagonisms than we used to: generation gaps, Yuppies, militant Christians. Diversity, not melting pot, is the theme of our time. In baseball too.

Then came expansion. In the American League, each team visits every other team only twice a year—six days out of 180 in each of 13 non-home cities.That also means only six days of contact with any set of visitors to your city. When a league had 200 players on eight teams crossing paths eight times a year, you had a fair chance to "know everybody"—or at least most of those important to you. In a 14-team league with 350 players (and more on disabled lists instead of back in the minors), encountered at most four times, you don't develop the same range of familiarity. And the same is true, of course, with respect to coaches, other writers, broadcasters, and non-baseball contacts in those cities.

Does all this sound as if baseball life is less fun?

I think it is less fun. I think neither the players nor the writers, nor all others in the expanded industry, get as much pleasure from the life they lead. Not less fun from what they do: Players love playing the game just as much, writers and fans love following and analyzing it, business people enjoy being proficient. But the ambience is less attractive. The atmosphere is more tense, testy, and antagonistic, on all sides. The big money is one reason—so much more is at stake that a paradox arises. On the one hand, players (and clubs) have a degree of economic security no one dreamed possible twenty years ago; on the other hand, maintaining the position attained is a great psychological pressure, making one more sensitive to vague, undefined threats (that is, change) even when direct challenge (to job security) isn't there.

Fun, of course, is not the be-all and end-all of life's activities (a sentiment with which, I imagine, many would not agree). The effectiveness of baseball operation is incomparably greater than it was twenty or forty years ago, and the difficulty of winning no less. Travel is more routine and more necessary than ever, but generally less pleasant. An inherently itinerant activity is bound to be less satisfying. The trouble with a technology that makes it possible to go much farther much faster is that it entices you to schedule activities you couldn't attempt before. My friend Harold Rosenthal, who was covering the Brooklyn Dodgers for the *Herald Tribune* when I first started to work on the desk there in 1948, came across a sociologist's statement he treasured: "The incidence of immorality among itinerant workers is highest."

"What that means," said Harold, "is that the road will make a bum out of the best of them."

It's true. Only now it makes a tired and grumpy bum.

CHAPTER
13

Noncombatants

One of the oldest show-business jokes and one of the most obvious military clichés contain truths too easily overlooked. The cliché is: For every soldier actually in combat, up to ten support troops are needed, engaged in supply, repair, transport, training, reserve, and so forth. The joke is the one about the fellow who cleans up after the elephants in the circus parade, complaining about his smelly, boring job. "Why don't you quit?" he's asked. "What, and leave show business?" he replies.

The truth is this: A lot has to be done by people out of the limelight to produce whatever it is the audience is paying attention to, and much of it is not pleasurable.

In baseball, the support troops are many and varied, and have become systematized according to their responsibilities. We'll look at (1) the medical establishment, (2) the quartermaster corps (supply and repair), (3) transport, (4) administration, and (5) the public relations department. We'll take them in reverse order.

Public relations is an elaborate profession that has grown, in the last fifty years or so, out of what used to be called, condescendingly, the "publicity man" or "press agent." Their role used to be the simple and straightforward one of getting attention—free advertising—to drum up business for the sale of tickets or patent medicine. The free, as distinct from paid-for, advertising need remains basic. But techniques and standards have been refined and expanded. And P.R. personnel nowadays spends as much effort on shepherding players to appointments, servicing executives and visiting V.I.P.s, and processing statistics and releases as on direct contact with media people.

Once upon a time a designated club official, usually the road secretary, performed the additional chore of notifying the press when the team had something to announce: a trade, a signing, the start of a ticket sale, yesterday's attendance, things like that. When only newspapers were involved, that was enough. When radio came in, the volume of work (including statistics) increased, and teams began hiring a full-time publicity man, usually a former baseball writer.

By now, every major-league team has an entire department handling its relations with the outside world, and "publicity" is only one aspect. The Dodgers, who pioneered and excelled at P.R. activities even before they left Brooklyn for Los Angeles, can be used to illustrate contemporary practice. They had, in 1989, the following job titles that speak for themselves:

Vice-president, communications.

Director, marketing and promotions.

Director, publications.

Director, publicity.

In addition, a community-relations unit consisted of three famous former players: Don Newcombe (director), Roy Campanella, and Lou Johnson.

And all these had appropriate (but overworked, of course) assistants and secretaries.

"Community relations" refers to the equivalent of social work: As club representatives, these people interact with the general population on a nonspecific, goodwill, public-service basis. They give talks and make appearances at schools, clubs, award dinners, gatherings of all kinds. They talk baseball, but not only to plug the Dodgers. Newcombe, for example, is a recovered alcoholic who is eloquent about recovery and prevention programs. This is not a commercially oriented effort: It is a corporation trying to be a "good citizen" to generate positive feelings toward itself. It hopes for (and gets) favorable fallout in political and business affairs, but it doesn't measure the department's value by ticket sales.

The publicity director travels with the team, deals daily with the regular writers and broadcasters, issues statements and information (collating and distributing those twenty-four pages of statistics), and handles seating problems and transmission equipment requests. He does the job that, thirty years ago, was the "publicity man's" whole job.

"Publications" refers to the press guide (once a 32-page pamphlet, now often more than 200 pages thick), elaborate yearbooks, promotional brochures, and so forth.

"Marketing and promotions" means stimulating ticket sales directly by arranging for the special shows (Bat Day, Cap Day, Camera Day, guest celebrities to sing the national anthem and throw out the first ball) and laying the groundwork for group and season sales (supplying speakers, especially in the off-season; maintaining liaison with surrounding smaller communities and special-interest groups throughout the area; selling club identity any way possible).

Above all that, the communications vice-president deals with policy: Along what lines will we carry out these tasks? What are our basic attitudes and accepted procedures to be? How do we accommodate (or influence) policies being handed down by the league and the commissioner's office? What political or press relations problems are we having? And (this one is always the bottom line) are we keeping the boss happy?

This Dodger pattern nowadays is typical rather than exceptional. Teams vary in effectiveness and effort (just as they do on the field) but all perform these functions somehow. And the Montreal Expos do it in two languages. Ron Piche and Jean-Pierre Roy were not only their "public relations representatives" but simultaneously their "relationnistes."

Arthur (Red) Patterson was one of the most energetic and creative developers of present standard practices. Before World War II he was a baseball writer for the *New York Herald Tribune*. When Larry MacPhail bought and took charge of the New York Yankees in 1945, he brought in Red as his publicity man. Some years later, Red switched to the Dodgers, went with them to Los Angeles, and was vital in laying the foundations of their tremendous success. Later, he became a top executive with the Angels in Anaheim. One of his early experiences indicates the scope, and possible frustration, of the P.R. experience.

When night games were still few and therefore special events (a team played only seven or fourteen a year at home), Patterson would dream up pre-game shows. One of his Yankee Stadium promotions was a dog show, prompted by his background associations formed while covering Madison Square Garden dog shows for the *Trib*. A former colleague on the *Trib*, Rud Rennie, was now covering the Yankees. They hadn't always enjoyed warm relations as colleagues and didn't at that time. The dog show was a big event: Red went all out, got a great cross section of fancy breeds, equally fancy handlers to march them around, a red carpet, and exciting competition for "best in show." It tapped into the trappings of "suburban society" when that had an aura of prestigious respectability hard to recall nowadays, and therefore lent "class" to baseball. Also, Red was eager to score points with his superiors by showing how much attention this unusual extravaganza could generate. So he pressed all the writers, including Rennie, to devote decent space to describing this rare and fascinating departure from simply the announcement of tonight's batteries. Rennie had a purist's attitude toward baseball, and was permanently affected by someone who had compared his spare writing style to Hemingway's.

Here is Rennie's note, in its entirety, as I processed it on the *Trib* sports desk:

"Dogs performed before the game."

The administration of a modern ball club is large in other areas. Here's the table of organization of the San Francisco Giants:

Administration—chairman (owner Bob Lurie); president and general manager (Al Rosen); executive vice-president; senior vice-president; staff counsel; government-affairs broadcast coordinator; three staff assistants.

Baseball Operations—three vice-presidents (baseball operations, assistant general manager, scouting operations); three directors (travel, player development, minor-league and scouting operations); special assistants (Willie Mays, Willie McCovey, Orlando Cepeda); four staff assistants.

Accounting/Finance—vice-president, finance; accounting manager; assistant accounting manager; payroll/benefits administrator; accounts payable.

Tickets—vice-president; three administrative staff members.

Public Relations—vice-president; three directors (media relations, graphics and photography, community services); assistant director of media relations; community representative; administrative assistant.

Marketing/Promotions—director of marketing; promotions manager; director of sales; sales representative; data coordinator; sales/administration; secretary.

Retail—director; distribution manager/buyer; retail sales/merchandising manager; information systems; retail operations assistant; warehouse manager; mail order; three Dugout Stores managers.

Stadium Operations—vice-president, stadium operations/security; assistant director; guest relations coordinator; maintenance (four people); secretary; switchboard operator.

GiantsVision (cable telecasts and operation of electronic scoreboard and message boards)—eleven people.

Clubhouse—four people.

And that doesn't include some twenty-five scouts and ten to fifteen minor-league managers, coaches, and instructors.

When Bob Fishel succeeded Red Patterson as the "publicity director" of the Yankees, he put out their first press guide (thirty-six pages) in 1956. It listed a total of sixteen people as executives, starting with "Co-owners" (Dan Topping and Del Webb) and ending with "Manager" (Casey Stengel). At that point, the Yankees had won seven pennants and six World Series in the preceding nine seasons.

Time marches on.

The transportation responsibility, of course, goes back to baseball's beginnings and has retained its overwhelming importance. The generic title is "road secretary," a job awesome in its responsibility and bewildering in its detail. Arranging for planes, buses, hotel accommodations, and individual travel needs of players and officials is only the beginning. In a real sense, the road secretary is everybody's nursemaid and problem solver, although not quite to the same extent as before the business became so departmentalized. In the old days, the road secretary was the ball club's chief contact with the outside world. (During Prohibition, he was also the caretaker of the bottle.) The scope of the road secretary's burdens has narrowed, but the routine tasks have expanded enormously in complexity and number. And it's still the road secretary who handles complementary ticket requests for the players and others, and who collects the check for the visiting team's share (and reviews turnstile counts) at every stop.

But the road secretary doesn't look after the luggage, equipment trunks, and other paraphernalia. The traveling clubhouse man does that.

The clubhouse man and his assistants preside over the care and provision of bats, shined shoes, repaired gloves, and all necessary clubhouse supplies (including food, chewing gum, and clean uniforms). They are proficient at sewing (including names and numbers on uniforms), laundry, handling messages, keeping order, doing housekeeping, and being discreet. If every country's military and civilian officials were as reliably close-mouthed as clubhouse men, all the spy establishments in the world would get nowhere.

They are also the first line of defense in clubhouse security, keeping out people who don't belong and monitoring the hallway activities of legitimate salesmen of equipment and trinkets, whose presence players welcome.

Baseball has developed its own customs concerning equipment. A player is supposed to supply his own shoes and gloves at his own expense, although at the major-league level he gets such items free from manufacturers in return for his endorsement. The club pays for bats, but the individual player orders them from a manufacturer who follows his exact specifications. The uniform (including batting helmet) is provided entirely at club expense. So are baseballs, which are not guarded as zealously as they used to be by a coach or clubhouse man. Mail is sorted into boxes (or sometimes large cartons) by the clubhouse man, but dealing with it is entirely the individual player's responsibility.

But it's the medical corps that is by far the most important unit of all. The most intimate place on any ball club, the inner sanctum sanctorum, is the rubbing table, and the trainer is its high priest.

To the outside world, a trainer is perhaps the least noticed and certainly the least-thought-about person in the ballpark. Even the batboys get more attention, because they are more frequently visible. What most fans see is a figure in long white pants, running out to administer first aid whenever a player gets hurt during the game, and they pay no more attention to him, once he disappears again, than to a groundskeeper.

To ball players, it's entirely different. The trainer is the man who takes care of their most important asset: their bodies. He is also, if he is a good trainer, a potential father confessor. If a player has any brains at all—and there are players who don't—he will be completely honest with any trainer he trusts, and will reveal and discuss many a minor ailment he wants to hide even from his manager. Proper care for a small injury soon enough can often prevent more serious trouble, without forcing the player out of action; neglect, or failure to follow prescribed treatment, can have crippling consequences.

The wise manager, too, relies completely on a trainer's good judgment. He lets the private player-trainer relationship exist without prying, and yet can be sure of accurate and pertinent information when he seeks it.

In other circumstances, however, a trainer can take on the aspects of a house detective. When he does, the ball club may or may not win, but life is a lot less fun—and in the long run, unhealthy.

A trainer's duties are more than applying Band-Aids and listening to moans. They form the focus of two of the major activities of a modern major-league organization: physical condition and logistics.

A trainer is the first line of diagnosis and therapy. Every team has a doctor, often an orthopedic specialist, because so many athletic injuries call for one. But the official club physician doesn't always travel with the team, and may not be in the ballpark at home at all games. Therefore, the trainer performs four separate functions as the physician-on-the-spot:

1. He applies first aid when an injury occurs.
2. He is the liaison to the doctor, in determining whether an injury calls for the doctor's care, in reporting various details to the doctor, and in carrying out the doctor's instructions in the treatment of a player afterward.
3. He looks after the special physical needs of uninjured players (like giving rubdowns, taping ankles, and loosening up a pitcher's arm).
4. He looks after the general health of the club, checking weight, diet where necessary, dispensing pills for everything from sleep to colds to vitamins, administering various injections, and so forth.

In the above respects, a trainer's tasks at home and on the road are similar, except that he has a better-equipped room, usually, at home. In addition, however, he assists the equipment manager while the team travels.

And on top of everything else, today's trainer is the twentieth-century counterpart of Figaro, the famous barber of Seville—the factotum of the town, the one on whom everyone calls for the solution of any unexpected little problem, from a broken shoelace on up.

Most teams today carry two trainers, a chief trainer and an assistant. During a game, one will be in the dugout and the other back in the clubhouse.

All this is a far cry from the legendary idea of a trainer, based on practices of three generations ago. In the early days, a trainer was some old friend of the manager, with a gift of gab and a collection of patent medicines, with some secret-formula liniment in his second-hand doctor's bag, and as much alcohol on his breath as in the bag. His education was strictly haphazard and based only on experience, often someone else's experience imperfectly understood.

The gift of gab was important: The old-style trainer had to have the ability to kid an injured athlete along. If the injury was painful but not too serious, this kind of applied psychology might keep the man playing; if it was serious, at least the victim's spirits might be kept up, or at least attention might be drawn away from his suffering.

Such a talent in a trainer today is also desirable, but it is no longer the main therapy at his command. Modern trainers have formal preparation, in a trainers' school or elsewhere, which gives them a working knowledge of physiology, drugs and medications, diagnosis, and various therapeutic mechanisms.

In the dressing room of a modern stadium, one will find a special room for the trainer, usually between the locker room and the showers. It will have at least two rubbing tables, on which a man can stretch out full length to be massaged or otherwise worked upon. There will be a rather large medicine cabinet, and several machines: a whirlpool bath (a four-foot-high metal tub in which hot water circulates violently while arms or legs are immersed), some sort of diathermy machine (which uses electric heat or ultrasonics for deep heat treatment), and something that makes plenty of ice (a refrigerator is part of the standard furniture). One may or may not find, however, X-ray machines—for such examinations or treatments, players are usually sent to hospitals, where qualified personnel can handle them. And in recent years, weight and exercise machines have been installed.

A trainer's bag usually has trays that set up when it opens, like some types of tool chests, and it is crammed with an incredible number and variety of objects: scissors, gauze, bottles of liquids and pills, cotton, spatulas, and ointments in bewildering combination.

Taping ankles, or wrists, is as much an art as a medical science, because the comfort of the athlete is as important as the structural support being given—and athletes can be pretty finicky about the comfort of a joint they have to use heavily. Good taping can keep minor strains operational and prevent injury.

Before a game, the starting pitcher and perhaps a couple of other players want their arms "loosened." This is a rubbing, kneading, stretching process that stretches the muscles about to be subjected to such unusual strain.

Every sport has its own pattern of common injuries. In baseball, in order of frequency, these are muscle-tearing injuries, twists at the joints (ankle, knee, wrist), bruises, and cuts. Broken bones are relatively infrequent, and when they occur are often "hairline" fractures.

The most common injury of all is a charley horse. Essentially, this is a hemorrhage under the muscles of the thigh—it can be the result of a blow, or of a stretching-tearing damage from excessive effort or insufficient warm-up. In general, because baseball is a game of quick starts (in fielding and in getting away from home plate or a base), legs are subjected to muscle pulls and tears. In a "tear," muscle tissue is literally torn, that is, separated at some point; a "pull" is a less severe version of a tear, and a "strain" is a stretch short of the breaking point. Because the ball must be thrown hard, often from awkward body positions, arm-muscle injuries are common—and pitchers, of course, generate their own exceptional pressures.

The twisting injuries happen mostly in hitting the ground or taking a bad step—while sliding, while trying to make an acrobatic catch, or while slipping on a rain-soaked or otherwise tricky surface. Sprained ankles are more common than sprained wrists, but both are standard baseball hazards.

Bruises, in baseball, can be inflicted in four ways: by being hit by the ball, whether it's thrown or batted; by collision with another player, either a teammate trying to make the same fielding play or an opponent guarding a base (especially the catcher); by running into a barrier, the outfield fence, or the box fronts in foul ground while fielding; or by contact with the ground in sliding or falling. Most of the ball-inflicted bruises, of course, involve the hands and fingers, but some pitchers and infielders take their share of painful whacks on the leg or body from line drives traveling 100 miles an hour or more. It's remarkable that they survive these as well as they do.

Cuts are, by and large, of two types (although any collision can also produce them): spike-inflicted and ball-inflicted. The spike wounds, which often require half a dozen stitches or more, are the result of slides the vast majority of the time. Ball-inflicted cuts are the special torture of catchers, who suffer innumerable "split" fingers from foul tips. A split finger is one in which the blow by the ball has caused the skin to split, usually lengthwise.

Catchers seem to be well protected by their chest protectors, shin guards, and mask, but there are many vulnerable points, and foul tips seem to find them all. When a bat deflects the pitch just a trifle, too much for the catcher's gloved hand to react in time but not enough to make it miss the catcher, the ball still has practically all of its original force behind it. The points of the shoulders, the insides of the thighs and of the knees, the neck and Adam's apple, and, of course, the arms— all these are places exposed to the foul tip. A flap hanging down from the mask offers partial protection to the throat, but this is limited. Movement opens theoretically protected areas to vulnerability.

And, it should be realized, the umpire behind the catcher is just as unprotected from the foul tip that misses the catcher.

The elbow is a potential trouble spot for those who must throw a lot—pitchers and catchers, especially pitchers, and some outfielders, third basemen, and shortstops. Pitchers are far and away in most danger, it goes without saying; not only do they throw harder and longer when they pitch, but, by trying to put special spins on the ball, set up particularly severe unnatural stresses. A most common pitching injury, therefore, is a loose bone chip in the elbow. This can be removed surgically, but many men pitch successfully for several years with this condition before it gets so unbearable that it has to be corrected.

And a batter is subject to a special kind of injury that often goes unnoticed from the stands: a bruised instep, ankle, toe, or shin from his own foul tip.

The degree to which a man is incapacitated by an injury is often out of proportion to ordinary standards of damage. A very small thing can put a man out of action—and he may be able to play with an intrinsically more serious ailment that would have an ordinary man home in bed. It all depends on how the particular problem affects the player's key actions.

For instance, just plain blisters on the palm of the hand—if raw and painful—can prevent a man from batting effectively. (That's why batting gloves became popular.) But a man with two broken fingers can play, and even bat a little bit—if the fingers happen to be the pinkie and fourth finger. One of baseball's most famous injuries was Dizzy Dean's broken toe, which ended his career as a top-flight pitcher. When he tried to pitch before the toe was fully healed, he used an unorthodox stride in favoring the toe, and thus permanently injured his arm by the unnatural motion that resulted. A charley horse may slow a man down, but not prevent him from playing; a pulled muscle in the back, though not even painful while running or throwing, may make swinging the bat impossible.

The trainer must judge all these things, or at least help the individual player judge for himself. He must help decide when pain is just pain, to be borne without danger of further damage, and when it is unsafe to ignore damage that doesn't seem to hurt much.

A good trainer, then, can forestall a certain amount of injury by precaution, and can get men back into the lineup a game or two sooner by effective treatment and proper understanding of the individual case. Every man has his own rate of healing, and his own psychological as well as physiological responses. The trainer who can read these accurately, and take appropriate action, is of immense value to individual careers and team success.

When a rookie arrives, the trainer is often the first friendly human being he finds. When a veteran is on the way down, the trainer may be the last sympathetic listener he'll have. And to the trainer, more than to anyone else connected with a baseball team, the star and the fringe player have equal status, and are of equal concern. The trainer sees men when they are in pain, with their defenses down, dependent and frightened. He may not become the best character-reader in the world, but he has the best opportunity to become one, and most trainers are pretty hard to fool in that respect.

They are the most unsung of the unsung heroes in the baseball hierarchy, and the standards of their profession—recognized only recently—are rising rapidly. It took club owners nearly a century of professional baseball to finally realize that since the main assets of their business are the physical capabilities of their ball players, it might be a good idea to put those bodies in the care of qualified people. Actually, for owners, that's about the normal rate of speed for seeing the light.

Why, then, the fan might ask, if trainers are better and more appreciated and given better equipment, do there seem to be more injuries than ever?

The answer is, there aren't more injuries. It just seems that way because today, through radio, television, better diagnosis, and a different reporting attitude, the fan hears all about every injury, sometimes *ad nauseam*. In the old days, not only were injuries to familiar players less documented, but no one was aware of how many careers ended prematurely, before the player in question became familiar. Today, many players, who simply would have had to quit under the conditions of two generations ago, are kept going, and some are thoroughly repaired.

The newest clubhouse feature is the videotape player and a burgeoning library of edited tapes. Baseball players are starting to study their own performances on film the way football players have for decades, and the full use of this training aid is just beginning. Among today's young stars, Tony Gwynn and Will Clark are two of the most dedicated practitioners.

So the scene behind the scenes is much larger than ever, and still growing in complexity.

CHAPTER
14

Scouts

Good scouting, on which all baseball success ultimately depends, has also changed dramatically.

It used to all begin back in the bushes.

Among baseball people, the word "bush" has special connotations. It is usually an insult, or at least an expression of disrespect. It's short for "bush league," the opposite of "big league," and it usually refers to behavior—being cheap, or mean (in the sense of cheap); showing up a teammate or a friend; showing off; acting, in whatever way, small, petty, unsophisticated, crude. A man who has "no class" is termed "bush"; so is a situation not worthy of major-league conditions.

But almost everyone in baseball used to start in the bushes, or come through them. The number of players who come from farms, tiny towns, or isolated areas is much smaller than it used to be, but with very few exceptions players still spend at least some time playing in the little towns that make up the lower echelons of the minor leagues. And the big-city boys, by and large, come from the poorer, and tougher, neighborhoods. More well-educated, upper-middle-class-bred young men are playing major-league baseball today than ever before—but they are still a minority. So "class," in the sense of polish, is something most players have to acquire, while "class," in the sense of character, is put to some severe tests on the way up.

It was in the bushes, then, where basic baseball attitudes were formed and hardened—and in the bushes, literally or figuratively, where most baseball talent was sought.

And the men on whom the whole elaborate structure of the multimillion-dollar business rested were the scouts.

It became an axiom, in the forty years between the development and the universal application of farm systems, that no major-league organization is any better than its scouts. Before that, this wasn't true. When most minor-league teams were independently owned, and when the majors were relatively young, scouting was a haphazard business, although great energy went into it. The key man, usually, was the manager, who hired and fired players (no general managers then); in the minors, and on some major-league teams, owners were very active. They used their own observation, word-of-mouth reports, and letters of recommendation from friends and former associates. It was common for one player to recommend others to his manager. The inducement of a proffered contract, and occasionally transportation, was enough in most cases up to World War I and beyond. Major-league teams then bought minor leaguers who had done well.

When farm systems began in the 1920s, the traditional methods of personal recommendation and brief tryout of self-professed prospects proved inadequate. To stock a farm system, one parent organization had to sign hundreds of players—and to do this, the organization hired full-time, professional scouts.

In 1965, the painfully constructed scouting-and-farm-system operation was knocked into a cocked hat by the adoption of a free-agent draft, patterned on the football and basketball drafts of college stars. This revolutionary step altered many of the accumulated skills and known conditions of scouting, and its eventual effects could not be predicted.

Some consequences could be seen right away. The basis of the farm approach Branch Rickey had pioneered was signing up everyone in sight, scattering dozens or hundreds of players through the low minors, and letting cream rise to the top. The number you could sign was unlimited, and since the amateur player had freedom of choice, your selling point was the quality of the organization he would be entering. With a draft, entirely apart from the order of choice, the key element is that everybody gets one pick before anyone gets another. Not only was your selection limited to who was available on that turn, but at the end of the process everybody had the same total number of prospects (not counting, of course, the insignificant number of those not highly enough regarded to be drafted at all).

But, unlike the football and basketball drafts, you weren't choosing almost-finished products as college stars are in those sports. You were projecting the eventual major-league possibilities of seventeen- and eighteen-year-olds, a risky proposition. Nevertheless, when you did draft a player in a high round, you had to offer a sizable bonus—not as large as when all clubs were competing for a few top prospects (which is what made them turn to a draft), but a systematized bonus list covering more people. Now a scout could cover less territory, but the pressure to guess right was greater.

This meant the minors were not a let-'em-play-and-see-what-happens operation, but a narrowly focused teaching scheme for those to whom a commitment had already been made. And powers of persuasion became almost irrelevant (although you still had to convince the family to choose professional ball over a college scholarship).

But that was only the beginning. American life began changing drastically in the 1960s on all sorts of levels. The young men being scouted were growing up with different attitudes, coming out of different environments, living in a different economic context. More and more were spending at least some time in college (thanks to the expansion of recruiting for other sports). As overt discrimination against blacks decreased, the exploitation of black athletic skills previously ignored became maximized (more by the colleges than by professional sports). Individuals grew up with greater expectations, more sophistication, more awareness of rights and opportunities, less respect for authority in any form. The minor leagues were dying at the grass roots, and semi-pro sandlot ball virtually ceased to exist, for non-baseball economic reasons. Little League and teenage organizations were a generation old. Television, other communications, more cars than ever, and the airplane were homogenizing America rapidly. The backwoods were shrinking and turning into exurbia. The bushes were ceasing to exist.

Then the major-league players made their breakthroughs in labor organization, and concern for working conditions began to trickle down, at least a little bit, into the high minors. When the lid came off the salary structure in the 1970s, the break with the past was complete. Combined with expansion, which meant job security for more major leaguers, it altered the role and status of minor-league players. They had become, in the farm system's evolution, raw material to be mined, like nuggets imbedded in a vein of ore, and the pre-signing scouting was in effect looking for promising mine sites (that is, stocking it with ore). Ore is cheap, mostly to be discarded, and the gold would be extracted. Now, they were clearly investments and apprentices; their gold potential had to be recognized earlier, because the veins would be less numerous and the extraction process too expensive to waste on unpromising beginnings.

So the focus of scouting, at the lowest levels, shifted. Quality took precedence over quantity. Supervision of scouts and collation of information became more important. In-system scouting—the evaluation of players who were already professionals, in the minors and also in the majors—became more important than uncovering unknown and undiscovered talents, at a time when less and less could be hidden anyhow.

But the basic structure of the scouting department remains.

A major-league team's scouting department has three major areas of operation. The most important scouts are still the ones who deal with the primary source of raw material—players who have not yet signed a professional contract. These scouts are assigned geographic sectors, and watch high-school and college teams, sandlotters, American Legion, and other organized amateur leagues, semipros, industrial teams, and so forth. Each scout has several "bird dogs" working for him—friends or associates who are his pieceworkers, not really part of the ball club's organization but a vital network to the scout himself.

The second level of scouting is the minors. A parent team must have some evaluation, preferably a detailed one, on every player on every minor-league team. This became all the more important under regulations that promote the drafting of players from rival organizations. Minor-league scouting has two basic purposes: knowledge of abilities of players who may be acquired in trades, and a standard of comparison for judging the performance and development of one's own players.

The third level has intensified the most: systematic scouting of other major-league teams. The practice of sending scouts to "get a book" on a prospective World Series opponent used to get a lot of attention; it was inevitable (under Parkinson's Law, that work expands to fill the time of an increasing staff) that this would spread to regular-season activities. If it was worth scouting the leaders in the other league before a World Series, why wouldn't it be just as useful to scout the teams you had to play to get into the World Series? It would.

The two purposes of major-league scouting, then, are to evaluate men for possible trades, and to keep up with current information on an opponent's form immediately prior to playing him. Since some players now become free agents, constant evaluation is more vital then ever.

The real work, however, is done at the lowest level: digging out raw talent in the first place.

No one in an important baseball position is more anonymous than a scout, yet for the success of an organization he is more important than well-publicized managers and front-office executives. The basic job of the front office, in fact, is to hire good scouts. In a way, that means scouting scouts, and, obviously enough, being willing to pay them better than some other organization.

Who are scouts? Former players, by and large, some with recognizable names because they played in the majors, most unknown because they didn't. Most of them have some local business interest at home, because most scouts aren't paid much. Their expense accounts, in fact, mean more than their salaries. They travel a great deal, within their areas, seeing as many games as they can, running down reports from bird dogs.

What makes a good scout? Judgment and luck.

What does he judge? Basic talents. Obviously, the records compiled by a high-school player don't mean much, because of the level of competition. And his skills, at that point, aren't really important; what count are the skills he can acquire. So a scout looks for certain fundamentals, and tries to project in his mind how far these can be developed. How fast can he run? How hard (in absolute terms) can he throw? How quick are his wrists when he swings a bat? How relaxed and sure are his hands when he catches a ball? How quick are his reflexes, responding to a batted ball or an unexpected situation?

Has he reached full growth? Is he skinny and not too strong, but likely to fill out? Is he strong now but likely to be heavy-legged or overweight by the time he's twenty-five? Is he effective now only because he matured faster than the kids around him, or is early maturity a permanent advantage for him?

What's his mental and emotional makeup? How competitive is he? How much does he really want to play baseball? Is he clean-living, reliable, teachable?

These are the questions scouts ask themselves.

Rickey, a great judge of talent, always spoke of five basic abilities: ro run, to throw, to field, to hit, and to hit with power. George Weiss, another fabulously successful farm-system operator, was less a judge of player talent than a skilled administrator of good scouts.

As one can imagine, it's a tremendous roulette game. No one can really tell what a seventeen-year-old boy will develop into as a thirty-year-old man. Yes, a Willie Mays or a Mickey Mantle is obviously a great talent, and you don't have to be a wizard to spot him; almost any fan, watching such superstars in the raw, could recognize their potential. But many others, perhaps equally gifted at seventeen, never went on for one reason or another—an injury, an illness, a lack of desire.

Discovering a Mantle or a Mays is luck—not luck in seeing them, since that's the product of hard work, but luck that they went on to fulfill their promise. The scout's bread and butter, though, is not superstars, but usable players—the ones who, alongside a Mays or a Mantle, can round out a winning team.

That's what's so tough, judging the eventual usefulness of a player with some clear-cut abilities, some evident weaknesses, and large gray areas of possibilities. Is this one worth signing, and (in the days of competitive bonuses) for how much?

Here's how tough it really is: The top vote-getter for the 1990 All-Star Game was Oakland's José Canseco, who had just become the game's first $5-million-a-year player. He had been drafted in 1982—in the 15th round, which means about 400 other players were chosen before him. The second-biggest vote-getter was Ryne Sandberg of the Cubs. He had been drafted by the Phillies in 1978, in the 20th round. Don Mattingly, all in all probably the best player of the decade of the 1980s, was drafted by the Yankees in 1979 in the 19th round—and was already good enough to be Most Valuable Player in his first full year (1980, South Atlantic League), and an All-Star each of the next two years up the ladder. So it wasn't a matter of "slow development"; some 450 "prospects" were ranked ahead of him by the scouting community when he was already what he was. At the same time, countless first-round draft choices have never been heard from again.

Before the free-agent draft, a scout's most important skill lay in signing the player he had decided was worthwhile. Twenty clubs, presumably, were in competition. After World War II, it was no longer likely that any "sleeper" could be turned up, that any player of promise existed anywhere without the full knowledge of at least a half-dozen organizations. The trick was not to know of his existence, but to persuade him to choose your organization over another.

This involved cultivating the family, befriending the boy, keeping others at arm's length. In a bidding contest, finally, the amount offered would be crucial, and the scout had to decide how big a bundle the particular prospect was worth, in the context of his club's yearly budget. And when he did decide, it was up to him to see that his bid was favored over any reasonably similar bid from another direction.

The free-agent draft eliminated persuasiveness as a basic consideration, since the player could negotiate *only* with the team that drafted him. A scout's analytic powers (and prophetic powers) became much more important in the scheme of things.

A major-league club today has approximately twenty-five full-time scouts. They file reports on all players in their areas, and on all the minor-league players they see, every year.

A typical reporting system (long used by the New York Yankees, for example) rates every prospect by the highest baseball level he may ever reach in the opinion of the scout. A player is rated single-A, double-A, triple-A, or major league *in potential;* then there is a final select category called "Yankee," presumably one step above major league. Until 1965, that was true enough.

Joe Garagiola, who has been known to exaggerate for effect but who also has as big a store of anecdotes as anyone in baseball, claims that Dave Philley, the former outfielder turned scout, used the notation "K.P."

"What's that mean?" Joe says he asked.

"Kain't Play," Joe says Philley said.

Each player is reevaluated every year as he moves up through the system, and his ratings may change—but it is astonishing how often original opinions prove correct years later. In the course of, say, three years in the minors, a player is evaluated by half a dozen scouts (including his manager and various roving coaches). And it is all, of course, fed into computers.

It is easy to be wrong, because living human beings, and very volatile ones at that, are the subject of these neat office procedures. Mistakes are made again and again. But very little is left to chance, and the amount of work done is prodigious.

It is safe to say that there is no baseball player in America, eighteen years of age or older, who has played a dozen games with any organized team at any level, who has not been written up (or viewed and rejected) by some major-league organization.

Though the bushes themselves are disappearing in an ever more urbanized society permeated with ever-improving transportation and communication, whatever the bushes turn into will continue to be the habitat of scouts as long as professional baseball exists.

Today, the competition for talent is against other facets of life—college, well-paying jobs (minor-league pay is laughably inadequate and out of date), and other professional sports. The most gifted athletes of 1900, by and large, played mainly baseball as kids and stuck to it as they grew older, because it was the only game in which one could make a living. Today, the talented athlete of fifteen or sixteen, not yet committed to any one game and exposed to all, may well choose football or basketball as a means of getting a college education, with the possibility of a well-paying pro career afterward.

At the same time, the players themselves are incomparably better educated about the game, exposed to fine points as children through television and Little League; much better coached at earlier stages; and much more sophisticated, more sensitive, more arrogant, more independent, bigger and more powerful physically, less able and less willing to put up with hardship. All this makes scouting more important, and more difficult, than ever. The veneer of too-early experience can be misleading; character, under pampered conditions, may be harder to read.

But for every player on a pennant-winning team, there is some scout, somewhere, who saw something in him and decided "sign him." It's an obscure, thankless job most of the time, but it is indispensable.

So it is the major-league scouts—"special-assignment scouts," most teams call them—who have emerged as the elite of their profession. Ever-increasing attention is paid to scouting opposing major leaguers, as managers process more computerized information (since they, too, belong to a later generation comfortable with available technology), and as ever more information is needed to make judgments about million-dollar contracts, player movement, and so forth.

Based in a big-league city, but not the home of the team they work for, they catch teams as they come through, and travel only when an immediate upcoming opponent has to be checked out. They file daily reports on the current form of opposing players for immediate use: How's this guy swing, what's this one throwing, who's slumping, who's hot, how, why, what are the variations from previously accumulated ideas. They also make more general evaluations for trades and other possible transactions, and double-check impressions about their own team's players. So they become pre-game press-room regulars in the base city, and the best conversational resource in America. They're in the fifty to seventy age range, have voluminous and indelible memories, and thus are living history books. Some love to talk, some love to listen, but they all share a religious dedication to the prime directive of their profession: to have an opinion. Mention anything—a player, a team, a car, real estate, today's lunch, somebody's clothing—and they'll give you an instant rating. If you care about the baseball scene, no better combination of informaton and entertainment can be found than these "superscouts," an affectionate-sarcastic designation first applied to Mayo Smith when he was between managing jobs in the 1960s.

Do they share information? No. That would be unethical. What they really do is sound each other out constantly, to make mental comparisons for their own evaluating process. What a scout says on a point of evaluation may not be exactly, or entirely, what he really thinks. But whatever he says, he'll say it forcefully, definitely, color-fully, very likely profanely, and without reservation. And most likely, it will be something well worth listening to.

Missing from their makeup is any hint of reverence—for higher authority, higher earning power, or what passes for conventional wis-dom. Maybe that's why writers feel so comfortable with them.

The late Garry Schumacher was not a scout, but an esteemed New York and Brooklyn baseball writer who went to work for the Giants and moved with them to San Francisco in a public relations function. Yet Garry, who was a history and opera buff, summed up a scout's viewpoint better than any actual scout I've ever met.

"Lee's problem was," he'd say, referring to the general of the Con-federate Army in the Civil War, "he couldn't win on the road."

"Napoleon," he'd say, describing the ill-fated attempt to conquer Russia in 1812, "had no bench."

"Ya oughtta hear this new tenor they got, Pavarotti," he told me when I came through San Francisco in the 1960s. "Belts those high notes into the third deck."

That's the flavor. As for substance, there's Charlie Silvera, who used to collect Yankee World Series checks as Yogi Berra's seldom-used replacement. He grew up in the Bay Area, and settled back there after his playing and active coaching days were over, acting as a major-league area scout for various organizations (Yankees in the late 1980s, Milwaukee in 1990). Charlie will give you an instant opinion on any player's current form and overall abilities, but that's not what makes him famous in this set. What Charlie has is a bottomless pit of infor-mation on every San Francisco, Peninsula, and East Bay high-school and college athlete of the last sixty years, along with a vast compen-dium of old Pacific Coast League lore. Drop a name and he'll scoop it up like the best infielder you ever saw.

But when he and Hank Sauer and Jim Davenport and Dee Fondy and Bill Wight and Whitey Lockman—and a dozen others—sit around and gossip, you can also learn why hitting and pitching work the way they do, what really happened on various memorable occasions long ago, how the game is changing, and all sorts of technicalities in a singulalry non-self-serving context.

If you listen.

CHAPTER
15

Statistics

"Statistics are the lifeblood of baseball," I wrote in the corresponding chapter in 1966. Since then they have become a veritable Red Sea threatening to drown us all. The arrival of the handheld calculator let loose forces of computation never contemplated in the past. Mainframe computers available to leagues, service bureaus, self-generated research groups, and even the media magnified them. But more is not automatically better, and more data doesn't guarantee more information, and more information doesn't necessarily mean greater understanding.

No one can deny that statistics play a greater role, get wider dissemination, and are accepted for use by more fans than was the case a generation ago. One need only utter the words "Rotisserie League" to prove how far the infection has spread. But if we want a sensible perspective on this subject, we have to go back to the beginning and start with basics.

Don't misunderstand. As one of the earliest exploiters and chief beneficiaries of the statistics explosion that really began in the 1930s, am I now bad-mouthing the hand that fed me? Am I renouncing the image and reputation that made the celebrated columnist Jimmy Cannon ask me if my attaché case was "full of decimal points"? (Later, when I had moved on to *The New York Times*, I told him, "No, Jimmy, now it's full of colons and semicolons," an honest bit of self-appraisal demonstrated again throughout this book.) Am I, of all people, putting down statistics and statisticians?

Definitely not. I am only continuing my lifelong battle for better comprehension and proper use of the statistical tool. Like a scalpel, if you don't use it sparingly and correctly, it can do more harm than good.

So let's go back to Square One.

What *are* baseball statistics?

They are the counting of discrete events easily identifiable—a time at bat, an out, a run, a hit, an error, a victory, an inning, a time of game, a particular pitch—and, after collating them, subjecting the totals to elementary arithmetical manipulations, mostly adding and dividing.

Why are baseball statistics more fascinating—and more valid— than statistics in most other sports?

Because baseball is a one-thing-at-a-time game, and therefore full of things easy to count. A batter's or pitcher's or fielder's record depends much more on his individual action, easily observed and un- ambiguous in its result, to a much greater degree than anything done in football (where 22 men move simultaneously) or the continuous- flow games (basketball, hockey, soccer). Extraneous factors do enter into it—fielders have to make routine plays for a pitcher to record outs, and a hitter or base runner can be affected by a teammate's action—but these are relatively small distortions in the counting pro- cess. It's easier to assign responsibility for the outcome of a particular play to a single player in baseball than in other team games.

Then what's the problem?

Forgetting the true nature of what's being counted.

The first thing to remember is that statistics merely count what has already happened; they say nothing about why.

The second is that the standard baseball statistics count only cer- tain selected items, ignoring the effect of other equally countable items that are obviously related. For example, a man's total of runs batted in, which is recorded, is obviously influenced by his number of op- portunities, that is, the number of men on base when he batted; but this is not recorded in the official box score.

The third is that many statistics have self-limiting factors, or other subtle mathematical relationships, that˙are universally ignored by baseball people. For example, if a team has a weak pitching staff, its total of double plays made may be high—because the weak pitching puts so many men on base that double-play opportunities are more frequent.

The fourth is that statistics, by their nature, are meaningful only for a large number of cases.

And the fifth, and by far the most important, is that baseball is played by human beings, whose actions cannot be described by simple numbers. A man's performance fluctuates whether or not surrounding circumstances appear unchanged.

Even with all these things in mind, however, the fiend for statistics can be led to totally incorrect conclusions, because there is one more fundamental flaw in the way standard statistics are kept. They record *how much*, but not *when*, and in the winning and losing of ball games, the *when* is all-important.

After all, the box score says that a man who got two hits in four times up had a good day. But the two hits may have been wasted singles, while the two times he made out, the bases may have been loaded with two out. His team lost the game, and he definitely did not have a good day. Another box score shows that a pitcher struck out 11, so he must have had "bad luck" losing the game, 3–2. But the box score won't show that with one out in the eighth inning, and the score tied, and a man on third, and a weak hitter at bat, our unlucky pitcher didn't succeed in getting one of his 11 strikeouts when he needed it, but gave up a long fly that scored the winning run.

The question of "when" permeates all baseball numbers, from the smallest to the largest scale. A run scored in the second inning of a game is not the same as a run scored in the eighth; scored early, it affects all subsequent strategy—it may keep a pitcher in the game instead of forcing him out for a pinch-hitter, it may alter bunt situations and defensive alignments. A winning streak early in the season, putting a team in first place, is not the same as a winning streak of the same number of games in September, when that team is already out of the race.

Statistics, by their very objectivity, can't reflect such things, but the reality of baseball is built on exactly such factors.

Here are some common, almost universal, misuses of statistics, showing how myths are promoted and realities misunderstood.

Fallacy No. 1: Statistics can be used to predict. They can't, except in terms so broad as to be self-evident.

Fallacy No. 2: Statistics can be used to prove a point. They can *convince*, which is quite different and important in its own right, but they can prove only the event they record, not something else about it.

Fallacy No. 3: Statistics can be used to compare. Again, it is a question of scale. One can say, of course, that a .300 hitter is better than a .200 hitter, but one hardly needs statistics to see that. Attaching value judgments, however, to the difference betwen .310 and .290 is simply invalid, on the basis of statistics alone.

This third fallacy goes to the heart of the difficulty. The underlying assumption, in all statistical comparisons, is "other things being equal." But other things are *never* equal.

If one tries to compare figures for different eras, one is immediately immersed in different conditions, many of which the statistic user doesn't even know. In 1930, the ball was different from the one used in 1920, or 1960. Parks were different, styles were different, even rules were different. Until 1950, even the height of the mound differed in various parks. (It was then standardized at 15 inches; and in 1969 it was lowered to 10 inches.)

Such differences have small consequences, it's true—but it is precisely these small consequences that are being compared when one argues about players of different eras. One doesn't, very often, compare a star of today with a nobody of yesterday, or vice versa; one argues about a .341 of Ted Williams and a .367 of Ty Cobb, and within that sort of statistical range the different conditions outweigh the difference in numbers.

But even within an era, and within the same season, comparisons must be made with care. An "average" is exactly that—an abstraction arrived at by "averaging out" a large number of cases. Only when a season is over is the true "average" for a player's performance known; the greatest of all statistical fallacies is extrapolation from insufficient data, the "at this rate" type of reasoning. A man who hits 10 homers in the first 20 games is *not* likely to hit 81 in 162 games, and, while every baseball fan recognizes the flaw in that example, dozens of similar mistakes are made every day in thinking about less familiar categories than homers. (In 1988, George Bell hit three homers on Opening Day. He wound up with 24, not 486.)

Furthermore, even in the same season, players on different teams play a different proportion of games in various parks, which are shaped differently, have different ball-carrying characteristics, and are in turn affected by changes of weather and time of year. Also, individual hitters don't all face the same pitchers the same number of times, and neither hitters nor pitchers face each other under identical conditions of fatigue, health, and efficiency, or in similar game situations.

Take a particular pitcher. Let's say he starts against the Yankees four times (once in each series). Already, we're dealing with a very small number. In those four games, he may pitch to Don Mattingly a total of 15 times. Suppose, this year, it happened that 13 of those times

Mattingly batted with no one on base, and that in two of the games a strong wind was blowing in. Our hypothetical pitcher, then, was usually able to avoid giving him a really good pitch to hit, and when he did, Mattingly hit two long flies that the wind kept in the park. That year, Mattingly got one hit in 12 at-bats, and three walks, off this pitcher—an "average" of .087.

Now this statistic becomes available to everyone (especially radio broadcasters, who need such statistics to fill their word volume), and the pitcher has been established as being "tough for Mattingly."

In reality, though, only Mattingly can say if this pitcher was tough for him. The next year, things break differently: The pitcher has the same equipment, but now Mattingly comes up often with men on base, and walks cannot be risked. The pitches are a little better, he creams a couple for three-run homers—and suddenly the statistics are reversed.

This is the sort of thing that goes on all the time, and especially for players not as prominent as Mattingly. It all *could* be recorded statistically, but it isn't—and it isn't worth the effort. The men who have to play know perfectly well how to allow for the immense number of variables involved; and the fans, who can get satisfaction from the illusion of order that rudimentary (but often invalid) statistics provide, would be merely overwhelmed by any attempt to give a truer mathematical picture of what goes on.

For this reason, many fans are perplexed, and hurt, when they find that baseball professionals pay little attention to some statistic the fan prized. On the other hand, players care passionately about those statistics that affect their salaries: batting average, home runs, runs batted in, errors, earned runs, victories.

The tone of the player's interest is quite different; he doesn't care what the figures prove, only what they say. He wants credit for a .300 average, does not want to be charged with an error or an earned run. But here, most players are just as misdirected in their attitudes as the fans. Actually, even these statistics—as distinct from slightly better statistics—have only a marginal effect on the player's earning power.

The fact is, ball clubs pay whatever they feel they have to. A star doesn't need statistics to prove his value, and the ordinary player has no special bargaining power anyhow. In the past, general managers, as professional businessmen, would *use* statistics as an arguing device when talking salary with players, very few of whom were professional businessmen.

Now the situation is somewhat different, but not as different as many commentators would have you believe. It is true that statistical achievements are now written into contracts for bonus provisions—a practice that was actually forbidden as an "unfair incentive" before the revolution of the 1970s—so that a 20th start, or so many plate appearances, or making the All-Star team, can mean lots of extra money. Realistically, however, these are mind games being played by general managers, players, agents, and arbitrators. They toss statistics at each other as bargaining ploys, knowing underneath what one is really willing to pay and the other is willing to accept—the famous market forces at work. Both hope, of course, to flim-flam some well-meaning but often naive arbitrator the way the general manager used to flim-flam the young country bumpkin, but it seldom works. The new factor in the equation is the capable agent, who can out-statistic the club on behalf of his client more often than not. And any club management that thinks it's being clever by writing in tease bonuses it intends to prevent the player from getting (by holding him out of games, or putting him in the bullpen only for that reason) is being just plain stupid. And old-fashioned. There's a key scene in *Eight Men Out*, the story about the Chicago White Sox of 1919 who became the Black Sox by throwing the World Series. The owner denies a bonus he promised a pitcher for 30 victories because he won only 29. So the pitcher joins the fixers.

Nevertheless, all players now are "ranked" according to a complicated formula in the Player Agreement, and their official status can be affected by being in the top third, bottom third, and so forth. It just doesn't matter too much except in rare borderline cases.

All this is not to imply that baseball statistics have *no* meaning. They have a great deal. The trick is to keep clearly in mind just which meaning is valid and which isn't. As a large-scale guide, they are quite sound. Over a period of several hundred times at bat, a man will perform quite in line with his lifetime average.

Also, to the professional baseball man, many implicit qualities go with the phrase ".300 hitter" or ".250 hitter" or "20-game winner," qualities not taken into account by the fan who uses the same terms. The fan's orientation, and knowledge, is focused on the numerical proportion involved; the professional is aware of a complex context—a certain degree of bat control and sensible hitting pattern, a certain proportion of luck, a balancing of hot streaks and cold streaks, a particular discipline and set of physical abilities. These make up a ".300 hitter." To the professional, an established .300 hitter whose average is .260 at the moment is still considered a .300 hitter, while a .250 hitter who has made 60 hits in his first 180 trips may have, incontrovertibly, a .333 average, but he is not yet a ".300 hitter."

The following checklist should help one keep the fascinating subject of statistics in perspective:

1. A man hitting .293 is not necessarily "hitting better" than someone hitting .286, or even .276—although he certainly is hitting better than someone at .222; in other words, a slight difference is not significant at all.

2. Relatively small differences on the field can seem like big differences in numbers. For a man who has 300 official at-bats with the season half over, the difference between .333 and .290 is 13 hits; the difference between .290 and .250 is 12 hits. Half a season is about 80 games. In other words, the difference between .250 and .290 is about one hit every seventh game—and lucky bounces, ballpark variations, scorer's decisions, luck of the draw in pitching opponent, and a host of other factors all must be figured in. Two slow hoppers and a fortunately placed pop fly, in the course of a month, can make the difference—or, in the other direction, four or five hard line drives that are caught.

3. All cumulative statistics—homers, runs batted in, strikeouts—should be considered in the light of opportunities, which are not included as part of that official statistic.

4. Comparisons within one team are most valid; within one league, next so; across the two major leagues, of doubtful value; to previous years, increasingly unreliable the more years involved.

5. Players are not automatons; they vary in ability from week to week, and especially over the years. The most common mistake, made even by managers sometimes, is to keep thinking that because a man keeps his identity he keeps his ability, that the reliable name is still reliable in action. But a .300 hitter one year, even while relatively young, may not be a .300 hitter the next; and to distinguish between a slump, which is temporary, and a permanent change in effectiveness is the hardest judgment to make in baseball.

All these warnings apply to the use of statistics to prove, analyze, or determine a choice. The guiding idea is that statistics are a by-product, not a cause; a description, not a law; and an isolation of a few, almost arbitrary, factors from dynamic reality. In fact, that's the best thing to keep in mind: The word *statistics* suggests the word "static," and, in the real world, events are dynamic, not static.

Statistics as *records*, however, are another story. They are not merely valid; they are the whole business, by definition. Categories of records may be carried to ridiculous extremes, or to amusing lengths, depending on your point of view, but a record is a record is a record— and, strangely enough, in this one indisputably appropriate area of statistics, people still tend to go wrong by introducing the very value judgments they ignore when dealing in comparisons for analysis.

The Roger Maris case is the best illustration.

In 1961, Maris hit 61 homers, breaking Babe Ruth's hallowed mark. Two-thirds of the way through the season, Commissioner Ford Frick had issued his famous "asterisk" ruling, although he didn't use the word *asterisk*. In 1927, when Ruth hit 60 homers, the schedule called for 154 games. In 1961, it was 162 games. Therefore, said Frick, to break Ruth's mark, Maris would have to hit 61 homers in the first 154 games.

Now, if you say that fast enough, it may sound reasonable. But if you start to think about it, the argument evaporates.

Let's start with semantics: A "season" record is either a record for one complete season, or it is nothing at all. Yes, 162 games is more than 154, but 154 is more than 140, and it just happened that during the same season, 1961, Sandy Koufax broke the National League record for strikeouts—which Christy Mathewson had set in 1903, when the schedule called for 140 games. Why didn't Frick insist on "asterisking" Koufax's record? Because he wasn't aware of it, and no one had paid any attention to such a difference since 1904; but Ruth's record had strong emotional overtones, so this number-of-games issue was not only raised but widely supported.

But what about the numbers themselves? When a tie game is played, all the individual records count, but the game is replayed to a decision. Thus the legendary 1927 Yankees, for whom Ruth hit 60, played 155 games that season—and Ruth missed four of them. But the Detroit Tigers, back before World War I, had played 162 games in one season, although the schedule called for 154 (they had 10 ties, and two scheduled games were unplayed); what about records that might have been set by that Tiger team?

And what about logic? If 154 games, why the first 154? If some equivalence is being sought, when can the question of schedule balance be ignored? In the 154-game schedule, the Yankees faced each of seven other teams 22 times; in the 162-game schedule, nine opponents are met 18 times apiece—already an irreconcilable difference. But taking the first 154 games of a 162-game schedule means that eight games— with only two or three opponents—are to be arbitrarily ignored. For that matter, why not the last 77 games of one year and the first 77 of the next?

Anyhow, the whole idea of using the same number of games is an attempt to level off opportunities—but the real opportunities are measured by the number of times a player comes to bat, not by the number of games his team happens to play. The 1927 Yankees had an exceptionally strong hitting team, which batted around more often, and players at the top of the batting order came to bat more frequently than the 1961 Yankees did. In fact, a little research shows that Ruth, in 1927, came to bat 692 times—and Maris, in 1961, came up 698 times.

Which standard should be used, then? Times up? Games played? Games scheduled? Official times at bat?

Why bother?

A season is a season is a season, and the Frick-Maris case—well-intentioned on Frick's part but quite unfair to Maris—is an instance of the mess that can result when statistics are used unthinkingly.

Also entirely legitimate is the *recreational* use of statistics: for trivia, argument, board games, contemplation, historical satisfaction, theorizing, or just plain love of numbers. Here the modern technology has been a blessing, because in this respect, the more elaboration the better. The great compilations in the encyclopedias published during the last twenty years were started by amateurs who were ahead of their time in being computer friendly. SABR—the Society for American Baseball Research—was started by people who had no official connection with baseball, and it now has thousands of members and does marvelous work. Its newsletter and larger publications have enriched baseball's archives and all those with more than a superficial interest in this aspect of the game. Self-starters like Bill James *(Baseball Abstract)* expanded the scope of such activity. But Allan Roth, hired by Branch Rickey for Brooklyn in the 1940s, is the real developer of detailed, beyond-standard stats.

The Smithsonian Institution of sports statistics is the Elias Sports Bureau, the official statistician for the major leagues, the National Football League, and National Basketball Association, and a host of private clients. The American League had its own statistics bureau for many years, but of course the two leagues coordinated through Elias. (The National used Al Munro Elias, father of the Elias Bureau subsequently presided over by Seymour Siwoff this last quarter of a century; the American used the Howe News Bureau of Chicago before creating its own setup in Boston.) Howe and Elias laid their foundations entirely with pencil and paper. Meanwhile, *The Sporting News* of St. Louis developed its own huge statistical operation.

The new, independent amateur statisticians (some of whom turned professional) created all sorts of analytic devices that attack the first deficiency mentioned: proportion of opportunities. Breaking down "when" something happens is harder, but less impossible now that a body of play-by-play material is being built up in the computers and in private files.

The trouble is, the more one tries to pursue scientific accuracy and completeness, the farther one gets from the thing that appeals to the ordinary fan (and especially children and teenagers): simplicity. A batting average is just long division. The number of homers or strikeouts is just a number, with more implying better. Those who enjoy complexity are drawn to baseball statistics because of their variety and availability; but many who enjoy baseball prefer to stay with old, familiar, traditional, straightforward categories that were begun in the nineteenth century precisely because they were the easiest thing to note down and count.

Al Campanis, every time we met, loved to remind me of a quote attributed to Disraeli: "There are lies, damned lies, and statistics." Numbers will certainly lie to you, but only if you let them.

The trick is to find the ones that are really relevant to some point you want to make, and exert the discipline to ignore the rest. The trouble is that in order to wind up with a few pithy, pertinent, illuminating, and intriguing statistical notes, you have to keep *all* the statistics all the time.

But just because you keep them, you don't have to use them all— and you don't have to draw totally questionable conclusions out of whole cloth.

My own view is that the SABR mania (and I speak as a member of the organization) has gone out of control. The Bill James approach, of cloaking totally subjective views (to which he is entirely entitled) in some sort of asserted "statistical evidence," is divorced from reality. The game simply isn't played that way, and his judgments are no more nor less accurate than anyone else's. The truly mathematical manipulations—regressive analysis and all that—do not, in my opinion, add to what is already known on the *working* level. They are perfectly valid and even brilliant as material for conversation, recreation, argument, trivia-hunting, and anything else one wants to enjoy about them. But they don't tell a professional—a player, manager, or scout—anything he doesn't know anyhow by observation. And when his observation conflicts with the printout, he—and I—will trust his observation every time, for two reasons.

The first is that no matter how you manipulate them, you're starting with gross counts of hits, outs, sacrifices, etc. If it helps you to rank players according to some formula, fine; but it doesn't alter what did (or will) happen. And what has been recorded was not fine-tuned in the first place, ignoring all sorts of factors that might have been (but weren't) counted. GIGO.

The second reflects my belief, already declared too often, that the reality of the game is dynamic, human, intuitive, and unpredictable, and that even the most elaborate numerical description barely scratches the surface of complex actuality. Most professionals feel the same way.

The other famous saying, of course, is: "Figures don't lie, but liars can figure." That brings us back to contract negotiations, and matters to be pursued in later chapters.

CHAPTER

16

Scoring

Before you can have statistics, you have to have someone keeping a record of what's happening. And to keep a record, you have to agree on certain definitions of how to categorize the separate incidents. And that's how official scorers were born.

The one man who, far more than any other, invented the box score, the profession of baseball writing, the keeping of records, and the role of official scorer was Henry B. Chadwick. He was born in England and came to Brooklyn at the age of thirteen as part of an affluent family. He began writing for newspapers at nineteen. When he was a twenty-three-year-old newlywed, he attended a baseball game being played by the Knickerbocker Club at Hoboken, New Jersey, across the Hudson River from mid-Manhattan, at a place called Elysian Fields. Only the year before—this was in 1847—the Knickerbockers had begun using a new set of playing rules systematized by one Alexander Cartwright. Chadwick, steeped in the English games of cricket (which was popular in New York then) and rounders, was enchanted with this faster game. He became the first full-time, and to this day still the most prolific, chronicler of baseball affairs. By the time he died (in Brooklyn) in 1908, he had worked for six New York newspapers, established the format and supplied the content for annual record books, and published countless volumes of baseball material. He's the only professional baseball writer in the Hall of Fame proper at Cooperstown, inducted in 1938, just two years after its establishment.

Chadwick's influence, and insight, established patterns that have never changed. He saw the usefulness of recording a summary of the game in tabular form, and thus in distinguishing between a hit (positive achievement by the batsman) and an error (a misplay by the fielder). But this point—and others—presupposed that someone would have to make an arbitrary decision about which was which. The lone umpire had his hands full running the game and settling arguments. A recorder affiliated with either side would naturally make interpretations favorable to his side, and if rival scorers disagreed, what would be the call? (Rival scorers did disagree; early box scores of the same game don't always jibe.) Obviously, a neutral judge was needed.

Chadwick was neutral, and respected, and set a good example. But when the professional, commercialized, catering-to-the-public leagues became established, they recognized that team-affiliated scorers would lack credibility, and that their output would lack uniformity. The only people present at every game who were officially neutral and reasonably knowledgeable were the newspaper writers covering the game. So the scoring function eventually passed to them.

It has, in recent years, passed away from them, too. The combination of expansion and fewer papers reduced the pool of experienced baseball writers. Newspaper managements, belatedly besotted with ethical questions in the turbulent 1960s and 1970s, decided a conflict of interest existed if a writer covering the game was also a part of it (able to end or continue a possible no-hitter, for instance), and in many cases forbade their writers to continue serving as scorers. Some still do, but in each city now the scoring assignment is meted out by the league to anyone suitable—a retired writer (most often), a local coach, a less-than-regular baseball writer.

What does a scorer actually do?

During the game, he makes a few decisions when necessary—hit, error, passed ball, wild pitch—but mostly he keeps an accurate record of every play (not every pitch) so that he can do his real job: fill out a summary form after the game that will go to the league office and become the "official" record of that game. It's *only* a tabular summary. Believe it or not, no *official* play-by-play record was deemed worth keeping through most of baseball history (although informal files began to exist when the Associated Press started a play-by-play service in the 1950s; the computers have them now).

Now, calling something a hit or an error is, unavoidably, an exercise in discretion. The element of opinion can never be eliminated.

But to have useful statistics, opinions have to be standardized as much as possible. Entirely apart from questions of favoritism and rooting interest, unless the play called a "hit" in Pittsburgh is determined on the same basis as in Cincinnati the added-up totals won't mean much. After all, the whole premise of the statistical approach is "all things being equal"; the principle of counting rests on ignoring all characteristics except the number of (assumed) identical objects.

So reducing to a minimum the individual scorer's area of discretion is a basic goal of systematized scoring. This leads immediately to a philosophical conflict. Since a hit is "good" and an error is "bad," the scorer can see himself as a judge awarding praise or blame, or a teacher giving a passing or failing grade. And this is how most fans, most players, and too many scorers look at it.

The other school of thought, to which I subscribe, sees the scorer as an instrument of uniformity, not moral judgment. Every similar play (already a fuzzy concept) should be scored the same way by different scorers in different places, to make the raw material of compilation as sound as possible. Avoidance of GIGO—garbage in, garbage out—should be a prime concern.

This outlook has led to official rules of scoring, included as Rule 10 of the Official Baseball Rules and running for twenty-five pages through twenty-four numbered subsections. It makes some calls automatic and spells out the approach to all.

On the key question of hit-error, the operative words are "ordinary effort" by the fielder. Forget "ought to" and "he's a major leaguer and should make that play" and how hard or softly the ball was hit. You must simply judge if ordinary effort would have resulted in an out. If you think it would have been a fine play if the fielder had made it, then it's not an error if he didn't.

One could adopt a much stricter standard, and it would be valid. But what counts is that every scorer observe the same standard. And there's a specific note emphasizing the point at the end of Rule 10.05, the one that defines hits: "NOTE: In applying the above rules, always give the batter the benefit of the doubt. A safe course to follow is to score a hit when exceptionally good fielding of a ball fails to result in a putout."

So a great stop followed by an off-balance, inaccurate throw is a hit; a slow roller that an in-rushing third baseman swipes at barehanded and misses is a hit; a ball an outfielder doesn't hold after a long run is a hit. Otherwise, you would be penalizing the fielder for making a good effort, and depriving the batter of something he earned.

There are myths, and ball players as well as fans (and ex-player broadcasters) cling to them. Must the first hit, especially after five innings or so, be a "good" one, since it breaks up a no-hitter? Definitely not. A hit is a hit, or it's not. Does it matter if a fielder touches the ball or not? Not at all. It was an ordinary effort or it wasn't, and letting a ball go through your legs untouched is a failure of ordinary effort, and an error.

Degrees of difficulty have been taken into consideration. A pitch that bounces before it reaches the catcher and then gets by him is a wild pitch by definition, not a passed ball; sure, the catcher blocks lots of those, but it's more than ordinary effort when he does. A foul tip not caught can't be an error. An inaccurate throw to a base trying to catch a runner stealing can't be an error (unless it's wild enough to allow an extra base to be taken) because a difficult play is being attempted. (If the runner didn't think he had an advantage, he wouldn't be running.) An inaccurate throw on a double-play pivot that fails to get the second out at first can't be an error; but if it's a good throw, and the first baseman simply drops it, it can be. A fielder evidently blinded by sun or lights is deprived of making an "ordinary" catch, so if he doesn't, it's a hit. Ordinary effort.

Players, whose capacity for objectivity is practically nonexistent (and objectivity is not a useful quality in a competitor), complain about scoring all the time. There is a basic conflict in motivation—the player wants what's favorable to his record, the scorer wants to call the play correctly—and it is complicated by several exceedingly human factors: Some scorers are less competent than others; some do not manage to give the job 100 percent attention; some do permit themselves to favor the home player at least a little. For the last-mentioned service, however, no scorer has ever been thanked; he has merely put some other scorer on the spot, having given a chance for all the players in other cities to yell at their scorer, "In every other town they give the home team a break, but not here, you no-good four-eyed little————." This sort of friction is not too bad if it stops short of physical assault, but sometimes it doesn't.

Fellow writers, also, are not above criticizing a scorer, and that can lead to noise in the press box. My favorite incident occurred in 1952, in old Yankee Stadium, and involved two of the legendary long-lived baseball writers of all time, Dan Daniel and John Drebinger.

It's August. Virgil Trucks is pitching for the Tigers. The Yankees don't get a hit in the first two innings and we know that Trucks has already pitched a no-hitter this year, back in May. The idea of a pitcher getting two no-hitters in one season is fresh in our minds because Allie Reynolds did it for the Yankees just last year.

Drebby is the official scorer. Phil Rizzuto hits a grounder to Johnny Pesky. The Detroit shortstop has trouble getting the ball out of his glove, and finally throws late to first.

Drebby has his head down—not unusual for any scorer—so he naturally looks to the rest of us for help. He has seen it, but not as clearly as he'd have liked.

"It's an error, John," we tell him plainly, and he is ready to agree. An error is announced.

But down at the right-hand end of the press box sits Daniel, the only man in the press box of Drebinger's own age (their sixties). He is shaking his head and waggling his forefinger in the traditional signal for "hit."

Drebby can't really trust the young punks who surround him. He's been working with Daniel (with whom he has argued incessantly) for thirty years. He changes it to a hit.

We (about half a dozen of us) think this is ridiculous. We ask Daniel why, and what did he think he was looking at?

"Ball stuck in the man's glove," growls Daniel. "That's always a hit."

It is? Why? Is this a tradition made up on the spot, or some ancient precept suddenly resurrected? If ever there was a routine play, this was it.

"Stuck in the glove," Daniel insists. "That's how you call it."

The argument rages on for four innings. At one point, we phone down to the dugout and get Pesky. Definitely an error, he says; easy play; just failed to get a grip on the ball.

Finally, around the sixth inning, Drebinger gives in to reason and changes it back to an error.

Of course, no one else has gotten a hit. No one else does. Trucks completes his second no-hitter. Great feat. Happened only twice before—Johnny Vander Meer, in succession, in 1938; Reynolds, 1951. (And only once since: Nolan Ryan, 1973.)

In the next day's *World-Telegram*, Daniel waxes appropriately rhapsodic about Trucks's achievement and makes note of the controversy. "At first," he writes, "the official scorer *for some strange reason* called it a hit."

My emphasis.

CHAPTER

17

The Owners

Here's how I described club owners twenty years ago:

Nowhere is myth more deeply entrenched than in the area of baseball ownership. The word associations of "sportsman" and "moneygrubber" represent the opposite ends of the scale by which our society measures the men whose money is invested in major-league teams. Neither term comes anywhere near the truth.

Baseball owners are capitalists, pure and simple, in an age when pure and simple capitalists are harder to find every day. Without exception, but in varying degrees, they are wealthy men, since only men who are already wealthy have the money to buy their way into this extremely exclusive company. But "wealth," of course, is a relative term: The millions commanded by a Phil Wrigley, who owns the Chicago Cubs, are incomparably greater than the hundreds of thousands a Walter O'Malley was able to control in acquiring the Brooklyn Dodgers. O'Malley was a successful lawyer with a shrewd eye for politics, finances, and promotional manipulaton, and he qualifies as a "self-made man"—but the point is that he made himself first, outside of baseball, and then got into it.

They are also, in attitude, closer to the robber-baron image of the nineteenth-century industrial autocrat than any other surviving segment of the business community. They exercise absolute power within each 24th of their monopoly, and collectively maintain a policy of internal *laissez faire* and external imperialism. In their prime commodity—player talent—they held off any taint of trade unionism until 1969. In matters of government subsidy and supervision, they have remained unsullied, while taking full advantage—like all good nineteenth-century capitalists—of governmental protective and favor-granting powers.

Thus baseball owners, as a group, tend to be extremely conservative politically, and—perhaps with all sincerity, perhaps not—to equate their peculiar ways of doing business with the Foundations of the Republic. Mom, apple pie, and the unhindered operation of the baseball monopoly are obviously equally sacred to the American Way of Life. That tax laws should make possible baseball profits; that antitrust provisions of the law must have exemptions for baseball; that municipalities and counties should indirectly subsidize a ball club by paying for a new stadium and roads; and that any attempt to set up a rival organization in the same business must be ruthlessly stamped out—these are the ideas taken for granted by the baseball community, and they are quite in tune with a philosopohy that sees the function of government as helping business and keeping its hands out of most other things. The principles of high tariff (restrictions of players' activity outside of Organized Baseball); colonialism (the farm systems); labor as a commodity (the reserve clause, trades, blacklists); *laissez faire* (free movement of franchises regardless of local conditions); a "public be damned" attitude whenever an owner's desires conflict with the public's; a certain amount of *noblesse oblige* charity (the pension plans); these principles are still the reality of baseball half a century after they had been modified or abandoned, or at least modernized, in most other activities.

Does this mean that baseball owners are ogres, to be shunned by liberal-minded contemporaries? Or to be looked upon as heroes by the new wave of conservatives? Not at all. It simply means that they should be seen for what they are: prosperous businessmen, each with his own character and mind, but sharing with all the others the common desire to make money and get personal attention.

How much must the picture be changed in the 1990s?
Less than you might think.

Nevertheless, it is significantly different in several respects, not the least of which is public exposure of their activities. We know much more than we used to about how clubs really operate, thanks to the Players Association, lawsuits, the television industry, revelations in other sports, and a cultural climate that pays less respect to the rights of privacy. And since they know we know, they give a lot more attention to how things look.

The central thrust of the above description remains valid. Owners own. That's the bottom line (a concept they cherish). While they can't have things all their own way as much as they used to, they still can't be forced to do anything they don't want to. It is their enterprise— lock, stock, and barrel.

However:

They no longer have absolute control over the movement of players and salary structures, although they still have a lot more than managements do in almost any other business.

They are a different mix of individuals than the groups of twenty or forty or sixty years ago.

They live in a different tax structure and national economy than they once did.

They have prospered beyond anybody's wildest dreams, but face some dangers that didn't exist in the past.

And they are part of a much more elaborate internal structure, with inter-club responsibilities, than ever before.

When Dick Young dubbed them "The Lords of Baseball" back in the 1950s, they were indeed similar to medieval dukes or local kings, with absolute power within each one's domain and only a loose allegiance to a central kingdom (the two leagues and the commissionership). Now they have delegated more authority to the center (through national television and labor relations necessities) while tempering their local rule with something like constitutional monarchy—not the figurehead monarchy of today's England, but the still muscular sort of the great European powers in the middle of the nineteenth century.

Two new myths have arisen, just as false as the old ones. The first is that ball clubs are now owned by "corporations" instead of "individuals." They are indeed, but they always were, for the most part. What has changed is the legal and financial pattern of how wealthy people arrange their affairs, and our ability to know about it. It's true that before the income tax (1913) it wasn't necessary to structure one's holdings in as complicated a fashion as it is now; but even then, the men who owned breweries or real estate or transportation companies and then bought baseball clubs thoroughly integrated both the cash and the motives of their various businesses.

The second is that, since the reserve system was cracked open in the 1970s, the owners are "at the mercy" of their unionized players who "demand" outrageous million-dollar salaries. Players certainly have a stronger bargaining position than before—they'd have to, since they started from zero—but they can't demand or force anything that club owners are unwilling to give them. Even with agents, players do not walk into a management office brandishing machine guns and yelling "Open that safe!" Nor could they, if they struck for ten years and shut down the baseball industry forever, seriously affect the financial health of their employers, few of whom depend on baseball for a living. (And those who do make baseball their primary business, like the late Walter O'Malley's son Peter, have other resources too by now.) The loss of absolute power does not imply becoming powerless. It just means that considerable power is less than absolute.

So some of the general characteristics outlined in the 1970s, which also applied in the 1930s and the early 1900s to varying degrees, remain valid in the 1990s.

All owners are in baseball to make money. It doesn't necessarily follow that the money they hope to make will come directly from the operation of the baseball club; the indirect benefits of baseball fame to other business are well known. The means of financial advantage—taxes, other business, publicity—may vary, but the goal is always the same: profit.

All owners want public notice, or at least the notice of some prominent local group important to them. If the owner wanted *merely* profit, he could make more in surer ways by other investments. It is the combination of profit *and* a certain kind of fame that brings an already successful man into baseball.

Most owners—but definitely not all—are sincere baseball fans, with a deep rooting interest in their club, and perhaps in baseball generally. What must always be remembered is that this emotional attachment, while real, always comes *second* to economic necessity. Owners will put up with financial loss in order to remain in action; they will rarely *choose* financial loss for sentimental or "sporting" reasons. The sad fact is that, with rare exceptions, when a clear-cut choice arises between more victories and more profit, the path toward more profit is chosen. (Fortunately, this wrenching emotional experience isn't confronted too often, since as a rule victory on the field promotes profit; but this isn't always and automatically true. Roy Eisenhardt, who presided over the building of the post–Charley Finley Oakland Athletics into the champions they became in the late 1980s, gives a fascinating lecture to law school students—he's also a law professor—on how the steps that produce a winning team and the steps that produce financial health are *not* the same and are often unrelated. Even in other businesses, the better product doesn't always mean the biggest commercial success, although most of the time it does.)

No one but an owner has any real, ultimate power on any gut issue—not the commissioner, not the league presidents, not the general managers, not the public interest, and not the press (which can manipulate public response). Much flim-flam surrounds the exercise of authority by all these other people, but it is illusory: It is true that 99 percent of the time the owners don't bother to interfere with routine matters. But when anything really fundamental is involved—expansion, or television money, or rules of operation, or pensions, or player relations—the owners and *only* the owners decide through committees and votes. The commissioner, theoretically, is at the top of the baseball structure, but in reality he is the *employee* of the owners. He can be more or less persuasive on any issue, and exert more or less leadership, but he can *never* act against their collective will. Anytime one loses sight of that fact, one loses the ability to comprehend clearly what is happening in baseball.

Some owners, sometimes, feel civic and public responsibility and act accordingly. Only some.

All owners are surrounded by employees, assistants, and advisers whose prime interest it is to keep the owner convinced that he has an excellent staff. It is the staff that handles the day-to-day details. This is what has grown so large recently, as we saw in an earlier chapter, and like any bureaucracy, it has increased influence upward and created tremendous inertia.

Most owners have little understanding of the nature of baseball, the feelings of its participants and spectators, or the true dimensions of baseball problems—because they did not spend their early or even youthful years around baseball, and because they can give it only a small portion of their time and attention now. Their assistants, at the general-manager level, do have the necessary knowledge, contact, and understanding of the ground roots, but often fail to make the right points to their employers because of the difficulty in making an unprepared boss—even a bright boss—grasp the subtler issues.

Another set of factors magnifies the gap between most owners' conception of the baseball world and the real thing. Since they are already capable, successful men in their own fields, with plenty of money, they tend to refuse to accept the idea that they *don't* understand. Like most successful people, they come to believe that methods they *know* have proved successful in the past can be used in a new situation. (We saw a similar problem in changing a hitter's style.)

The successful industrialist, or the heir to a fortune, is usually confident of his own judgment: He has the money to prove it, and he is accustomed to having his orders followed unquestioningly. Whatever else Fitzgerald might have had in mind in the opening words of his story "The Rich Boy"—"The very rich are different from you and me"—he was dealing with one pertinent facet of this chapter: The habitually rich live in an environment different from ordinary people, and therefore develop different responses—but while this difference can be more or less sidestepped in other pursuits, in baseball the very rich man or woman (the owner) is dealing directly with the emotional reactions of the definitely not-rich (the fans), and it's not surprising that an empathy gap results.

And this is further complicated by the probable character of a man who chooses to buy a baseball club. He is money-oriented, if he is self-made, because that's what it takes to be self-made; he then tends to measure success and failure in money terms. He is not of deeply intellectual bent, since he has chosen being a baseball owner over collecting art or endowing symphony orchestras. He is outgoing to some degree, at least within his peer group, or he wouldn't have chosen so public a position.

Such men, with such interests, are likely to make mistakes precisely when it counts: in those few but important situations in which the subtle peculiarities of baseball life require a solution different from that called for in apparently similar circumstances in other fields. Such men find it hard to accept that they *don't* know, and hard to listen to those who do.

So let's sum it up by asking the six traditional journalistic questions: who, what, why, when, where, and how.

Who are they? Men and women with already available financial and local political clout, which invariably pre-dates and outlasts their baseball connection.

Why are they club owners? Because they want attention for themselves (as ego satisfaction), or for their other activities (business, politics, charity). Some may shun the spotlight on a personal level, but in a peer group or social setting *all* want to be identified and envied as members of this exclusive club.

Where do they come from? The white conservative establishment.

When did they get into baseball? Relatively recently. Of the 12 National League ownerships in place at the end of 1989, half were not there in 1979; of the 14 in the American League, only six go back the 10 years. Since 1969, when the expansion to 24 teams set modern patterns—divisional play, new ballparks, recognition of the player union, active marketing—only five principal ownerships remain unchanged: the Angels, the Royals, the Dodgers, the Expos, and the Cardinals.

What are they worth? Personally, in the tens and hundreds of millions; corporately, in the tens of billions. But the baseball industry itself, in total revenues, reached $1 billion annually only at the end of the 1980s—a small fraction of their aggregate holdings.

How do they maintain control? By a monopoly status, certified by law only for baseball but culturally acceptable for major-league sports in general because the nature of the activity—defining a closed group of "the best" teams in any sport playing a coordinated schedule— seems to justify it.

By far the most important of those six items is the "when."

Up to 1960, the exclusive club was exclusive indeed: Sixteen clubs, the same number established in 1901, had absolute autonomy. In beating off a rival league (the Federal) in 1914–15, Organized Baseball not only established its economic base but won its antitrust exemption.

Expansion then began to dilute individual power, but collective absolutism remained in place until the early 1970s. Then collective bargaining, accepted as the price of preserving the antitrust exemption in the Curt Flood case (we'll come to that in the next chapter), loosened the owners' grip on the players—but not on the public or the ability to move franchises.

The fact that so few of today's owners have direct experience with the full reserve system, while so many of their high-ranking employees still come out of the absolute-control mindset that prevailed for so long, is the source of many of the difficulties club owners faced in the 1980s.

And there's a big cloud on the horizon. As recently as 1973, George Steinbrenner's group could buy the New York Yankees from CBS for about $12 million. The Haas family paid that in 1980 to Finley for the A's. No club on the open market cost as much as $20 million up to that time.

But when the New York Mets were sold in 1986 the price was in the $80-million range, and since then more such deals have made $100 million a reasonable round number for a first-class franchise in 1990.

This changes the ball game. If you buy a team for $8 million, no matter how you finance it, the debt burden is not overwhelming. (If you don't borrow the money, you commit the same amount that stops earning elsewhere, so the interest-cost factor is roughly the same.) But when you buy one for $80 million, the need for cash flow becomes entirely different—more pressing—and the types of business decisions you are likely to make will be driven by different imperatives. This will affect player relations, marketing, the prospects of resale to "the next biggest sucker," and needs for new parks or locations. I believe that all major-league sports will face this unprecedented set of circumstances as the new century approaches.

The "danger" I referred to above is the lack of experience and guidelines for dealing with such a situation in what has always been—and still is—a trial-and-error business of holding and building (especially building) the public's affection for the product.

No matter how this and other problems may be met, however, only the owners can meet them. The "game" does not belong to the fans, the players, historical tradition, kids, a home city, philosophical fascination, or anything else writers and commentators romanticize, with self-serving rhetorical encouragement from the industry. It belongs to the club owners, period. We can root for them to choose wisely, but rooting is all the rest of us can do.

CHAPTER
18

The Players Association

Now we come to the part everybody hates: labor relations.

But if we ignore it, we blind ourselves to a large segment of baseball reality. The Players Association, its activities, and management's response to it are as central to the conduct of the major leagues as the commissioner's office or the individual clubs. Salary standards, grievances, work rules, and drug testing make dull enough reading compared to game heroics, personality features, and statistical gems. But actual strikes, lockouts, defection by a player from your favorite team, and constant reminders of how much even inferior players make while ticket and beer prices creep ever upward—these infuriate most fans and poison the atmosphere they turned to for enjoyment in the first place. When sports pages become choked with this sort of material, crowding out "real baseball news," most readers wind up angry, frustrated, and ultimately bored.

Take my word for it: Most writers feel the same way.

There's a remark attributed to various prominent persons: "On Page One, I read of mankind's failures; I turn to the Sports Page to read of mankind's triumphs." If you relate to that sentiment, and love the romance, poetry, drama, intriguing detail, and game variety of baseball as most of us experience it, and are content to live within its satisfying mythology, and don't want to be aggravated—then by all means skip the rest of this chapter. You won't miss anything that has to do with the game itself.

But if you hope to understand anything at all about the reality of baseball life, and the reasons for so many unwelcome developments, you have to wade through this employer-employee stuff. It's the mountain that has to be climbed not only because it's there, but because only from its summit can you get a glimpse of the lay of the land.

And the best way to approach it is historically.

We need a bit of ancient history as background. The prototype of major-league competition was the National Association of Professional Base Ball Players. (Yes, "baseball" was two words then.) It operated from 1871 through 1875, and as its name indicated, made players the ruling element in the clubs they played for. The trouble was, they kept shifting from club to club in a way that bewildered a team's followers; the best ones tended to cluster on a couple of teams to the detriment of even competition; there was no effective discipline on such matters as gambling, contract-jumping, and "rowdyism"; and precious few had any idea of how to handle a club's finances, let alone their own.

So in 1876, perfectly in tune with the entrepreneurial capitalism of that day, there was formed the National League of Professional Base Ball *Clubs*. Each club was to be run by professional businessmen, not players, and these managements, banded into a league, could honor each other's contracts, live up to schedules, enforce discipline, and create enough stability to keep customers. Most of all, a club would have permanent continuity, while players came and went.

The central problem remained competition for top players. Each club sought the best players it could get, and each of the leading players had clubs bidding for his services. If they shifted around too often, fan loyalty could not be created. So, within three years, the business-minded club managements came up with a system of "reservation." They were already not tampering with one another's stars while under contract during a season. Now they decided each club could "reserve the rights" to sign a player for *next* season so that no other club would even try to hire him.

At first, only a few (I think five) players could be "reserved"—that is, retained *between* contracts—so it was something of a distinction to be one of them. It meant you were among the best, and guaranteed employment for the next year.

It also meant, of course, that you—one of the best players, by definition—suddenly had no bargaining power, since there was no other club *inside the league* willing to make you an offer. In pursuit of "stability," the new club owners found a way to hold down salaries by avoiding bidding wars.

Pretty soon the number of players you could put "on reserve" went up, to nine, eleven, and fifteen (which was more or less the whole roster in those days). Meanwhile, because the National League was being successful and because plenty of capable players were not reserved, a second major league quickly developed, the American Association, modeled on the club-control system the National had devised. It had its own reserve system, and it didn't take long for the two leagues to agree to observe each other's contracts.

Of course, such a conspiracy to refuse employment and to "assign" workers to associated firms would violate the very heart of antitrust law—but, in the 1880s, there wasn't any antitrust law yet. The system thrived.

By 1885, all players in both leagues were subject to the reserve. The provision in the player contract establishing this club right came to be known as the famous, and eventually infamous, "reserve clause."

With such a weapon, the club owners had a degree of control no one had originally imagined. Why not use it to put a ceiling on salaries and enhance profits (which were still modest and risky)? The National League decided to try. In 1888—just twelve years after the whole concept of club government had been invented—it put forth a salary classification system at much lower levels than were then current.

The players rebelled. They didn't exactly strike, since this was a time when the idea of a labor union was still sheer radicalism. They did better. They found backers, started their own league, quit the National en masse, and, in effect, tried to return to the essential feature of the old Association that had failed—player-investors running their own clubs.

All this happened in the year 1890. The Players League challenged the National not only by putting teams in the same cities, but by scheduling games at the same time. Three leagues operated that year, with most of the established stars in the Players League and the American Association (in smaller cities and with a smaller financial base) relatively untouched.

Naturally, everyone went broke.

There was interest, all right. Total baseball attendance was the highest ever, but it was split three ways. By the end of the year, the Players League teams were financial busts, the National was barely breathing, and the American Association was a wounded bystander. The National took back the stars. The Players League folded. The American Association folded a year later.

All that was called the Brotherhood War, since the players had called their proto-union the Brotherhood of Professional Base Ball Players.

And that traumatic experience fixed attitudes and established unquestioned assumptions that ruled baseball (and other American sports) virtually unchallenged for the next seventy-five years. Those attitudes remain strong in many club owners, fans, and writers to this day.

Axiom No. 1: A reserve system is necessary to prevent suicidal competition for talent.

Axiom No. 2: Therefore it is justifiable, no matter how much it offends laws, civil rights, freedom of choice, personal needs, or moral principles.

Axiom No. 3: Orderly (and therefore commercially attractive) competition can be constructed only with players so bound.

Axiom No. 4: Any loosening of the reserve clause is unthinkable, un-American, probably blasphemous, certainly ruinous, and positively out of the question.

These attitudes persisted despite a good deal of contradictory evidence. When the National League was left in a monopoly position (with 12 teams) in 1892, it entered a decade of internal turmoil and falling receipts. In 1901, a rival league, the American, claimed major status and started signing up established stars. Salary levels doubled and tripled, and by 1903 the two leagues reestablished control by interleague agreement. In 1914, an even better financed third league, the Federal, set up shop. Again, star players were enticed away and all salary levels shot upward. But this time, Organized Baseball (as the two leagues and the minors affiliated with them had come to be known) was in a stronger position. First, there were two existing leagues, not one; second, World War I was complicating the economic picture for everyone, even though the United States wasn't in it yet; and third, now that federal antitrust laws did exist and the Federal League was challenging the old leagues under them, the baseball establishment had found a friendly judge in Chicago named Kenesaw Mountain Landis. He immobilized the case until the Federal League backers gave up and sold their teams and ballparks as best they could. (Wrigley Field was built as the Federal League Chicago team's home.)

That was in1915. One of the promised opportunities to buy in was repudiated, and that led to another antitrust suit (for damages) which didn't reach the Supreme Court until 1922. That produced the exemption still in force today, the Court finding that baseball was not the sort of "interstate commerce" Congress had in mind and therefore not subject to the Sherman Act.

This opinion, a strange one even then and completely counter to the direction the Court took within a few years, was conveniently interpreted and enthroned in the mythology as "baseball is a sport, not a business." Such a formulation lent emotional (though not logical) support to further justification of the reserve clause.

But the players, despite a passive majority, were not deaf, dumb, and blind. They knew that when teams could bid for their services— in 1884, 1890, 1901, 1914—salaries went up dramatically; that when a monopoly reserve was reestablished, pay leveled off and sank. (The depressed pay scale of the 1919 Black Sox, cited by some historians as a cause of the willingness of some players to throw the World Series, was partly a consequence of the elimination of the Federal League.) When the 1920s turned out to be a boom decade, and the 1930s a depression in which anyone felt lucky to have any job, their lack of bargaining power stayed on a back burner. But after World War II, in 1946, things started to move.

An attempt to unionize in Pittsburgh was squelched immediately. But new forces had been turned loose. Millions had been in the military, industrial unions had become respectable, the GI Bill displayed how helpful collective policies could be to individuals, and Jackie Robinson's arrival highlighted new concerns for people's rights. The deepest post-depression and postwar yearning was for "security," and pension plans became the focus of attention for workers everywhere.

The baseball players could, and did, organize themselves to establish a pension plan. The owners could live with that and didn't feel threatened. Thus the Players Association was born, concerning itself almost exclusively with pension issues and a few details about spring-training expenses. Almost incidentally, it got an agreement on a minimum salary for major leaguers ($5,000). It did hire legal advice, but it explicitly rejected any "union" flavor and was administered by prominent players. The pensions were financed by All-Star Game receipts and World Series radio-television money, then extremely modest.

But the antitrust issue came up again, and this time in connection with player rights. Minor leaguers opposed being shunted around and prevented from advancing. Players who had gone to a short-lived, independent Mexican League in 1946 had been blacklisted when they tried to return. So throughout the 1950s, trouble was brewing more and more obviously on two fronts, the courts and Congress.

Lower courts found the antitrust exemption ludicrous, especially when used to control players (which had never been an issue in the original case). But the Supreme Court, in 1953, upheld it, 7–2, "without re-examination of the underlying issues" on the grounds that it was up to Congress to make any change, since "the business had been left for 30 years to develop, on the understanding that it was not subject to" antitrust law.

At the same time, throughout that decade, the same Court rejected antitrust exemptions for boxing, football, all sorts of other sports, movie theater and studio relationships, and so forth. Baseball, and baseball only, retained its unique exemption.

But Congress *was* getting into the act. In extensive public hearings in 1951 (a House Judiciary subcommittee headed by Emmanuel Celler of Brooklyn), much information about the baseball business was revealed for the first time. But almost all witnesses, including prominent and ordinary players, testified to the "necessity" of the reserve system. (One obscure witness was so captivating that exposure of his gift of gab led to a great later career: Joe Garagiola.) The myth was alive and well.

Nevertheless, congressional hearings scared baseball authorities out of their pants. They were so sure they were going to lose in court that they had fired their commissioner, Happy Chandler, in 1951 for letting things get that far. Having dodged that bullet, they felt threatened every moment by possible congressional action as called for in the very decision that saved them. Lobbying against that possibility became their prime concern. And it has been successful lobbying to this day.

The message to the players, of course, was clear: We won't get bargaining power through lawsuits. The idea of becoming better organized began to percolate, slowly but irresistibly.

By the middle of the 1960s, the Players Association had a structure and history, and pensions were better (since World Series revenue had increased). The antitrust threat, through congressional hearings, had forced expansion in 1961–62 as an alternative to a third major league (the stillborn Continental, triggered by the move of the Giants and Dodgers out of New York), so the creating of new jobs and the enthusiasm of new cities eased some of the pressure on player control. But "union" remained a dirty word and the reserve system was as rigid as ever.

This was the Middle Ages of baseball labor history. Modern times began in 1966.

As their principal adviser, the players replaced Judge Robert Cannon, who considered himself part of the baseball establishment trying to represent player interests, with Marvin Miller, an "outsider" who had been an economist for the steel workers' union and an experienced labor negotiator. Miller had three things going for him: (1) exceptional ability to educate his own members combined with great personal integrity; (2) a clear understanding that the player-owner working-condition relationship was adversarial, always had been, and couldn't be otherwise; and (3) more brains in this particular field than all the baseball executives put together.

But the most significant sign of change was the fact that the players hired such a man. They were, at last, psychologically prepared to act together and to accept the need for expertise in their leadership.

What Miller knew was that negotiation is impossible without some minimum equality of weaponry, and that for employees, that weaponry was lodged in labor laws—which hadn't existed in the 1890s or 1920s. Only by functioning as an authentic labor union could players bargain instead of beg, and begging had left them far behind the rest of society (including sports) in dollars and degree of freedom in career choices. The average major-league salary in 1950 (the Celler committee had revealed) was $10,500. In 1966, after two decades of inflation, it was still only $23,000 with more than half making less than $17,000. (At that time, half of *all* self-employed males were making more than $15,000 a year, while only 500 had the special talent to be major-league ball players.)

Even within sports, the baseball players were out of step. In 1963, Willie Mays was the highest-paid player at $105,000. At the end of the 1964 football season, the New York Jets, unsuccessful members of an upstart American Football League, gave Joe Namath a $400,000 package before he had played a single minute as a professional. In 1966, the Green Bay Packers, champions of the National Football League, shelled out $650,000 for a running back named Donny Anderson, drafted but not signed the year before. (These were multi-year agreements, but the numbers made their impact anyhow.) But when Sandy Koufax and Don Drysdale, in the spring of the same year, held out for $165,000 apiece after pitching the Dodgers to two World Series championships in the preceding three years, they were vilified for their greed and regarded as a danger to the Republic. They had to settle for $125,000 (Sandy) and $110,000 (Don).

So against the resistance of myth, media, management hostility, and misconceptions, Miller led his constituency to acceptance of an inescapable truth: If you act like a union, talk like a union, pursue and gain goals like a union, you'll look like a union. But to do that, you have to *be* a union to enjoy its legal privileges and protections.

It was a constituency quite ready for such conversion. If it hadn't been, it wouldn't have looked for, hired, and continued to support such a man. They were lucky they found one with Miller's particular capabilities. But management, which went on deceiving itself for years that he was a pied piper leading naive and loyal ball players astray, failed to grasp that if it hadn't been Miller it would have been someone else. The historical details would have been different and, most likely, would have progressed more slowly. But the end result would have been the same.

The rest of the story leads to events still unfolding.

In 1967, for the first time, a "players agreement"—a collective-bargaining contract—was signed. This was an orthodox labor agreement, entirely apart from pension matters (taken care of in a separate, already existing, contract). Its big achievement seemed to be a raise in the minimum salary from $7,000 to $10,000, but its really important provisions were the following: (1) a grievance procedure for violations of the agreement; (2) a prohibition on arbitrary rule or regulation changes during the life of the two-year agreement; and (3) a joint study, to be completed in two years, of "possible alternatives to the reserve clause as now constituted." The first introduced the concept of arbitrating disputes (with the commissioner as the first arbitrator). The second asserted the right of the players to have input when rule changes might affect them. The third openly mentioned the "unmentionable" subject.

In 1969, the opening of spring training was threatened while a new pension plan agreement was being negotiated, but a settlement was reached before the first exhibition game. This caused a tremendous fuss at the time, but virtually unnoticed—at first—was what happened that December: Curt Flood, traded by St. Louis to Philadelphia, challenged the reserve clause itself by asking to be allowed to seek employment with any club and, when he was routinely refused, filing an antitrust suit.

Neither Miller nor the player representatives were looking for so direct a confrontation so soon, but when Flood told them he would go ahead anyhow on his own, they couldn't afford not to give his suit all the support they could. They backed him.

A three-week trial in the spring of 1970, in New York, was a media circus with a preordained result: The lower court had no jurisdiction because of the exemption; only appeals all the way up to the Supreme Court could make the merits of the case open to a ruling. The appeals were pursued.

But a booby trap had also been set. Baseball stepped into it by contending, in post-trial public statements and in arguments presented to higher courts, that the reserve issue had nothing to do with antitrust; it was really a question of working conditions to be worked out in collective bargaining.

As Pyrrhic victories go, this was a classic. Labor law exempts collective-bargaining agreements from antitrust restrictions (so that unions can exist and employers can deal in concert). But they also demand good-faith bargaining. As a defense against antitrust, baseball not only put the reserve system on the table, it committed itself to subject it to the give-and-take of negotiation. What had been unmentionable was now untenable.

In 1972, the comedy-drama came to a climax.

Negotiations to renew the pension agreement actually did lead to a strike, the first in baseball history (if you don't count 1890). Over the trivial issue of how surplus funds were to be allocated, on which the players (but not the owners) agreed to take an arbitrator's decision before they struck, the first two weeks of the season were wiped out. The settlement made was the one available in the first place. But the players had proved their unity and established their self-confidence; the owners appeared not only disunited but inept.

But even before the strike began, in oral arguments before the Supreme Court on the Flood case, the management side repeated its commitment to bargaining on the reserve clause.

And in June, the Supreme Court handed down its verdict. Once again, it refused to reverse its previous rulings, apologizing publicly for the "anomaly" this exemption created, but insisting it was up to Congress to straighten the matter out (although Congress had never hinted at any exemption in the first place).

So the exemption was preserved—and a new general agreement was up for negotiation in 1973.

The first question was: How about loosening up the reserve?

The management side was stuck. The players had just shown they could handle a strike, if necessary, and the owners had shown they couldn't. Under the labor law they had invoked, the owners had to offer something. But any kind of open market was still unthinkable. Still, even they couldn't deny that a player prevented from seeking another employer had no leverage in asking for more money from the only one he was allowed to have.

So they accepted an alternative put forth by Miller. A salary dispute would go before an impartial professional arbitrator (definitely *not* the commissioner). This would cost them money, but the reserve itself would stay intact, pending "further study."

And arbitration worked. The salary level rose.

But not too much.

Now, what *was* this reserve clause? How did the mechanism work?

In order to be eligible to play, every player had to sign a "standard" playing contract for year X. The reserve clause was a simple option. It said that if no agreement were reached on a salary (or other terms) for year $X + 1$, the existing contract would simply be renewed automatically for year $X + 1$.

What if you didn't sign and "played out" the option year? Wouldn't that make you free?

No, said baseball and its lawyers. When the option renewed the old contract "for one year," it also renewed the option provision, plugging it in for the year after that.

You mean, Miller asked, it's a *perpetual* option?

Yep, they said.

But it says "one year," Miller pointed out. How can one year mean forever?

That's what it means, they said.

Well, gentlemen, said Miller, we have a disagreement about interpreting the contract, and under our labor agreement, such a disagreement has to be settled by an outside arbitrator.

After the 1974 season, Andy Messersmith and Dave McNally, both pitchers, refused to sign new contracts and played out the 1975 season on their option year. (McNally retired halfway through.) They claimed free agency. Their cases went to an arbitrator, Peter Seitz. (Technically, Seitz was chairman of a three-man committee: Miller, John Gaherin of management, and Seitz.) At the same time, negotiations for a new general agreement (which could, of course, contain any kind of modified reserve arrangements the parties agreed to) were in progress.

Seitz, an experienced and respected arbitrator, had no trouble with English so plain that even players and writers could understand it. "One year" did not mean "forever." Yet he understood the fears a free market generated, and accepted the myth that some kind of reserve system was essential. He urged the parties to work out a negotiated settlement—say, a ten-year limit or something like that on reserve rights, or some other adjustment short of absolute, perpetual control of players when they are not under any existing contract. He informed the management side that if they insisted on a decision, he would have to rule against them, thus wiping out all restrictions, unless some had already been agreed to in bargaining.

No deals, said baseball. Go ahead and rule.

Seitz did.

At one stroke, some 600 players were free agents, able to deal with anyone. The few still bound by multi-year individual contracts would be free whenever those expired.

That's okay, said baseball. We still think Seitz is wrong. We'll take his ruling to court and get it overturned.

The courts threw baseball out on its ear. When you submit a labor dispute to an arbitrator, you can't go over his head unless you can show he did something dishonest or improper. Reading plain English correctly did not constitute malfeasance.

And that's how things stood in February 1976. As management appealed to a higher court, and bargaining sessions continued, the clubs, at last, offered a nine-year limit on the reserve. Several star players said they'd sue Miller if he accepted, since they had just been given a zero-year limitation. The owners said they wouldn't open spring-training camps until they had a labor agreement. It was mid-March before one was reached in principle, and after an abbreviated training season the regular schedule began on time. But the new agreement wasn't actually concluded until July.

And what was it?

All the current players were given one shot at free agency, after either 1976 or 1977.

Then a reserve-option system would apply to every player for the first six years of his major-league career. When he did exercise his free-agent rights, after the sixth year or later, he couldn't do so again for another five years.

There were all sorts of complicating details (a free agent couldn't deal with all clubs, just some, and a five-year man could demand to be traded, and some veterans could refuse trades) but the essential pattern was set.

A player can be a free agent sometimes. Reserve rights remain in force most of the time for most players. And salary arbitration is available to those who aren't free agents (except for the first couple of years of major-league life).

Has this wrecked baseball? Well, in the thirteen years between 1977 and 1990 baseball made more money, had better attendance, got more favorable public approval, and took a firmer grip on the ancillary marketplace—by a wide margin—than in the eighty-six years the reserve system was in force (after 1890).

But when a new general agreement had to be negotiated in 1980, a squabble over the new system's details produced another strike threat. Spring training was shut down a week early. The strike deadline was postponed until May. The day before the strike was to start, it was agreed to "study the situation" for another year. The study got nowhere.

In June 1981, the players went on strike for two months. The clubs had bought strike insurance. When it ran out in August, a settlement was reached with nothing important changed. The issue was "compensation" to a club losing a free agent, a version of football's Rozelle Rule blasted by the courts years before, which would inhibit the signing of a free agent. The players would have none of it. The owners insisted they couldn't go on without such a concession. But they did go on, and continued to prosper faster than ever.

In July 1985, the same factors and the same issues produced another strike. But this one lasted only one day because the commissioner, Peter Ueberroth, imposed a solution favorable to the players. (Soon he was no longer commissioner.)

As 1990 began, another strike-lockout threat loomed, over the same issue—"takebacks" from the limited reserve system worked out in 1976—but with radically different details.

This time the management side was locked into a strategy devised in response to the 1985 humiliation. Unless the players agreed to terms before spring training began, the camps would be kept closed, and the season itself would not be played until and unless the players signed. They would be given no chance to start play and then strike late in the season when it would hurt.

If even the best-laid plans gang aft a-gley, this one was doomed from the start because it was a very bad plan indeed.

To begin with, a "lockout," as distinct from a "strike," put management on the wrong side with the fans, whose only concern was that their entertainment not be disrupted. Since management talked openly, for 18 months, to 650 players about its intention to enforce a lockout, a weak attempt at trying to make the media refer to it as a "strike," when the time came, lacked conviction.

Second, the biggest single obstacle to reaching any agreement, regardless of terms, was the distrust engendered by the collusion cases (which we'll describe a few paragraphs further down). The essence of these decisions by two arbitrators was that the 1985 labor agreement had been deliberately violated by the management side shortly after it was signed. How do you sit down to bargain in good faith with someone who has just been convicted of bargaining in bad faith last time around? With that antagonism already in the air, threatening a lockout was not a way to make matters move more smoothly.

Third, the threat was an empty one. To "force" players to miss spring training was like saying to your teenager: "You can't have your vegetables at dinner, but take two helpings of dessert and go to your room to watch television the rest of the evening." Spring training is no treat to ball players. They don't get paid until the regular season starts, so they don't lose income. They'd have to be given some training time, sooner or later, because their individual contracts require it and there would be damage suits for injury if they were forced to play without it. So how would keeping them out frighten them or put pressure on them to bargain?

Only if a lockout extended several pay periods into the season could it have any effect on the negotiators, even theoretically. But the players, and everyone else, knew that management had no intention of shutting down its operations in the very year that they would be getting twice as much money (from a new television deal) as ever before.

Fourth, as twenty years of experience had shown, any attempt to intimidate the players, who were individuals carefully selected for their aggressive and competitive natures and who had already been paid high salaries for many years, was bound to fail. That made a patently empty threat like this one not only silly but self-defeating.

Fifth, in the context of this self-created blind alley, the management side floated an elaborate trial balloon: an obviously unacceptable salary-limit-and-share-of-the-gross scheme that wasn't even worked out. All this did was increase the impression of bad faith, delay matters, and enhance the players' belief that the owners didn't know what they were doing.

Sixth, even while talking lockout between the seasons, the clubs had gone wild in signing free agents for double the dollars they had offered before, contradicting all talk of the need for austerity and "reason."

Seventh, the management side was in disarray. The plan had begun to take shape under Commissioner Ueberroth. It was intended to proceed under Commissioner Giamatti, who was at least familiar with it as National League president under Ueberroth. But Giamatti had died of a heart attack in September 1989. His deputy, Fay Vincent, was made commissioner with no firsthand experience in this plan or previous player negotiations. The professional negotiator brought in also had no baseball experience, while the union leadership was directly descended from Miller (who had retired) and knew firsthand all the intricacies and atmospherics of the preceding fifteen years.

It was no contest.

Spring training was delayed—devastating to local merchants in Florida and Arizona, and to the psyche of baseball fans everywhere, but no skin off the nose of either players or management. When it became clear that some sort of training must begin by mid-March if the 162-game schedule was to be preserved, an agreement was reached, curtailed camps were held, the schedule began a week late, and the missed games were interspersed through the remaining 25 weeks of the regular season.

The agreement? All the newfangled revenue-sharing ideas had long since evaporated. The players got more, in dollars and in adjustments to the arbitration system for younger players, than they would have accepted in November.

And what lay behind all this continuing turmoil? The awkward position the clubs had put themselves in originally. They were being whipsawed by the combination of salary arbitration and free agency that they had brought on themselves.

Even a little yielding on the reserve in 1973—say, the later nine-year proposal—may have fended off arbitration. Negotiation before Seitz handed down his decision might have traded arbitration for limited free agency. This way, they had the worst of both worlds. Players unable to move could get raises from an arbitrator to "prevailing rates" for their experience, record, and position, as compared to other players. This raised the floor. Then free agents (the desirable ones) went out and created bidding wars that raised their level—and that became the standard of comparison for the next round of arbitrations, which became the jumping-off point for the next set of free-agent auctions. The escalator kept gaining speed.

What Miller had perceived was that a limited free agency was better for the players than free agency for everybody every year. It created a shortage of available free-market players. Any reserve rule does "protect" your own roster—but it also prevents you from hiring anyone on someone else's roster. In any given year, only about 10 percent of the player population is going to be on the open market, so 26 clubs may be bidding for two first-class catchers. If everyone were a free agent, they'd have 52 catchers to choose from, and many of them would be eager to be assured of a job. At the same time, there would no longer be any justification for salary arbitration for anyone.

Charley Finley, the maverick owner of the Oakland A's, whose teams had won three straight World Series in 1972–74, saw that right away in 1976. He was as eager as anyone to keep the old reserve intact. But when it was breached, "Make 'em all free agents!" he declared. But who wanted to listen to him? In the long run, that may still be the right solution, but whatever the practical effect may be, baseball is not ready emotionally for such a world.

One final piece of the puzzle remains to be described. The first wave of free agency, 1977–81, had produced the million-dollar salary and a $150,000 major-league average. After the long strike, by 1985, stars were getting $2 million and the average was $350,000, with four- and five-year deals plentiful (Dave Winfield got a 10-year deal from the Yankees).

Commissioner Ueberroth urged his club owners to show "good business sense" by restraining their competitive urges, and to take a good look at how terrible each club's balance sheet looked. Suddenly, the long-term deals stopped, and free agents found other teams remarkably unwilling to offer more than their original team was offering, or even to talk to them.

This was, the union cried, "collusion." As it happened, the general agreement specifically forbade such collective action by either side—at the insistence of the clubs, who were afraid several star players (perhaps with the same agent) might band together and insist on mutually determined salary levels (high). (They remembered what Koufax and Drysdale had tried.) Now the clubs were trying to maintain levels (low, relatively speaking) "voluntarily."

The alleged collusion, if actually engaged in, would be a contract violation. Contract violations go to an arbitrator. Sound familiar?

Collusion I dealt with negotiations for the 1986 season. Collusion II concerned similar actions for 1987. Two different arbitrators found that the clubs had, indeed, engaged in the forbidden practice. (Among other things, they left a paper trail.) Collusion III for 1988 came out the same way, and the total damages (not yet determined) will be more than $100 million.

But there will be no Collusion IV, because after the 1989 season, the wildest bidding so far has produced $3-million-a-year stars, long-term contracts, an average salary pushing $500,000, and expressions of disbelief all around. One might say that club behavior at the end of 1989 removed any doubt that Collusions I, II, and III had been real, and not just simultaneously applied business wisdom by independent managements who—if that had been the case—were struck with simultaneous stupidity after losing two arbitrations.

What does all this mean, and where does it lead?

New Axiom No. 1: Since baseball's exploding gross income can't be concealed, with billion-dollar television deals and attendance records announced publicly, there's no way to deny a "fair share" of the increase to the players, whose agents can do arithmetic even when a player can't.

New Axiom No. 2: If rock musicians, movie stars, other entertainers, Wall Street hotshots, corporate executives, lawyers, and tennis players make the kind of money they do, ball players are no more "overpaid" than a lot of others.

New Axiom No. 3: Any idea that baseball can ignore laws, rights, and procedures that apply to everyone else because "sports are different" is no longer tenable.

New Axiom No. 4: The American appetite for sports entertainment—not stereotypes preferred by club owners, players, agents, commentators, or talk-show hosts—will determine who can afford to pay whom how much for what in the future. If it shrinks, salaries and franchise resale values will shrink; if it doesn't, neither will they.

What should we, the true lovers of our national game, do about it?

Nothing. Go back to reading about the ball games, and leave the financial stories to those who are obliged to deal with them.

CHAPTER
19

The Commissioner

So far, we've been trying to separate a few myths from a lot of reality. When we look at the commissionership, we find almost nothing but myth. Nothing in baseball is so thoroughly misperceived, by fans and media especially, but also by many within the industry, as the role of the commissioner.

To say that it is a mythological post does not negate its true importance. It just doesn't work the way most people think it does. And the power of myth should never be minimized in human affairs.

The image is "czar," attached so convincingly to the first one (Kenesaw Mountain Landis) in the early 1920s that it became a generic term for an organization's head granted exceptional powers to control an activity. We now speak of a "drug czar" in charge of our war on drugs. It means "autocrat" (derived from Caesar) and is more properly spelled "tsar" when referring to the late Russian emperor, whom the label-makers had in mind in 1920.

But the commissioners of baseball—or of other leagues—are anything but autocrats. They are servants, hired by the only people who have money invested in these extremely private businesses: the club owners. No matter what some lawyers try to tell you, a commissioner has *no* formal power to make owners, as a group, bend to his will against their will. All his powers are delegated to him voluntarily, subject to change and withdrawal, and he faces the most direct form of recall: He can be fired on the spot.

At the same time, he can and does wield enormous power through two less formal weapons: persuasion and myth. Internally, he can persuade his employers, or a key group of them, to do what he thinks is right and to back up the decisions he makes—and after all, if they didn't have some respect for his judgment they wouldn't have hired him. (Is that true? Not always, as we'll soon see.) Externally, the prestige created by the myth of his power gives him tremendous influence with the public, whose opinion can be mobilized against an opponent or in favor of a goal. The owners can threaten—privately or tacitly—to fire him; he can threaten—privately, tacitly, or publicly—to resign. Short of that, even a declaration of condemnation from his pulpit carries tremendous weight.

So the importance of the position is indisputable. What needs sharper definition is its function.

It is the commissioner's job to represent the "best interests of baseball" to the best of his ability. But the word "baseball" in that phrase is a euphemism, or code word, for "club owners." It is to their interests, and only theirs, that he is ultimately responsible. If the public believes he's looking out for its interests, that's obviously good for the owners. If, as used to be possible, the players believe he's "for" them, that's even better. But in any showdown and authentic conflict, if he doesn't protect his employers' interests above all others, he's not doing his job.

But times do change. Landis, in his era, acted as prosecutor, judge, and jury in supra-club disputes. He operated within a tight group of owners who thought "my league" first and "baseball" a distant second, with few administrative duties and virtually no staff. Today's commissioner is, in effect, chief executive officer of a large and varied business in which the 26 clubs see themselves more as corporate subsidiaries than sovereign fiefdoms. He runs a complex and expensive business, negotiates big deals (with television), and, all but stripped of judicial powers, faces players and public more as a delegate (from the owners) than as a representative (of player and fan constituencies).

Once again, we have to run through the history to see how today's office works.

The original National League idea of member clubs automatically required a central office and a presiding officer not connected with one of the clubs: a president. When the National and American leagues decided to work together in 1903, another level of hierarchy became needed to deal with inter-league questions. A three-man "commission" was formed, consisting of the two league presidents and a third chosen by them to act as chairman. The agreement binding the two leagues and most minor leagues (essentially, to honor each other's contracts, boycotts, and rules) was called the National Agreement, so at its top was the National Commission.

Dedicated as the club owners were to relying on insiders—the minors had no representative on the commission—an automatic imbalance emerged. The third member would be from one league or the other, when mutual trust was still fragile. The American League had the stronger president, Ban Johnson. So the chairman selected was Garry Herrmann, president of the National League's Cincinnati club (and a good friend of Johnson, who had been a Cincinnati sportswriter; when it came to "insiders," they didn't deal in half measures).

The commission system never worked well, for many reasons, and collapsed in 1919. It wasn't the fixed World Series that did it, but a civil war inside the American League about conflicting rights to a player, and similar player-control questions. At an internal political impasse, the owners had to look for "outside" leadership and settled on Landis, who had protected them so well in the Federal League antitrust case.

In 1920, Herrmann resigned in February, the Black Sox scandal became public in September, and Landis was elected in November. He didn't actually take office until January 1921. The Black Sox trial took place in July 1921, and only after they were acquitted did Landis act against them. He barred them for life, displaying his judicial experience, instinct, and frame of mind with these ringing words: "Regardless of the verdict of juries . . ." You can't get much more czarist than that, and the public approved.

The regime of Landis lasted until his death in 1944. It was, in fact, autocratic. He had insisted on "absolute" powers in his contract, but what made them absolute in practice was the situation the owners had created. Having put him before the public as their "savior," their guarantor of the game's "integrity," the man on a white horse who would end twenty years of all-too-open squabbling, the Solomon from the federal bench who embodied impartiality, the fearless judge who had fined Standard Oil $29 million and would be equally unhesitant to protect players and fans from robber-baron owners—having publicized such a portrait, how could they resist anything he might want to do? All he had to do was declare publicly what he favored, or even indicate it indirectly through some favored newspaper outlet, and any opponent would appear evil in the eyes of the nation. His trump card, a threat to resign, didn't even have to be picked up, let alone played. The image of a benign czar who loved his peasants (players and fans) and kept his nobles (the owners) in line proved to be a monster that made club owners think Dr. Frankenstein's problem had been trivial.

The fact that the image was built on exaggeration only made it more effective. He hadn't saved them from anything; Babe Ruth had. He not only entered the Black Sox situation late, but subsequently swept under the rug gambling and fixing scandals involving none less than Ty Cobb and Tris Speaker. The civil war among the owners had been settled by the decision to hire him, not by anything he did afterwards. His famous fine (imposed in 1907) had been overturned by higher courts, along with many of his later decisions. His career on the bench had been marked by prejudicial outbursts, bias, procedural irregularities, and threats against attorneys. One critic wrote of him, "Few men have been as zealous in their suppression of minorities, and his charges to juries were dangerously similar to patriotic addresses."

Another insight into his temperament can be gained from his struggle over his own compensation. His salary as a federal judge was $7,500. He was hired as commissioner for $50,000—but insisted on clinging to his judgeship at the same time. The U.S. Senate had to actually threaten him with impeachment before he would resign.

As commissioner, he had three main policies.

1. Keep baseball problems out of court, no matter what it takes to do so.
2. Oppose the development of farm systems on all fronts, often by declaring minor-league players free agents.
3. Maintain a militant air of respectability (which some might call prudery) about baseball by speaking stridently against gambling (symbolized by horse racing) and liquor (during Prohibition, which he supported ardently) and for jingoistic Americanism.

The first was wisdom of the highest order, since he knew baseball's vulnerabilities better than anyone. The second was decent impulse, but backward-looking economics. The third was very much in tune with widespread cultural attitudes of his era.

His successor had to be chosen while World War II was still on, when everyone concerned had bigger problems to worry about. The choice was Albert B. (Happy) Chandler, a U.S. senator from Kentucky (which meant, in those days, automatically a Democrat and, in his case, a loyal enough New Dealer). Already, the desire to have someone "who knew his way around Washington" was strong.

Chandler's contract was far less "absolute" than the first one—they weren't going to give away such power again—and he had none of the public relations capital Landis had started with and built on. He tried sincerely to play the (false) role of being commissioner of players and fans as well as owners. He was on the right side in supporting Branch Rickey's fracture of the color line. He tried to continue the purity atmosphere by suspending Leo Durocher for a year for "being in the company" of a well-known racetrack figure (an excessive and silly action that did score public relations points). He substituted down-home warmth ("Ah loves baseball!" was his identification in parodies) for the patriotic and moralistic posturing of Landis.

But he didn't keep baseball out of court.

No one can say what the radically different world that started in 1946 would have brought forth for baseball if Landis had still been alive. Perhaps he, too, could not have avoided the litigation let loose. But Landis was safely dead. Chandler didn't—probably couldn't—prevent it. There were other reasons why his employers became disenchanted with his regime, but that one was enough. In 1951, they forced his resignation by denying him an extension.

Then they turned to an ultimate insider, Ford Christopher Frick, reverting to their deepest in-group instincts. Frick had been a sportswriter and early sports broadcaster, at times a ghostwriter for Babe Ruth. In 1934, he had become the National League's publicity director (a pioneering post in those days) and within a year the league's president. As such, he was creative and effective. He helped teams in trouble during the depression, he was vigorously on the right side in Jackie Robinson's ordeal, and he saw his circuit, perceived as inferior to the American when he took over, become accepted as equal and on its way to dominance before he left.

As commissioner, Frick had circumscribed powers, as had Chandler. He let the stronger club owners have their way, upheld the dignity of his office, gave his advice in private, and was increasingly overtaken by the pace of developments (television, the growth of football, franchise shifts, the move to California, new marketing concepts). His was a "caretaker" regime, performing that mission capably, at a time when the mission was inappropriate, inadequate, and impossible. His first seven-year term was happily renewed. His internal relationships were excellent, his public image benign but not impressive. The sarcastic label attached to him was "That's not my jurisdiction." When it was time for him to retire in 1965, the baseball map and economy were inconceivably different than they had been in 1951 (as was the rest of the world).

The fourth commissioner was a joke, and not a very good joke. He was the consequence of twenty years of increasing dominance by individual club owners, creating almost as weak a central core as the pre-Landis period had produced.

His name was William D. Eckert—General William D. Eckert. He was a retired air force general whose expertise had been procurement and contracts. He had no previous connection with baseball and knew nothing about it. The story was that the search committee had confused his name with that of Eugene Zuckert, former secretary of the air force. A New York newspaperman, seeing the story of his appointment coming over the wire, cried out, "My God, they've hired the Unknown Soldier," and that reaction was all too valid.

The truth was, the owners at that time saw no need for a commissioner at all. It was an office that had become a burden with no useful function. They were merely stuck with it because the public was wedded to the images created under Landis, and they didn't dare abolish it. But they handled their own business affairs (like franchise moves, television contracts, and player relations) through committees, they didn't want or need any central watchdog, and they certainly didn't want policy input from a non-investor. In Washington, they had their lobbyists. Eckert's lack of qualification and background suited them fine.

He was a totally sincere and decent man, unaware of the extent of his unawareness. His military career had made him orderly and cautious, not autocratic and belligerent. Asked at a get-acquainted news conference what his favorite comic strip was, he replied, "I'd rather not single one out." He was supplied with heavyweight insider assistance (notably Lee MacPhail and John McHale), but his contractual powers were as limited as those of his two predecessors.

But the figurehead philosophy that went into his selection didn't work. Within a couple of years, the emptiness of his office and the increasing disunity among the owners were putting the baseball industry further and further behind other sports in marketing, television ratings, and public esteem. The owners had intended a weak commissionership to provide an obstacle-free environment for their activities behind a public-interest front. Instead, they had a see-through facade and no leadership even when they looked for it.

So at the December meeting of 1968, they simply fired him. And the battle that developed over choosing a successor pushed them—unintentionally—into modern times.

It took more than six weeks to resolve it. They decided pretty quickly to go back to an insider—they had just seen that a weak outsider was no good, and they certainly didn't want a strong one—and thus they had a dilemma. Any insider had roots in one league or the other, and they were in a distrustful mood that precluded opposite-league support. Several meetings and votes ended in stalemate. Finally, in February 1969 in Florida, they hit upon an answer. They'd make a "temporary" appointment for a few months of housekeeping while they restructured their voting system to get around stalemates, and find a "real" commissioner later.

And the "commissioner pro tem" they chose was an insider's insider. Bowie Kuhn was one of their lawyers. It's true, he was with the firm that represented only the National League. But he had led their successful fight against an antitrust action when they wanted to move the Braves from Milwaukee to Atlanta in 1966, and he had been representing them in labor negotiations opposite that newcomer, Marvin Miller. He was as sincere and ingrained a baseball fan as anyone could be, having worked in the Griffith Stadium scoreboard in Washington as a youth, and had plenty of political connections after schooling at Princeton and Virginia. He was a tall, imposing figure who handled himself beautifully in front of the public. That the public knew nothing about him and had never heard of him was something of a bonus.

For this, 24 clubs voted unanimously.

But Kuhn had to deal with serious matters immediately. Spring training was being threatened by the pension plan dispute, mentioned in the preceding chapter. The splitting of both leagues into six-team divisions was going into effect, untried, for the first time. The mound and strike zone had been tinkered with because offense had all but disappeared in 1968. Players sent to expansion teams were balking at the transfers. In all these areas he had to act, and he did, quite constructively. His popularity-poll rating soared, the media heaped praise on him, baseball's business went forward—and he discovered he liked the job.

The owners had cut back the term to four years and kept the pay low. But at the August 1969 summer meeting, Kuhn had the seven-year term restored, the pay substantially increased, and his appointment made permanent (for seven years). The internal politicking that had required would come back to haunt him, but on the whole his first year was a rousing success.

By December, with the help of business school experts, he had a reorganization plan ready. It would have centralized the administration in the commissioner's office, bringing the two league presidents directly under his wing (and ending a practice of having the league headquarters in different cities, at the convenience of each current president). It would have given the commissioner structural authority that Landis had exerted informally, and that the next three after Landis didn't enjoy. It was not an illogical plan, but it did shift power from clubs with an easily controllable president's office to a commissioner who could play one league against another.

The club owners said no, in no uncertain terms.

So Kuhn embarked on thirteen more years of commissionership in essentially the old pattern. Since he was incomparably more knowledgeable than Chandler or Eckert, and far more forceful than Frick (who had been equally knowledgeable), he managed to build piecemeal the centralized organization that baseball had to have in a television, labor-relations, product-marketing age. But he had to do it by persuasion, maneuver, and compromise. And since along with his numerous assets he had one fatal shortcoming—so little feel for other people's responses that he was a terrible negotiator and a poor convincer—he produced pro-Bowie and anti-Bowie factions that aggravated more problems than they solved. Before being reappointed in 1976, he had to beat back a "dump Bowie" movement in which Finley was most prominent. Rather than face another such fight in 1983, he accepted a graceful, drawn-out retirement of the sort Frick had conducted.

His fourteen-year regime had deeply ironic aspects. He started with a terrific public image, which didn't last long, and ended by being the target of persistent vilification. Yet he was far better at his job, in understanding what he was doing, at the end than at the beginning. He made many mistakes early that didn't get appropriate attention, and then was blamed unfairly for things he couldn't control or actually did right. When he could have played a constructive role (in management councils) in the Flood, pension, strike, and free-agency disasters, he didn't; but from the time of the 1981 strike on, he advocated better approaches—and wasn't listened to by his own side. Meanwhile, he did install and expand the central organization that simply had to be created, and presided over television and attendance growth. He learned a great deal on the job (in my opinion) and when he got good at it he was discarded because too many rifts had remained open too long.

In a way, he reversed the Landis pattern. Landis, always a hero in public, became increasingly out of touch with the world around him and left the baseball industry in shakier condition than it had been in his early years. (Not that the depression and the war were his fault, but serious difficulties simply weren't being confronted—notably segregation.) Kuhn, the butt of increasing criticism after a brief honeymoon, turned over an industry in 1984 incomparably healthier than it had been in 1969. (Again, it wasn't all his doing, but he certainly did his share.) One might say that if the Judge was his own best publicist, Bowie was his own worst enemy.

Kuhn played a role in the search for a successor, and stayed on until one could be found and installed. He turned out to be another outsider because, by then, no insiders of potential stature had been produced for a long time. (That's not meant to be a snide remark: As any organization grows larger, older, more bureaucratic, more compartmentalized, and more complex—as baseball did throughout the 1970s—it's less likely to bring to the surface charismatic insiders.)

272 ♦ LEONARD KOPPETT

He was Peter Ueberroth, riding the crest of a great personal success as the man in charge of the 1984 Olympic Games in Los Angeles. These were universally deemed to be a miraculous financial success, a dazzling Hollywood production, an artistic success (although the Soviets did boycott), and the most thoroughly publicized sports extravaganza ever staged up to that time.

He was certainly an outstanding organizer, and his public image was excellent. He had no firsthand experience in the baseball business, but had an extensive background in American athletics in general and in ancillary fields. (His own business career, before his Olympic appointment, was in the travel agency field.) He had been dealing extensively with politicians, media and advertising executives, and the publicity machinery at the highest levels. No one questioned his "competence."

And he certainly had a capacity for decisiveness. He took office, right after the Olympics, on the eve of the 1984 playoffs and World Series. The umpires, who also had a union, who had lost whenever they tried to strike in the past, and who lagged far behind others in baseball in getting their share of the prosperity, were threatening to strike—and World Series umpires are the direct province of the commissioner. (Up to that point, their bosses are the respective league presidents.) Ueberroth immediately settled with them, on generous terms—which the two leagues, of course, then had to carry out and which they could have negotiated for themselves before that if they had wanted to.

The public and the umpires loved it. The owners weren't so sure. They were girding up for another showdown with the players in the coming months—another "we have to have this if baseball is to stay in business" confrontation—and a hint of unilateralism by the commissioner was not what they were looking for.

Those who were apprehensive were right. When the players came to the moment of strike in mid-season again in 1985, Ueberroth stepped in and said, in effect, "Settle it or I'll go public against the clubs' position"—and it was settled, in one day, largely (but not 100 percent) on the players' terms.

Ueberroth, it turned out, took the "czar" concept seriously. He was as American as apple pie—growing up in the Midwest, moving to California, going to college at unpretentious and urban San Jose State, settling in Los Angeles—but his instincts were definitely autocratic. He ran his Olympic organization like a dictator, which may be necessary in that context, and feasible for a once-every-four-years event with the whole world clamoring for admission. But the practices of secrecy, red tape, arbitrariness, and lofty pronouncement didn't fit as well in a business trying to sell tickets (and sponsors' products) every single day in endless competition for the entertainment dollar. Waving the flag was a surefire Olympic device, but less automatically effective for commercial baseball.

Nor does the Olympic movement have anything comparable to 26 club owners.

On the surface, in a time of unprecedented prosperity with the 1985 stoppage aborted, things seemed serene enough. Owners spoke well of their new commissioner, and his sophisticated P.R. operation worked the way it was supposed to. Privately, the same sort of pro and anti cliques that developed under Kuhn quickly formed under Ueberroth.

And Ueberroth had a unique and effective way of solving serious difficulties: declaring them solved.

Drug use, he said, was baseball's biggest problem—and the nation's—and he would eliminate it by drug-testing minor-league players and office workers. (The major-league players, of course, would have to agree to random testing, and they didn't.) When prominent players confessed involvement and testified against a minor dealer who had been supplying them, the commissioner "punished" them with mild fines, suspensions, and a demand for community work. A couple of years later, on the verge of leaving, he announced that baseball no longer had a drug problem. So that was that.

The same technique applied to economics. Baseball was in terrible shape, with most clubs losing money when he came in, he said. Every club was in the black and the industry was "healthy," he said, on his way out early in 1989. His two main actions in this respect had been getting the players pretty much what they wanted in 1985, and orchestrating the thrifty approach of 1986–88 that led to the collusion penalties still to be paid; the arithmetic didn't seem to add up (either things weren't so bad in 1984 or so good in 1988), but how many fans and writers do the arithmetic?

By 1988, it was clear that he would not be asked to serve another term, but there was no question of his being dismissed. He beat everybody to the punch by announcing that he would resign to pursue other interests, and that he wouldn't answer pleas to stay on—because his mission had been accomplished. He had solved baseball's problems.

But even those club owners who had steadfastly insisted that their commissioner was doing "a great job" the four years he was in office were remarkably restrained in whatever pleas they might have made to beg him to stay—at least in public.

They seemed, in fact, extremely happy to move on to Commissioner VII—an outsider-insider.

A. Bartlett Giamatti was certainly an outsider: a professor of literature who had been the president of Yale University. But he had become an insider in 1987 by leaving Yale and taking over the presidency of the National League. From the start, there were those who said he was embarking on a two-year apprenticeship for the commissionership. Such a crazy idea was roundly denied. But that's exactly what happened.

As passionate a fan on the personal level as Kuhn, as accustomed to operating on a larger landscape as Ueberroth, Giamatti brought unusual qualities to the office. Bowie read literature—Bart taught it. Ueberroth had run big businesses—Giamatti had run a world-class university. (Eckert, who read "Facts on File" and an undisclosed comic strip, had run only subunits of the most elaborate miltiary organization on earth.) Ueberroth had been a celebrity—Giamatti moved easily and naturally among celebrities. Landis had been an assertive judge— Giamatti was a contemplative intellectual. Chandler had been a professional politician—Giamatti had lived among professors of political science. Frick had been a journalist—Giamatti was a student of history.

No one will ever know what kind of commissioner Giamatti would have made. He took office in April 1989 and died in September. His time on the stage was consumed entirely by the Pete Rose gambling case—protracted, distasteful, somewhat ambiguous, painful to all concerned. But he was commissioner long enough to do something, unintentionally, that had never been done before: He chose his successor.

The office Giamatti inherited was unrecognizably expanded from the one Kuhn took over twenty years before. It had far-reaching responsibilities and daily operations that had been accreting, bit by bit, all that time. It had pure business aspects that Landis and Frick would never have dreamed of touching, and its demands on a commissioner's time were almost impossible to meet. What Giamatti needed, he felt, was a deputy—a second-in-command to help execute whatever policies were adopted. In creating a position that had not existed before, he automatically created a path of succession, although that was certainly not anyone's intention.

It had to be someone close, on the same mental wavelength, and a man with as much larger-world business experience as possible (because most of baseball's business now involved the larger world). He had a close, lifelong friend, who had grown up with him in New Haven, who fit the bill. Francis T. (Fay) Vincent was a product of Williams College and Yale Law School. He had become prominent in Wall Street investment circles, then a federal regulator, then president of a motion picture company: If a college president could turn to baseball, a childhood love, for a midlife career change, so could an industrialist with the same interest.

The whole point was for Vincent to be relatively invisible, rarely official, an adviser on an entirely personal level to whom important tasks could be delegated. In a few months, Vincent became known and respected within the upper echelons of the club-owner world, but virtually anonymous otherwise. He popped up a bit in the papers during the Rose case, but there wasn't one baseball fan in 10 million who had any idea what he looked like.

When Giamatti suddenly died, the owners could have started looking for a replacement. There was plenty of machinery in place to run things without a formally appointed leader. Vincent certainly could have done a lot while retaining the "deputy" title, as Kuhn had once been labeled a "pro tem." But this time, they didn't beat about the bush. They had liked Giamatti, had believed he would be taking them in the right direction, had decreased their factionalism under him. They liked Vincent and appreciated his background. If they wanted continuity—and they did—here was the way to get it. They named Fay Vincent Commissioner VIII.

The spotlight hit him with unexpected force in unforeseen circumstances when the San Francisco earthquake, on October 17, 1989, interrupted the World Series. Would the Series be canceled? Moved? Resumed soon? Resumed after how long? His decisions and announcements on this matter put him on view, through television and the press, as no purely baseball matter could have.

He made an excellent impression—sensible, low key, displaying a fine sense of proportion about the delicate questions raised in the midst of such serious larger considerations. He cited the right priorities, showed patience, didn't overreact, dealt properly with various authorities, and arranged to let matters run their course. The resumption after ten days went so smoothly that the very forgetability of the 1989 World Series (for those not intimately involved) is the best proof that the situation was handled well.

But his honeymoon was a short one. By mid-winter, he was deep into the player negotiation mess, ducking shrapnel from all sides. When the disruption began, the public and media automatically blamed him (as they had Kuhn, and Pete Rozelle during football's strikes) for not "stopping" it—a mindless demand but a natural consequence of the commissioner-czar myth.

Realizing that the only way to get things off dead center was to remove the cockamamie revenue-sharing plan from the table, he injected himself into the bargaining to that extent. Those owners who had long nurtured their mindset of having a showdown didn't thank him for doing something constructive. The union side, not really letting go of its suspicions, found him "disappointing" when he didn't do more (from its point of view). The fact is, the 1990 season was preserved intact (and public complaint was forgotten within two weeks), and his contribution to a labor settlement, whatever it was, proved more constructive than anything previous commissioners had done in comparable circumstances.

But as this is being written, it is much too early, of course, to try to evaluate or analyze or even describe the new commissioner's place in the succession. What can be said is this: The position itself entails much less myth, and much more executive leadership reality, than it ever did before.

CHAPTER
20

Agents and Lawyers

To complete a picture of baseball's structure, we have to mention groups that had no role at all twenty-five years ago—agents, arbitrators, and professional marketing people—and some who used to function much further in the background than they do now: lawyers.

A few top players always did have an agent who served as an adviser if not actually as a face-to-face negotiator. Babe Ruth had Christy Walsh. But until free agency became a reality in 1976, a player with no bargaining power had little need for an agent, and a club official could (and would) refuse to talk to one. Nevertheless, right after World War II prominent players started to acquire agents to handle their non-baseball activities, like endorsements and public appearances, and thus became familiar with the advantages of having professional representation.

Salary arbitration and free agency, in the 1970s, made the agent's function all but mandatory for every player. The relationship can vary. One may have a traditional agent, as actors and authors do, taking a percentage of every transaction, or a "personal manager," or a legal adviser (or all three and more), but the important word is "representation." The image of the slick general manager outfoxing the naive country bumpkin ("Sure you knocked in 100 runs, but you only hit .275"; "Sure you hit .330, but you only knocked in 67 runs") belongs to history. Management now has to deal with a player-agent team, not simply an individual player.

By the same token, the stereotype of an agent "manipulating" his player is overdone. Like other humans, agents come in all degrees of astuteness, sensitivity, honesty, skill, drive, and experience—but each has to retain the confidence of his client. Players don't hesitate to change agents if dissatisfied. An agent who doesn't try to do the best for his client will cut his own throat, because his reputation will suffer within a very tight world of players who talk to each other. The nature of the business does attract sharpies, but the ones who last display integrity and sound judgment.

The Players Association has tried to monitor agents and their practices, but this involves tricky legal and personal areas. It does most of its good by education, spreading the word about what's fair and customary, and calling attention to those who are demonstrably unreliable.

Management has developed its own corps of what can be called "counteragents," specialists in preparing the management side of an arbitration case.

All these people acquire more inside information about what's happening than most media people ever can—so they become primary sources for the media. Unquestionably, they have lots of information—but just as unquestionably, they have loyalties and obligations to a client that outweigh loyalty to journalistic objectivity. They do (and should) put a "spin" (as political writers put it) on what they disseminate to favor their point of view. A careful journalist finds them enormously helpful and informative, as long as he or she keeps in mind their vested interests. But the general result is that much more material reaches the public, with less assurance of the accuracy of any particular item, than used to be the case.

Arbitrators are non-baseball professionals from the fields of law, labor mediation, or academia who are brought in to settle grievances as well as salary questions. By far the most important achievement of the Players Association under Marvin Miller was the establishment of grievance machinery that replaced the arbitrary power of the commissioner as exercised by Landis.

Because arbitrators have little experience, and no stake, in the baseball business, they introduce an unpredictable element into fundamental decision-making. Their rulings can be of overwhelming importance, as we saw with Peter Seitz and the perpetual-option case that led to free agency. An arbitrator is chosen by both sides (usually the executive directors of the Players Association and the owners' Players Relations Committee) and cannot be fired during the case at issue; but he can be rejected for future cases if one side doesn't like the way he acted. The power of the arbitrator rests in the fact that the courts won't overturn (or even consider) his decisions unless there's some indication of impropriety on the part of the arbitrator.

It was Miller who proposed the salary arbitration methodology that management has found so onerous. The player and the club each submit a proposed salary figure, and the arbitrator, after conducting a hearing, must choose one or the other. He cannot "split the difference," which would encourage extreme requests from the rival parties; since he has to choose one or the other, each participant feels pressure to submit a figure expected to seem more reasonable to the judge. And free agents raise the standards arbitrators use for comparison.

Non-salary arbitrations (like the option matter) have even greater effect. In the collusion cases of the late 1980s, the significance of the rulings against management went beyond whatever the eventual cost may be in tens or even hundreds of millions of dollars. By confirming the view of the players—to themselves—that the clubs had consciously conspired to violate the agreement they had just signed in 1985, these decisions strengthened the distrust that has made all baseball negotiations so difficult for the last thirty years.

Marketing experts, on the other hand, have little direct effect on player-club relations, but a very large indirect effect on the interests of both groups. It is they who have made possible the unforeseen and explosive growth of revenue, which has meant salary escalation, expansion, and profit. In 1965, when Frick retired as commissioner, baseball had no central marketing office, and few clubs marketed themselves, even locally—and major-league baseball's gross receipts were less than $200 million. Now the commissioner's office lists, by name, eleven people who deal with marketing activities, and gross receipts exceed $1 billion. Sales from marketed items (souvenirs, emblems, licensed products, films) are substantial but not the real difference. What marketing techniques do is increase the value to sponsors of radio and television, triggering the huge increases in those fees, and help raise ticket sales at higher prices.

Lawyers, it goes without saying, have always played key roles in all business affairs. But there has been a subtle (or not so subtle) change in the nature of that role in our society in general, and it has had some striking consequences for baseball (and all sports) in particular.

In an earlier time, club owners, individually or in a group, would decide "We want to do this," and ask their lawyers "How do we do this legally and stay out of trouble?" The lawyers then worked out the blueprints.

But nowadays, laws and regulations are so complex (concerning labor, discrimination, taxes, leases, municipal relationships, pensions, insurance, travel, and so forth) that a tendency has arisen to ask the legal adviser "What can I do?" as well as "How can I do it?" This has shifted decision-making to the legal department and—more to the point—has made legal advisers prime recruits for executive positions (as in making Kuhn commissioner). And no individual club owner now makes a move without his own legal adviser alongside.

Now, the essence of baseball promotion—of ticket-selling in all its forms—is attention-getting originality, as exemplified by Bill Veeck and described marvelously in his books. A good promoter is action-oriented and fast-moving.

A lawyer, on the other hand, is trained to be cautious, quite properly and with good reason. The attorney's job is (a) to keep you out of trouble and (b) to resolve it in your favor when you get into trouble.

That frame of mind leads to an instinctive "No" or "Let's wait" in the face of any new or radical proposal. It is exactly the opposite of the "let's try it today" frame of mind a promoter needs. As lawyer-thinking input increases, flexibility and response time decrease. As promoter types are replaced by lawyer types, the talent for making deals starts to replace the talent for staging events.

This is not inherently good or bad, it is merely inevitable in the way our society has evolved since the early 1900s. The men who built the baseball business were not concerned with antitrust, federal regulation, tax advantage, or civil rights questions. Because what they built worked so well for so long, it lagged behind adapting to a changing culture because it didn't have to. When it was time to catch up and adjust to reality, the need for proper legal guidance was inescapable. So there's no sense bemoaning the fact that legal minds and attitudes have become dominant in running baseball. But there's no sense ignoring it, either.

The central importance of the grievance machinery set up when the Players Association began acting as an authentic union is too little appreciated. It goes far beyond the surface fact that some neutral arbitrator hands down a decision after listening to both sides, instead of having an employee of the owners (a league president or the commissioner) making the decision and pretending to be evenhanded. The psychological aspect, from the player point of view, is even more fundamental.

In the old, paternalistic system, a player was always "asking" for whatever he got—not just salary, but better showers in the dressing room, travel expenses when traded, a padded fence and warning track, more towels, anything. Not only was there no guarantee that a request would be granted, but the very act of having to ask put the player in an awkward position. If he asked too often, or too much, or when the authority was in a bad mood, or of a truly mean boss, he was branded as a "troublemaker" and subject to the countless retributions the old complete-control system provided.

With grievance machinery in place, it is the union—a collective, continuing, impersonal body—that is taking the dispute before the authorities, not the individual (exposed and vulnerable) player. This removes a great deal of tension from the daily life of every player. If he has a request that is truly trivial or unsuitable, his own union can point out that it's inappropriate. (To be honest, I couldn't think of a good example.) But, as is usually the case, suppose it's something at least arguably legitimate—a dress code, a medical problem, unfair treatment under some existing rule. The player then makes his case to a friendly and supportive representative of *his* interests, who can then pursue it as a skilled professional. He doesn't have to confront directly the employers who are the cause (in his eyes) of his problem—and who can retaliate against him later even if he wins his point.

The mere existence of such a mechanism reduces the frequency of arbitrary regulation ("Shave that mustache" or "We don't allow our players to have their wives come along on road trips"), and effectively prevents chiseling on expenses or imposing excessive fines (which used to happen more than you'd think, with little practical recourse for the players). But when there is an actual dispute to be settled, it becomes a matter of business and quasi-legal adjudication, not a personal conflict.

Dignity is important, and with a union and agents, a player now has it—and needs it, since the club has so many lawyers. At the same time, many general managers and club owners consider it an indignity that they have to deal with a player's dignity.

So it is not all one happy family behind the scenes. It never was. But the antagonisms are more overt than they used to be, and much more widely reported by the media, a process that feeds upon itself and exacerbates the friction. The myth of paternal benevolence and carefree players lasted as long as it did, and became as entrenched as it did, because players knew enough to keep their complaints to themselves most of the time under the old system, while owners and management often mistook subservience for satisfaction. Those conditions have changed, and now players don't hesitate to complain and managements don't deny resenting it. Both sides exaggerate, and are more eager than they once were to seek public support for their version through an all-too-willing gossip-happy media establishment. And this, in turn, creates an impression of greater turmoil than actually exists, and of a greater difference from some imagined golden past.

The truth is, there is more understanding on both sides in the 1990s than there used to be. Management has learned, after some resistance, to treat employees with greater respect and more consideration—and at least some players, having become plutocrats early in life, feel a more profound affinity for big money and those who have it than Ring Lardner's country bumpkins could ever relate to. It is, in effect, a more closely knit business community making a lot of discordant noises, rather than the one-sided "family affair" whose deep divisions used to be concealed by a conspiracy of silence.

So in morale, as well as in material wealth, major-league baseball in its second century is healthier than it has ever been before.

The Whole
BALL GAME

CHAPTER
21

Spring Training

No civilization that has produced baseball spring training can be all bad.

Of all the delightful aspects of what baseball people call "our great game," spring training has its own special quality. For many years, I have marked its beginning by writing a column extolling its virtues. Since I came closest to saying what I mean in one I did for *The Sporting News* in 1975, I won't try to rewrite it but simply reproduce it:

> PALO ALTO—This is a hymn of praise, a paean, a celebration, a jubilation for baseball spring training, a glory of the Western World not found in any other time and place but America of the last 80 years.
>
> It has been written (by me, years ago, and I'm sure by many others) that Florida is a state of mind, not a geographical location. Arizona and Palm Springs are, of course, equivalent in this sense. The very special combination of attitude and surroundings, of work and play, of hope, enthusiasm and occasional discomfort that make up spring training just doesn't exist in any other context.
>
> Let us ruminate on the three words: baseball, and spring, and training.
>
> Of all the major team games, baseball is the most leisurely by nature. It is often attacked for this by people who, I am

convinced, must be incredibly obtuse or selling some other product. The comparatively slow and relaxed pace of baseball is one of its greatest assets, not a drawback; it is what makes possible those elements that make baseball enjoyable. You don't have to like baseball, of course; many people don't. But if you do, it is the leisurely element that underlies your enjoyment—and no other game offers that particular complex of enjoyments.

But put that aside. If we have to talk about what makes baseball enjoyable at this stage of the game, our minds won't meet anyhow. Let's go on to "spring."

The depth of mankind's feeling about the spring season goes back to pre-history. Re-birth, the warming of the seasons, the revival of nature after a cold winter—such concepts are built into earth's creatures, including us. The imagery of a new beginning around the time of the vernal equinox permeates religion, art, psychology and even science.

What better time, then, to start a new season, a hopeful new year? Baseball is the only sport (among the large promotions) that has its competitive schedule coincide with the subliminal feelings of a new year.

Both geography and history have played a major role in forming this pattern. Baseball began, grew and developed in the northeastern quadrant of the continental United States, where winter weather is too severe to contemplate playing an outdoor game requiring fine control of a ball in flight.

People who live in Boston, New York, Philadelphia, Cleveland, Detroit, Pittsburgh, Cincinnati, Washington, Chicago and St. Louis know how deep the yearning can become, by mid-February, for sunshine and warmth and beaches and gentle breezes. And for more than 50 years, that's where all major league baseball teams were located.

So the annual ritual of baseball clubs going south in the spring struck deep resonances in the hearts of all the fans back home. It might be sheer envy, it might be the most fully experienced vicarious thrill, but it was a response, and a response that reached far into the subconscious. Spring is here, and another baseball season is starting.

This is something that Californians don't really understand, since they live in a much more even climate all year round, in the populated areas. Spring, in California, means less rain, but not a long-awaited respite from a long, dark, confining mini-ice age. I've felt this change myself. To go from Palo Alto to Arizona for a few weeks is certainly pleasant, but it is in no sense an escape, as it used to be to go from New York to Florida. The destination is nice—but the contrast is not as compelling.

Which brings us to "training," and that's probably the most striking difference of all with respect to other sports.

Anyone who has been through basic training in the Army has a good idea of what a football training camp is like, and if you went through a Marine boot camp, you have a better idea than others. Basketball and hockey camps may not be quite as confining, but they are, like football, at isolated locations under fairly strict supervision.

But baseball teams train at resorts. That's right, resorts. Think about that a minute.

Miami, Fort Lauderdale, St. Petersburg, Tampa, West Palm Beach, Orlando, Palm Springs and Phoenix, with its satellites of Scottsdale, Tempe and Mesa—these and the other spring training locations are communities that have made recreation a primary business. They are good at what they do. Their goal is to make visitors happy and comfortable, because that's how a resort makes its living.

And the baseball crowd gets all the benefits of such surroundings.

Each person, of course, makes use of it his own way. Club owners don't go to the same restaurants, or golf courses, that clubhouse attendants do—but on whatever level, from rookie through super star, there is something in a resort setting for everyone: entertainment, good food, recreational facilities and, above all, an atmosphere of people trying to have a good time according to their tastes.

The effect on everyone of such an atmosphere should not be underestimated. It is a pleasure that football, basketball and hockey players don't get during their training seasons.

Baseball practice also is far more pleasant—batting and throwing—than scrimmaging in those other games. The type of physical conditioning sought is less painful. A large proportion of practice time is devoted to actual games (30 or so exhibitions). And with relatively few exceptions, jobs are not really on the line during spring training.

Besides, baseball mystique calls for brandishing confidences. Everyone starts out expecting great things. (In football, by contrast, the prevailing approach to every game is carefully stimulated apprehension. A football coach always talks of how tough the other team will be; a baseball manager shamelessly overpraises his own team.)

So, we have optimism, untarnished by any result that will count in the standings; springtime, with all its overtones; and resort setting, with all their opportunities and time to enjoy them. One word sums up the whole baseball spring training scene: Beautiful.

My sentiments remain unchanged. The real world, of course, continues to change a good deal.

Back in 1975, and before, the exhibition-game setting still retained an uncrowded sleepiness that was part of the charm. In the 1980s, spring-training games began to sell out and turn people away. This didn't decrease the relaxed aspect of the game on the field, but it made hanging around more of a hassle—in the ballpark, around the hotels, in the parking lots. A packed house, even when it's a small-capacity house, creates a different atmosphere and different logistics than half-empty stands. Again, whether this is better or worse is a matter of taste, but it is undeniably not the same.

And the reasons have little to do with baseball as such. What has happened, over the last twenty years, is a change in American demographics and recreation choices. We have a larger number of older people, reasonably affluent, who have settled or retired in Florida and Arizona—and these are not only already on the scene, but precisely the age group whose childhood was still in a time when baseball was unquestioned king of the major-league hill. So March is their "season" in their new year-round homes, and they make the most of it.

In addition, vacation planning and tourism are more organized, and a bigger business than ever. More people arrange to make a holiday coincide with spring-training dates, and travel agencies stimulate the practice. As television has increased the in-season viewing audience up north, it has produced a larger fallout of those who choose a spring-training venue over ski slopes or just beaches.

And as clubs have improved their marketing operations in all other respects, they have also improved their exhibition-game marketing, and reaped the benefits.

The original idea was to find milder weather for a bit of pre-season conditioning. In the 1880s, they tried places like Hot Springs, Arkansas, Charleston, South Carolina, and Jacksonville, Florida. Then they went to a lot of places in Georgia and Texas, and other southern locations. They found out very quickly that newspaper stories from training camp stirred up ticket-buyers back home. This was free publicity and promotion that could not be surpassed, and the emphasis shifted very early from mere conditioning (which was necessary and beneficial) to the promotional element. Remember, all the teams (and most of the country's population) were concentrated in the Northeast, experiencing harsh winters. Up to World War I, once the World Series was over, there was no sustained big-league reading material for cooped-up city dwellers and farmers. Football, strictly a college activity, ended around Thanksgiving. Basketball was entirely local in its focus, in schools and YMCAs. Hockey had not yet come south of the Canadian border. Even horse racing had to stop, and boxing was limited to small arenas in the winter. The sports-news habit, created in the first place by daily box scores, had millions of readers looking for the next fix. Spring training provided it.

In the 1920s, when the Florida boom took place, it became the natural habitat for spring training, and the connection to fancy resort areas was institutionalized. California also had a piece of it; Arizona didn't get established until after World War II.

When there were only 16 teams and the minor leagues were still numerous, a regular feature of spring training was "the trip north." The regular season wouldn't start until mid-April (often the third Tuesday), so around April 1 teams would leave Florida and barnstorm their way north, playing in a different minor-league town each day, perhaps against the local team, perhaps against another major-league team hooking up for the tour. Such games, of course, would be once-a-year sellouts in those towns. The trip would end in large cities (like Baltimore) that didn't have major-league teams. Travel was by train, and for a couple of weeks the whole entourage would live in Pullman cars.

Two neat anecdotes are attached to such trips. The New York Giants were one of the first teams to train in Phoenix, and the Cleveland Indians used Tucson. Then they would travel east together, through Oklahoma, Texas, and so forth, playing what amounted to an 18-game series. One year in the 1950s, the Giants had a player named Clint Hartung, who had been built up as a "pheenom" back in 1947 ("the next Babe Ruth"), but turned out to be less. Like Ruth, he was both a pitcher and an outfielder, but that was the extent of the resemblance. He eventually earned a place in baseball history for the following feat: When Bobby Thomson hit his pennant-winning three-run homer in the ninth inning against the Dodgers in the Polo Grounds in the third game of the 1951 playoff, Hartung was the runner on third, having gone in as a replacement for Don Mueller, who had injured his ankle sliding into third on the Whitey Lockman double that preceded Thomson's home run.

This spring, however, Hartung was struggling to make the team, and Bill Roeder (yes, the same Bill Roeder who wanted to bat against Stu Miller), who wrote for the New York *World-Telegram and Sun*, did a piece about his unfulfilled promise. It was a nice enough story, with a human-interest angle focusing on a player just hanging on in obscurity after having been so publicized for what turned out to be unrealized potential. It was, all in all, a routine spring-training, non-game story.

But it was good enough to be picked up by the Associated Press, and circulated nationally.

Along the barnstorming route, in half a dozen towns, half a dozen local sports editors knew exactly when the Giants and Indians would be coming through. Here was an ideal feature for that day's paper, so they spiked it for use at the right time. (In ancient times, when newspaper offices actually handled pieces of paper instead of computer terminals, a "spike" was a desk implement—a long inverted nail attached to a flat base—on which material to be saved could be "spiked." That this has to be explained helps show why this book has had to be rewritten.)

So every day for a week, when the teams pulled into a new town, there was the local paper with Roeder's Hartung story prominently displayed.

Hartung was furious. He looked for Roeder throughout the train, wanting to kill him.

"I don't mind your saying how I didn't make it, 'cause it's true," Hartung yelled at him, "but do you have to go and write the same damn story every single day for a week?"

The other happened in 1934, and was repeated proudly by Don Heffner, its subject.

This was Ruth's last year as a Yankee player, and Heffner was a rookie second baseman. He wasn't about to displace Tony Lazzeri, but manager Joe McCarthy wanted to see as much of him as possible, intending to keep him as a utility man. And Ruth had to play at least part of every game because he was the drawing card on the tour.

The last stop was Baltimore. This was, of course, Ruth's hometown. It was also the International League city in which Heffner had played the year before. A young Baltimore columnist had a fine idea for a local-angle story: He'd ask Ruth, the Baltimore-born legend, what he thought of Heffner, the recent Baltimore star, who had just played a whole series of games only about 150 feet in front of Ruth's position in right field.

So the writer asked Ruth:

"What do you think of Don Heffner?"

Ruth said:

"Who the hell is Don Heffner?"

Then there was the day in Mesa, Arizona, in the 1970s, when Bob

Fishel locked himself out of his car. Fishel, once a publicity man for Bill Veeck in St. Louis and then for the Yankees through the glories of the Casey Stengel regime, was now public relations director for the whole American League, and was standing in the parking lot embarrassed, frustrated, and confused. The game was still on, and he had to get to another game a half-hour away, and there was no attendant, and he was stuck.

Along came a prominent player (never mind who) whose day's work had ended early.

"What's the trouble, Bob?" the player said.

"I've locked myself out of the car," said Fishel, mortified.

"That's no problem," said the player. "Look, you just go and stand over there for a moment, will you? Just look away."

Fishel obeyed. Within thirty seconds, the car door was open.

"Come on back," said the player.

"Thank you," said Fishel, impressed even though he had lived in New York for many years by that time.

"Any time," said the player, "any time at all," and went his way as Fishel drove off.

But isn't there a serious side to spring training? Certainly. For each player, it means getting ready for games that count. For each club management, it means making personnel decisions. So they develop patterns.

Hitters can't start getting their timing down until they face live pitchers (and pitchers who really pitch, not just batting-practice tossers). And pitchers need to loosen and strengthen their arms gradually before they can throw the ball with something on it. So pitchers have to be brought in earlier than the rest, in order to give the hitters something to swing at when the hitters come in. And pitchers have to have catchers.

So pitchers and catchers are usually brought in ten days or so before the rest of the squad. Players undergoing rehabilitation from an injury, or learning a new position, or of borderline status, may come in with this group.

The full squad needs only a week or so before it can start playing exhibitions. And this entire early-camp period is used for practicing "fundamentals"—cutoff throws, pitcher covering first, bunt plays, and so forth.

The exhibition schedule calls for about 30 games (and nowadays there is no tour toward home, just a final weekend in some other major-league city). Its main business is to set up the pitching rotation. A pitcher will usually work two or three innings the first time, three the second, three the third, then five, then seven. If you do that on a four-day cycle, you can work 12 pitchers twice each in the first 8 games. But if you're going to have five starters, and you want each to have a seven-inning outing before the season starts, you have to reserve the last five games for that, and the five before those for the five-inning tests. What matters is not how they get hitters out in those games, but how many pitches they throw and what sort of mechanics they work on. So that disposes of the first 8 and the last 10 games. The 12 in between are juggled accordingly.

Regulars may play a lot, a little, or irregularly. It's an individual matter, between player and manager, and minor injuries are nursed along in ways they wouldn't be in the regular season.

For this reason, spring-training results and box scores are totally meaningless. But fans devour them just the same, and springtime optimism never wavers. If a team loses a lot, it simply doesn't matter (and year after year the regular season proves this to be true). If it wins a lot, you start talking pennant even if the same bunch lost 100 games last year (and will again). Either way, the whole spring season produces all winners and no losers.

Beautiful.

CHAPTER
22

The Post-Season

First there was the World Series, a set of games between champions of different leagues, for the baseball championship of the world. They did it in the 1880s, had to abandon the idea when only one league existed in the 1890s, resumed it in 1903, and set it up on a permanent basis in 1905. It is, by definition, custom, and preference, the capstone of the entire competitive structure.

Then came the All-Star Game, invented in 1933, putting on the same field the best players from each league, for a single exhibition game that decides no title, produces no prize money, affects no one's earning power—but romanticizes star appeal in a way not even the World Series can match.

Then came the playoffs, a demeaning word that baseball authorities tried to shun by emphasizing their official title of League Championship Series. They had to be created in 1969, when each league split into two divisions, to produce each league's representative to the World Series: the league champion, or pennant winner.

These are the three great events of the baseball season that fall outside the regular schedule, and they have developed their own distinct mystiques.

The World Series, for all its climactic significance, means more to the public than to its actual participants.

The All-Star Game, a mid-season interruption, means a great deal to the public and virtually nothing to the players and even less to the business hierarchy.

And the playoffs, despised in anticipation by traditionalists but now accepted by the LCS designation even in newspaper stories, are the most dramatic, most intense, most absorbing baseball competition on earth, so regarded by both public and players with equal fervor.

There are perfectly good reasons for what appears to be a contradiction. How can the qualifying round for the World Series upstage the World Series itself, and what's wrong with an All-Star Game? The answers lie in the word "profession." The people who play and stage major-league baseball make their living by doing that activity, and one's success—and level of income—is defined by victory on the field. So while it is a great honor to be *selected* for an All-Star team, it is both a nuisance and a danger to actually play in one. At worst, one can suffer an injury (as one can in any game, at any time) that will interfere with the season-long effort to win games that count for your own team and improve your personal record; at best, you have to travel, play, and travel again in a three-day interval that the other 90 percent of the players get as a vacation just when time off would be most welcome, in mid-July. And the outcome of the game, as well as your performance in it, has no significance whatever with respect to any championship or compensation. Everyone else associated with any particular club has to live through the apprehension that an injury to an outstanding and important member of your club (since only these are invited) might wreck your own season—as has happened more than once.

So the price one pays for All-Star honors is high. There are other reasons, as we'll see, why it's something that has to be done, and one might as well learn to make the best of it; but what is catnip to the fan can taste like bitter fruit to the player.

In the World Series, the professional stakes are real, but less than they appear. Each team is already its league champion, a suitable achievement for honor and reward, and the difference in prize money between winning and losing is not so large. Of course, it's better to win than to lose, and everyone tries as hard as possible to win. But to lose is neither terrible nor a disgrace. You're still, forever, your league's champion for that year, and your future earning power won't change that much on the basis of the outcome of one seven-game series after you have nailed down such 162-game success.

What really counts in the World Series is getting there. You always hear players, especially older players, say, "I've always wanted a chance to play in the World Series." They say "play," not "win" (although of course they want that too). From the professional's point of view—including the club treasurer—the year-long goal of all that effort is to reach the World Series. Then the result is in the lap of the gods.

Ah, but to get there, you have to win the League Championship Series.

And if you lose that, you're nobody.

The financial rewards, in prize money and in bargaining power, take a tremendous jump if you do get to the World Series. If you lose the LCS, that whole six-month struggle is wasted and your season is down the drain.

You want tension? Games for big stakes? Crunch time? The League Championship Series is where you get it.

This is neither logical nor fair. What all baseball people know is that "anything can happen in a short series." The true competition is a season-long test, in which attrition and team depth—especially in pitching—form a vital part of the process. It's a game of averages, of evening out, of trends and repetitions. Any game can be decided by a bad bounce, a bad call by an umpire, bad luck with the weather. You simply don't judge baseball excellence by one-day, or even one-week, performance. The one true measure is the league standing.

That's why a World Series can be approached with a degree of satisfied equanimity by its participants. They know its outcome won't "prove" as much as their presence.

But exactly the same thing should apply to the division races. If you spent six months finishing in first place in your group, why should that be undone any more in a best-of-seven series (which used to be best-of-five)?

It shouldn't be, but it is. A divisional title has simply never acquired the prestige it deserves. One reason is that the divisions themselves are artificial groupings, composed of teams that play almost as many inter-division games as intra-division games (actually, more inter-division games in the 14-team American League). The won–lost record isn't "pure": You have faced different opponents in irregular combinations, and the second-place team in the other division may actually have won more games. The league's championship—the hallowed "pennant"—is on the line only when the division leaders meet. The winner goes on to the World Series and more limelight, more money, more honors; the loser goes home, and is perceived as just another second-place finisher.

What has happened, of course, is that the divisional setup has produced a season-end climax that used to occur rarely and by accident. Books are still being written about the 1949 season, when the Yankees and Red Sox happened to face each other in the last two games with the Red Sox one game ahead. The Yankees won both, in eventful fashion, and established legends. But it was strictly the luck of the draw that brought the schedule up in that fashion; most years back then, on those last two days, the Yankees would be playing the Senators and the Red Sox the Athletics, or vice versa. In 1908, 1946, 1948, 1951, 1959, and 1962 playoff games were required to break ties in the standings, creating more legends—but six-month races don't end in flat ties very often. Most pennants, in single-standing days, were clinched some time before the last weekend and occasionally a couple of weeks ahead, and even races that went down to the last day usually didn't have the two contenders playing each other.

But the LCS guarantees that. Even when the New York Mets won their division by 21½ games in 1986, they had to start the LCS against Houston all even, with opportunity and stakes equal for both. So the close finish, head-to-head, has been built in, and it adds to the psychology that makes the loser so quickly forgotten.

The reason baseball people shied away from the term "playoffs" was that it had a minor-league connotation. During the depression, when every dollar was so desperately needed, minor leagues devised a system to prolong their schedules with artificial excitement by having the top four teams engage in "playoffs" (actually Shaughnessy Playoffs, named after Frank Shaughnessy, president of the International League at the time). No. 1 would play No.4, No. 2 would play No. 3, and then the winners would play for the league championship. This became the standard system in basketball and hockey and it does, one must admit, reduce the full-season record to a jockeying for favorable position in the playoffs. But fans have always loved it, and proved their love by buying tickets—and, of course, it keeps interest alive even for a team in fifth or sixth place while it tries for fourth, because once you qualify even as a fourth-place team, who says you can't go on to win the whole thing?

The major-league divisional system in 1969 was nothing like that, but it encompassed the same principle. In 1968, for instance, each league had 10 teams in one standing. The Cardinals and Tigers were far, far ahead by July, and while fans in a couple of cities might cling to the hope that their team would somehow catch up, there wasn't much to keep folks fascinated in the teams that were in fourth to tenth places. If they had kept a 12-team standing in 1969, it would have been that much worse.

This way, each six-team division had its own race—four races now instead of two—and if a third-place team still offered hope in August, 12 of the 24 clubs might be "in contention."

At the end, however, only the first-place teams kept going, so the "impure" element of the Shaughnessy system was not present. Only "first-place teams" could get to the World Series, although two of them wouldn't.

But we may yet see the basketball-hockey-football type of extended playoff system in the baseball world of the 1990s. Expansion will come, and probably some sort of realignment. The American League schedule for 14 teams has been highly unsatisfactory, and there will be a gravitational pull to get each league up to 16 teams. (If you have 15, you have to have inter-league play or an idle team every day.) When you have 32 teams playing with only four qualifying for post-season, you've got the same lopsided discouragement you moved away from in 1969. A 16-team league with four four-team divisions would produce four divisional leaders—and an extra round of playoffs. But if it stayed in two divisions (or went to three), second-place teams would have to be brought into the picture, at least as "wild cards" analogous to the football system.

Playoffs have proved themselves, beyond argument, as unfailingly popular with the customers, with television, and with the public in general. Only writers, intellectuals, and rock-ribbed traditionalists knock them. The fact that baseball's club owners were so resistant in the first place, so slow to appreciate what was actually happening, and so grumpy about the future shows us once more how backward-looking the baseball establishment tends to be.

And television, more and more, determines the patterns to be adopted.

Television networks know what pulls a big audience—that's their business. They want the World Series, the playoffs, and the All-Star Game. They don't care about regular-season games on a national scale (because in-season interest centers on the local team in each area, and is a great show for local television). The only reason they do any regular-season games at all (on weekends) is that baseball makes it a tie-in sale with the World Series. Baseball wants the exposure, and the network doesn't mind a little continuous promotion for the end-of-season payoff. But the value of the package—hundreds of millions of dollars—rests almost entirely in the three glamorous segments.

The All-Star Game does well on television, which is a star-focused medium. And, for all the reservations already mentioned, players take a more positive view of it than they did about twenty years ago. They certainly like the honor of being selected (and may have cash bonus provisions in their contract for making the team). They like socializing with their peers. They like the national television exposure (which might help in some endorsement deal). And they are aware of their group obligation: The gate receipts go to their pension fund. So it would be wrong to think they have a wholly negative view, and since individuals are different, some out-and-out love it. But the really great thing would be to be voted to a starting role and then have the game rained out.

When the LCS started in 1969, it had a 3-of-5 format, to distinguish it from the 4-of-7 World Series. But there's a reason why the World Series settled into a 7-game set, and why 5-of-9, tried in 1919–21, proved excessive. The starting pitcher is the dominant individual in any game, and in championship contexts, at least one team is likely to have a couple of truly outstanding pitchers. The standard rotation used to be four days. In a 7-game series, with two off-days for travel, the No. 1 pitcher can start the first, fourth, and seventh games, and two others can start two each. That's a "fair" distribution of team strength. (If the series goes fewer than seven games, some sort of superiority has been clearly established apart from starting-pitcher dominance.) If there are no travel days, the first three pitchers can work Games 1 and 5, 2 and 6, and 3 and 7, or the No. 1 superpitcher can try the seventh game with short rest (in the old days).

In any case, a third starter has a more significant role in a 7-game set than in a 5, so it's more of a team test. Nine games doesn't change the situation all that much, and such a series drags on too long, especially if a team gets ahead 3–0 or 4–1. So seven is a good number for a series in which the starting pitcher makes each game so different. (In basketball and hockey, of course, the same lineup can play every game.)

When the LCS, for 16 years, was in the 5-game format, only 9 of the 32 series reached a fifth and decisive game. When it was extended to seven games in 1985, four of the first eight series went to a seventh game, and in three of those four the team that finally won had trailed 3–2 and would have been eliminated in the 5-game format.

Meanwhile, the money has changed dramatically, but not the proportions. Right at the start, it was decided to set aside the bulk of the receipts from the first four games only for the prize-money pool, to advertise to the public that the players had no interest in extending the series on purpose. Between the two world wars, the difference between a winning and a losing share was on the order of $2,000, which represented less than 10 percent of a star's pay but more than half a season's pay for many of the lesser players. (In round numbers, it was usually $6,000 for winners and $4,000 for losers.) In the middle 1950s, a big jump in ticket prices pushed it into the $8,000–$6,000 category with a few more extreme cases. (The actual payout depends on how many shares a team votes, so if the winners vote few and the losers many, the gap can grow to $11,100–$6,700, as it did in 1954 when the

New York Giants swept the Cleveland Indians in four games in two large stadiums.)

In 1973, I used the following example:

The players on any pennant-winning team can be divided into three classes: a superstar or two or three, making between $75,000 and $150,000 a year in salary; a group of established regulars, earning between $20,000 and $50,000; and the remainder, rookies and marginal players, making under $20,000.

To a man earning $100,000 a year, the $20,000 extra he may make by winning the World Series is a significant amount, worth working for all year. Such a player also makes considerable outside income through endorsements, and being on a pennant winner greatly enhances his value in this area.

But whether the final payoff for the Series is $20,000 or $15,000 doesn't matter very much. In his tax bracket, he probably can't keep more than half the difference anyhow. So, in real money, the difference between winning and losing that seventh game is $2,500—and he has spent about 10 extra days beyond the end of the regular schedule to play those seven games. The money, then, is simply not that important.

Pay no attention, then, when you read over and over about "money players" coming through in the World Series. They were "money players" getting there, perhaps, but by the time the seventh game comes around, they are almost pure amateurs: Only the honor of winning is left.

And that is what is hard to emphasize correctly: The honor *is* important, it is an incentive, and pride runs deep—but failing to get it just doesn't carry the same disappointment that failing to win a pennant does.

On the other hand, to the man working for $20,000 a year, winning the World Series means doubling his pay, as well as establishing his status on a new level. To him, the financial difference between winning and losing is considerable; he may keep $4,000 of that $5,000 difference, and that's a very large portion of his total income. But it is precisely these low-paid, marginal players who get little opportunity to do anything decisive in a World Series, if they play at all. The spotlight is on the stars, most of the time.

The established pros in between, in the $50,000-a-year bracket, aren't as hungry as the newcomers, nor as blasé as the stars, but they too have been around for a while, and know that the big job was done when they got into the Series.

In the late 1980s, the numbers were quite different. The LCS and World Series money is pooled (according to formulas) and also covers teams that finished second and third in each division (as the World Series pool did for second-, third-, and fourth-place finishers in the old days). But it's big money, because ticket prices are so much higher. In the 1988 World Series, the victorious Los Angeles Dodgers got $108,664.88 a man, and the losing Oakland A's $86,222.89. A $22,000 differential between winning and losing sounds like serious business.

However, by that time, many of the prominent players were earning more than $1,000,00 a year, and the average major-league salary was around $400,000. So in actual bank-balance terms, the prize money difference is less important than ever, and pride and prestige are the fundamental motivators.

Yet the world is different in many ways. Today's players have grown up in a television age, and are so conscious of what national TV exposure means that they react even more intensely to the limelight factor than did previous generations. At the same time, television conditions all of us to short attention spans, an endless succession of highlight shots, and a brand-new program (sports or not) starting the minute this one ends, so the "memorable" isn't memorable as long or as deeply ingrained, even though it is more permanently available on tape if you choose to look at it.

This combines with what I call the "accumulated history factor." In 1924, when only 21 World Series had been played, a grounder hitting a pebble and becoming the winning hit had a cosmic significance not possible for an event—any event—in the 80th World Series. Elmer Smith of Cleveland, in 1920, hit the first World Series grand-slam homer, and 30 years later he was still being mentioned because only one other (by Tony Lazzeri in 1936) had been hit. Now there have been 15, each successively less unique. It's just as much of an accomplishment for the one who does it, but it's less memorable in the scheme of things. And so is everything else about each additional Series (and season) as time goes on.

Worse still, since the 1970s most World Series games (and most LCS games) have been played at night. This increases the live TV audience, but it wipes out newspaper coverage because of deadline requirements, and lasting romance (myth, legend, tradition, nostalgia, gilded memory) is created by writers and readers, not viewers with an itchy finger on the remote-control button. In a less poetic age, less daily poetry about baseball is being produced. (It turns up more than ever in larger forms—novels, plays, feature films, articles, and documentaries—but not automatically in mass journalism the way it did when the World Series was not only younger but also not challenged by Super Bowls and other home-delivered championship events.)

Richer, bigger, more accessible, more sophisticated, less "special"—that's what baseball's showcase events have become entering the 1990s, and that's true of just about everything else connected with the game.

CHAPTER
23

Where Did the Hitters Go?

If hitting is an art, is it being lost? The proliferation of published encyclopedias has made it easy for any fan, and any writer, to notice how much more imposing were the batting statistics of the past. Are today's hitters less skillful? Less dedicated? Less developed? If so, why? If not, why does the question come up? And, if so, can anything be done about it? Should it? Will it?

To get a handle on this topic, we must become familiar with the concept of eras. Baseball statistics, like dollars, change value with time. To compare 1980 dollars with 1930 dollars, we have to account for inflation. To compare 1980 batting averages with 1930 batting averages, we have to account for differences in the conditions of play.

But before doing that, let's give the answers outright. Then we can look for explanations.

Is the art being lost? Certainly not. Has it changed? Sure.

Are today's hitters less skillful, dedicated, and developed? Yes, to a degree, but an important distinction must be made: This doesn't mean they are less effective or don't try as hard. They are facing conditions their fathers didn't. (The mention of fathers prompts a digression. Are the sons better or worse hitters? It depends on the fathers, naturally. I would say that Earl Averill was a much better hitter than Earl Averill Jr., that Ray Boone was a bit better than his son Bob, that Gus Bell and Buddy Bell were just about the same, that Mike Hegan might have been just a bit better than his father Jim, that Terry Kennedy was definitely better than his father Bob, and that Tom Tresh was much better than his father Mike. And only in the 1990s will we find out how Barry Bonds and Ken Griffey Jr. eventually stack up against their papas. Trying to be specific can ruin any general argument.)

Why does the question come up? Because the statistics are dramatically different.

Can anything be done about it? Sure, lots. Should it? Maybe. Will it? Almost certainly not.

Now let's get down to business. To make sense of the statistics, we have to divide the past into specific eras and establish the norms for each era. Then, when we find (as we will) that the contemporary numbers are appreciably lower than those of some imagined Golden Age, we will list (deep breath) eleven reasons why.

For convenience, we'll use three aggregate measures: batting average, runs scored, and home runs hit. We'll lump both leagues together, and express runs and homers in terms of both teams per game. All sorts of more refined measures are possible, and all sorts of conclusions can be debated, but we're not trying to "prove" anything or make value judgments, we're just trying to get a bird's-eye view of the terrain over a very large temporal area.

Here are the eras, starting in 1903 because before that there were so many differences in playing rules that comparisons are not meaningful. (It was in 1903 that both leagues adopted the current foul-strike rule, that a foul counts as a strike up to two strikes.)

Years	Characteristics	Batting Average	Runs per Game	Homers per Game
1903–19	Dead ball, trick pitches	.252	7.68	.29
1920–41	Lively ball	.280	9.69	.96
1942–45	Wartime	.257	8.18	.81
1946–62	Postwar lively ball, more relief pitching	.259	8.87	1.61
1963–68	Enlarged strike zone	.245	7.72	1.59
1969–76	Expansion and re-stored strike zone	.253	8.13	1.46
1977–89	With designated hitter	.261	8.62	1.61

All this looks more complicated than it really is.

In the dead-ball era, the ball itself wasn't as resilient, pitchers were allowed to scuff it up and make it really wet, one ball was kept in play much longer, and batters concentrated on a level swing for maximum contact to hit line drives safely without worrying about distance. Home runs simply weren't a factor, and the dead ball kept averages low.

In 1920, the lively ball was introduced, trick pitches were banned, a fresh ball was put into play more often, and hitters who had been trained to concentrate on contact rather than free-swinging were still in the majority. Averages soared and homers became common.

During the war, the quality of play was simply inferior, and hitting suffered more than pitching.

After the war, there was a major change in orientation. Everyone wanted to hit homers, and they got them at the expense of some batting average points. And the use of relief pitchers as specialists instead of emergency mop-up men became widespread.

In the 1960s, we had the disaster we'll examine in detail in a moment.

In 1969, the strike zone was restored and expansion (4 teams added to 20) thinned out talent, so the offense didn't get back to the normal postwar effort, and the American League adopted the designated hitter in 1973. The full effect of this took a few years to develop.

So since 1977, we've had a better balanced game essentially in the healthy postwar pattern (compare 1977–89 to 1946–62), but nowhere near the offensive production of the 1920–41 Golden Age.

And here are my eleven reasons:

1. Better pitching.
2. Distance-oriented hitting.
3. Bigger and better gloves.
4. More attention to fielding alignment.
5. Bigger or more symmetrical ball parks.
6. Expansion.
7. More travel through more time zones.
8. Night games.
9. Lighter and thinner bats.
10. Higher salaries.
11. Batting helmets.

The importance of this list is not that every item is of equal influence, or beyond dispute, or a sudden and radical change in itself. It is that they all point in the same direction, each contributing to forces that work against better batting records. Their cumulative effect is enormous.

And remember what I said way back at the beginning: What counts in baseball reality is *when*, not *how many*. For winning and losing, the clutch hit is no more or less important than it ever was, and no harder or easier to achieve. It simply comes up in a different context. So I'm *not* saying "hitting is worse." I'm saying "hitting *statistics* are worse." There's a difference.

Finally, there is a tidal pattern that seems to apply to all team games: Defense always catches up with offense, and when it does, some sort of rule change or other adjustment is made to restore a desired balance. In baseball, this cycle has manifested itself repeatedly. The original idea (in the early and middle 1800s) was for the pitcher to put the ball in play, not stymie the hitter—that's why he was required to throw underhand and why the term was "pitch" and not "throw." When they learned to throw curves and throw hard, even underhand, they had to move the pitching distance back (from 45 feet to 50), and when overhand deliveries were allowed, it had to be moved back to 60. By the early 1900s (thanks in part to the foul-strike rule) pitchers were dominant again, and the big change came in 1920. And so forth.

The current era is quite stable, but the underlying trend will always be there: Defense learns to predominate until you do something about it.

Now, the reasons.

1. Pitching is tougher in four distinct ways: (1) There are more "good" (but not "great") pitchers than there used to be, and, even more important, many fewer "poor" pitchers in the majors; (2) a much larger repertoire of pitches is used; (3) relief pitching has been developed as a specialty; and (4) more systematic attention is given to choosing the right pitch to throw.

There are more good pitchers than ever, and fewer bad ones, for one usually overlooked reason. Listen to Eddie Stanky, who spent years developing minor-league players for the Cardinals and Mets before returning to managing with the Chicago White Sox, then turning to college coaching: "You can teach pitching much more effectively than you can teach hitting," he said. "Therefore, as we spend more time and money on instruction, we produce a larger number of better pitchers, but we don't produce better hitters at the same rate. There is a lot you can show a pitcher; there is very little you can do to help a batter make contact with the ball."

Also, a pitcher can practice and improve on his own. A hitter can develop only against good pitching.

Today, the major leagues are full of pitchers who have seen big-league baseball on television all their lives, with its frequent reliance on the revealing center-field camera angle, who have had systematic instruction from Little League up, and other superior instruction in high-school, college, American Legion, and rookie-league ball. In the minors, their managers are men chosen for ability to teach—not fading older players, as was so often the case in the old days.

Today's pitchers, at nineteen, are thoroughly familiar with the philosophy of choosing pitches and studying hitters; they know the importance of keeping runners close to bases, and what to do in bunt situations; they have realized, from childhood on, the importance of good control instead of just throwing hard; and, on the average, they are physically bigger and stronger than their fathers.

All these things don't necessarily help a man throw harder, or more strikes, or give him a better breaking ball—but they contribute to poise and they help win ball games. Thirty years ago, pitchers had to learn the same things—but often, they learned them in the majors, in their mid-twenties, and while they were learning, many hitters added to their own personal records.

At the same time, the accent on youth, the careful handling, and the reduction of the minors have left fewer and fewer places for the pitcher who isn't so good, or at least promising. In the old days, there were four or five regular starters, and the other five pitchers on any team represented quite a drop in ability; today, the relief men may be more talented than most of the starters.

In other words, while the best pitchers in any era were equally tough, the proportion of "patsies" is much smaller now than it used to be—and in the records, the hits off patsies are indistinguishable from the hits off good pitchers.

Before World War II, fastball and curve, with a change of pace, constituted standard equipment. There were a few knuckleball specialists around, and Carl Hubbell was famous for his screwball. The slider was just coming into use.

Then the slider became a standard pitch, and the pitcher who used it increased the effectiveness of his fastball and curve, since the slider comes right between. Various types of sinkers—including a mild version of the spitball—also became prevalent. Knuckleballers became somewhat more common, and left-handers who threw the screwball were plentiful.

Today, the hot pitch is the split-fingered fastball, or "splitter," which is a nasty sort of sinker that drops sharply. Knucklers are in disfavor because there is more stealing to worry about.

Still more important, the pattern of pitching is more daring and more confusing. It is no longer possible to count on a fastball with the count 3–0, 3–1, and 2–0; even young pitchers throw breaking balls in such situations.

The biggest change of all is in relief pitching. A reliever used to be the man who took over when the starter failed, a measure of weakness. Today, the manager who has a good relief pitcher can't wait to get him into the game—and he has tough middle-inning relievers, too.

The hitter is affected adversely in three ways. First, the starters don't have to pace themselves, because they know (and the manager assures them) that relief will be available if needed, so they can throw "as hard as they can as long as they can." Second, the relief pitcher who comes into the game in the seventh, eighth, or ninth is fresh, so the hitter doesn't get a crack at a tired pitcher. Third, if the situation is crucial at the time of the pitching change, the relief pitcher is often chosen precisely because he is particularly tough for the particular hitter.

What this means to averages is readily seen. In 1930, when the aggregate batting average peaked at .296, there were 538 complete games pitched in the National League and 560 in the American, a total of 1,098 games in which batters got to face the starter a fourth or fifth time. In 1968, with so much less hitting, there were only 897 complete games—even though there were some 400 more games played because of expansion and longer schedules. In 1989, only 483 of 4,212 starting pitchers finished. In 1930, almost half of all starters went the distance; in 1968, little more than one-fourth did; in 1989, one-ninth. In other words, the 1930 hitters were getting a crack at a tiring starter much more often, even though the starters were getting hit harder in the first place.

Now do a little arithmetic: If a man gets one hit in his first three trips to the plate every day, and then makes out the fourth time, he is hitting .250. If he also gets a hit the fourth time up every third game, he is hitting .333. In 1930, his fourth trip was against the starter approximately half the time; in 1968, he was facing a fresh and qualified reliever about three-quarters of the time. Thus the 1968 hitter, even if equal to the 1930 hitter in all other respects, might not get a hit the fourth time up every third game, but every fifth game. But that, over 150 games, would bring his average down to .300 instead of .333—and that's the 30-point difference we see.

The above is an idealized example, for the sake of simplicity in numbers, but it illustrates a very real situation. The more times a good hitter can face the same pitcher in one day, the more of an advantage the hitter has (as a rule); not only does the pitcher get tired and increase his chance of making a mistake, but the batter gets more of a chance to adjust himself to that pitcher's motion and stuff. So the steady stream of relief pitchers has a definite effect on averages—and, in fact, that's precisely why relief pitchers are used so much: They get the job done.

All these factors—better pitching, more deliveries, more relief—are enhanced by the increasingly elaborate records managers keep, and the amount of scouting done. Outstanding pitchers always did study every opposing hitter—but many mediocre pitchers did not, or did so carelessly. And managers and coaches relied entirely on memory, which is fallible. Today, charts are kept of where every batter hit every pitch off every pitcher, and the conclusions are not left to the individual initiative of the run-of-the-mill pitcher. Managers make sure that *all* pitchers are told what only the better pitchers knew for themselves in the past.

So much for pitching. It's tougher, and it will continue to be tougher.

2. Almost as important is the psychology of the hitters. With very few exceptions, today's hitters are home-run minded, and have been from Little League on. They take a big swing, and a big swing means less bat control, which means a lower average—and more homers. There were plenty of homers in 1930, when Hack Wilson set the National League record of 56; but there are many more today. Through the 1930s, when the combined major-league batting average was about .280, there were about 110 homers hit in every 100 games played. Throughout the 1960s, when the batting average was just under .250, there were about 160 homers for every 100 games, or almost 50 percent more. And it has stayed that way since.

So the situation is plain enough. Hitters, as a class, are sacrificing, quite consciously, average for power. Hitters used to feel ashamed of striking out and managers would punish them for doing it too often (since putting the ball in play somehow, by making contact, helps the team in ways a strikeout can't). But nowadays, while paying lip service to making contact, hitters are neither embarrassed nor disturbed by striking out, considering it just one more out and the price one pays for hitting an occasional home run. If as many of them concentrated on just meeting the ball and trying for singles as hitters did in 1930, their averages would be closer than they are.

3. Gloves are important in their own way. Originally, and into the 1940s, fielders wore comparatively small-finger gloves whose prime function was to protect the hand. Now they have evolved into highly effective traps that extend a fielder's range by a few inches. Infielders smother hot drives. Outfielders snare long flies that might have gone off the fingertips of the old gloves. One reason outfielders catch routine flies one-handed—a style that inevitably draws criticism from older observers—is that in the huge pocket, almost like a lacrosse stick, the bare hand only gets in the way.

For any individual hitter, this may turn half a dozen potential hits into outs in the course of a season—but for 500 at-bats, 6 hits is a difference of 12 batting-average points, which may mean the difference between .303 (terrific) and .291 (not bad, but certainly less impressive in the documentation for salary arbitration).

4. Fielders not only have a better chance to grab a batted ball, they have a much greater chance of being in its path. Position play has been developed to a degree of accuracy undreamed of forty years ago, when the "Ted Williams Shift" gave Lou Boudreau the reputation of genius. Today, extreme shifts according to batter-pitcher-pitch are routine— and again, it's not left up to the individual's initiative as much as it used to be, but centrally directed by the manager. The outstanding players, of course, always did place themselves properly; today, the ordinary players are made to do it as well.

5. Also, the parks are different, and the universally improved quality of pitching takes better advantage of them. In 1930, the National League included Ebbets Field, with a 296-foot right field; the Polo Grounds, with its 250- and 278-foot foul lines; Baker Bowl in Philadelphia, with a 280-foot right field; and Braves Field in Boston, with a 297-foot right field. In such parks, the danger of home runs in one direction often promotes a pitcher to risk giving up only a hit in another, and promotes walks. By 1972, the picture was entirely different. Of the 12 National League parks then in use, 11 had been built since 1960, all were symmetrical, and none had a foul line shorter than 330 feet. (The only "old" park, Chicago's Wrigley Field, was always a good hitting park, but its dimensions were symmetrical and reasonable.)

In 1989, only Boston's Fenway and a modified Yankee Stadium had notably lopsided configurations. Domed stadiums in Seattle and Minneapolis were home-run havens in their own way, but symmetry was the rule in 23 of the 26 parks.

6. The effect of expansion has to do with batting orders. One might say, if larger leagues include more "lesser" hitters (who used to be consigned to the minors), don't they also include more of the "lesser" pitchers," and doesn't that even things up?

It does not. A pitcher, at any level of ability, can "pitch around" a more dangerous hitter. If the best hitter isn't "protected" by a fairly dangerous hitter coming up next, he won't often get a good pitch to hit. Expansion has thinned out batting orders, so that instead of sending up five or six really tough hitters in succesion—one protecting the one before—most teams can only send up three or four. Aside from the effect on any particular game, this works against large-scale averages, which is what we're talking about. When the 1927 Yankees sent up Combs, Koenig, Ruth, Gehrig, Meusel, and Lazzeri, or the 1950s Dodgers sent up Reese, Gilliam, Robinson, Snider, Hodges, Furillo, and Campanella, whom did you pitch around? In 1989, when the San

Francisco Giants had the two hottest hitters in baseball in Will Clark and Kevin Mitchell, despite all their prodigious feats while hitting third and fourth, the team wasn't able to take command of the pennant race until Matt Williams came back from the minors and started doing damage in the fifth slot. Concentrations of power improve batting orders by more than the sum of their parts. Expansion works against that. If you reduced today's major-league population to 16 teams, you'd have batting statistics that would look more like those of the 1930s.

7. Travel, of course, started to get worse even before expansion, when the Dodgers and Giants opened California. Until 1955, the longest jump was Boston to St. Louis, twenty-five hours by train. But the main thing was that there was some regularity to life: You took a sleeper from one town to the next, spent three or four days there, and moved on. Even twelve hours on a Pullman train is less wearing than a two-hour flight in the middle of the night with its to-and-from-the-airport legs added—and there is no jet lag comparable to coast-to-coast flights.

Since expansion, you make more trips to more places, sometimes staying only a day or two, and what's disrupted is routine—the time you eat, sleep, practice, play, relax. Since a batting average is exactly that—the *average* measure of your consistency over a six-month season—it is affected more by irregular life patterns than by one-shot actions (like a home run) or the performance of a pitcher, who doesn't work every day anyhow.

In 1930, Bill Terry of the Giants was the last National Leaguer to hit .400. On his 154-game schedule, 88 games required no travel (11 in Brooklyn); 22 more were in nearby Philadelphia and Boston; and there were three western trips, continuous swings through Pittsburgh, Cincinnati, Chicago, and St. Louis, with each stop taking four days twice and three days once. These involved 44 games.

In 1989, when Will Clark hit .333 for the San Francisco Giants, his team had 81 home games out of 162, but made the following trips for the other 81: San Diego, Cincinnati, home; Los Angeles, St. Louis, Pittsburgh, home; Chicago, Montreal, Philadelphia, New York, home; Atlanta, Cincinnati, home; San Diego, Houston, home; Pittsburgh, St. Louis, home; Chicago, Atlanta, Houston, Los Angeles, home; Montreal, Philadelphia, New York, home; Cincinnati, Atlanta, Houston, home; Los Angeles, San Diego—and off to Chicago to begin the playoffs.

Check that out with an atlas. If you don't think it makes a difference, think again.

8. Night baseball exacerbates the irregularity. We used to think that the problem was visibility, that lighting systems, even good ones, didn't give the hitter as good a look at the ball as daylight. ("It only lights the top of the ball, and the shadows are different," they'd say.)

But by now, all ball players have grown up playing under lights, and many say they prefer it: They're more accustomed to that than twilight (which is sometimes dictated by television needs, as in West Coast All-Star Games and World Series) or scudding clouds, or whatever. And certainly modern lighting systems (which have to satisfy color television cameras) are superb.

The big problem, now, is more irregularity. Terry, in 1930, went to work (when the umpire called "Play ball!") at essentially the same time every day: mid-afternoon. Clark and his contemporaries play roughly two-thirds of their games at night, but at least once a week, and often twice, they must have a day game after a night game. That sort of cycle shakes up the system of even a writer, so you can imagine what it does to an athlete who has to face 90-mile-an-hour pitchers. The same things—meals, sleep, habits—are disrupted, as they are by the travel. Net result? A few more lost batting-average points at the bad times.

9. Now we return to the frame-of-mind factor. The homer-oriented, free-swing hitters started switching to lighter bats with thinner handles. These are easier to swing, and when they connect they create a whiplash effect (like a pole vaulter's fiberglass pole) that propels the ball farther—*if* they connect. A heavier, thicker bat, with a larger area that can make solid contact, will produce a hit off the handle once in a while, and enforce the discipline of a controlled swing. The thin bat won't, and it will often break even when it does make contact. Here again, players have sacrificed average for power—or at least the pursuit of power.

10. And higher salary structures have encouraged such attitudes. Long ago they said "Home run hitters drive Cadillacs," when a Cadillac was a symbol of wealth. Because of the previously unimagined level of compensation for the ordinary ball player (not only the star), certain mental frameworks gain strength. There is a sense of security. ("I'm not going to be sent down, and even if I am I've got plenty of money in the bank.") This promotes yielding to ego satisfaction with less sense of risk, and less receptivity to managerial advice—and hitting a homer is more fun than hitting a ground single. Most of all, however, it makes possible lapses in concentration, an acceptance of a certain amount of failure, and a giving in to minor injuries to a degree that didn't exist when fear of the consequences was greater. No one lacks conscious desire to try to win, but not everyone keeps bearing down as hard every second when victory is not on the line. And batting average, we keep reminding ourselves, incorporates all the lapses with all of the hits. Finally, since statistics have become such a vital feature of contracts and negotiations handled by agents, 10

more homers on your record is going to make a bigger impression—on arbitrators, All-Star voters, and your friends—than 10 more points of batting average.

11. The helmet factor is a new, recent idea of my own, and highly questionable, but I'll mention it anyhow.

I started this whole book with a discussion of the fear that has to be overcome. The helmet is a wise and practical protective device of which I wholeheartedly approve. Getting hit with a hard-thrown baseball is painful and dangerous enough, and extra protection for the vulnerable head is fully justified.

What I wonder about is this: If hitters are thrown at less frequently and less malevolently (as they are) and if they feel an added security that the helmet can prevent the worst, does that lessen the *habit* of maximum concentration while at bat? This is not a matter of decreasing the *instinctive* fear that has to be overcome to hit at all. The helmet doesn't affect that. But if, among all the things you do have to worry about, you can worry about one specific possibility a little less, a certain kind of *maximum* alertness may be weakened. *May* be. And in terms of concentration, it may shift the *type* of concentration to a different set of proportions: more on what you expect, less on being prepared for the unexpected—and that can spill over into dealing with the unexpected pitch, not only an unexpected threat.

I don't suggest it happens to everyone, and I certainly don't mean hitters get complacent. But if just a little bit less physical alertness is demanded, does a little less mental alertness seep into the equation? I doubt if anyone consciously relates the one to the other, but subconsciously? Do I then fail to develop my mental reflexes—what's he throwing? what am I looking for? how is he getting me out?—as fully as possible?

I don't know. I'm not qualified to talk about the subconscious. But I do know that the baseball authorities did something unconsciously that made a terrible mess. They killed offense in the 1960s.

Here's the story:

In 1961, a record number of home runs were hit. Baseball old-timers were outraged at the idea that Maris broke Ruth's record of 60, and there was talk that the ball had been juiced up. There was also a relatively big offensive year in 1962 (although still far below the levels of the 1930s). At the same time, the competition of pro football on television was making baseball people sensitive to the charge (promoted by Madison Avenue people selling football to sponsors) that baseball was "too slow."

Someone got the idea that fewer walks would speed up the game, and the definition of the strike zone was rewritten. The actual wording didn't make much difference. The clear message to the umpires, that their employers wanted a bigger strike zone, did.

The results were dramatic—and no one paid the slightest bit of attention. See for yourself:

	1962	1963	Difference
Runs scored	14,461	12,780	1,681 fewer
Home runs	3,001	2,704	297 fewer
Batting average	.258	.246	12 points less
Walks	10,936	9,591	1,345 fewer
Strikeouts	17,567	18,773	1,206 more

Now, in the two adjacent years, exactly the same number of teams played the same number of games in exactly the same ballparks, with exactly the same dimensions and conditions—and with substantially the same players (taking the total population of both leagues). Also, for decades up to 1962, there had never been any change from one year to the next of the magnitude of the 1962–63 changes, up or down.

So when, all of a sudden, there are 1,345 fewer walks and 1,206 more strikeouts, it's hard to believe in coincidence or a sudden mass hitting slump. Furthermore, the 1963 figures quickly became standard for the next few years—and in 1967 and 1968 plummeted still further. By 1968, the runs were down to 11,099, homers down to 1,995, batting average down to .236, walks down to 9,156, and strikeouts up to 19,143.

What had happened was simple enough for anyone willing to lift his head out of a sandhole to understand: A bigger strike zone gives the pitcher a bigger target, and it also forces the hitter to swing at pitches he shouldn't. Worse yet, umpires, being human, enlarged the strike zone down and away, as well as up and down, and it's the low outside pitch that causes all the trouble. All of a sudden one started to hear of strikes "on the black"—that is, on the black-rubber border half buried in the ground around the plate itself.

But if a hitter has a strike called on him on a low outside pitch, he is helpless. Now he doesn't know what's a good pitch and what isn't, and the whole art of hitting depends on avoiding "bad" pitches. Every pitcher hopes, 90 percent of the time, to hit that low outside corner. ("If a man could do that on every single pitch," Bob Lemon once said, "he'd win every single game.") Now that spot was a whole area, and a vague area at that. No wonder hitting died.

The ultimate ridiculousness of this situation was made vivid by the 1966, 1967, and 1968 All-Star Games. With the greatest hitters in baseball gathered together, and pitchers limited to three innings apiece, the games wound up 2–1, 2–1 in 15 innings (with 30 men striking out), and 1–0.

When the final figures for 1968 were in, even baseball officials couldn't ignore them. So they took a bold step: They restored the strike-zone definition (which they didn't think was important), and they lowered the mound from 15 inches to 10 inches (which they did think was important).

Sure enough, in 1969 and 1970, offense revived—but only partially, because the umpires didn't shift back so quickly and, at least in part, because there was another expansion (which, *temporarily*, brings more poor pitchers into action).

By 1971, however, the long-term downward trend was asserting itself again; and finally, in 1973, the American League took the drastic remedy of the designated-hitter rule.

There are those (from my generation) who will tell you that a true, tight strike zone has never been restored, that today's umpires are woefully inconsistent, and that even though the excesses of 1963–68 are behind us, a fluctuating strike zone leads to more called third strikes and hurts the best hitters disproportionately. Be that as it may, the fact is that offense did not revive fully until 1977, when the ball itself was juiced up—a topic to be dealt with in a later chapter.

So if you want to compare the records of hitters from different eras, my advice is, don't. If you insist, relate it to the different-eras table here and do some mental arithmetic. In general, comparison to the league average for that year is the best guide.

But if you tell me that hitters like Will Clark, Tony Gwynn, Don Mattingly, José Canseco, and some of their contemporaries aren't the equal of any who ever played, regardless of numbers, I simply won't believe you.

CHAPTER
24

Who Was the Greatest Pitcher?

To single out someone as the "best" of anything in sports is silly—and irresistible. It's silly because the idea itself is undefinable, even beyond the unshakable reality that comparisons across different eras and leagues are simply invalid. One can identify the "most" in some category, or the "best by definition" (such as a champion), or the "best record," or "most remarkable achievement." But a generalized "best" is nothing more than a subjective assertion.

And that's probably why it's so irresistible. We love subjective assertions. We enjoy wallowing in contemplation of the qualities and feats of the greatest players, to discuss and compare the greatest accomplishments, to share dreams of approaches to perfection, to exercise the memory banks that are the fundamental product all those ball games create.

Along those lines, in the original version of this book, I had a chapter on "The Greatest Pitcher." The subject is worth reviving for two reasons. One is that the statistical picture of pitching history is entirely different from the way it looked twenty years ago. The other is that the conclusion I came to then still stands.

The new elements are named Nolan Ryan, Tom Seaver, Gaylord Perry, and several others, who have rewritten the record book. Men with high totals of strikeouts and victories have emerged in the last couple of decades—naturally enough, in light of the discussion just completed about the decline in hitting statistics. This is the other side of that coin. Just as poorer batting statistics are not exactly the same thing as poorer hitting, so better pitching records are not the same thing as better pitching.

Consider two benchmarks: 300 victories, and 3,000 strikeouts.

At the end of the 1968 season, the last before divisional play began, 14 pitchers had posted 300 or more victories. Of those, only two pitched after World War II, Warren Spahn and Early Wynn. And only one in the entire history of baseball had as many as 3,000 strikeouts: Walter Johnson, with 3,508.

By the end of 1989, there were five additional 300-game winners and nine more in the 3,000-strikeout class.

We know what happened. Expansion produced more games and innings available, and changes in the strike zone and hitting styles inflated strikeout frequency. Also, better conditioning, five-day rotations, and the enormous salaries enabled (and encouraged) top-rank pitchers to stay in action longer, boosting their cumulative totals. And this generation of pitchers faced no career interruptions, like World War II, which deflated the possible career totals of their predecessors.

But to explain it is not to discount it. Records are records, and if we're going to engage in subjective comparisons, we can't ignore them. What we're trying to do is put them into perspective.

So let's set some ground rules. Longevity is fundamental. We're trying to single out one man, among the thousands who have pitched in the major leagues over many decades. However distinguished the achievements of any of them may be, only those who could maintain superiority over the full span of career possibility—about twenty years—can be considered for a No. 1 ranking.

For example, Sandy Koufax was so overwhelming in the 1960s that those who saw him then, and those who still talk of batting against him, rarely dispute the idea that if you can't call him the "best ever," you can certainly say that there was "none better."

When forced to retire because of chronic elbow trouble in 1966 at the age of only thirty-one, Sandy had broken every conceivable single-season strikeout record, had won the Cy Young Award three times in four years, had pitched no-hitters in four consecutive seasons, had led the league in earned-run average five years in a row, and had pitched the Dodgers to three pennants by winning season-end showdown games while posting a won–lost record of 97–27 in a period of four consecutive years.

Yet Sandy made the point about longevity himself, most vehemently, in 1964. His season had been cut short by what was then called "an inflamed elbow," but it was already the chronic arthritis that was to be diagnosed as such only the following spring. Almost prophetically, Sandy said: "Before you compare me with the great pitchers of all time, let me be around awhile. Let me prove what I can do over a long period of time. Don't put me in a class with pitchers like Warren Spahn and Whitey Ford until I've shown I can win games for 10 or 15 years. Spahn has been doing it for 20. That's what it takes to rate as a great ball player, not a couple of good years, but a whole career."

At that time, Sandy was twenty-eight years old, and had been a full-fledged star for only three seasons. He signed with the Dodgers (then in Brooklyn) for a modest bonus in 1955, and never spent a day with any other team because bonus players had to be kept on the varsity, but he didn't become a consistent winner until 1961.

After 1964, of course, Sandy immensely strengthened his claim to a place among the full-career men. That's why, among all the records he set, the ones that meant most to him were career totals. He finished up having struck out more men than all but six other pitchers—Johnson, Cy Young, Spahn, Christy Mathewson, Bob Feller, and Tim Keefe, who pitched back in the 1880s.

So if we accept a two-decade career (approximately) as a standard, we immediately rule out some famous names whose moments of glory were every bit as bright as Koufax's. Dizzy Dean, in 1933–37, was as commanding a figure as any pitcher could ever be. But in the 1937 All-Star Game, a line drive broke his toe. When he tried to resume pitching too soon, he favored his leg and strained his arm, and was never great again.

Less celebrated, and certainly less remembered, is Addie Joss, who won 155 games for Cleveland in his first eight major-league seasons, and pitched two no-hitters, one a perfect game. But in 1911, at the age of thirty-one, Joss died of tuberculosis.

Then there was Herb Score. Only a few years before Koufax, he was the magnet for all the same superlatives. After the 1956 season, the Boston Red Sox offered Cleveland $1,000,000 for his contract— and were turned down. But, the very next season, a line drive hit Score in the eye. His sight was saved, but he never could regain his pitching rhythm and soon developed a sore arm. He finally retired to become a broadcaster for the White Sox in 1963—still only thirty-one years old.

Those who can qualify, therefore, must be blessed with continued strength and good health. Pitchers' arms are notoriously fragile; the wear and tear are tremendous, the risk of injury always present—as Koufax demonstrated.

All right, then, with the field narrowed down to the twenty-year men, what are the other elements of pitching greatness?

There are four: stuff, control, craft, and poise.

Stuff is the physical element: How hard can he throw? How big is the break on his curve? Stuff is the product of strength and exceptional, hair-trigger coordination, and seems to be an innate quality, perhaps improvable by practice and technique, but not acquirable.

Control is the ability to throw the ball—with stuff on it—exactly where the pitcher wants to, with extraordinary accuracy.

Craft comprises the knowledge that comes with experience, analytic powers, meticulous observation, and resourcefulness. Craft is what tells a pitcher where and how to apply the stuff he can control.

And poise includes the ability to apply one's craft under the most severe competitive pressure, to rise to an occasion, and to produce best when the need is greatest.

Both the practice that perfects control and the experience that perfects knowledge and poise are time-consuming. In the process, age and the attrition of muscular strain take their toll. Usually, by the time a pitcher masters his craft, some degree of his physical gift has been lost.

It is very rare, therefore, to find a man who possesses the highest degree of stuff, control, and craft simultaneously. It is so rare, in fact, that our list of eligibles for the "greatest pitcher" designation is quickly reduced to quite manageable terms.

Spahn and Ford were the most distinguished pitchers of the post–World War II era. Spahn pitched until he was forty-four years old and won more games (363) than any left-hander in baseball history. Ford, until the circulation in his arm (and his Yankee support) gave out in 1965, owned the best career winning percentage in the history of the game.

But neither of them, outstanding as they were, ever had speed and power even remotely comparable to that possessed by Johnson, Feller, and Koufax. The same was true of Carl Hubbell, Herb Pennock, Ted Lyons, and a dozen others. They were artists, fully worthy of Hall of Fame membership, but not contenders for No. 1.

Others, like Dean, Lefty Gomez, and Rube Waddell, did have overpowering stuff. But they never perfected the craft. Untouchable for a while, they became merely very good pitchers when their exceptional speed was lost.

Among the more recent elite, the same split appears. Don Sutton, Phil Niekro (a knuckleballer), and Gaylord Perry, who passed 300 victories, were not in the overpowering class. Bert Blyleven, who had moved up to fourth place in career strikeouts by the end of 1989 and was still active, used a legendary curveball. Bob Gibson and Ferguson Jenkins were certainly power pitchers, but notably less effective when their fastball slowed. Jim Palmer, Juan Marichal, and Robin Roberts, for all their distinction, don't stand out that much from each other, and from their top contemporaries, to be considered *the* No. 1.

More thought has to be given to Ryan, Seaver, and Steve Carlton. Ryan passed 5,000 strikeouts in 1989, retaining his 95-mile-an-hour fastball at the age of forty-two, and if the label we were dealing with was "most remarkable," he'd get it. Rarely with winning teams, he compiled a won–lost record that doesn't do him justice, and his hits-allowed ratio (around 6.5 per 9 innings) is the lowest in baseball history; plus he topped it all off in 1990 with his sixth no-hitter. But he also walked more batters than anyone (more than 2,500, with no one else at 2,000), so the "control" requirement wipes him out.

Seaver had stuff, control, craft, poise, and 311 victories, and a winning percentage of .603. You certainly have to count him among the finalists. And Carlton also had all those qualities, with 329 victories and a strikeout total (4,136) second only to Ryan's. His 1972 season, when he was 27–10 with a 1.91 earned-run average for a last-place Philadelphia team that won only 32 other games (and lost 87), may have been the greatest single-year achievement ever.

So my list is down to the seven: the three legends of an earlier time, Walter Johnson, Grover Cleveland Alexander, and Christy Mathewson; Bob Feller and Lefty Grove of the heavy-hitting era; and the two moderns, Tom Seaver and Steve Carlton.

Cy Young must be considered a special case. He won more games than anyone else, 511. But his career began in 1890, when conditions of play (and rules) were simply too different to allow meaningful comparison. Only in 1903 was major-league baseball stabilized into its familiar form. All those being considered started to pitch after that (although Young did pitch until 1911).

Feller is the next to be eliminated, partly by fate. To his blinding fastball, he added one of the biggest, most explosive curves ever used. He joined Cleveland at the age of seventeen, in 1936, and started breaking strikeout records right away. In all, he won 266 games, pitched 3 no-hitters and 12 one-hitters, and set a single-season strikeout record (348 in 1946) that stood until Koufax surpassed it in 1965.

But Feller was robbed of nearly four full seasons, at the very height of his powers, by World War II. He was only twenty-three years old when he went into the service, and took up right where he left off when he returned at twenty-seven. Granted peaceful times, he might have posted 100 more victories and 1,000 more strikeouts. He might have made his claim to No. 1 undeniable. Even when his fastball was long since gone, in 1951, he was able to win 22 games. But the lost years eliminate him.

Grove, according to most testimony, was faster than Feller.

"He was the fastest pitcher who ever lived," said Ford Frick, who was a baseball writer in the 1920s before moving up through the National League hierarchy to the commissionership of baseball.

Grove never had Feller's curve, but he kept his fastball longer. In 17 American League seasons, he won exactly 300 games (and lost only 140) and was still the league leader in earned-run average at the age of thirty-nine (in 1939).

But Grove did it all on power. Mathewson had that too, and more finesse. He used a famous "fadeaway," a pitch that would be called a "right-handed screwball" today. His career with the New York Giants ran from 1900 to 1916. Of his 373 victories, 365 came in a 14-year span, which means he *averaged* 26 victories per season.

Still, Mathewson was usually with a winning team, and so was Grove. Alexander and Johnson were not.

And that's where Seaver and Carlton drop out too. Carlton was on a first-place team eight times, and a contender in other years. Seaver had his share of non-support, but was with a winning team about half his career. It was different for Alexander and Johnson.

"I would have to say," said Casey Stengel, who ought to know, "that Johnson was the most amazing pitcher in the American League and Alexander in the National. Alexander had to pitch in the little Philadelphia ballpark, with that big tin fence in right field, and he pitched shutouts, which must mean he could do it. He had a fastball, a curve, a change of pace, and perfect control. He was the best I batted against in the National League."

Alexander was twenty-four years old when he joined the Phillies in 1911. To a right-hander, the 280-foot distance to the right-field barrier in Baker Bowl presented a special hazard, since left-handed hitters were the ones who had a crack at it. It's true that the lively ball was not yet in use, but, by the same token, hitters who weren't swinging for the fences were much harder to strike out—and that fence could be hit even if the batter wasn't particularly trying to reach it.

In his first seven seasons with the Phillies, Alexander won 190 games. He moved on to Chicago and St. Louis, and in 1926, at the age of thirty-nine, was the World Series hero for the Cardinals as they defeated the Yankees in seven games—well into the lively ball era. Then he won 21 and 16 the next two years.

Altogether, Alexander won 373 games. He pitched 90 shutouts, still the National League record, and this is a particularly significant statistic.

"A good pitcher's main job," Sal Maglie once observed, "is not to give up the first run." If a pitcher holds the opposition scoreless, his team can't lose. Once his own team scores, the pitcher's job is to give the other side one less. A shutout is proof positive that the pitcher has performed his team function to perfection.

Strikeouts are important in this respect, too. Base runners can't advance on a strikeout (generally), and winning runs can't score from third, as they can on flies and ground-outs. That's why stuff is so important. Alexander struck out 2,199 batters, ranking sixth when he retired.

At the same time, control is even more important than stuff—and Alexander walked only 951 men, averaging about one walk for every six innings pitched. And he pitched in 696 games.

If I were choosing the "most complete pitcher," Alexander would be it.

But Johnson was greater still.

Walter Perry (Barney) Johnson was strictly a fastball pitcher, the fastest of all. Eventually, he developed a pretty good curve, of which he became inordinately proud; but mostly, he just leaned back and fired the fastball with a three-quarter-arm motion that was almost sidearm.

"You might know it was coming," said Stengel, "but you couldn't hit it. And he had perfect control, too."

"When I batted against him in 1921," said Fred Haney, who was a Detroit infielder then, "he looked so fast I couldn't believe it. When I got back to the bench, they told me, 'Hell, you should have seen him ten years ago, he was twice as fast then.' Hell, I was glad I *hadn't* seen him ten years before; I didn't want to see him the way he was right then."

"Johnson," said Frick, "always worried that his fastball might kill someone if it hit him in the head. His control was so perfect, though, that he didn't even have to throw close to hitters. He just kept throwing it over the plate."

This is a noteworthy statement, since the record book shows that Johnson hit more batters than anyone else (206). But I interpret this in his favor. Since, by all accounts, he didn't *try* to brush hitters back, in an era when that was the universal practice and hitters expected it, the fact that so many failed to *avoid* getting hit by normal inside pitches demonstrates how hard it was to react to his speed. Don Drysdale, who holds the National League record for hit batsmen, was consciously intimidating hitters; Johnson was not. So I see this statistic as analogous to Koufax's record strikeout totals achieved when he was not trying to strike people out (because he wanted to make fewer pitches with an aching arm). They just couldn't hit him—and they just couldn't get out of the way of Johnson's fastball.

Johnson came out of Humboldt, Kansas, in 1907. He was nineteen. He went straight to the Washington Senators and never pitched for any other team in Organized Baseball until he worked one inning for Newark in 1928, when he was managing the International League club.

The Senators then, as ever, were seldom successful. During his first 16 years with them, they finished in the second division ten times. They were last or next-to-last seven times. He didn't get a chance to pitch in a World Series until 1924, when he was almost thirty-seven years old. Then he lost two games to the Giants, but got credit for winning the seventh and deciding game to give Washington its first— and only—world championship.

And, despite this minimal support, Johnson won 416 games—more than anyone but Cy Young.

"He was, besides, a wonderful man," said Frick. "The scene that sticks in my mind is the end of the 1925 World Series. Johnson was at the end of his career, and pitching the seventh and deciding game against Pittsburgh. Roger Peckinpaugh, a great shortstop who was having a terrible series, made an error. Then Kiki Cuyler hit a bases-loaded double, and Johnson was beaten.

"When the inning was over, he waited at the mound until Peckinpaugh came by on the way off the field—and he put his arm around Peckinpaugh's shoulders in a comforting gesture. That was Johnson the man."

And this was Johnson the pitcher.

He pitched 110 shutouts, a record that stands by itself. To this day, only Alexander (whose 90 is next), Mathewson, Young, and Eddie Plank, whose careers ended at least 60 years ago, have reached even 65.

He struck out 3,508—about 1,000 more than anyone else had 30 years after he pitched his last game.

He once pitched 56 consecutive scoreless innings, a record that stood until Don Drysdale surpassed it in 1968 and Orel Hershiser surpassed that twenty years later—both with the aid of disputed umpiring decisions in their favor.

He won 16 games in a row in 1912, an American League record that has been equaled but not exceeded.

He pitched more innings and completed more games than any other pitcher in this century.

From 1910 through 1919, he won 264 games, or more than one-third of all the games won by his team in those ten seasons (the Senators won 755).

He won by a 1–0 score (the ultimate pitching test) 38 times—more than twice as often as anyone else. (Alexander did it 17 times, and ranks second.)

His earned-run average is the lowest in baseball history for 3,000 innings or more. (Alexander's is second.)

And those 416 victories are 137 more than his 279 defeats, working for teams that lost 180 games more than they won on the days he didn't get the decision.

And oh, yes, control. He walked 1,406 in 5,923 innings. That's less than one walk every four innings, and a strikeout-to-walk ratio of 5 to 2.

To me, such statistics are beyond quibbling, even though I am so suspicious of statistics by themselves. When I call Johnson "the greatest of all pitchers," I may get an argument and be judged wrong, but I can't be accused of coming to an unreasonable conclusion.

And, of course, I never saw him pitch.

Of the ones I saw, Koufax and Feller were the best.

Finally, no discussion of this sort would be complete without mention of Babe Ruth.

Many fans, even today, are aware that Ruth was a pitcher before he became the home-run king, but few realize just how remarkable a pitcher he was.

From 1915 through 1919, Ruth was a regular starter for the Boston Red Sox. (He was a left-hander.) In 1915, his 18–8 record constituted the best winning percentage in the league. In 1916, his earned-run average of 1.75 led the league and his won–lost record was 23–12. In 1917, he won 24 and lost 13.

He pitched less than half as often in 1918 and 1919, posting records of 13–7 and 9–5. Then he was sold to the Yankees and became strictly an outfielder.

How good a pitcher would Ruth have been if he had remained one? Probably one of the best. He pitched in two World Series, in 1916 and 1918, and ran up a string of 29 consecutive scoreless innings, a record that stood until Ford broke it in 1961. Ruth's career earned-run average, for 163 games, was 2.28. He won 94 games and lost only 46, and was only twenty-four years old when he gave up pitching seriously. (Subsequently, at the end of a season, he would pitch an occasional game for the Yankees—and he never lost one.) At the age of twenty-four, Alexander was just starting, Koufax had more defeats than victories, and even Johnson had only 82 victories (to Ruth's 89). Grove won his first big-league game at twenty-five, and so did Spahn.

Certainly Ruth's native ability was prodigious. He might have become the greatest of all—but baseball history would have been inconceivably different.

On the other hand, imagine if they had the designated-hitter rule in his day. Every fourth day he'd pitch (and bat). The other three he'd be the DH. He'd wind up with 400 victories and 800 homers, wouldn't he? And that would make him a double Hall of Famer.

CHAPTER
25

Who Belongs in the Hall of Fame?

Speaking of the Hall of Fame, Babe Ruth is one of its five original members. When it was set up in Cooperstown, New York, in 1936, Walter Johnson, Christy Mathewson, Ty Cobb, and Honus Wagner were the others. And Ruth is, as a matter of fact, listed as both pitcher and regular player in at least some reference books.

But exactly what is baseball's Hall of Fame? Who's in it? Why? How do they get there? And what's it doing in Cooperstown?

When we come to mythology, the Hall of Fame both embodies and perpetuates it. Its location and origin are a response to pure myth, its purpose is to confer mythological status on its enshrinees, and its own status is shrouded in mythic significance.

It is not, actually, an official part of baseball but a private foundation that has baseball's approval and the full cooperation of baseball's administration.

Cooperstown is a small town in upstate New York (between Albany and Syracuse) that was identified as the place where baseball "originated" by a report prepared in 1907 and sponsored by Albert Spalding. Supposedly, in the year 1839, a local lad named Abner Doubleday laid out "the first true baseball field" in Cooperstown.

This story was made up out of whole cloth for various emotional, political, and commercial reasons we need not go into here, and was accepted uncritically for nearly half a century until historians turned the spotlight on its fictionality. Abner Doubleday grew up to be a Civil

War general in the Union Army and had nothing whatever to do with the development of baseball. But his myth was going strong in the middle 1930s when a family in Cooperstown, not insensitive to deep-seated currents of boosterism and tourist possibilities that run so often through American entrepreneurial instincts, had some property it could donate to set up a shrine. The guiding light behind the idea was Ford Frick, then president of the National League, who was planning to celebrate the league's sixtieth anniversary in 1936—an extremely forward-looking promotional idea in those days. Arrangements were made and in due course a small red-brick building was opened to house memorabilia and plaques, with a playing field alongside. Subsequently, it has developed into a full-scale museum of imposing proportions.

The method of selection, basically unchanged from the start, works this way:

Those members of the Baseball Writers Association of America who have been active for ten years are entitled to take part in an annual election of "modern" players. Those with fewer than ten years of experience can't vote, but once you qualify, you remain eligible to vote even when you pass on to "inactive" status upon retirement or movement into another job.

A "modern" player is defined as one who played his last major-league game at least five years before the election but not more than twenty years before. This creates a fifteen-year window during which the player can be considered. The five-year delay guards against emotional enthusiasm at the moment of a player's retirement, provides the voters with a chance for perspective, and prevents competition for cashing in commercially on the honor. The twenty-year limit keeps the decision within the range of those who have seen the man play. A first-time voter, therefore, overlaps at least the last five years of the career of the most recent eligibles. But if a player's career ended twenty years ago, most of the active members probably were not covering baseball when he played. In recent elections, about two-thirds of the voters have been in the active category.

To be elected, a player must have his name appear on 75 percent of the ballots cast.

That's it: 75 percent. There are no other qualifications. In any particular election, you don't have to vote for anyone; you can vote for one, two, or any number up to ten, but you don't list them in any order, so a name is either mentioned or it's not. The number of voters fluctuates from year to year, but in the late 1980s it was around 400.

So the baseball writers have fifteen chances to elect any particular player. Once he passes out of their jurisdiction, twenty years after the

end of his career, he becomes the province of the "old-timers committee," a body of appointed voters (former players, officials, a couple
of retired writers) who can vote on him again. This is an eighteen-
member committee that also has the three-quarters approval requirement. So a player passed over by the writers can be voted in by the
special committee, and this has happened many times.

It's a terrible idea, a perversion of its original purpose. Back in
1936, the writers were asked to choose those who had played after
1900 (considered a major dividing line in baseball history at that time),
with a special committee set up to consider nineteenth-century players.
That made perfect sense, and for the next twenty years or so, there
was a legitimate need to include players from before 1936 for whom
the writers did not have appropriate opportunities to vote.

But once the fifteen-year-window system had been in place for a
long time—let's say, by 1960 or so—and when all the players whose
careers pre-dated the writer-voting system had been duly considered,
there was no excuse to have a separate small committee, no more
qualified than the writers, to second-guess the collective decision expressed fifteen times that so-and-so did not belong. Right or wrong, a
vote is a vote. If you want the writers to vote in the first place (because
their supposedly objective status as non-employees of baseball lends
credibility to the process), then accept their decisions. If you want a
committee to do the choosing, fine: Pick a committee and let it choose.
But the second-guessing machinery has led to abuses that, in my opinion, have greatly detracted from the validity of the honor and, therefore, have done a disservice to the most distinguished members.

Special committees have also chosen non-playing personnel, and
members of the Negro Leagues who were barred from Organized Baseball before Jackie Robinson. This seems to me an entirely proper way
to deal with those categories.

How does a voter go about making a decision? Any way he wants.
There are no specific guidelines dealing with any statistical achievement, although there is a general statement about suitability, character, etc. The absence of explicit instruction seems to me a great
virtue: If you could spell out qualifications, you wouldn't need a vote.
That such voter freedom leads to disputes, and leaves room for argument, is just dandy. Argument is the lifeblood of sports interest and
myth-making. If you don't want it (which baseball officialdom has
every right not to want), don't let people vote. But if you ask for their
judgment, accept it, and don't try to tell them how to arrive at it.
Different people have different views and different ways of evaluating.
That's why 75 percent is considered a broad enough consensus to war-
rant admission.

As a voter since 1961, I can tell you what standards I use, and I know that at least some of the other writers agree with me. But I can't speak for others and can't describe universal rules, because no universal rules exist. And shouldn't.

My first question (asked of myself) is: Was this player the dominant one at his position for a substantial period of years during his career? Or, if more than one player was of comparable excellence at that position during that era, were they close enough so that there is no point in trying to make distinctions between or among them? If yes, put his name down. This covers Mays, Mantle, Musial, Spahn, Bench, Joe Morgan, etc.

The second question is: Did this player, even though he didn't quite meet the first standard, have such an impact because of personality and role in historic events that you could not write a sensible summary of his era without devoting considerable attention to him? If yes, put him down. (Dizzy Dean is an example of someone in this category, and so is Yogi Berra.)

The third question is: If I don't think he belongs this time (when I first vote on him), how can he get better in subsequent elections? The answer is, he can't. Now, it's possible for me to be wrong. I may, in subsequent years, realize some aspect of his importance that I overlooked the first time. Then I could and should change my mind; it's possible to learn more and become convinced. But by and large, if it doesn't become already clear in my mind that I think this player is a Hall of Famer during the five years before he reaches eligibility, the answer remains no.

In all this, I pay little attention to statistics or dramatic events. After all, I'm judging people whose careers I've followed all along. If I don't know—in my own mind—that this player belongs by the time he finishes playing, what sense is there in comparing lifeless numbers with others who are (or are not) already in? I had plenty of time to do that while he was playing (and for five years afterward).

Nevertheless, some numbers are such great benchmarks that they have acquired, among my contemporaries, the status of automatic tickets: 300 pitching victories and 500 home runs are examples. But can I honestly say to myself that I wouldn't choose this man if he wound up with 299 or 499, but I would if he went to 301 or 501? Of course not. Such numbers are just general confirmation of quality and quantity or performance.

We have discussed in earlier chapters the booby traps contained in comparative statistics. For something so special as the Hall of Fame, numbers that look the same from different eras simply shouldn't influence judgment. Unless you already believe a player is outstanding, you wouldn't be considering him in the first place. That someone was installed twenty-five years ago with lesser (or greater) numbers is simply irrelevant. Is today's candidate one of the very, very best players of his time or not? If he is, put him in. If he's not, don't.

One other standard should be applied, and is generally accepted. Hall of Fame status is not related to one historic feat or season—Don Larsen's perfect game, Roger Maris's 61 home runs, Orel Hershiser's string of scoreless innings. It is a recognition of a total career. The great feat (like Bobby Thomson's homer) is memorialized in the Hall in various ways through exhibits and descriptions. But a player, as an individual, goes in on the basis of his total achievement, not his peak moments.

The views I've just expressed are not widely shared these days. There is a tendency to see the Hall of Fame honor as the fair reward for every outstanding player, for two reasons. One is that everyone has favorites, and people we like are visibly disappointed at not being honored. The other is the comparative-statistics trap: So-and-so is already in, so why shouldn't my man go in?

Here we have the true evil of the old-timers committee at work. They have broadened the base by bringing back players who were passed over, and have done a dreadfully inconsistent job of it. The former players and club officials doing the voting certainly know baseball, but have no training or tradition in objectivity—in fact, they have a lifetime of experience of thinking "us versus them." They vote in their friends (who have credentials, of course), and pass over some they don't like (who have absolutely equal credentials), and in the process lower the credential base for all. Two outstanding inequities in this respect are Pee Wee Reese in and Phil Rizzuto out, and Bobby Doerr in and Joe Gordon out. All four were passed over by the writers, which may have been wrong, but at least it was evenhandedly wrong. But there is no rational way to separate Reese from Rizzuto or Gordon from Doerr on the basis of their records when they played at the same time and one against the other (and especially since Rizzuto and Gordon were usually on the winning side when they met head-to-head with Reese and Doerr among teammates of equal reputation).

Back in the 1960s, Frank Frisch was a member and leader of the old-timer committee. Frisch was an opinionated, persuasive, highly intelligent, well-educated, and passionate man, enormously knowledgeable about baseball as only a great player and long-time manager can be—and a Hall of Famer himself. But we used to joke that if he had remained on the committee long enough, every member of McGraw's Giants of the 1920s (with whom Frisch played) would have wound up in the Hall of Fame. It's not that the people he lobbied for weren't deserving—at a certain level, dozens and dozens can be considered "deserving"—but that this procedure passes over so many others equally deserving (by that standard) and lessens the distinction between them and Ruth, Cobb, Johnson, Mathewson, and Wagner—and Mantle and Mays and DiMaggio and Williams and Musial and Spahn and Ford and so on and so on. Dave Bancroft, Freddy Lindstrom, George Kelly, and Ross Youngs, estimable players all, are not in the same class—and there are at least a couple of dozen others in their class. If you include all, the honor is diluted; if you don't, it's arbitrarily unfair.

I look forward to voting for Tom Seaver and Nolan Ryan and Steve Carlton and George Brett and Reggie Jackson and others when the time comes. There's a large supply of what I think of as the "unquestioned" qualifiers, and it isn't fair to them to come down a notch for the "worthies." At the same time, I can't understand why Maury Wills, whose impact on the way baseball is played was so great, hasn't been voted in (or how my colleagues could, one year, vote Bob Gibson in but not Juan Marichal, whose accomplishments were so nearly identical in the same years; at least they did add Marichal two years later).

But that's fine. Disagreement is what this is all about. That's why we have the three-quarters requirement.

And what about Pete Rose? He is in disgrace because of his betting activity, and deserves to be in disgrace because he shouldn't have been doing what he was. (I don't mean whatever actual bets he made, because I don't know that; I mean hanging around with the people he admitted hanging around with.) But disgrace is one thing, playing ball is something else. The transgressions came late in his career, when he was no longer playing or at the tail end of his playing career, and even worse transgressions—fixing games—were ascribed to Ty Cobb and Tris Speaker toward the end of their careers. Meanwhile, Rose got more hits (and set a flock of other records) than anyone else in the history of the game. What in the world would a Hall of Fame for player excellence mean if it didn't include Rose? If we were judging off-field character and behavior, we'd have a tough time justifying Cobb and Ruth. Rose did a bad thing, and the appropriate punishment—exile—was imposed. (He went to jail for tax evasion, not betting.) To carry that on to a Hall of Fame question seems to me either irrelevant, excessively self-righteous, or impossibly inconsistent. If I'm still there when his name comes up, I'll certainly vote for him.

Meanwhile, there is one oversight that is so ridiculous, and unaccountable, that I must call attention to it.

The non-player list of Hall of Fame members, as of 1989, had forty-two names, starting with Walter Alston (for managing the Dodgers)

through Tom Yawkey (for owning the Boston Red Sox), including umpires, Negro League players, and one Morgan G. Bulkeley, who, history
records, was the first president of the National League in 1876.

Missing is the name of William A. Hulbert.

Who?

If that was your reaction, that's the essence of my complaint.

All he did was invent major-league baseball, and therefore all major
professional sports leagues in America.

We saw, in an earlier chapter, how the essential step was shifting
from the player-controlled, unstable, and uneconomical National Association of Professional Base Ball Players of 1871–75 to the concept
of a league of *clubs*, with control vested in management, in 1876.

Well, Hulbert was the Chicago businessman who conceived and
worked out the plan for that change, who made it work, and who set
up the National League and made Bulkeley a figurehead league president to accommodate older interests back east while he himself was
running the Chicago club. After the first year, Bulkeley left his Hartford
club (of which he was president) and went on to run the Aetna insurance company and become mayor, governor, and U.S. senator. He had
more to do with baseball than Abner Doubleday, but not much.

Hulbert, meanwhile, was the driving force behind the new league.
He was the one who persuaded Al Spalding and three other Boston
stars of the early seventies to come back to Chicago (Spalding's home
area). Spalding already had his sporting-goods business going and had
a pretty sharp organizational brain of his own. He can be considered
a co-architect of many features of the new enterprise. But Hulbert was
the central figure.

And the main thing he did was not simply think up the idea of
salaried players, with no say in business matters, working for club
owners. He understood the basic necessity of a set schedule and league
discipline—and made it stick.

Toward the end of that first season, the New York and Philadelphia
clubs, with indifferent won–lost records, declined to make their final
western trips, because they could make more money playing exhibition
games at home. That had been customary in Association days.

They were the two largest cities in the league.

Hulbert insisted on their expulsion.

At the meeting to do so, in Cleveland that December, Bulkeley
wasn't even present, and Hulbert was elected league president, a position he then held until his death in 1882. He guided the National
League through the first few years that established not only its own
stability (1990 was its 115th season) but the model for all stable
leagues.

He had the league operate in 1877 with only six teams, but didn't completely neglect the New York market. The expelled team, the Mutuals, had actually played its home games in Brooklyn, then still a separate city. Hulbert helped arrange for the Hartford team (to which Bulkeley was no longer paying attention) to play all its home games in Brooklyn, even though it kept the Hartford name. He also applied his theme of discipline in another vital area: When Louisville players were discovered fixing games, he expelled them. He kept his six-team league going through 1878, with three franchise shifts, and brought it back to eight clubs in 1879 (adding two and moving two). In 1880, it was so successful that a rival league, the American Association, was being formed in imitation, and fighting for players. In 1882 it went into business and was winning acceptance when he died. The two-league system flourished for the rest of the 1880s, and New York and Philadelphia reentered the National League (today's Giants and Phillies) in 1883.

Why is a man who played such a vital role in the sport's true beginnings not identified in the museum situated at the site of its purely mythical origin?

I don't know, and neither do any of the baseball officials—league presidents, commissioners, club owners—I have asked. There is no record of any particular hostility to Hulbert's memory, no hidden political problem (since Spalding was his protégé), no hint of any impropriety. It seems to be sheer inertia, indifference, ignorance, injustice, and insensitivity at work.

It shouldn't take a committee or any other complex procedure to correct the oversight. The Hall of Fame hierarchy itself, or the commissioner, can do it by edict. If they care.

CHAPTER
26

Expansion and Its Consequences

I've been mentioning, in passing, the effects of expansion. It thinned out batting orders, adding to the decline in offensive statistics. It created an upward pressure on salaries, and helped the players organize their bargaining position, by increasing the demand for top players and a feeling of security in many others because more major-league jobs were created. It constantly increased the value of the national television package because it brought home-team identity to more markets.

Now let's try to get a more coherent view of what it has actually done, and how. Expansion is *the* determining force and greatest change in baseball in this century, more far-reaching in its effects even than the lively ball.

The causes of expansion, which are still at work, are the demographic, economic, and sociological changes that have altered all American life during the second half of this century. Baseball has had to react to them, against its will, and adding teams (in new locations) has been the simplest and most natural response.

The results of expansion have been more balanced competition, more money for everyone, some alterations in style of play, and distinctly different attitudes on the part of fans as well as participants.

Causes and results interact, of course.

We're going to deal with statistics—about ballparks, about population, and about pennant races. We may seem to wander, but, as Perry Mason likes to say, "I'll connect it up."

Babe Ruth hit 708 American League home runs in his twenty-year career between 1915 and 1934. All of them were hit in only nine ball-parks: the Polo Grounds and Yankee Stadium, in New York, his home fields during that time; Fenway in Boston; Shibe Park in Philadelphia; Griffith Stadium in Washington; Comiskey Park in Chicago; Navin Field in Detroit; League Park in Cleveland; and Sportsman's Park in St. Louis.

Hank Aaron broke the single-league record when he hit his 709th home run in 1973, playing for the Atlanta Braves. He was also in his twentieth season—and he had hit those home runs in 22 different parks.

By the time he finished with 755 home runs, Aaron had connected in 31 different parks, having spent his last two seasons (1975 and 1976) with the American League Milwaukee Brewers—ironically, in the same ballpark that he had started from in 1954 with the Braves, before they left Milwaukee for Atlanta.

But that's not the record. Frank Robinson and Rusty Staub, who played in both leagues at various times, hit homers in 32 different parks. Robinson even hit one in Jersey City, where the Brooklyn Dodg-ers played a total of 14 games in 1956 and 1957, bringing in each opponent once each year. Robby, with Cincinnati, had only two shots at those fences, and connected once.

What's the point of all this?

Well, to understand the baseball world's mental habits that still persist, and are handed down by older players and officials to younger ones, one has to get some feel, however vague, for the stability baseball used to project.

In 1916, the Chicago Cubs moved into Wrigley Field, a remarkable modern park built two years before for the Whales of the Federal League, which had folded after 1915. In the preceding seven years, a flurry of ballpark building in the new style—steel and concrete, often double-decked—had produced new stadiums for 14 of the other 15 teams. And during the 1920 season, the St. Louis Cardinals moved into Sportsman's Park with the Browns.

In the thirty-six years from 1916 through 1952, only two new major-league venues appeared. Yankee Stadium opened in 1923, across the Harlem River from the Polo Grounds, in which the Giants remained. And in 1932, Cleveland's Municipal Stadium was first used for Sunday games, then for night games, and eventually (after World War II) for all games instead of League Park.

For that generation of baseball fans, the name and location of those parks seemed as permanent and natural as the planets in their orbits.

Oh, a name could change: Navin Field became Briggs Stadium, and Shibe Park became Connie Mack Stadium, and Redland Field became Crosley Field in Cincinnati, but that didn't fool or bother anybody.

And the parks themselves, of course, were constantly being altered, as seats were added, contours changed, fences moved, and scoreboards expanded. But these were mere details.

What's more, by the end of the 1952 season, not a single major-league franchise had moved in 50 seasons, since Baltimore had become the New York Yankees in 1903.

Then the Braves went from Boston to Milwaukee, at the start of the 1953 season.

During the next twenty-one years, a different ballpark appeared on the major-league scene in seventeen of them, and never did three consecutive seasons go by with the same set of parks in use. Only in 1957, 1959, 1963, and 1967 were there no changes from the preceding year.

Imagine a fan—or writer, or coach, or general manager, or even a player—at the age of forty in 1952. If his active memory of baseball went back to the age of five, he had never experienced a franchise move and was aware of only two new stadiums, in Cleveland and New York. Is it any wonder that the next two decades left him bewildered?

There were 26 new parks during this period, 32 in use altogether.

It may seem strange even to today's younger fans, because after 1974 things settled down. In the seventeen years from then through 1990, only three seasons produced new playing sites—four of them domes. In 1977, Seattle and Toronto presented expansion teams and the Montreal Expos moved into Olympic Stadium; in 1982, the Minnesota Twins moved into their downtown dome; and in 1989, in mid-season, the dome-to-end-all-domes was opened in Toronto. This one is a domed city, rather than a roofed ball field. It includes a hotel, restaurants, shops—what O'Malley envisioned for Brooklyn back in 1955.

Of those 1952 parks, the only ones still in use in 1991 were the ones in Detroit, Boston, Cleveland, Chicago, and New York in the American League (acknowledging the fact that Yankee Stadium was completely rebuilt in 1974–75), and Chicago (Wrigley Field) in the National.

But it's no time for complacency. Chicago's Comiskey Park, which became White Sox Park, is history and a new one (financed by the city and state) has gone up in an adjacent block; serious explorations for a new park are in progress in Detroit and Boston; the Yankees are threatening to move (to New Jersey nearby, or to another part of the Bronx); Baltimore's new one will be ready in 1992; and Wrigley Field, which had lights added in 1989 after fifty years of resistance to what romanticists call sacrilege, is not guaranteed to last forever either. In addition, expansion is coming again in the middle 1990s, one way or another.

So if the actual ball fields themselves change so much so often, the games cannot be unaffected and the statistics they produce can't be treated as hallowed, uncontaminated numbers representing perpetual verities.

Population figures tell their own story, and it's a neglected one. In 1952, the 16 major-league teams occupied 10 cities (counting Brooklyn as part of New York). The aggregate population of their metropolitan areas was 35.3 million. That's an average of 2.2 million per team, regardless of geographic distribution.

In 1989, the 26 teams were located in 22 different cities, with only New York, Los Angeles, Chicago, and San Francisco–Oakland housing two teams. The aggregate population was 98.3 million, or 3.8 million per team.

So the potential market for ticket sales—people within transportation range of the ballpark, which is how metropolitan areas are defined—is two and a half times as big.

But the teams of 1952 averaged 900,000 ticket buyers a year, while the 1989 teams averaged 2,200,000 each. Even if we ignore higher ticket prices as simply a reflection of inflation (they're actually more than that), it's still a tremendous increase in revenue. The 1952 figure can be expressed as 41 percent of the available population. (This is statistically false, since comparing ticket sales, with repeaters, to population is an apples-and-oranges impropriety, but it does convey the idea.) But the 1989 rate is 58 percent. And the actual average attendance—2.2 million—happens to be equal to the average total population of 1952. That's a coincidence, but a provocative one.

If the potential market is so much bigger, and enhanced by telecasts whose value depends on size of market, it is less surprising that baseball in the 1980s has seen its revenue grow from about $300 million to beyond $1 billion, a rate of growth that eclipses even what happened before World War I, when the starting point was so low.

Look at it this way: In the first half of the century, live customers were the main source of income, and the vast majority of these came from the central city in which the club was located; after that, a larger proportion of live customers could be drawn from suburbs and exurbs, which contained a larger proportion of the affluent willing to pay more—not just for tickets but for concessions and parking. At the same time, this same enlarged base of customers increased the possibilities of cashing in on their interests as well as those of other followers through radio and television (making baseball programs more attractive to advertisers). "Growth" before 1960 or so meant simply "larger cities." After that, it meant tapping regional resources in unprecedented ways.

But this also means a fundamental change in the promoter's targeted audience. He used to care primarily about those who could reach his turnstiles, one way or another. Now he had to consider millions of consumers-at-a-distance who might seldom, if ever, actually buy a ticket but whose existence and interest could contribute to profit.

It also means a fundamental change in the nature of political pressure. Senators and representatives, as well as state governors, hear from their enlarged constituencies about getting (or keeping) a piece of the major-league pie, and bring their influence to bear on promoters who would prefer to keep the monopoly as small as possible.

This also explains what happened to franchise values. With more people per team, and more cities reaching a critical size which they believe can support a major-league operation, the demand for franchises is intense. Cities without a team want one, and offer a lot to get one; those that have one must make a comparable offer to keep it. This usually involves providing, one way or another, a new and improved ballpark in place of an older one wearing out.

The New York Mets paid a $2-million entry fee (in the form of expansion-draft roster-stocking) in 1961. They were sold, in 1980, for $20 million. They were sold again in 1986 for $80 million. The original Yankee franchise in 1903 cost $14,000. It was sold in 1915 for $460,000. After Colonel Rupert died, it was sold in 1945 for $3 million. In 1964, the remaining two partners of that deal sold it to CBS for $14.6 million. It was passed on in 1973 to a consortium including George Steinbrenner for only $12 million—and its 1990 value is something between $100 million and $200 million, or even more. (The Yankees have a local cable television contract that brings them more than $40 million a year just from that.)

And such numbers make it more comprehensible—not less awesome, but more comprehensible—that ball players can get $4 million a year for one season's play. Ruth's salaries for his entire career totaled $910,900, at least double what anyone else had accumulated at that time (1934). Even accounting for inflation, that's still quite a difference.

But do the above figures about the two New York clubs lend substance to the prediction that "the rich clubs will get all the best players and kill competition"?

No. It doesn't work that way.

The bugaboo of killing competition was always used as the rationale for preserving reserve-system restrictions on player movement. The implicit reasoning is that general managers making trades will be infallibly wise about strengthening their teams, but that players acting on their own will be stupid about making the most of their opportunities. (Management doesn't say it that bluntly, but that's what it means.) But let's see.

If only management can control where players go, and tries honestly to make every transaction contribute to increasing its own chance of victory, the net result of these free-market (for management) decisions should be a wide distribution of success. No team can "lose" its good players except at its own discretion, and can build up winners as generations (about five years in sports teams) change.

If, on the other hand, players can choose where to play, and are motivated entirely by who offers the highest salary, all the best players will wind up on the rosters of those who can pay the most and the result will be a few superteams with a majority of losers.

And in the old context of stability with only 16 teams, those two propositions were unchallenged.

But history exists.

We know that the dominance of the Yankees, with 29 pennants in 44 years between 1921 and 1964, happened entirely under the old, absolute-control, maximum-restriction reserve clause. And we know that since free agency, achieved in modified form in 1976, there have been no dynasties. But that's anecdotal. Let's make a table, in cycles of 16 pennant races (counting divisional races since they came into being), and see how many different teams were able to finish first.

Years	Teams in Action	Number of Different Winners		
		American	National	Total
1921–28	16	2	3	5
1929–36	16	4	3	7
1937–44*	16	3	5	8
1945–52*	16	4	6	10
1953–60	16	3	4	7
1961–68	20	5	4	9
1969–72	24	4	5	9
1973–76	24	5	5	10
1977–80	26	4	5	9
1982–85†	26	7	6	13
1986–89	26	6	6	12

*As World War II was ending, normal rosters were disrupted. In 1945–48, each league had four different winners in four years. In 1949–52, normal patterns were restored, and in those four years, the American League had only one winner (the Yankees) and the National had three.

†1981 is not included because a two-month strike caused a split season without true first-place finishers.

Since 1976, in the free-agency era, 11 of the 12 National League teams have finished first at least once, and the 12th, Montreal, reached the special playoffs in the split season of 1981. Of the 14 American League teams, 11 have finished first with only Cleveland, Texas, and Seattle failing to do so. One might say that 23 different winners among 26 teams indicates a fair distribution of competitive balance in a 14-year period. On the other hand, in the 14 years from 1950 through 1963, the Yankees and Dodgers won 18 of the 28 races, the Giants 3, the Braves 2, 5 others 1 each, and 7 none at all (not counting 4 expansion teams, which also didn't win any).

But what does all this have to do with expansion?

First, expansion created more jobs and more demand for players to fill them at the major-league level—and this was a key element in giving players the chance and the frame of mind to create the union that cracked the reserve system.

Second, expansion brought new thinking into the "club" of owners, shifting weight away from the hidebound complacency elsewhere that let something like a Yankee dynasty flourish.

Third, the opening up of new revenue sources "leveled the playing field" to some extent outside the megalopolis locations of New York and Chicago (and in an earlier time, Philadelphia). Inner-city population was the *total* determinant of potential sales in the old days—and since even the most profitable team had relatively modest resources, the less profitable couldn't operate the same way. After the breakout, each locale not only had additional ways to raise cash, but the higher level of the floor of revenue made it possible for even the "poorest" to be "rich enough" to maintain good scouts, coaches, farm systems, and star salaries. The big-and-rich always have an advantage, but after expansion it was a smaller advantage, relatively speaking.

Fourth, many of the new owners, because they had to buy in on what was historically a high entrance fee, had greater financial resources than earlier club owners did. Gene Autry (Angels) and Joan Payson (Mets) represented a different level of economic power than Charley Finley (in Kansas City) or Walter O'Malley (in Brooklyn) or the Griffiths (moving from Washington to Minnesota). They were no less dedicated to the reserve, but they also brought with them new kinds of considerations about taxes, debt, ancillary activities, and boosterism.

Finally, the mere fact of expansion, from 16 teams to 20 to 24 to 26, set in motion mechanisms that tend to even out competitive ability even apart from reserve systems and other rules. Dilution means leveling off, almost by definition. The aging star is harder to replace, because more teams are competing for good prospects. Players of mid-level capability who used to be locked for life in the minors get more chances to play in the majors and some of them, after a few years, become better than they would have been in the smaller system. No matter how you do it, if you divide the best 650 players among 26 teams you wind up with a smaller difference, top to bottom, than when you take only the best 400 on 16 teams. The larger sample enhances the luck-of-the-draw element in any season's set of games, making it easier for any team to be good one year, bad the next, within a narrower range.

In these ways, expansion aided competitiveness and made change seem more normal. It created new ballparks, in the old cities as well as the new. It made viable huge television deals that nationwide networks didn't want when too few cities were involved. And it forced ownership to confront modern times: new schedules, playoffs, marketing, player autonomy, less parochial policies.

So the point here is not to rehash arguments about the effects of free agency. It's to show how different fan experience is now than it used to be, and like most things, the difference has its good and bad aspects.

Spreading joy, in turn, to more cities certainly seems like a good aspect. Close competition and uncertainty of outcome certainly seem desirable. The chance for more players to get a moment at the top is surely good.

On the other hand, dynasties have an appeal and create a glamour that is missed when no team clearly establishes itself as the "best" and the "one to beat" over a period of time. Millions of fans, especially in the television age, are not that wedded to one home team, and even if they are, they are attracted to some superteam when their own is consistently mediocre or worse—even if it's only to hate the superteam. So that feature of myth creation can be called bad.

But while traditionalists and the less committed may yearn for old Yankee, Notre Dame, Green Bay Packer, or Boston Celtic syndromes, the people in Minneapolis, Kansas City, Chicago, Toronto, San Diego, Houston, and elsewhere are never heard to complain about their occasional taste of victory.

So the changing scene keeps changing, and granting the innate human resistance to change, it's hard to conclude that the changes of the 1970s and the 1980s haven't been for the better. We can be sure that more changes will come in the 1990s, and can only hope they turn out as well as these did.

27

The Ball's the Same, the Bat's the Same—Or Are They?

But wait. Certainly something must stay the same. What about the ball and the bat? Aren't they the way they've always been? Isn't the ball still the same size it was 100 years ago? Isn't the bat still round (or, if you want to quibble, cylindrical)?

Yes, but.

The *size* of the baseball hasn't changed significantly since the 1850s and not at all since 1876. It has to be between 9 and 9¼ inches in circumference, and weigh 5 to 5¼ ounces. The significance of this lies in the ease with which a normal hand can grip it so that fingers can impart various types of spin.

But the *composition* of the ball, and how it is wound, has changed appreciably from time to time, and these factors determine how it flies when hit.

The bat has changed more, but by choice rather than regulation. Originally, it couldn't be wider than 2½ inches in diameter at its widest point, with no limit on length, and had to be a solid piece of wood. From 1885 to 1893, one side was allowed to be flat. Now it has to be round, it can't be longer than 42 inches, its handle can have grip-aiding material, its end can be cupped, and it must be wood but not necessarily a single piece. Its diameter can be 2¾ inches.

But that's a *professional* bat. Throughout the school and amateur systems, aluminum bats are used, and they're very different indeed.

Since we're concerned only with major-league baseball, the aluminum bat's influence is indirect—but very great. It has changed the nature of the player's preparation for his profession and the scout's way of judging talent.

Aluminum bats don't break, which is the economic cause of their popularity. They also make the batted ball behave differently. The ball comes off harder and faster upon contact, and most professional players believe that if a metal bat were allowed at their level of play, some pitchers and third basemen might be killed or maimed. But the main thing is that they produce a greater consistency of result along the whole length of the bat than wooden bats do.

All bats are tapered, narrower at the handle than at the head. The weight of a metal bat is more evenly distributed, and the handle isn't quite as narrow. If the point of contact is with the "fat part" of a bat, not quite to the end but well up from the handle, the ball is hit with maximum force. The closer the point of contact is to the hands, along the handle, the more a hitter is "handcuffed," with his power decreased.

This difference, between hitting the ball with the fat part and hitting it off the handle, is less with a metal bat than with a wooden bat. The hitter benefits because he doesn't have to be as accurate about the point of contact (longitudinally), and has a better chance to hit the ball still fairly sharply "off the handle."

This better chance decreases the advantage a pitcher can gain by pitching inside. The batter has a better chance still to do some good by making contact with the inside pitch.

In terms of physics, these differences may not be immense, but they're enough to have a major effect on style—especially since the players using this implement aren't as skilled, proficient, developed, and strong as major-league pitchers and batters.

The result is that, in developmental stages of amateur, school, and college ball, pitchers don't learn to pitch inside and hitters don't learn how to handle the inside pitch. And scouts watching them have to try to translate what they're seeing—the hits and outs recorded under these conditions—to wooden-bat realities that will arise in professional play.

Many scouts believe that this has led to an overall decline in hitting skills among major-league players. Even the most talented—perhaps especially the most talented—must make an adjustment that takes time. And pitchers, too, must develop patterns that did not become ingrained when they faced aluminum-wielding hitters, since inside pitches didn't provide as much advantage.

But the entire fear factor we started with exists only for a close pitch. Young players, therefore, don't develop as much tolerance for it, and get angrier when confronted with it in the professional setting. All sports activities are first of all habit: trained reflex, honed by repetition. Less experience with inside pitching, and better success when confronted by it (because of handle hits), results in less, or at least later, ability to deal with it on the major-league level. At the same time, fewer pitchers have become proficient in using that dimension in their early stages.

These are not tremendous, obvious, dramatic differences, but they count.

What is obvious is the shift of players to lighter and smaller bats, a movement that began in the 1960s. The theory is that bat speed, rather than bat mass, determines force at the point of impact. The old-time players knew this, of course, and "choked up" on the bat, gripping it an inch or two up from the bottom to increase control. Long-ball mania, as it became universal, made players fond of gripping the bat all the way down at the nub, so by swinging a lighter bat held at the end you got the same velocity of the fat end as swinging a heavier bat from a choke-up position.

Of course, if you don't connect just right, with the fat end, you don't get handle hits at all; this is what we just talked about with respect to aluminum bats, and the old "heavy lumber" produced effects somewhere in between (but without the metal bat's extra resiliency). So we're back to the prevailing willingness to sacrifice average for power.

Babe Ruth used bats that weighed 40 ounces or more. Today, 33- and 31-ounce bats are common. Length doesn't make as much difference, so the 42-inch-long limitation is not a practical consideration. But shorter bats—say, 34 inches instead of 36 or 37—are also more common today for their lighter weight.

Does a shorter bat make you less able to reach an outside pitch? Yes, but you can take care of that by standing a little closer to the plate. And if a lot of pitchers are less assiduous about driving you back with a close pitch, you can do that and get away with it. But if a pitcher does drive you back, and then works outside, he's got you.

It's a complex set of interactions that never ends.

Throughout the 1980s, players moaned and groaned more and more about broken bats. Thin-handled bats break easier, and more often, than thicker and heavier ones, not surprisingly, and today's bats often shatter even when you hit the ball with the fat part. There was actually speculation about an eventual shortage of wooden bats, as the destruction of rain forests and other public issues of lumber harvesting made the nightly news. The cost of bats is insignificant to a major-league team's budget. But schools will never go back to wooden bats.

In answer to complaints, Nobe Kawano, the long-time equipment manager of the Los Angeles Dodgers, showed his players some reproductions of bats used in Ruth's era. They couldn't believe it. For all the modern players' absorption with building muscle by working with weights, they couldn't imagine swinging such things effectively.

"But they did," Nobe told them. "And they didn't break many."

He's not likely to make converts.

While the bat story is vague and controversial, the ball story is specific and partly documented, and no less controversial.

Do authorities tamper with the liveliness of the baseball while vehemently denying that they do? Or do manufacturers turn out livelier and deader batches with or without official requests?

Yes.

But not as often as, and not always in the way that, ball players and the public come to believe.

We know that major changes in the ball were made in 1910, 1913, 1920, 1929, 1931, and 1977. It was widely believed that the 1987 ball was juiced up. In other years, the evidence is less definite, but the complaint that the ball is artificially lively comes up every time a lot of home runs turn up early in a season.

Before examining the specifics, to separate rumor from fact, several general principles must be stated.

Although baseballs are manufactured by machines, no two baseballs are exactly alike. The covers are hand-sewn. Variations in wool yarn, from yard to yard, are unpredictable. And even within the specifications, the quarter-ounce range amounts to a 4 percent permissible variation.

Proof that balls are different is visible to everyone in every game. Pitchers, who make their living by becoming expert at the feel of a baseball with extremely sensitive fingers, often reject one ball and ask for another (and get it). Whatever it is that makes them uncomfortable with a particular ball, this shows that another ball isn't exactly the same—and therefore, may behave differently when hit.

Since this is true, the luck of the draw distorts statistics from which conclusions can be drawn. Suppose that in a box of a dozen balls, some are a bit livelier than others, or that one whole box is a bit different from another box. In the course of a game, several dozen balls get into play. Now, suppose this liveliest ball in the sample is fouled into the stands, and the next ball, not as lively, is used for a fat pitch that the batter hits squarely—and an outfielder hauls in at the fence. If the balls had been used in reverse order, the dead one fouled off, the lively one might have gone two feet farther for a home run.

These are completely random possibilities. It is a convention of statistics to say that in a very large number of cases, such variations will even out. And that's true if the number of cases is large enough. But ball games are made up of discrete events whose impact on memory and attention does not even out; it depends on their importance. A home run that flies farther than you expected from that particular batter's ability makes a greater impression than the big hitter's less-than-expected out (or even homer).

But there's a still greater random factor: the atmosphere itself. Weather—wind direction and strength, rain—is obvious enough. But how a ball "carries" varies not only with every park, but with time of day in each park, and from day to day, and actually from hour to hour or even minute to minute. Players know this and allow for it. Catfish Hunter, in accepting induction into the Bay Area Sports Hall of Fame at a gala San Francisco dinner in 1990, said: "I'm thankful the ball didn't carry in the Oakland Coliseum at night the way it does in the daytime, or I might have given up 600 homers instead of 300 and I wouldn't be standing here." José Canseco made the same observation, but as a complaint, when he hit 42 homers in 1988 and felt he could have hit more. For winning and losing, these are conditions both teams must confront on an equal basis, as best they can. But for statistics, they create uncertainties that become hard to account for.

So to talk realistically about dead and live baseballs, we can't rely on anecdotal evidence or the convictions of players and managers. One way to be sure is to examine actual documentation and testimony. This is analogous to the question of fixed basketball games: You can't prove a game is dishonest by looking at it or citing the play-by-play, because honest mistakes are indistinguishable from purposeful ones; unless you have external evidence that a deal was made, you are left only with unprovable suspicions. That's why those games can be fixed and why coaches whose teams were fixing them could be unaware of it, or at least able to doubt. So statistical comparisons that show a sudden increase or decrease in homers don't "prove" anything. The ball may have been made differently, or random factors may have accumulated in one direction.

In some cases, though, we do have external evidence, and statistics confirm rather than reveal what we know.

Late in the 1910 season, a cork center inside the hard-rubber center (around which the yarn is wound) was introduced. Using our three standards, batting average, runs per game, homers per game, here's what happened:

Year	Batting Average	Runs	Homers per Game
1909 (rubber)	.244	7.09	.21
1910 (transition)	.250	7.67	.29
1911 (cork)	.266	8.98	.41
1912 (cork)	.269	9.05	.38
—	—	—	—
1914 (cork)	.254	7.49	.33
1915 (cork)	.250	7.59	.31
1916 (cork)	.248	7.13	.29

They had decided, in 1913, that the new ball was *too* lively, that it was producing "too much" offense. So they deadened it, not by eliminating the cork necessarily, but in other subtle ways. (The simplest way is not to wind it quite as tight.)

In 1920, the ball was made livelier again, along with the other steps already mentioned (no trick pitches, a fresh ball in play). That bit of history is well known:

Year	Batting Average	Runs	Homers per Game
1919	.263	7.75	.39
1920	.276	8.73	.51
1921	.291	9.71	.76

Ruth led the way, of course: 29 homers in 1919, 51 in 1920, 59 in 1921; but others caught on. Statistics always lag behind a change, to a certain degree, because players must adjust habits to new conditions even when they recognize them.

The 1920s were so prosperous and wonderful for baseball, and so clearly benefiting from the new emphasis on hitting, that the owners proceeded to that universal human fallacy: If a lot is good, more must be better. So in 1929 they juiced up the ball even more. But that turned out to be too much of a good thing, so in 1931 they had to tone it down some:

Year	Batting Average	Runs	Homers per Game
1928	.281	9.46	.89
1929	.289	10.37	1.09
1930	.296	11.07	1.27
1931	.278	9.62	.86
1932	.276	9.83	1.02

That 1931–32 level came to be considered the norm when I was growing up.

Much was made, in those days, of the fact that each league had its own ball, the National's manufactured by Spalding and the American's manufactured by Reach. What wasn't known at the time was that the two sporting goods companies were secretly a part of a trust cartel formed back in the 1890s, and that baseballs came off the same machines and were taken out of the same bins to be sent to the cover-sewers and given different stamps. By the 1950s, with a certain amount of fanfare, it was declared that the leagues had agreed to use a "uniform" ball.

The manufacturing process is inconsistent. The quality of wool can change. The glue that holds the cover on can be of different resiliency. Stitches can be uneven (the most common reason a pitcher wants to change balls).

In 1977, baseball did go to a new manufacturer, Rawlings instead of Spalding. Officials, from Commissioner Bowie Kuhn down, swore the ball itself was sacrosanct and made to "exactly the same specifications." But here's what happened:

Year	Batting Average	Runs	Homers per Game
1976	.256	7.99	1.15
1977	.264	8.94	1.73

Strange to say, players and fans did notice a difference.

The manufacturer then offered an explanation. The specifications were unchanged, but the new company was being more conscientious and efficient about living up to them, while the old company had become careless and sloppy. So the balls were coming out livelier, because they were better made.

In 1978, offense dropped off just a bit from 1977, and that general picture has remained consistent to this day.

Except for 1987.

In the 1987 season, home runs soared to a record 2.12 a game (by both teams). Runs went to 9.44—a jump, but not unprecedented; and the batting average of .263 was on the high side but less than in 1979 and 1980 and, actually, the exact average of the preceding ten-year period.

So the whole thing seemed to center around a sudden excess of homers (which produced more runs automatically, but not higher averages), and the screams about an artificially juiced-up baseball echoed across the land. And when in 1988 and 1989 homers went back to 1.51

and 1.46 respectively, runs down to just under 8.30, and the batting average to .254, it was considered proof that the 1987 ball had been manipulated and, just as purposely, deadened in mid-August because the results were out of hand.

But I wondered. In all the earlier cases of a change in the ball, the averages increased or decreased by a substantial amount, as well as the homers. This time, only home runs seemed to be affected.

A closer look uncovered some interesting patterns.

All the extra homers seemed to be confined to certain ballparks. If the ball itself were different, one would expect the change to show up pretty uniformly wherever games were played—as had been the case with past changes. But the 1987 distribution was peculiar.

If you defined 1985 and 1986 as "normal," and then compared 1987 to that, you found that home-run inflation (a long-term trend) had behaved this way: 1985 was 10.6 percent higher than 1984; then 1986 was 5.9 percent higher than 1985; and then 1987 jumped 16.9 percent above 1986. Well, that was a big jump, but not nearly as big as the years when we know the ball changed. Those were in the 50 percent range.

But almost all the 1987 increase was confined to certain ballparks: San Francisco, Texas, Cleveland, Baltimore, Detroit, both Chicagos, Cincinnati, and Montreal accounted for almost 70 percent of the total increase. If the ball's construction was making it fly farther, why didn't it fly farther in other places?

Could some other factor be at work?

How about the atmosphere?

What if 1987 happened to be a year when the weather was unusual in the vicinity of those ballparks?

I knew of no way to track that down, because weather-station records by region wouldn't be a fine enough measurement. All that mattered was the actual atmospheric effect on balls in flight inside a particular park during the hours a game was in progress.

But there were two suggestive indicators.

There were three indoor ballparks, in Houston, Minnesota, and Seattle, where the weather could have no effect. Each of them, in 1985 and 1986, had produced more homers than the year before. But in 1987, homers were actually down in Houston and Minnesota, and up in Seattle by a smaller percentage than in the previous two years. So in the face of this tremendous increase, the total of homers hit indoors was actually less.

If the ball was juiced up, what happened to the juice indoors under controlled atmospheric conditions?

The other indicator was geographic. The biggest increase of all had taken place in San Francisco, but the Giants had a better team than in the past. But there were 11 ballparks located in the middle of the country, away from both seaboards, from Atlanta to Texas. In those 11 parks, the change from 1985 to 1986 had been zero: exactly the same number of homers. But in 1987, in just those parks, there were 369 more homers, an increase of 24 percent. Since these were in both leagues, and since all teams came in and out of them as visitors, you couldn't ascribe that to personnel changes.

Maybe there was abnormal summer weather in the middle of the continent.

Was there? I have no idea.

All I'm trying to show is that the question is not as simple as it appears. When the ball is changed, the statistical reflection is greater and more uniform than what we saw in 1987. Does this mean they didn't change it? No, it just means you can't prove it by numbers. (If you hold a gun to my head and force me to give an opinion, I'd have to say I suspect there might have been a bit of tinkering; but I wouldn't be surprised if there wasn't.) The word "random" deserves more respect than it gets. All sorts of coincidences can come into play in a particular year. In 10,000 tosses of a coin, a run of 10 straight heads is not only not unusual but a virtual certainty; we just don't know *when* it will come up. By the same token, a combination of funny weather, manufacturing inconsistency, which balls are in play when they get hit, a succession of poor pitching performances, and hitter confidence boosted by seeing that last little guy hit one out could all come together to produce an abnormal year without Machiavellian intervention by the authorities.

And, of course, it makes a great difference how balls are stored, in a cold or warm or dry or humid place, and for how long. We don't know that, in any particular case, either.

Or maybe Peter Ueberroth really was Machiavelli. We'll never know until and unless some historian digs out correspondence, tape recordings, or work orders, or someone squeals. But statistics alone won't tell us.

Fluctuations aside, lighter bats and livelier balls mean lower averages. Here's one other way to look at it, for sweeping panoramic impression, as if it were a satellite photo. Counting only those who played enough to qualify for a batting title, we find:

In the 1920s and 1930s, there were between two and three .300 hitters per team. In the 1940s and 1950s, there were one or two per team. In that 1963–68 offensive blackout, it fell to .7 per team for the six years, and as low as .3 in 1968 (one American Leaguer, five National Leaguers). Since then, it has held fairly steady at just under 1.0.

Think back to what I said about batting-order density, and free-swinging mentality, and you can put the ball and bat controversies in proper perspective. Their construction matters only after—and if—you make contact.

CHAPTER
28

The Evolution of the Playing Rules

The baseball game we see didn't just happen. It evolved by trial and error, consciously adopting certain rules and discarding others. One of the fundamental characteristics of its development, quintessentially American in its response to entrepreneurial needs, is that these choices were influenced very early on by what would make the game attractive to spectators as well as to the players. To appreciate fully the beauty of the game we have, and why it has remained stable in so many respects for so long, we should contemplate the course of its evolution and the thinking behind various principles we take for granted.

For instance, why is a ball caught on the fly an out? Why not on one bounce? Well, a caught fly is an out in cricket, and baseball comes directly from cricket, among other ancestors. But a one-bounce out was the rule in early baseball. The trouble with it was that it was too easy. What's wanted, by spectators as well as players, is people running around the bases—an exciting feature that was an improvement on cricket.

And what about the strike zone? Why have it? Or the force-out. Or the infield fly. Or the balk. Why three strikes and four balls?

All these ideas were arrived at gradually, so let's start at the beginning.

The single step that made baseball as we know it possible was a change in how a runner could be put out between bases. In many of the varieties of rounders, "base" or "town" ball played in America from Colonial times on, an out could be recorded by throwing the ball at a runner and hitting him when he wasn't in contact with the base or within some designated safe area.

This one provision, aside from all other considerations, required the use of a fairly soft ball. And a soft ball won't go very far, or very fast, when hit by a bat.

When this rule was abandoned, in favor of the "tag" play—a runner off base could be put out by having a fielder touch him with the ball while holding it—it became practical to play with a harder ball. Players might suffer more painful bruises if hit by a batted ball, but that would be accidental. The likelihood of repeated blows by deliberate hard throws was eliminated.

A harder ball changed everything. It put a premium on basic athletic skills: quick reflexes, strength, footspeed. It enlarged the field of play. It made a much more exciting game for the participants—and for spectators. And, gradually, it made the pitcher the dominant figure in the game instead of merely the one who started the action.

A special circumstance arose, by trial and error, in making a tag play at first base. With a harder ball, and increasing batting skill, fielders had to back up to sufficient depth. Those who caught the ball had to throw it to the guardian of first base, who, in order to take most throws, had to face away from the runner approaching from home plate. If ball and runner arrived at about the same time, the physical application of tag would lead to nasty collisions.

It was decided, then, that it would be enough for the first baseman (or any player) simply to tag first base with the ball in his possession, before the batter-runner touched it, to retire the batter. After all, the idea was to have the batter reach first base safely before the fielders could prevent him, and only if the ball reached first base before he did could he be tagged with it, even in theory. So, strictly for practical reasons, tagging the bag was deemed good enough, and the standard play at first evolved.

But the principle involved could be extended.

The batter *must* go to first after hitting the ball. Reaching first safely is the only alternative to being out. He is, in that sense, "forced" to try to beat the ball to that base, and that's why it is sufficient for the ball-holding fielder to touch the base without touching the player.

When first base is occupied, and the batter hits the ball, a runner on first is "forced" to try for second (with exceptions we'll come back to). First base must be vacated for the sake of the batter-runner, so for both players to be safe—to avoid an out—the first one must reach at least second base.

But if tagging the base is good enough to retire the batter at first (because he is forced to try for it), why shouldn't the same method be applied to the runner "forced" to try for second?

It should. It is. And it applies at third base when first and second are already occupied, and at home plate when the other three bases are full. The force play, eliminating the physical tag, made possible the special beauties of the double play (and even a triple play), avoided unnecessary collisions, speeded up the game, and gave the defense a better chance in a game that, in its primitive stages, was tilted heavily in favor of the offense.

If a runner is not "forced" to advance, however, it is neither fair nor reasonable to have him declared out merely because the ball reaches the next base before he does—for the simple reason that he has the right to return to his own base. When a runner is on second, with no one on first, and the batter hits the ball, the runner could stay at second if he wanted to and be safe. If he tries for third, and the ball is thrown there, he must be tagged with it to be out.

These rules grew out of a larger philosophy stemming from the tag-play principle. If you have to tag a runner between bases, you need a reasonable chance to touch him without having to chase him all over the field. So the concept of a baseline emerged—a straight line, not too strictly determined but essentially direct, between bases. The runner may not wander away from the baseline *to avoid being tagged;* if he does, he's declared out. (But this is true only if he is *avoiding* a tag play; otherwise, he can run anywhere he likes on the way from one base to another. He takes a straight line because it's the shortest distance, not because the rules demand it, and when he can gain speed by making a wide turn, usually at third, he has a perfect right to do so, unless someone with the ball is trying to tag him.)

On the other hand, a fielder *without* the ball has no business getting in a runner's way in the baseline, not even unintentionally or accidentally. Any such contact or impedance entitles the runner, automatically, to the next base—unless the fielder is in the act of fielding the ball, in which case it is the runner who must get out of the way.

This business of giving runners and fielders a fair chance—equalizing offense and defense in some reasonable manner—led to special rules concerning fly balls.

The difference in elapsed time between a hard-hit bouncing ball and a slow roller reaching some infielder is not very great. But the length of time a high pop-up or long fly stays in the air—out of everyone's reach—is much longer. The advantage gained by a runner who takes a lead and starts for the next base as soon as the ball is hit is only a slight advantage on a grounder. If the grounder is hit sharply and goes through the infield, normal quick retrieval by an outfielder may stop the runner from taking an extra base or it may not; if the ball is hit so softly that the batter beats it out, infielders have converged upon it in time to stop other runners from getting more than one base. And if a force situation is involved, the runner needs as good a start as he can get.

On a fly ball, however, the fate of the batter is not determined until the ball is caught or hits the ground. If caught, the batter is out, and runners aren't forced at all.

Now, suppose there were no restrictions on the runner. As soon as the ball is hit, he leaves first base. He may be all the way to third base by the time the ball comes down and is caught. So although the defense accomplished its goal—getting the batter out—the offense gained two bases strictly through the courtesy of the force of gravity: It takes a ball as long to come down as to go up, and all that time the runner has been running.

The unfairness here is self-evident. The defense *wants* batters to hit high, soft, easily caught flies (if flies at all), and the offense isn't supposed to benefit from them.

On the other hand, if the fly ball is not caught (especially if it's a long drive), the offense should be entitled to anything it can get.

So the runner is allowed to try to advance while the ball is in the air—at his own risk. If it is caught, he is obliged to try to advance only *after* it is caught. That means if he has already started, and the ball is caught, he'd better get back to his original base before trying again to advance.

In practice, this excellent rule creates what we're familiar with. If the runner thinks the fly ball won't be caught, he does, indeed, run all the way. If he's pretty sure it can be caught, he'll wait in contact with his base, and take off the minute the ball touches the fielder's glove (if he thinks he can make it to the next base). If there's a doubt, he'll go "halfway" and watch, having time to retreat if it's caught, and having a head start on an advance if it's not.

But if he guesses wrong, and has already left the base before the fly is caught, he can be put out by having the ball thrown to the base he left before he can get back. He is, in this sense, "forced" to go back, and doesn't have to be tagged in person, the base itself being enough as in other force situations.

We take it completely for granted that if there are men on base when the third out is made, retiring the side, they are wiped off the books and the team's next turn at bat starts with no one on base.

But why should that be? They earned their way on, didn't they? Why shouldn't runners be carried over from one inning to the next?

In theory, there is no reason why they shouldn't be. A perfectly consistent type of baseball game would result if they were carried over—but it would be, of course, a much higher-scoring game.

And that's the historical reason for the clean slate each inning. Originally, baseball *was* a very high-scoring game, too much so. The offense had too many advantages, once a hard ball came into use, and the fairness concepts applied to baserunning developed in the interest of "balance." The idea of "three out, all out" reflected attempts to give the defense a better break.

Why was the offense so far ahead? Mainly because modern pitching techniques had not yet developed, in terms of physical skills. But there was another reason. Baseball evolved not only from the English game of rounders, but also from cricket—and in cricket the batter is supreme (for complicated reasons we needn't explore).

The essential point was, in the primitive forms of baseball, that the pitcher was perceived as merely one who puts the ball into play, with his fielders responsible for executing the outs. And it took the highly distinctive concept of balls and strikes to change that dynamic.

Originally, a "strike" meant a swing-and-a-miss (they said he "struck *at*" the ball) and three misses retired the batter.

But nothing required the batter to swing at a delivery he didn't think he could hit. In fact, he was allowed to indicate to the pitcher whether he wanted a "high" or a "low" ball, and the pitcher was supposed to comply.

We can all see the flaw in that—now. But it took a while for the early players to realize that a patient (or timid) batter could simply stand there and not swing at all until (1) the pitcher got exhausted, (2) the pitcher served up something so soft that no batter could resist it, or (3) everybody got bored and went home.

By the same token, the timid pitcher could simply keep throwing the ball out of reach until darkness came.

What's surprising is how long it took them to work out the solution.

As usual, the burden was placed first on the pitcher. If he kept tossing the ball out of reasonable reach, the batter was eventually awarded first base. But if the batter didn't want to swing at "good" pitches, he still didn't have to. Now look at some of these dates:

1845—Alexander Cartwright codifies the rules for New York's Knickerbocker club.

1871—First organized professional league.

1876—The National League is formed.

1880—The number of balls required for a walk is reduced from nine to eight.

1882—Seven balls for a walk.

1884—Six balls for a walk.

1886—Seven balls again.

1887—The batter may no longer order a high or low pitch, and the called-strike, strike-zone concept is introduced. Now five balls mean a walk. Three strikes are still out—unless, after two strikes, the next one is a called strike. In that case, the batter gets a fourth strike (swung or called).

1888—The batter gets three strikes, period. And for the first time, the batter gets first base if hit by a pitch.

1889—Four balls for a walk.

This is forty-four years after Cartwright and thirteen years into the life of the National League. If you were twelve years old when you became a fan of professional baseball in 1871, you are now thirty.

But we still haven't reached the game we know.

One of the changes Cartwright made permanent was to lay out the field as a square, with home plate at one corner, instead of as an elongated diamond, as was often done before that. The field of play, then, was defined by the 90-degree angle made where the first- and third-base lines meet at home plate. If a batted ball landed outside these baselines, and their extension into the outfield, it was out of play—unless it was caught on the fly or (as the early rules provided for all batted balls) on one bounce.

In other words, a foul ball could not help the offense. This was to put a reasonable limit on the acreage the fielding team had to cover. But if the fielders were good enough to get a ball that was hit foul, the batter could be retired—again, an attempt to even the odds a bit in a game still totally favoring the hitters.

But if a foul fly was not caught for an out, the foul ball simply didn't count. There was no limit to how many could be hit in any time at bat.

Now, once the called-strike concept came in, and the number of balls required for a walk was reduced to four, the batter acquired an interest in fouling off any strike-zone pitch he didn't really want to hit. He had just lost the right to demand high or low deliveries. Suppose he preferred a high one (in the strike zone). If he could foul off low pitches (in the strike zone) indefinitely, he'd get his high one sooner or later.

And there's one easy way to foul off a pitch deliberately:

Bunt it.

It took about six years to close this loophole. In 1894, the batter was charged with a strike every time he bunted the ball foul.

That's why, to this day, a foul bunt on the third strike automatically makes the batter out.

But at first, the foul-strike rule applied *only* to bunts. A full-swing foul, unless caught on the fly, simply didn't count.

The next year, 1895, another kind of foul-strike was added—the foul tip. A foul tip is defined as a ball merely deflected by the bat, and continuing back in almost a straight line. It wasn't considered a fly ball, so the batter wasn't out even if the catcher caught the ball before it hit the ground. But it now became a strike, if the catcher did hold it.

But not until 1901—the National League's twenty-sixth season—did the present foul-strike rule come into being. Now any foul, not caught on the fly, counted as a strike for the first two strikes. Only on the third strike could fouls prolong the batter's life, and then only if he took a full swing and did more than merely graze the ball.

The American League, which began functioning as a major league in 1901, did not adopt the foul-strike rule until 1903.

And only at that point, fifty-eight years after Cartwright's rules, do we have "baseball as we know it."

During this long evolution of a proper balance between the hitter's and pitcher's opportunities, two other dimensions had to be dealt with: the style of a legal delivery, and the distance from which the pitcher faces the batter.

Originally, the pitcher was required to toss the ball underhand, letting it leave his hand below the level of the hip, from a distance of 45 feet. The idea was, remember, to have the batter hit the ball to begin play, not to overpower him. Since the fiendish abilities of such underhand throwers as Kent Tekulve and Dan Quisenberry had not yet been developed, the underhand toss really did make it easy for the hitters.

Even so, 45 feet was pretty close, and in 1881 (when it took eight balls to get a walk and three missed swings to strike out) the distance was moved back to 50 feet.

Gradually, pitchers kept lifting their arms in the act of throwing, shaving that hip line ever closer. In 1884, the restriction was raised to "shoulder high," and in effect straight overhand pitching became possible.

This explains, among other things, why those nineteenth-century pitchers were able to pitch every game, or almost every game, for their teams. An underhand toss is a "natural" movement, arms being hinged at the shoulders the way they are, and causes little strain; throwing from 50 feet, one didn't have to throw all that hard anyhow to reach the strike zone in a time span that would put pressure on the hitter's reaction time. (What we now call a 90-mile-an-hour fastball covers 60 feet in .5 second; from 50 feet, the same half-second interval is achieved by a ball traveling about 68 miles an hour—a very modest fastball indeed. (We'll get back to this.) But an overhand throw is "unnatural" (ask any pitcher), although it can provide more power and velocity (and allow a greater variety of breaking-ball pitches). For a while, the 50-foot distance made it possible to avoid fatal arm strain even with an overhand motion; but as pitchers (and their managers) saw how devastating they could become by throwing harder, they applied more pressure on themselves—and on the hitters.

So by 1893, it was evident that the overhand thrower had too big an advantage being that close, and the pitcher's plate was moved back to our famous distance of 60 feet 6 inches.

A few historical statistics can give a feel for what such changes mean.

In 1883, before overhand pitching was allowed, there were about 7 strikeouts a game in the National League. In 1884, with the new style, there were about 10, a 43 percent increase. When you see that Hoss Radbourn, a Hall of Famer, won 60 games while starting 75 that season, and struck out 441 batters in 669 innings, you now know the reason. What Radbourn and his peers didn't know yet was that you can't go on throwing overhand that much for very long.

Then, in 1892, the last year of the 50-foot distance, the league's batting average was .245. In 1893, with the pitcher set back 10 feet, it became .280, and stayed over .290 for the next four years.

However, as everyone adjusted, 60 feet 6 inches turned out to be the "right" distance, for two reasons. Not only did it turn out to be the right reaction time for the hitter's response to the strengthened pitcher, but it also conformed (unknowingly) to the laws of physics. The aerodynamics of a thrown ball—its spin, velocity, trajectory, and so forth—are extremely complicated. The 60-foot distance proved to be the correct one for the best mixture of control and stuff when the ball reached the strike zone. It's far enough for spin and gravity to take effect, and close enough to exploit a human's good aim, especially when you let the human throw from a small hill, which he started to do in the 1880s.

Now, baseball fans have known from childhood that the pitching distance is 60 feet 6 inches. (Lefty Gomez, asked by manager Joe McCarthy what kind of pitch he threw when Jimmy Foxx connected for a 450-foot grand slam, said, "Best pitch I ever threw, Joe, for the first 60 feet; the last 6 inches weren't too good.")

But do we know what that distance is? From where to where?

Actually, it's from the front edge of the pitching rubber to the back corner of home plate—the point at which the two foul lines meet.

This makes the effective pitching distance a good deal shorter. The pitcher must keep his pivot foot, the one he balances on, in contact with the rubber. He strides forward in the act of releasing the ball, so by the time it leaves his hand it is a foot or two closer to home plate. And a strike is defined as a pitch on which *any* part of the ball passes through *any* part of the strike zone. But the plate is 17 inches deep (as well as 17 inches wide), so from the point of release to the front of the strike zone may be only 57 feet—or 55 or even 53.

But before the change, there was no rubber. The pitcher had to stay within a "box" whose front line was 50 feet from the back of home plate. So the *effective* change was from 50 to approximately 55.

And here's another thing we take for granted: Home plate is a five-sided figure, while the three bases are square. Why, and when did it get that way?

Originally, home plate was a square, 12 inches on a side, set into the 90-degree notch of the two foul lines. A 12-inch square has 17-inch diagonals, so the maximum width was 17 inches (and so was the depth, in line with the pitcher).

A fairly straight-line pitch that just catches the outside corner is a strike.

A curving pitch, breaking so that it winds up outside the 17-inch width at the point of the diagonal, may have passed inside the 17-inch width at the front half of the plate without touching the slanted line of the square's side.

This didn't seem fair—and, more to the point, it was virtually impossible for either the umpire or the pitcher to fine-tune his depth perception so perfectly that he could tell at which exact portion of a 17-inch-wide, knees-to-shoulders imaginary rectangle the ball was "over the plate" or not.

The remedy was to "fill in" the corners facing the pitcher with two triangular pieces.

Now the pitcher and the umpire have a full-width target, and the breaking ball that catches the front corner of the pentagon is a legitimate strike.

But this wasn't done until the year 1900.

So the front of the plate is 17 inches across. The new sides—now pointing straight out toward the pitcher's mound—are each 8½ inches "deep." The old "sides," running along the insides of the foul lines, are still 12 inches long along the lines, but are now connected to the new 8½-inch-deep sides running in the pitcher-to-batter direction.

Why didn't they simply make it a 17-inch square? Because then the back portions of the square would extend into foul territory, and all bases to be touched—including home—are intended to be entirely in fair territory.

All these little bits of geometry have a profound effect on the game we see. The whole art of pitching has grown up out of finding ways to use the corners of the plate, and the batter's job in protecting the strike zone is much harder with a full 17-inch front than it used to be when home base was a bare 12-inch square. Once again, we see that the interests of offensive-defensive balance have been served—by trial and error.

In pursuit of fairness for the base runner, some adjustments had to be made. If the batter were retired on a fly, any runner was required to tag up after the catch, or to return to his base if he had taken a lead. But if the batted ball was a grounder, a runner on first was obliged to advance to vacate first base for the batter.

What if a fly ball became a ground ball? That is, what if a fielder dropped a fly?

Obviously, the ground-ball rules would apply.

But that put the runner on first in an impossible situation. If he moved far enough toward second, and the ball was caught, he could be doubled up off first; if he waited at first and the ball was dropped, he would be easily forced at second.

On a fly ball hit fairly deep into the outfield, the dilemma isn't so bad: The runner can go halfway, and have a good chance of making it to whichever base he has to after the play develops, because the outfielder will have a fairly long throw.

But on a high pop-up, within reach of an infielder, the situation is different. The infielder can drop the ball (or let it fall) on purpose, with plenty of time to pick it up and make a force play on the runner who holds first.

Since leaving the base too soon can result in a double play (batter out on the fly, runner doubled up getting back) while holding the base can mean only one out (either the batter is out on the fly, or the force play at second is the only out because the batter has had time to reach first), it's clear what the runner must do. He holds his base and, one way or the other, only one "deserved" out (the pop-up) is recorded.

But what if there are runners on first *and* second?

Both face the dilemma, and the alert defense can get two outs by dropping the pop-up with time to make force plays at third and second (if the runners don't go), or by catching the pop-up and doubling up any runner who does go.

This would be an "undeserved" double play.

And it's especially bad if it happens with one out, because then the manipulated double play retires the side.

This was recognized in 1895, and an "infield-fly rule" was adopted. If, with one out and men on first and second—or first, second, and third—the batter hit a pop-up over the infield (in fair territory), the batter would be out automatically, whether the ball was caught or not, and the runners were not obliged to leave their bases (although they could, if they wanted to risk it).

But it wasn't until six years later, in 1901, that the infield-fly rule was applied also to a nobody-out situation.

With two out, of course, it doesn't matter. One more out, caught pop-up or force, ends the inning.

Baseball, however, is populated by ingenious people and is always evolving. The infield-fly rule as written applied to "infield" flies. As late as the 1930s, clever outfielders (like Tommy Henrich of the Yankees) would race in on a pop-up or looping fly just beyond the infield, let their infielder back off, and trap or drop the ball to create exactly the situation the infield-fly rule was supposed to prevent.

How could you rule it an "infield fly," the legalists argued, if an "outfielder" was catching it on the outfield grass?

So the rule was changed to make it a matter of umpire's judgment. If the umpire thinks an infielder could routinely handle the ball, he declares "Infield fly" and the automatic out takes over, no matter who actually fields it.

In fact, it is even an automatic out if an infielder purposely drops a line drive with less than two out and men on first and second or the bases full.

However, the infield-fly situation does *not* apply to a bunt. A bunt (with runners on) is a purposeful tactic by the offense to advance runners, who leave their bases even before the ball is bunted as part of a designed play. If the bunt is popped up, and the ball caught, and two runners can be caught off their bases, the defense "deserves" this double play. And if the popped-up bunt is allowed to hit the ground while runners, undecided, get hung up between bases, the chances are there will be time to force only one of them. If both do get caught this way, it is considered insufficient alertness by someone on the offense, not automatic helplessness as in the ordinary infield-fly situation.

Aside from these special circumstances, a runner at first base is particularly vulnerable to deception by the pitcher, and needs protection.

The runner has a legitimate need to take a lead, and needs a "fair chance" (there's that idea again) to steal a base. He can do either—get a head start to advance on a hit, or steal—only if the pitcher actually does pitch to the batter. If the pitcher, pretending to throw home, can actually hold the ball and then throw it to an infielder, the runner is trapped.

In the early days, runners did what you now see small children do when first introduced to the game: They stay in contact with the base to feel "safe." This produces a very static style of play, and much of baseball's basic appeal lies in the aggressive activities of base runners. This is one of its main differences from cricket.

So, to give the runner a chance, restrictions are put on a pitcher's movements. A violation of these restrictions is called a "balk," and when a balk is committed, every runner is automatically given the next base.

The current rules list thirteen varieties of balk.

This is an area of persistent controversy between players and umpires. No matter how specifically the rules are written, some elements of defining a balk are a matter of judgment. As a note in the rules says:

"Umpires should bear in mind that the purpose of the balk rule is to prevent the pitcher from deliberately deceiving the base-runner. If there is doubt in the umpire's mind, the 'intent' of the pitcher should govern."

Baseball people will tell you again and again that this pitcher "has a great move," or that another pitcher "always balks and they don't call it." There's a handy rule any fan can follow: If *my* pitcher does it, it's a great move; if the *opposing* pitcher does it, it's a balk.

The basic principle is that there must come a point when the pitcher is committed to throw to the plate, and that this moment must be recognizable to the runner. Up to then, it's up to the runner to protect himself against being picked off; but after that moment of recognizable decision, he must feel free to run or take a big lead.

This is why the big balk flap of the 1988 season was so silly. An attempt was made, by league office edict, to have umpires call balks "by the book," and to fine-tune the type of balk that occurs when the pitcher, in his stretch motion, doesn't come to a full stop. The strict interpretation was that the stop had to be "discernible," although what it meant to have a stop that one couldn't discern was not explained. But the trouble resulted from having umpires, each a different human being, making such a decision from various angles of vision on the basis of how the pitcher actually made his motions, without regard to the situation.

So you had balks called with the bases loaded (costing a run), or a man on second when one team was five runs ahead. What had been lost sight of, in concern for technicalities, was the *purpose* of the balk rule. If there was no sense in, no attempt to, and no possibility of *deceiving* a runner who wasn't going anywhere anyhow, why call it?

After enough hassling and spoiled ball games, the practice was abandoned (or at least decreased) before the season ended, and the umpires went back to calling the intent of the rule: only when it seemed to matter.

What all the turmoil really proved, however, was that baseball people have short memories and that newcomers don't always know history. Exactly the same kind of nonsense had marred the early part of the 1963 season—and the 1950 season. Even the dumb things baseball authorities do go in repetitive cycles.

In 1950, for reasons now obscure (to me), it was decided to tighten up on calling balks. For the preceding twenty years and more, the frequency had been between two and three per team per season. By the end of May, there had been many more than that called, and pitchers were going crazy. Halfway through the season, both league presidents sent down orders to stop the nonsense, and things returned to normal. At season's end, the National League average was 9.5 per team, and the American League 5.8, all a reflection of the first two months.

In 1963, legend has it (I can't prove this), the Dodgers convinced league president Warren Giles that balks should be called strictly. (Because they had Maury Wills as their chief weapon the year after he stole 104, and because Mr. O'Malley was very influential? Who knows?) By May 7, National League umpires had called 96, shattering the full-season record of 76 set in 1950. The American League umpires, working for President Joe Cronin, had called a perfectly normal 8. (Right: 8.) At that point, Commissioner Ford Frick called the two prexies together and said, "Cut it out." Uniformity was important, he told the public, because there was a World Series coming up in only five months.

The 1988 situation was not quite as simple. I believe there was a concerted effort, through the 1980s, to help base runners because they add to the attraction of the game. Just as the discovery of Babe Ruth's gate appeal in 1920 led to the lively ball, so the feats of Lou Brock and Rickey Henderson (who pushed the record to 130 steals in 1982) promoted a desire—less drastically, less universally, but consciously—to help that aspect of the game. Gradually, pitchers were not allowed to use some of the tiny movements that held runners close in the 1950s and 1960s; the book never did permit them, and now enforcement became tighter.

In 1988 specifically, it got out of hand because the authorities, like Giamatti, didn't really understand baseball-on-the-field. Reading the letter of the law, they thought they were doing something proper by focusing on the word "discernible," and lost sight of the *purpose* of the balk rule. That did get straightened out by mid-season—again—but in general, balks are called much tighter today than in the previous generation.

All these intricacies exist for one purpose: to be fair to the runner, and therefore to the offense. Yet it wasn't until the 1950s that one glaring injustice was corrected.

Imagine: bases full, pitcher doesn't come to a stop, umpire yells "balk," but in the meantime the pitcher goes through with the pitch, which the batter hits over the fence.

Do you nullify the four-run homer on the grounds that the cry of "balk" ended everything, allow one run, move the runners up, and make the batter hit again?

That's exactly what they used to do. Some "fairness" to the offense, eh? The defense did something illegal and the offense lost three runs.

Now, however, the offense is given a choice. Whatever happens to the completion of a play that involves a balk—a wild throw to a base, a hit, a wild pitch—the offense can take the result of the play if it's to its benefit, and the balk is simply ignored.

A final rule to consider, which also sets baseball apart from other team games, is the batting order, which requires every member of a team to bat in turn. In other games, there is no requirement that offensive actions must be evenly distributed (unless you count serving in tennis doubles): The offense is free to choose which players it wants to try to score how often. In baseball, the potential scorers must take their turns; none gets a second chance until all the others have had one. This, too, comes from cricket.

What counts in the batting order is SEQUENCE. Burn that word into your baseball brain: s-e-q-u-e-n-c-e.

A team is penalized if its players bat out of order, but not as simply as you might think. I have seen major-league games in which both managers and the umpires messed up proper application of the batting-out-of-order rule, because it's so easy to lose sight of its central provision.

The key thought is: The correct batter, at any moment, is the one listed immediately after the last who completed a legal turn at bat. That's it. No exceptions.

At the start of the game, each manager lists his nine hitters in the order he wants them to bat. This is the "official batting order," handed to the umpire and to the opposing manager.

Incidentally, it's *only* a batting order. No fielding positions are indicated, and officially no player is assigned to any fielding assignment. Fielders can shift positions every play, if they want to—the starting catcher can pitch, a man can play left field for one inning and shortstop for another, and so on. What they cannot do, *ever*, is change their position in the batting order, no matter what positions they play and no matter how substitutes come into the game.

Both teams are responsible for paying attention and seeing to it that the right man gets up. The umpire is *forbidden* to call attention to any mistake in order; he must act only if the opposing team protests, or the team at bat discovers and corrects its mistake.

Each player must remember one thing and one thing only: who hits before me. Suppose the order is A, B, C, D, E, F, G, H, I. All D has to know is that if C is at bat, he's next. No distractions, no other considerations.

Now somebody makes a mistake. B goes out or gets on, and D steps up (instead of C).

The umpire does *nothing*.

If the opposing team doesn't say anything, D completes his turn at bat. Then, but *before* a pitch is made to the next batter (or a play is attempted on a base runner if one is on), the opposing team can still appeal to the umpire.

If it does, the umpire must declare the proper batter—C—out, and wipe out whatever it was D did. Who comes up? Well, the last *correct* batter was C, who has just made an automatic out (for failing to bat after B). So the next hitter is D, who always follows C.

But if the opposing team does not protest, the first pitch to the next batter legalizes whatever D did. And the next hitter is E, who always follows D.

Suppose the team at bat discovers the error while D is still up there, incorrectly, with (let's say) the count 1–1. It can call him back and send up the right hitter, C, without penalty. C simply inherits the count and completes the turn at bat. Then D comes up.

The thing to remember is that the batting order's numbered slots, 1 through 9, have nothing to do with it. The rule is not that No. 4 bats after No. 3; it's that D bats after C any time C completes a legal turn at bat. And there's a reason for this.

A leads off. By mistake, G goes up instead of B. Then C, who knows he's "No. 3 in the order," follows. But as soon as one pitch is thrown to C, anything G did is made legal.

And that means C is the wrong batter. After G comes H. Always.

If the opposition protests now, H is declared out—he was the proper hitter—and the next correct batter is I. So C, D, E, and F have all been passed over. Since the last legal batter to complete a turn was H (automatically out), the batting order picks up with I.

It seems incredibly complicated, and the more you think about it the more mixed up you can get. But just concentrate on "who was the last legal batter?" The name after his is the correct next batter.

One can see why the opposition is in no hurry to protest. A singles. Then C (wrong hitter) hits into a double play. Fine. Throw a pitch to the next man (whoever steps in) and accept the two outs. If it's D, he's the right man (since C was just legalized), and that's that. If it's anyone else, it's the wrong hitter again and the opposition can protest or accept the outcome.

However, if C had hit a home run, the opposition would protest, wipe out the two runs, and pick up an automatic out. But the automatic out would be B, who should have come up—and the correct batter would be C again.

The tricky part is that the batting order handed to the umpire is the one that counts. Suppose A, C, and B bat in that order the first two times around, and the opposition doesn't protest. If they do it again in the seventh inning, it's still wrong and they can be penalized. But if they're alert enough to realize what's been happening, and this time B comes up after A, there's no longer anything to protest and the team is clean.

The penalty, then, can never extend beyond one batter, which is why the rule is made the way it is, according to names instead of numbered slots. Either the improper batter's action is nullified by having the proper batter called out, or he becomes recognized as the proper batter, so that only one automatic out can be recorded. If it were defined by slot numbers, you could run into situations where four or five consecutive batters could be "wrong," and automatic outs would pile up.

But that would be unfair.

And all the baseball rules have been devised to be as fair as possible.

And they are.

And that's why it's as wonderful a game as it is.

CHAPTER

29

The Windup, and the Pitch

In 1986, I wrote a piece for *The New York Times Magazine* that I want
to reproduce here, because to wind up this book I want to take up
where that one leaves off. Some of it repeats what I've already said,
and some of it contradicts it. But it's relevant because it is a fair
statement of how things looked to me exactly twenty years after I began
writing the original version of *The Thinking Man's Guide*, and leads
into our final topic: What can we expect in the years ahead?

Here's the reprint:

Baseball fans have witnessed many developments in their game
of choice during the 40 years since the end of World War II,
some favorable, some not so. In my opinion, the three worst
have been:

    1) Artificial turf.

    2) Expansion.

    3) The evisceration of the minor league system.

The three best developments have been:

    1) The televison camera.

    2) The playoffs.

    3) The return of the stolen base.

It is also my opinion that, unfortunately for fans, the worst
far outweigh the best.

Before zeroing in on these developments, I should begin by making the following four assumptions:

First, fans dislike change. One of baseball's greatest assets is continuity. If a time machine whisked you back, say, to the 1912 World Series between the New York Giants and the Boston Red Sox, you would have no trouble following the game. All the basic rules and techniques would be the same as they are now. But a 1912 football or basketball or hockey game would mystify anyone who knew only today's rules and styles.

Second, fans like action they can see, which means scoring. A steady diet of 9–7 games with 20 or more hits and the lead changing hands a few times is more enjoyable than a steady diet of 2–1 games, as tense and artistic as these may seem to the professionals involved.

Next, fans like identifiable heroes and exceptional performances. The sports industry pays lip service to "parity" these days, which means spreading victory around to as many markets as possible, but the price of parity is the absence of champions who fire the imagination the way the old New York Yankees, Green Bay Packers, Joe Louis, Muhammad Ali and Arnold Palmer did.

And finally, every fan has a personal Golden Age, coinciding roughly with the first decade of that person's interest in baseball, whether it starts at the age of 6 or 26. That era, for that individual, sets the norm to which everything afterward is related.

For me, that was the decade of the 1930's. But after some 35 years of being paid to watch and report baseball for daily newspapers, mostly in New York, and interacting with those who make their living playing or promoting the game, I've gotten too close to things ordinary fans have no access to. So I no longer qualify as an unadulterated fan and it would be presumptuous to speak as one. On the other hand, all my training, inclination, job requirements and accumulated data have centered on the question, "What does the fan want to know about what happened?" So I don't share the myopia of those who live entirely within the baseball community. I can identify fan concerns with no ax to grind.

All that said, here are my reasons:

ARTIFICIAL TURF: This hard, smooth, homogeneous surface distorts the basic principles of the game: hitting, pitching and fielding. A fundamental esthetic is altered as well: Because of the way artificial turf makes a baseball bounce, the game often looks as if it's being played with a tennis ball.

We think of pitchers as trying to get "outs" and hitters as trying to get "hits." Of course. But outs and hits are consequences of more basic conscious intentions.

A pitcher actually tries to accomplish two things. He wants to upset the batter's timing, so that he can't hit the ball squarely. And, according to the game situation, he wants to induce the batter to hit either a fly ball or a grounder.

A hitter can do nothing more than try to hit the ball hard. He can control its direction to some degree, but he must still hit the ball sharply enough to get it by a fielder.

Traditionally, hitters have wanted line drives and long drives that enable them and base runners to advance more than one base, and pitchers want grounders most of the time. On natural grass, each bounce takes some steam out of a batted ball. Under ordinary conditions, the four infielders and three outfielders can cover the gaps and field balls that aren't hit too sharply, while the offense benefits from balls hit very sharply and very far.

But artificial turf spoils all the formulas and ruins the rhythm of the game, especially in the outfield. A soft fly—in a sense, a victory for the pitcher—that falls in front of an inrushing outfielder may well bounce over his head. And a modest line drive (or even a grounder) into an outfield gap cannot be cut off before it skids to the fence. To compensate, outfielders must play deeper and come in more cautiously, making the gaps between them even wider. At the same time, though infielders can play deeper—since a bouncing ball reaches them a little sooner, leaving them a bit more time to throw to first—grounders still scoot by them more quickly than they do on natural grass.

The result is more "undeserved" hits, particularly extra-base hits—and a much less attractive game to the spectator's eye. Artificial turf decreases the possibility of the most elegant plays, when fielders move laterally to intercept the ball and throw to a base for a close play.

The surface is enough like a running track to enhance running speed, so fleet outfielders can reach just about any long drive that doesn't hit or clear a fence. But the difficult shoestring catch has become a bad gamble. So we see countless two-base hits on grounders past the second baseman, or pop-fly triples that bounce away, and fewer "authentic" doubles and triples hit over the outfielders' heads or out of their reach in the alleys.

If all baseball were played on artificial turf, we would simply adapt to the new parameters. But only 10 of the 26 major league parks have it—enough to make everyone deal with it, not enough to create a new norm. And, of course, in all the habit-forming years from Little League through the minors, players hone their reflexes on natural fields.

EXPANSION: The usual argument against expansion is that it "dilutes" playing talent. This is true but misleading. It is not true that there aren't enough "good" players to go around. Players with enough natural ability to reach the majors improve with the chance to play regularly. The player who would have been on the bench or in the minors behind someone slightly better in the old days now may surpass his original rival after developing on another team.

What *is* true is that, by definition, the best 400 players, when there were 16 teams, formed a higher density of excellence than the best 650 players on today's 26 teams.

More teams mean basic changes in statistics and schedule. Statistics are a key feature of baseball enjoyment, more so than statistics in other sports, and they became embedded in well-known regularities that existed, roughly, from 1903 to 1960. The 154-game schedule, in each league, had every team playing every other team 22 times. Such milestones as 20 victories for a pitcher or 100 runs batted in for a hitter acquired their significance in that context; but, more important, the frequency and uniformity of matchups among the teams in a league enhanced the "breaks-even-up-over-time" concept that adds to the validity of statistics.

In 1961, the year the American League expanded to 10 teams, the schedule had to be increased to 162 games (with each team meeting each opponent 18 times). And a celebrated flap arose right away, when Roger Maris and Mickey Mantle launched an assault on Babe Ruth's record of 60 homers, set in 1927. Commissioner Ford Frick, once a close friend of Ruth's, declared that a new record "wouldn't count" unless it was accomplished in 154 games—an emotion-driven, illogical, unjustifiable restriction that would poison Maris's achievement of hitting 61, and would make "asterisks" into confusing addenda to all of baseball's record-keeping. The issue had real emotional force, and after leagues were broken into divisions, and more teams produced more players who did not face opponents an equal number of times, many statistics lost their power to excite.

Also weakened has been the fan's capability for attention. In the 16-team days, true fans knew the regular players on all teams, their records and characteristics of their play. Not only were there far fewer players, but each team came to town more often. Now, with 26 teams in action and other sports having gained in both media attention and viewer interest, and with an Oakland coming to New York for only two series three months apart, no fan can keep up with all the players. This increases home-team-only rooting, intensifying partisanship, but attenuating fan involvement in baseball as a whole.

Expansion, of course, benefits fans in cities with new teams. But it does so at the expense of the potential enjoyment of the game by those who had local teams in the old setup, and by the millions who don't live in any major league city but follow the game passionately with free choice of favorites.

In an eight-team league, 10 superstars (in fan perception, aside from statistics) may well be scattered among six teams; in a 14-team league, more than half the teams are likely to be without a superstar.

And too, more sparsely sprinkled talent means that offense suffers. With fewer teams, more good hitters are concentrated in any one batting order, and they "protect" each other. But when a batting order has only one or two outstanding hitters in it, the opposition pitches around them and gives them less opportunity to do damage. It wasn't a coincidence that when Maris hit 61 homers, Mantle (with 54) was hitting behind him, or that Lou Gehrig was on deck when Ruth came to bat.

THE MINORS: It used to take several years of minor league seasoning to produce a major leaguer, and the proportion of top-level minor to major league teams was about 2 to 1. Now the proportion is 1 to 1, and every minor league system is strictly a developmental device for the majors, arousing little local interest.

Why does this concern the major league fan? Because the present system tends to depress offense and retard the development of hitting stars. Pitchers can, by and large, perfect their craft by practicing their deliveries; hitters can become good hitters only by honing their reflexes against good pitchers. A young hitter with natural talent can be ruined if he is overmatched too early, i.e., by bringing him to the majors; but he will stagnate at a certain level if the minor leaguers he faces aren't good enough to keep testing him.

In the old days, the high minors had many experienced pitchers who had been in the majors or would have been there if there had been 26 pitching staffs instead of 16. Young hitters faced them for a couple of years, and either improved or dropped out. Today, minor league rosters consist only of promising youngsters and temporary major league convalescents, with only a few marginals—who are marginal in the context of 26, not 16, teams. Today, potentially talented hitters get minimum minor league experience and rapid promotion to the majors. The best do well enough, but not as many develop to their highest potential as did in the days of the strong minor leagues.

O.K., those are the worst developments. Now what about the best?

THE TELEVISON CAMERA: Thanks to television, fans like my son, who was born in 1967, see more major league baseball and hear more sophisticated discussion of it before the age of 12 than I was exposed to by the time I was 30.

Television's greatest gift to baseball is the camera angle that lets fans see the pitcher-hitter battle as it really takes place.

This, after all, is the whole ball game. It takes exceptionally sharp and well-trained vision to judge the speed and path of a thrown baseball. Managers learn to do it from the dugout, and professional scouts operate behind home plate or in a press box. But how many people sitting in the stands can really pick out the fine, individual qualities of a pitched ball, aside from noting that it is too high, in the dirt, or wild? Fans react to the umpire's signal, the batter's and catcher's movements, and the flight of the batted ball, but they don't really "see" pitching.

On television they do, and with slow-motion replays no less. Fans see it from the catcher-umpire angle sometimes, from the pitcher's angle sometimes, but with center-of-the-screen clarity always.

That alone is blessing enough. But when you add to it close-ups of facial expressions, split screens of base runners taking leads, replays of long hits and funny bounces and spectacular catches—well, television has opened up the richness of baseball details to all fans in a way that only a few professionals actually on the field used to know.

THE PLAYOFFS: Purists scoff at playoffs, but if you think you'd be fascinated watching teams battle for 11th place in late August, or just playing out the string in September, think again. Breaking up leagues into divisions has its drawbacks, as we've seen, but it is the only sensible solution to too many teams. The same forces that created a World Series between two league champions operate to create and hold interest in preliminary rounds. Four "pennant races," whatever their quality, are better than two of the same quality. And the kind of excitement a one-survivor playoff series generates is not obtainable any other way.

THE STOLEN BASE: When Babe Ruth proved what home runs could do, a whole baseball generation converted itself to long-ball thinking. In the process, the attempt to steal a base, a basic scoring weapon before the 1920's, was put aside as a poor risk. The homer or double will score a man from first; a man thrown out stealing won't score when the next man hits a homer, and that out will decrease the number of times the home-run hitters get to bat.

The stand-around-and-wait-for-a-homer style, which prevailed through the 1940's and 1950's, promoted unwanted byproducts: strikeouts and walks. Hitters, swinging from the heels, didn't mind striking out if they connected a few other times. Pitchers, fearing the homer, stayed out of the strike zone.

But fans want to see the batted ball in play. Walks and strikeouts are stop-action plays. By the late 1960's, as factors such as the increasingly effective use of relief pitchers made homers harder to hit, stop-action reached a peak. In 1968, when scoring slumped to a low of 6.8 runs a game (by both teams), about 25 percent of all the players coming to bat walked or struck out— no action one-fourth of the time.

Beginning around 1960, Maury Wills of the Los Angeles Dodgers and Luis Aparicio of the Chicago White Sox initiated a base-stealing revolution. In the last 25 years, after standing pat for more than four decades, the record for stolen bases in a season has been broken three times, by Wills, by Lou Brock, and finally by Rickey Henderson, who stole 130 for the Oakland A's in 1982. And as a result, many managers have plugged stealing back into their strategies. The threat of a steal worries the pitcher and affects what he throws. It makes infielders move around and affects defensive strategy. Willingness to steal means that the walk ceases to be a stop-action play; it is now perceived as the prelude to a steal attempt.

If you went to 10 games in 1958, you saw, on the average, 86 runs scored, 18 home runs and 6 stolen bases. In 1985, you saw 87 runs scored, 17 home runs and 15 stolen bases. In other words, we haven't lost any of the pleasures of power or production, but we're seeing more action.

Needless to say, there have been other developments that have affected the fan, many of them well-publicized. There is the recent outrage, for example, over drug use by players, and other factors that have served to alienate the fan from the game: ever-escalating ticket prices; exorbitant player salaries; two

player strikes and one umpire strike during the 1980's; the uncertain economics of many franchises; and rowdyism in the
stands. But drug abuse, price inflation, labor strife, bad behavior
and selfishness are not peculiar to baseball, besides being concerns that are tangential to the actual playing of the game,
operating outside the baselines.

So what about the ones I've cited? Has the game itself improved for the fan? Is the effect of the bad balanced by the good?
I would say no. Artificial turf and expansion have caused far
more damage to the game than television and playoff excitement
can compensate for. Fortunately, it hasn't been enough to spoil
the special pleasures baseball affords, as constantly rising attendance and impassioned literary expressions continue to
prove. But is baseball somewhat less fun than it used to be?
Alas, yes.

And this raises another question, for each reader to answer
alone: what isn't?

My distaste for artifical turf is as great as ever. I don't share the
objection many people have to playing indoors: A roof and air conditioning seem to me just fine. It's the floor I don't like. Why they can't
figure out a way to make grass grow indoors I don't understand.

But an interesting aspect of how the carpet affects actual play came
up after this article appeared. The boys at Elias Sports Bureau—Seymour Siwoff and the Hirdt brothers cubed (Steve, Tom, and Peter)—
had started publishing their *Baseball Analyst* annually. One of its features is a breakdown of hitting on artificial turf and on grass, for
individual teams and players.

Everybody knows the carpet helps hitters, and that anybody's batting average must benefit from being able to play on the carpet at
home.

So I was puzzled when I noticed, in their book covering the 1984
season, that every one of the twelve National League teams had a
higher batting average on grass than on artificial turf—including the
six that had carpets at home. And in the American League, which had
ten grass fields and only four synthetics, seven teams hit higher on
grass, five did not, and the other two were exactly the same.

A 19–5 for grass with 2 even seemed too much for coincidence, so
I confronted some of my favorite experts with my new information:
Chuck Tanner (then managing Pittsburgh), Sparky Anderson (managing Detroit), Billy Martin (on one of his Yankee tours), Whitey Herzog
(managing the Cardinals), and Gene Mauch (managing the Angels).

Now, that's a pretty imposing list of baseball intellects. And they all had the same reaction:

"Nah! You're kidding. That's really true?"

It was true, all right. What I wanted to know was, how come?

Bob Skinner, then one of Tanner's coaches, was the first to point out what they all agreed to after they'd thought about it for a while.

"Infielders play deeper on the carpet, because the ball gets to them faster and they still have time to make a longer throw, so they take away more hits if they're placed right," said Skinner. "And you don't get any hits on slow rollers and topped balls. You may get more doubles and triples that bounce around in the outfield, but you lose singles."

That seemed plausible. The next thing to do was to check out the possibility that 1984 just happened to be a fluke. By the end of the 1988 season, I had a five-year sample. That didn't prove anything (statistics don't), but it certainly provided food for thought. After all, these were always the same teams with the same players, facing the same opposing pitchers, home and away, on grass and on turf, wherever it happened to be, so a team's ability was not at issue. It was being compared only to itself under different conditions.

Here's how it came out:

In the National League, where exactly half the games were played on grass, there were 38 cases of a team hitting higher on grass and 22 on artificial turf. The teams with grass at home were 20–10—but the teams with artificial turf at home were also 18–12 for grass.

In the American League, the 10 teams with grass at home were 29–20 in favor of grass, with one tie. But the four teams with carpets at home—Kansas City, Toronto, Seattle, and Minnesota—had higher batting averages on the carpet 16 times, on grass only three times, with one tie.

So the general proposition stood up, although not as dramatically as at first: Teams do hit higher on grass.

I tried one final refinement. Sometimes the difference was only a couple of batting-average points, which didn't seem significant. Five batting-average points at the .250 level amounts to one hit a week for any particular team. So I counted only those cases where the difference, in either direction, was at least six batting-average points.

It came out 29–14 for grass in the National, 26–24 for artificial turf in the American.

What does it all mean?

Don't jump to conclusions, and don't swallow conventional wisdom too uncritically.

But I still dislike baseball on a carpet for all the reasons I mentioned in the first place.

Complaining about expansion is about as fruitful as yearning for the nineteenth century. You have every right to wish for whatever you consider the Good Old Days, but they're not coming back. What's coming, in fact, is more expansion.

I hope they get to 32 teams as soon as possible, although it's going to be difficult to develop enough playing talent in a few years to prevent a visible decline in the standard of play, and it's not perfectly evident that there are 32 viable markets. But all the arithmetic is awkward for leagues between 12 and 16 teams. You can't have 13 or 15 without committing to inter-league play (which creates its own problems), and 14, as the American League has shown, is awful. It's bad artistically with the balanced schedule they use—13 games against 6 fellow division members, 12 against 7 in the other division—because you play 84 games outside your own race and only 78 inside it, and because it brings every visiting team around too seldom (two series a year, so that they are either bunched or too far apart). With 32 teams, you can have four 8-team "leagues," or eight 4-team divisions in two 16-team leagues. Either way, you can have 8 playoff qualifiers neatly arrived at.

Any way it happens, however, I hope realignment is part of the deal. Some of the present division memberships were silly from the start and exist only because of shortsighted prejudices by some club owners then, who seemed to think that year's "good team" gate attractions would never change. Atlanta and Cincinnati don't belong in the National League West and Milwaukee doesn't belong in the American League East. New cities, whatever they are, should present the opportunity for more rational groupings.

The minors had an economic revival in the 1980s, but there's little reason for optimism in the long run. The big success stories, like Buffalo, are clamoring for graduation into the majors, and it was the first round of expansion that killed off the high minors then. Also, more major-league teams will attenuate, not increase, the density of developmental teams, unless a new approach to farm systems is developed. I still believe (hope? fantasize? misconceive?) that sooner or later baseball will have to adopt a centralized low-minors development scheme not tied to individual major-league clubs, which would then stock themselves by drafting from the lower minors. Such plans have been kicking around for twenty-five years. Maybe one will materialize in the twenty-first century.

But it may be that aluminum bats will prove to be a bigger drawback to developing hitters than insufficient minor-league experience.

Of the three positives, playoffs and base-stealing can only improve, but television has a down side.

Playoffs will expand with expansion, and by now you know why and how I think that's a good thing.

To measure the A.Q.—Action Quotient—of baseball styles, I tried adding homers and stolen bases together. Historically, one eclipsed the other, and a falling off in power prompted the revival of the steal. Sheer human speed is a factor (and in this respect artificial fields *help*). The difference between a good chance to steal second and a bad risk is tenths of a second, and a large number of players who are one step faster is enough to tilt the balance, and make managers decide accordingly.

My A.Q. turned out this way:

How many homers and stolen bases would you see in 10 average games?

1906—26.5, 2 homers and 24.5 stolen bases.

1911 (remember that first lively ball?)—31.5, 4 homers and 27.5 stolen bases.

1921—20, 8 homers and 12 stolen bases.

1935—18, 11 homers and 7 stolen bases.

1949—20, 14 homers and 6 stolen bases.

1961—26.5, 19 homers and 7.5 stolen bases.

1968—21.5, 12 homers and 9.5 stolen bases.

1975—30, 14 homers and 16 stolen bases.

1982—31, 16 homers and 15 stolen bases.

1987—38, 21 homers and 17 stolen bases.

1989—30, 15 homers and 15 stolen bases.

That seems to me like a game in pretty good shape for spectating. To get a more meaningful A.Q. you have to plug in walks and strikeouts (non-action plays) and extra-base hits and double plays, and perhaps a few other things, but I leave that to the statisticians. I just think baserunning is back to stay.

The television problem is a subtle one. I stand by all my praise for camera angles and insights, and the number of former ball players who have turned out to be excellent commentators is ample and growing. But the medium itself, with its projected cable program, contains a danger.

Television is a highlights medium. Baseball is not a highlights game.

In news programs, as well as specials and the replays during live telecasts, the exceptional physical-action play is shown over and over—and all the "boring" routine stuff is edited out or glossed over. That's perfect for football and basketball, where the most significant plays also coincide with the most balletic movements—a drive, a dunk, a touchdown pass, an interception, a long run, a blocked shot. But in baseball, the significance lies in the situation more than in the physical occurrence: A grand-slam home run or a strikeout with the tying run on third is not a pictorial climax but a conceptual one. Neither lends itself as well to highlight presentation as it does to verbal description.

But that's only the tip of the iceberg. Television is conditioning everyone, especially children, to short-attention-span, quick-action, let's-get-on-to-the-next-thing viscerally visual responses—not just to baseball or sports, but to everything. (I need only mention MTV and the quick-cut technique of commercials and movies.) The coming generation's interest in baseball *results*, in its heroes, in its playoff and World Series epic-making events, will certainly continue to grow as more games—and highlights—are delivered by television.

Will this audience, however, ever develop a taste for the ball game itself? For the three-hour, slow-paced, long-buildup, growing-tension peculiar rhythm of a ball game in the flesh?

So far, the love of baseball has been instilled in people who have experienced it entire. Even today's youngest fans have contact with, and receive input from, older fans whose response was formed in a pre-television, pre–brief-segment, pre-highlight age. What will be the response of the second all-television generation?

Those who are already baseball fans translate, for themselves, what the screen brings them into a form of enjoyment to which they adapt. Today's televised baseball is preaching to the already converted, for the most part. But what will future converts expect? One tumbling catch after another? A ball flying over or against a fence every ten seconds? What in their television experience—not just with ball games, but in toto—will prepare them for three hours in a ballpark? What if the capacity for enjoying a relaxed pace—in anything—no longer exists?

It's an axiom of baseball promotion that the club is selling back to the customer an echo of an enjoyable early experience, which he in turn is supplying to his children, because at some point he (or she) was exposed to ballpark excitement by a friendly adult. But what will you sell to an aging generation whose associations were formed to a television set at home?

When outgoing Commissioner Peter Ueberroth announced the 1990s deal with cable television, a disturbing suggestion surfaced. The cable network would have access to several games the same night, and would be able, we were told, to switch back and forth to wherever the most dramatic moment happened to be. "If there's a no-hitter in progress in Baltimore," we were told, "we'll be able to switch to it in the sixth inning when Wade Boggs comes to bat."

No doubt. But what will that really mean? The whole point (the ambience and unforgettability) of a no-hitter is the mounting tension you feel as it unfolds. And the same is true of a hitting streak, of hitting for the cycle, or any other statistical feat. Baseball is a game of anticipations. The most exciting possible moment is bases loaded, two out, 3-and-2 on the hitter, just *before* the pitcher throws the ball. Then the action resolves the situation in a matter of seconds, making it indelible history. How can television, hopping back and forth between supposedly "key" moments, instill the emotional response we have come by naturally, in a way that people have been doing for 150 years?

My basic view that "different" does not define "better" or "worse," but only "different," applies here, too. The accessibility that television has already provided, and will continue to provide, is a boon to baseball consumers, not just to its producers. But the character of that accessibility has hazards, too.

Baseball's unique virtue has always been that it lends itself so well to being talked about, and therefore written about. The content of a book of this sort, no matter how one evaluates it, is in the mainstream of baseball chatter as begun by Henry Chadwick thirteen decades ago. Will it be in the mainstream of such expression two decades from now? We'll see.

The myth formation and romanticization of baseball were supplied automatically by people who wrote about it. From now on, that verbal tradition will have to be fostered consciously by the game's promoters in a visual-image age. That's my last pitch, the spin I want to put on whatever message this whole discussion may contain.

In one of the late Bill Stern's radio fantasies, he had Abraham Lincoln on his deathbed saying to General Doubleday, "Abner, keep baseball alive—the country is going to need it some day."

I hope someone says to baseball authorities, over and over again, "Keep baseball *talk* alive—you're going to need it, not just some day, but every day. And soon."

Meanwhile, we'll just have to keep doing that for ourselves.

About the Author

Leonard Koppett, in writing about baseball and other sports for more than forty years, has earned a reputation as a leading intellectual in the field, lighthearted enough to pursue jokes incessantly, opinionated enough to be thought-provoking, often cited by other authors. Known best for his work with *The New York Times*, he has also served as editor-in-chief of a newspaper, taught college courses, and had a dozen books published. He is now editor emeritus of the *Peninsula Times Tribune* in Palo Alto, California, for which he writes general-opinion columns on the editorial page as well as sports columns. He had earlier tours of duty with the *New York Herald Tribune* and the *New York Post*.

His baseball experience stretches from the New York scene of Yankees-Dodgers-Giants of the 1940s to the Yankees and Mets of the 1970s to his California base established in 1973. From the 1960s into the 1980s, his columns in *The Sporting News* presented provocative views on issues usually glossed over in daily baseball coverage. The original *Thinking Man's Guide to Baseball*, published in 1967, was one of the first books to describe the game and scene in depth, and this book is a thorough reworking of those topics from the perspective of twenty-five years later.

Born in Moscow, Russia (shortly before Lenin died), he was brought to New York at the age of five and began writing about sports while an undergraduate at Columbia in 1942. He has also done extensive magazine, radio, and television work. Since moving to California, he has taught at Stanford and San Jose, participated in law forums, and retained connections with *The New York Times*. He and his wife, Suzanne, a teacher specializing in expository writing, have a daughter (Katherine) and a son (David), both in their twenties.